Commercial Property Risk Management and Insurance

Commercial Property Risk Management and Insurance

Edited by

Mary Ann Cook, CPCU, MBA, AU, AAI

Arthur L. Flitner, CPCU, ARM, AIC, AU

2nd Edition • 2nd Printing

The Institutes
720 Providence Road, Suite 100
Malvern, Pennsylvania 19355-3433

2nd Edition • 2nd Printing • June 2015

Library of Congress Control Number: 2014948974

ISBN 978-0-89463-796-4

Foreword

The Institutes are the trusted leader in delivering proven knowledge solutions that drive powerful business results for the risk management and property-casualty insurance industry. For more than 100 years, The Institutes have been meeting the industry's changing professional development needs with customer-driven products and services.

In conjunction with industry experts and members of the academic community, our Knowledge Resources Department develops our course and program content, including Institutes study materials. Practical and technical knowledge gained from Institutes courses enhances qualifications, improves performance, and contributes to professional growth—all of which drive results.

The Institutes' proven knowledge helps individuals and organizations achieve powerful results with a variety of flexible, customer-focused options:

Recognized Credentials—The Institutes offer an unmatched range of widely recognized and industry-respected specialty credentials. The Institutes' Chartered Property Casualty Underwriter (CPCU) professional designation is designed to provide a broad understanding of the property-casualty insurance industry. Depending on professional needs, CPCU students may select either a commercial insurance focus or a personal risk management and insurance focus and may choose from a variety of electives.

In addition, The Institutes offer certificate or designation programs in a variety of disciplines, including these:

- Claims
- Commercial underwriting
- Fidelity and surety bonding
- General insurance
- Insurance accounting and finance
- Insurance information technology
- Insurance production and agency management
- Insurance regulation and compliance

- Management
- Marine insurance
- Personal insurance
- Premium auditing
- Quality insurance services
- Reinsurance
- Risk management
- Surplus lines

Ethics—Ethical behavior is crucial to preserving not only the trust on which insurance transactions are based, but also the public's trust in our industry as a whole. All Institutes designations now have an ethics requirement, which is delivered online and free of charge. The ethics requirement content is designed specifically for insurance practitioners and uses insurance-based case studies to outline an ethical framework. More information is available in the Programs section of our Web site, www.TheInstitutes.org.

Flexible Online Learning—The Institutes have an unmatched variety of technical insurance content covering topics from accounting to underwriting, which we now deliver through hundreds of online courses. These cost-effective self-study courses are a convenient way to fill gaps in technical knowledge in a matter of hours without ever leaving the office.

Continuing Education—A majority of The Institutes' courses are filed for CE credit in most states. We also deliver quality, affordable, online CE courses quickly and conveniently through CEU. Visit www.CEU.com to learn more. CEU is powered by The Institutes.

College Credits—Most Institutes courses carry college credit recommendations from the American Council on Education. A variety of courses also qualify for credits toward certain associate, bachelor's, and master's degrees at several prestigious colleges and universities. More information is available in the Student Services section of our Web site, www.TheInstitutes.org.

Custom Applications—The Institutes collaborate with corporate customers to utilize our trusted course content and flexible delivery options in developing customized solutions that help them achieve their unique organizational goals.

Insightful Analysis—Our Insurance Research Council (IRC) division conducts public policy research on important contemporary issues in property-casualty insurance and risk management. Visit www.ircweb.org to learn more or purchase its most recent studies.

The Institutes look forward to serving the risk management and property-casualty insurance industry for another 100 years. We welcome comments from our students and course leaders; your feedback helps us continue to improve the quality of our study materials.

Peter L. Miller, CPCU
President and CEO
The Institutes

Preface

Commercial Property Risk Management and Insurance is the textbook for CPCU 551, one of the required courses in the Commercial Concentration track of The Institutes' Chartered Property Casualty Underwriter (CPCU) designation program.

The purpose of CPCU 551 is to provide the learner with an understanding of how risk management techniques, including commercial property insurance, can be used: to address an organization's property loss exposures, as a basis for developing the organization's complete property and liability risk management and insurance program, and to promote better decision-making practices enterprise-wide.

Highlights of this textbook include educational objectives that are directly linked to key content in order to assist the learner in mastering relevant topics. Special exhibits link learning content to real life by using practical, current-event illustrations. Case-study educational objectives based on business scenarios are solved in the learning material to provide students with practical applications of the core content.

The Institutes are grateful to the many individuals in the insurance and risk management community who contributed to the development of this content, including F. Scott Addis, CPCU; Christopher Amrhein, AAI; Cheryl Koch, CPCU, ARM, AAI, AAM, AIM, AIS, API, ARP, ACSR; and Francis A. Menna, CPCU, ARM, ALCM, CIC.

For more information about The Institutes' programs, please call our Customer Service Department at (800) 644-2101, email us at CustomerService@ TheIntitutes.org, or visit our website at www.TheInstitutes.org.

Mary Ann Cook

Contributors

The Institutes acknowledge with deep appreciation the contributions made to the content of this text by the following persons:

Richard Berthelsen, JD, CPCU, AIC, ARM, AU, ARe, MBA

Pamela J. Brooks, MBA, CPCU, AAM, AIM, AIS

Kenneth R. Dauscher, PhD, CPCU, AIM

Doug Froggatt, CPCU

Nancy Germond, MA, ARM, AIC, ITP

Valerie Ullman Katz, CPCU, MBA, ARM, AIM

Lynn Knauf, CPCU, ARP

Pamela Lyons, BA, FCIP, CRM

Ann Myhr, CPCU, ASLI, ARM

Karen Porter, JD, CPCU, ARP, AIS

Kathleen J. Robison, CPCU, ARM, AU, AIC, CPIW

Jerome Trupin, CPCU, CLU, ChFC

Judith M. Vaughan, AIM, BA

Andrew Zagrzejewski, CPCU, CLU, ChFC, AIC

Contents

Direct Your Learning ▶▶

Introduction to Commercial Property Insurance

Educational Objectives

After learning the content of this assignment, you should be able to:

▷ Describe the importance of risk control in a commercial property risk management program.

▷ Describe commercial insurance policy formats in terms of the following:

- Multiline policies and monoline policies
- Standard forms and nonstandard forms
- Commercial package policy
- Businessowners policy
- Output policy

▷ Explain how each of the conditions contained in the Common Policy Conditions affects coverage under a commercial property coverage part.

▷ Explain how each of the following affects coverage under a commercial property coverage part:

- Commercial Property Conditions
- Other common conditions

Introduction to Commercial Property Insurance

1

COMMERCIAL PROPERTY RISK MANAGEMENT

Every organization is exposed to the possibility of accidental loss. The physical and financial consequences of accidental loss can prevent the organization from achieving its objectives or even bankrupt it. Therefore, organizations must manage their loss exposures through prevention/reduction and by establishing a plan to finance any unavoidable losses.

Because organizations are exposed to accidental losses, they attempt to manage their loss exposures through risk control measures, such as preventing accidents, applying risk control techniques to reduce the size of losses that occur, and purchasing insurance or using some other method to finance those losses that cannot be prevented or reduced.

Despite organizations' efforts to prevent losses using other risk control measures, some losses still occur, after which risk financing techniques can be used to pay for the losses. A predominant risk financing technique is insurance. The phrase "commercial property insurance" is used in two ways in this commercial property discussion, from a broad to a narrow definition. See the exhibit "Definitions of Commercial Property Insurance."

Definitions of Commercial Property Insurance

Broad—Aggregate Definition	Narrow—Singular Definition
All types of commercial property insurance covering property loss and related net income loss	One particular type of commercial property insurance that covers loss of or damage to buildings and business personal property at specified locations
Broad definition encompasses all types of commercial property insurance, such as commercial property, crime, and inland marine insurance	Narrow definition denotes one of the specific types of commercial property insurance, such as commercial property, crime insurance, or inland marine insurance

[DA06034]

Organizations use a six-step risk management process to prevent or reduce property losses. The Risk Control and Commercial Property Loss Exposures section presents a sampling of common property loss exposures and suggests appropriate loss control measures for each exposure.

Risk Management Overview

Organizations must effectively manage four categories of loss exposures: property, liability, personnel, and net income loss exposures. Understanding the definitions of these loss exposures helps insurance personnel to properly identify and analyze them. See the exhibit "Loss Exposure Definitions."

Loss Exposure Definitions

Property loss exposure: A condition that presents the possibility that a person or an organization will sustain a loss resulting from damage (including destruction, taking, or loss of use) to property in which that person or organization has a financial interest.

Liability loss exposure: A condition that presents the possibility that a person or an organization will sustain a loss resulting from a claim made against that person or organization by someone seeking money damages or some other legal remedy.

Personnel loss exposure: A condition that presents the possibility of loss caused by a key person's death, disability, retirement, or resignation that deprives an organization of that person's special skill or knowledge that the organization cannot readily replace.

Net income loss exposure: A condition that presents the possibility of loss caused by a reduction in net income.

[DA05225]

The loss exposures that an organization faces can be handled by applying a six-step risk management process. See the exhibit "Risk Management Process."

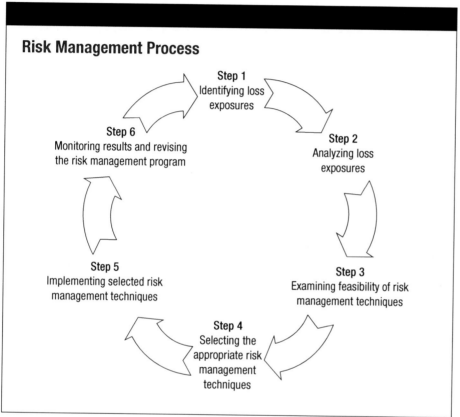

Risk Management Process

Step 1
Identifying loss exposures

Step 2
Analyzing loss exposures

Step 3
Examining feasibility of risk management techniques

Step 4
Selecting the appropriate risk management techniques

Step 5
Implementing selected risk management techniques

Step 6
Monitoring results and revising the risk management program

[DA05226]

1. Identifying loss exposures—First, the organization must identify its loss exposures within each of the loss exposure categories. For example, property loss exposures could include losses resulting from damage, such as costs to rebuild or repair damaged or destroyed office buildings and to restore computer data; losses resulting from taking, such as potential theft losses that could occur from persons inside and outside the organization; and loss of use costs to relocate the business during rebuilding and to store equipment and supplies until the damaged building and property have been repaired or replaced.

2. Analyzing loss exposures—These exposures should then be analyzed to determine the likelihood of loss and its probable extent. For example, techniques for managing these property exposures might include loss reduction, such as installing a sprinkler system to prevent fire damage and establishing a security system with the local fire department; loss prevention, such as establishing internal security controls to prevent employee theft and installing a security system to avoid robbery; separation, such as

establishing an arrangement with another nearby organization to enable work to continue during any business disruption and establishing offsite storage for computer data backup tapes; and risk transfer, such as purchasing property insurance.

3. Examining feasibility of risk management techniques—The costs associated with each technique should be considered to determine which are feasible and which are not—for example, installing a sprinkler system might not be feasible because of the cost and potential work interruption, while purchasing insurance and establishing arrangements for temporary relocation of the business and for offsite storage for backup tapes might be feasible.

4. Selecting the appropriate risk management techniques—The feasibility study should assist the organization in choosing the best techniques.

5. Implementing the selected risk management techniques—Implementing the selected techniques could include arranging meetings with organizations with which the organization could potentially establish a resource sharing arrangement, selecting a partner organization, and establishing the plan. It could also include meeting with an insurance agent to procure the best policy to meet the organization's needs.

6. Monitoring the results and revising the risk management program—Monitoring the results might involve staging trial runs with the resource organization to make sure the systems could handle the increased workload that such an arrangement could entail, reviewing organizational policies that could influence the success of such an arrangement, and annually reviewing insurance coverages and limits to ensure that the organization's needs continue to be met.

As demonstrated, application of the risk management process results in the implementation of appropriate risk management techniques. All risk management techniques can be classified as either risk control (avoid or minimize the loss) or risk financing (methods of paying for the loss). See the exhibit "Risk Management Techniques."

A brief example incorporates these risk management techniques into the risk management process.

John Smith is the risk manager for a group of motels. One of the loss exposures is risk of armed robbery in late evenings. His analysis indicates that such robberies occur most frequently between midnight and 2 AM when only one employee is on duty and when conventions are in town. John reviews the possible risk management techniques. Separation, duplication, and diversification are not applicable. Avoidance is not practical. Loss prevention technique possibilities are bulletproof glass partitions, better lighting, Web cams, and increased security. Loss reduction techniques could be making bank deposits before midnight and accepting only credit card payments from guests. John implements the glass partitions, increased security, and bank deposits before midnight. Because these measures will not completely eliminate the exposure,

---

Risk Management Techniques

Summary of Risk Control Techniques

Avoidance eliminates any possibility of loss. The probability of loss from an avoided loss exposure is zero because an entity decides not to assume a loss exposure in the first place (proactive avoidance) or to eliminate one that already exists (abandonment).

Loss prevention involves reducing the frequency of a particular loss.

Loss reduction involves reducing the severity of a particular loss.

Separation involves dispersing a particular activity or asset over several locations. Separation involves the routine, daily reliance on each of the separated assets or activities, all of which regularly form a portion of the organization's working resources.

Duplication involves relying on backups, that is, spares or duplicates, used only if primary assets or activities suffer loss.

Diversification involves providing a range of products and services used by a variety of customers.

Summary of Risk Financing Techniques

Retention involves generating funds from within the organization to pay for losses.

Transfer involves generating funds from outside the organization to pay for losses and includes insurance and noninsurance transfer.

[DA05227]

the organization purchases crime insurance with a deductible. The insurance policy uses the risk financing transfer technique, and the organization establishes an account to pay for the deductibles, which is a risk financing retention technique.

Risk Control and Commercial Property Loss Exposures

Most losses result from a chain of events. In some cases, a combination of unrelated events converges to cause a loss. Risk control measures are designed to address the links in the chain of events and the unrelated events that converge. Organizations apply risk control measures appropriate to the particular cause of loss and the conditions being addressed. Specific risk control measures provide valuable property protection and are applicable to property losses caused by these events:

- Fire
- Burglary, robbery, and employee theft
- Explosion
- Windstorm

- Flood
- Earthquake

Accidental losses generally result from chains of events. Many times the loss and its severity result from a combination of unrelated events that occur during the same time frame. Risk control measures are designed to deal with links in the chain of events leading to loss. Their use depends on the nature of the particular perils and hazards being addressed. As used here, the word "peril" is synonymous with cause of loss, and the word "hazard" refers to a condition that increases the frequency and/or severity of loss.

Generally, risk control measures take one or both of two approaches: the engineering approach and the human behavior approach. The engineering approach attacks hazards by reviewing and improving the design and location of properties and equipment, to reduce the number of hazards. The human behavior approach attacks hazards by modifying people's behavior to reduce the frequency of unsafe acts. Although losses are usually caused by unsafe acts, engineering often can be used to exclude or limit the opportunities for unsafe acts committed and to limit the losses that may result from unsafe acts. For example, automatic sprinklers can successfully interrupt fire loss chains that people have started.

Fire

A fire requires three elements: an initial source of heat, oxygen, and fuel. A fourth element, an uninterrupted chain reaction, causes the fire to flame up and spread, rather than just to smolder. This chain reaction causes greater fire damage.

Fire prevention efforts focus on removing one or more of the four elements. Heat sources may be electrical, chemical, mechanical, or nuclear. The source of oxygen for most fires is ordinary air; as more oxygen is supplied, the fire burns more rapidly. Fuel includes both contents and construction materials used for the building. As more fuel burns, the amount of heat present usually increases. Strong fires create their own air drafts, bringing more oxygen and allowing the fire to spread by engulfing more fuel.

Construction type influences fire control. Insurance Services Office, Inc. (ISO) defines several construction types. These definitions indicate the fire resistance of these types of construction. For example, in a "wood frame" construction, exterior walls are constructed of wood or other combustible materials. Wood frame construction is more combustible than "joisted masonry," in which exterior walls are constructed of masonry materials (such as brick, stone, or concrete) and other supporting elements (such as joists and beams) are wood. Joisted masonry construction is more combustible than "noncombustible" construction, in which exterior walls, floor, and roof are constructed of, and supported by, metal, gypsum, or other noncombustible materials.

Pre-loss fire control measures focus on controlling heat sources and keeping them separated from fuels. Separation also reduces the damage when a hostile fire breaks out. Various building design features can help prevent the spread of a hostile fire. For example, a "fire stop" is solid pieces of material that are inserted between wall studs or other supporting members to delay the flow of heat through spaces that would otherwise be open, a "fire wall" is a self-supporting solid wall that prevents a fire from passing through or around it, and a "fire division" is a space in a building that is separated from other spaces in the building by a fire wall.

Fire extinguishment methods can be classified as either internal or external fire protection. Examples of internal protection include automatic fire detection/suppression (sprinkler) systems, portable fire extinguishers, standpipe systems, guard services, and fire brigades. External fire protection (such as the public fire department) offers meaningful protection only when fire hydrants are accessible and adequately supplied with water and when fire department personnel are capable of responding to a fire at the organization's facility.

Burglary, Robbery, and Employee Theft

Theft is one of the most severe and pervasive causes of property loss. Any type of property may be targeted for theft. Thieves are most attracted to money or any other property that has high value and low weight and can be easily converted to cash.

Theft risk control often focuses on the three most common types of theft:

- Burglary is theft by someone who forcibly enters the place where the property is kept.
- Robbery involves the use (or threat) of force against the person from whom the property is taken.
- Employee theft (also called employee dishonesty or embezzlement) is theft that an employee commits against his or her own employer.

Various means can be used to keep burglars out of a building or at least delay their entry enough to allow security services to intervene. Deadbolt locks, bars on windows, and breakage-resistant glass are examples. After a burglar gains entry into a building, safes and vaults can deny him or her access to valuable items or at least make it difficult for the burglar to obtain the items. Burglar alarm systems can deter burglars and increase the chances of catching them. Holdup alarms, featuring buttons or foot pedals with inconspicuous access, can enable personnel to alert a central station or the police that a robbery is occurring. Guards, security patrols, surveillance cameras, and various protection procedures can be used to provide further protection against burglary and robbery.

Employee theft losses are difficult to control because the dishonest employee may have access to the property, understands the employer's procedures, and may even be highly trusted by the employer. Risk control measures include accounting controls, access controls, background checks, and separation of duties.

Explosion

Many explosions have the chemistry of extremely rapid combustion—almost instantaneous fire engulfing a large quantity of materials in its entirety. Examples include explosions of flammable liquids, vapors, or gases; explosions caused by excessive dust as in grain elevators; and the action of commercial explosives. Explosion suppressors can activate the instant an explosion begins. They detect a sudden abnormal increase in pressure and automatically flood the incipient explosion with a suppressing agent.

Explosive materials should be properly handled to prevent initial combustion that leads to explosion. The material may be kept in a low-oxygen or an oxygen-free atmosphere, where most of the air in a chamber is replaced with inert gas, such as carbon dioxide or nitrogen. For explosions that are not prevented or suppressed, venting is the standard method of control. Venting uses solid barriers, such as an earthen bank, to direct the force toward open air and away from other property. For example, dynamite is often stored in structures, called "igloos," with concrete or steel walls and light roofs (so the explosive force is directed upwards) and that may be surrounded by earth or concrete banks.

Explosion of pressure vessels, such as steam boilers, occur when the pressure exerted exceeds the vessel's capacity to contain pressure because of an increase in pressure or a decrease in the vessel's strength. Proper operation, maintenance, and inspection are important.

Windstorm

The energy source in windstorms cannot be controlled. Although an organization can locate away from areas that experience frequent severe storms such as hurricanes and tornadoes, doing so may be impractical, and no location above ground avoids windstorms entirely.

Most well-engineered and -maintained structures will generally not incur damage from winds below fifty miles per hour. A high-velocity wind can break glass, tear away exterior trim, and create forces that lift the roof. If the roof is not adequately anchored, it can blow off, and exposed contents can be damaged or destroyed. Even when the roof remains, its surface can suffer considerable stress, with damage to shingles, tiles, or other attached coverings.

Pre-loss actions for windstorm include these:

- Design structures to withstand anticipated wind loads
- Provide storm shutters and blinds for windows and openings rated to handle high wind loads
- Maintain roof and wall systems, including roof tie-downs

- Secure materials and equipment located outside the facility
- Locate trees and utility poles away from structures

Flood

Flooding can occur and cause water damage when low elevation is combined with rising water levels. Flooding can occur from high tides; rising water in rivers, streams, and lakes; and inadequate runoff of rain water (flash floods).

The best method of treating this exposure is to avoid locating in areas with prior flood experience. Because construction and rearrangement of the landscape changes natural runoff and flood patterns, building plans must assess how these new patterns may affect property, and such assessments should be completed before construction begins.

These flood risk control measures or devices may be implemented:

- Dams and other impoundments of water
- Channels designed to direct the runoff and open areas over which flood waters can spread out
- Property protections, such as dikes and sand bags (or other barriers), that divide flood waters
- Equipment designed to resist the pressure of flood waters and the effects of dampness, such as pumps to remove water and allow for runoff
- Structures constructed in flood-prone areas with the lowest floor above the 100-year flood level
- Plans to move property to higher ground when needed

Earthquake

When an organization is located in a geographic area with a history of damaging earthquakes, most risk control attention is diverted to the earthquake loss exposure. The effects of an earthquake can be reduced through careful attention to building design and construction and through close consideration of the conditions of the soil on which the structure will rest.

Earthquake-resistant structures are designed to withstand the forces of earth movement. Most collapses occur from the violent side-to-side, or lateral, shaking associated with earthquakes. The most common design for an earthquake-resistant building is a rigid structure with walls, columns, and pillars tied securely to floors and roofs by horizontal and vertical cross members that extend through the structure to the foundation. Construction of some modern high-rise buildings allows them to sway with an earthquake. See the exhibit "Risk Control Benefits."

> ### Risk Control Benefits
>
> Despite insureds' best efforts to prevent losses through risk management programs, some losses still occur. Most organizations use insurance (a form of risk financing) as a risk control technique to pay for losses that cannot be prevented.
>
> Risk control is a crucial consideration in the risk management process, even when insurance provides risk financing. Effective risk control reduces expected losses, and insureds' efforts to reduce expected losses are often rewarded through reduced insurance premiums. In addition to providing monetary benefits, risk control measures can reduce uncertainty and help the organization meet its risk management objectives.

[DA05968]

COMMON POLICY FORMATS

An insurance professional should understand common policy formats in order to properly structure commercial insurance coverage for insureds.

A basic distinction in the format of a commercial insurance policy is whether the policy is a multiline policy or a monoline policy. Another basic distinction is whether the policy is a standard form or a nonstandard form. Beyond these basic distinctions, three common formats for commercial insurance policies are the commercial package policy, the businessowners policy, and the output policy.

Multiline Policies and Monoline Policies

Insurance professionals commonly use the phrase "line of business," or simply "line," to refer to a specific type of insurance. This usage has resulted in the common insurance terms "multiline policy" (a policy covering two or more lines of business) and "monoline policy" (a policy covering only one line of business).

The phrases used to denote different lines—such as "commercial crime" and "commercial inland marine"—vary by insurer, but often follow the terminology used by either of two insurance advisory organizations: Insurance Services Office, Inc. (ISO), and the American Association of Insurance Services (AAIS).

Both of these organizations develop insurance forms for use by their member insurers and provide many related services. Most organizations are insured under a multiline policy (also referred to as a package policy) for most of their property and liability loss exposures but may also have one or more monoline policies for coverages that cannot be included in their multiline policies.

For example, many organizations purchase specialty coverages, such as flood insurance, in monoline policies because such coverages can sometimes be obtained only from an insurer other than the one writing the multiline policy.

Standard Forms and Nonstandard Forms

Although many insurers use the standard forms developed by ISO, AAIS, or other insurance advisory organizations, some insurers develop their own forms either because they want to write a type of insurance for which no standard form is available or because they want to differentiate their products from the standard forms.

Additionally, large insurance brokerages have developed their own insurance forms, referred to as "manuscript forms" [1] or "broker forms," using provisions that are more favorable to insureds than the provisions in standard forms. Generally, insurers accept broker forms only for the largest accounts.

In contrast with ISO or AAIS standard forms, insurers' or brokers' independently developed forms are often referred to as "nonstandard forms." One of the benefits of studying standard forms is that they serve as benchmarks for analysis of comparable nonstandard forms, enabling one to spot important differences from the standard forms.

Commercial Package Policy

A **commercial package policy** (CPP) is a multiline policy composed of two or more coverage parts, each coverage part providing a separate line of insurance.

Under ISO *Commercial Lines Manual* (CLM) policywriting rules, widely used by insurers, one of the coverage parts of a CPP must cover buildings and/or business personal property, and another must cover commercial general liability. Other coverage parts for property and liability lines can be added. Examples of additional property coverage parts are commercial crime, commercial inland marine, and equipment breakdown.

Each coverage part consists of these components:

- One or more declarations forms (containing information about the insured and the particular loss exposures insured)
- One or more coverage forms (containing most of the essential terms of coverage)
- For some lines of insurance, a general conditions form
- Any applicable endorsements (modifying the terms of the coverage form or general conditions form)

In addition to coverage parts, a CPP also contains a "common declarations form" for the entire policy and the Common Policy Conditions form. In many cases, insurers combine the common declarations form with the separate declarations forms that apply to the individual coverage parts.

The exhibit shows the coverage parts and forms that might be included in a particular CPP. An insurer can write a monoline commercial insurance policy (such as a monoline equipment breakdown policy) by combining the selected

Commercial package policy (CPP)

Policy that covers two or more lines of business by combining ISO's commercial lines coverage parts.

coverage part with common declarations and the Common Policy Conditions. See the exhibit "Components of a Sample Commercial Package Policy."

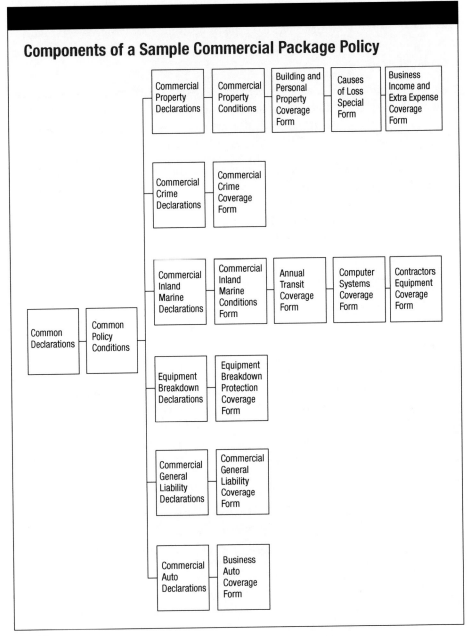

Components of a Sample Commercial Package Policy

[DA02871]

Businessowners Policy

Many small and midsize businesses have similar and relatively uncomplicated insurance needs. Insurers therefore offer policies specially designed for such insureds as an economical alternative to regular commercial package policies.

Such policies are known generically as "businessowners policies," although many insurers use proprietary names to establish brand identity. A **businessowners policy**, or BOP, is a multiline policy that includes most of the property and liability coverages needed by small and midsize businesses.

Businessowners policies typically provide building and business personal property coverage, business income and extra expense coverage, and the equivalent of commercial general liability coverage. Other coverages are either included automatically or available as options.

Businessowners policies resemble homeowners policies in the way they package standard coverages and in their simplified rating procedures. BOPs have a broad-based public appeal because of an economical packaging of the types of coverages that are most needed by a wide variety of small to mid-size businesses. At the same time, BOPs provide insurers and producers with a highly competitive product that is highly automated with streamlined underwriting.

The first businessowners policies were independently developed by individual insurers. ISO introduced a standardized businessowners program in 1976 and has revised it several times.

AAIS also offers a businessowners program as well as its Artisans Program, which uses a businessowners-type policy tailored to meet the specific coverage needs of eligible contractors. Many insurers, including the market leaders for this line, use independently developed BOP forms. Some insurers have developed specialized BOP forms for specific classes of business, such as contractors, printers, or places of worship.

Output Policy

The coverages in an **output policy** might include buildings and business personal property, business income and extra expense, crime, inland marine, and equipment breakdown. In a CPP, each of these coverages would have to be provided by a separate coverage part or coverage form. Thus, an output policy uses a more seamless approach in providing commercial property insurance.

Also, output policies often provide property coverage enhancements not contained in the standard forms used in CPPs, particularly broad coverage for property while away from the insured's premises, whether in the course of transit or at a location not described in the policy.

Eligibility for output policies includes most types of commercial organizations, and specialized output policies have been created for certain market segments such as agribusinesses and developers.

Output policies are generally used only for midsize and larger businesses. The CPP, the BOP, and the output policy, although different in their formatting, are composed of similar policy provisions. Policy provisions can be categorized as declarations, definitions, insuring agreements, exclusions, miscellaneous provisions, and conditions. A policy condition is any insurance policy provision that qualifies an otherwise enforceable promise of the insurer.

Businessowners policy (BOP)
A package policy that combines most of the property and liability coverages needed by small and medium-size businesses.

Output policy
A policy that combines, in one form and associated endorsements, all or most of the commercial property coverages that the insured organization needs, and uses a flexible rating plan.

Of the various types of policy provisions, conditions are the least likely to vary among different types of commercial property policies.

COMMON POLICY CONDITIONS

The Insurance Services Office, Inc. (ISO) *Commercial Lines Manual (CLM)* requires that a common policy conditions form be attached to every Commercial Package Policy (CPP) or monoline policy. The Common Policy Conditions (IL 00 17) form contains six conditions, which apply to all coverage parts in the policy unless a particular coverage part states otherwise. This approach avoids the need to repeat these common conditions in each coverage part. These are the six conditions contained in the form:

- Cancellation
- Changes
- Examination of Books and Records
- Inspections and Surveys
- Premiums
- Transfer of Rights and Duties Under This Policy

Cancellation

The insured may cancel the policy at any time by mailing or delivering written notice of cancellation to the insurer. If two or more insureds are listed in the declarations, only the one listed first (called the first named insured) can request cancellation.

The insurer can cancel the policy by mailing or delivering written notice of cancellation to the first named insured. To provide time for the insured to obtain other insurance, the insurer is required to give advance notice of cancellation. The notice must be mailed or delivered to the insured at least ten days before the date of cancellation if the cancellation is for nonpayment of premium. The notice must be mailed at least thirty days before the date of cancellation for any other reason. If the cancellation results in a return premium, the insurer will send the refund to the first named insured.

In almost every state, the Cancellation condition is superseded by state law and an endorsement is added to the policy. The endorsement modifies the cancellation provisions to conform with the applicable law.

The state laws commonly address permissible reasons for cancellation and a longer advance notification period if the cancellation occurs for a reason other than nonpayment of premium.

Changes

The Changes condition states that the policy constitutes the entire contract between the insurer and the named insured, and that the policy can be changed only by a written endorsement issued by the insurer.

In practice, changes are often first made by verbal communication and confirmed afterwards in writing. In most states, such verbal changes are binding because an authorized agent of the insurer is viewed as having the power to waive the written endorsement requirement. Such changes may be made, with the insurer's consent, upon the request of the first named insured.

Only the first named insured has the authority to request policy changes, and the insurer is authorized to make changes upon the request of the first named insured without specific permission of any other insured.

Examination of Books and Records

The insurer reserves the right to examine and audit the insured's books and records related to the policy at any time during the policy period and for up to three years after the policy's termination. This provision is included because many commercial insurance policies are issued with estimated premiums. The final premium is determined after the policy expires, based on reported values of the insured property, the amount of the insured's sales or payroll, or some other variable premium base. The insured is required to report the final figures to the insurer, and the insurer may accept the insured's reports without verification.

However, if the insurer prefers to verify the reports by making an on-site inspection of the insured's books and records, the condition permits the insurer to do that. An insurer may also choose to exercise its rights under this condition in the process of investigating a claimed loss.

Inspections and Surveys

The insurer has the right, but not the obligation, to inspect the insured's premises and operations at any reasonable time during the policy period.

The inspections may be made by the insurer's own personnel or by another organization acting on the insurer's behalf. Such inspections are important in determining the insurability of the insured's property and operations, in setting proper insurance rates, and in making risk control recommendations.

The insurer may inform the insured of the results of such inspections and may recommend changes. However, it does not have a duty to do either. The condition makes it clear that the insurer does not make safety inspections, does not guarantee that conditions are safe or healthful, and does not guarantee that the insured is in compliance with safety or health regulations.

These disclaimer clauses have been included in the policy to protect the insurer against suits made by persons who allege that their injuries would not have occurred but for the insurer's failure to detect a hazardous condition or a violation of laws or regulations, and that the insurer is therefore responsible for the resulting damages, fines, or penalties assessed against the insured.

Premiums

The first named insured is responsible for paying the policy premium. If the insurer owes a return premium, it will make payment only to the first named insured.

Transfer of Rights and Duties Under This Policy

The insured cannot transfer any rights or duties under the policy to any other person or organization without the insurer's written consent. For example, if the insured sells a building covered by the policy, the insurance cannot be transferred to the new owner of the property without the insurer's written consent.

Such a transfer of insurance is generally referred to as assignment of the policy. The condition also provides specifically for the automatic transfer of coverage if an individual named insured dies. (An individual named insured is a person whose name is listed on the "Named Insured" line in the policy declarations.) In that case, the insured's rights and duties under the policy are automatically transferred to the insured's legal representatives or, if the insured's legal representatives have not yet been appointed, to any person having proper temporary custody of the insured property.

COMMERCIAL PROPERTY CONDITIONS FORM

Conditions in commercial property policies can limit or expand coverage, determine how a loss payment is calculated, and place requirements on all parties to the insurance contract.

Commercial Property Conditions

A required component of the commercial property coverage part that contains conditions applicable to all commercial property coverage forms.

Policy condition

Any provision that qualifies an otherwise enforceable promise made in the policy.

The **Commercial Property Conditions** (CP 00 90) form is attached to every commercial property coverage part in a CPP or monoline policy written under *Commercial Lines Manual* (CLM) rules. In addition to the Commercial Property Conditions, several other **policy conditions** commonly appear in commercial property coverage forms. It is important for insurance professionals to understand how these conditions affect coverage.

Commercial Property Conditions

The Commercial Property Conditions (CP 00 90) form is attached to every commercial property coverage part in a CPP or monoline policy written under CLM rules. Many non-ISO commercial property forms contain comparable conditions. The conditions are outlined in the exhibit. See the exhibit "Commercial Property Conditions."

Commercial Property Conditions

Condition	How the Condition Affects Coverage
Concealment, Misrepresentation or Fraud	Policy or coverage part is void if any insured commits fraud related to the insurance. Intentional concealment or misrepresentation by any insured of a material fact with respect to the coverage part, covered property, the insured's interest in the property, or a claim under the coverage part voids the policy.
Control of Property	If the insured does not have control of the property (for example, when an entire building is rented to another firm or when the insured is a tenant in a building where the protective systems are controlled by the building owner), any act of neglect by others will not affect coverage.
Insurance under Two or More Coverages	When two or more of the policy's coverages apply to a property loss, the insurer will pay no more than the actual loss amount.
Legal Action Against Us	Before an insured can sue or bring legal action against the insurer under the terms of the insurance policy, the insured must comply with all the policy's terms. The action must be started within two years of the date of the loss (this will vary by state).
Liberalization	If the insurer, during the policy period or up to forty-five days before policy inception, adopts any revision that would broaden coverage without requiring additional premium, the insured automatically benefits from the broadened coverage. If the broadening would require additional premium, the insured does not automatically receive the benefit.
No Benefit to Bailee	The insurer will pay the insured(s) for any covered loss while the insured's property is in the temporary custody of a commercial bailee, but will not treat the bailee as an insured. The insurer may exercise its right to take action against the bailee to recover the amount paid to the insured. Coverage is provided to the insured when the insured is the bailee if there is coverage in the policy on property of others in the care, custody, or control of the insured.

Condition	How the Condition Affects Coverage
Other Insurance	When another applicable policy is subject to the same terms, conditions, and provisions as the coverage part, the insurer agrees to pay its share on a pro rata basis (calculated by dividing the applicable policy limit of the coverage part by the total of all policy limits covering on the same basis, and multiplying the result by the amount of the loss).
	If the other insurance does not have the same terms, conditions, and provisions, the insurer pays only the amount of loss in excess of the amount due from the other insurance, whether collectible or not.
Policy Period and Coverage Territory	The policy period is determined by the date(s) or time period shown on the policy Declarations sheet, generally beginning at 12:01 AM standard time for the address listed.
	The coverage territory is the United States, Puerto Rico, and Canada. Property located in other parts of the world is not insured unless the coverage territory is modified.
Transfer of Rights of Recovery Against Others to Us (the Subrogation Condition)	After an insurer has paid its insured for damage to covered property, the insurer has the right to seek recovery from any responsible third party to the extent of the payment made to its insured. The insured is not permitted to take any action that will hinder the insurer's ability to recover from the third party; except:
	If the named insured waived its right of recovery in writing before a loss occurs.
	After a loss has occurred, the insured can waive its recovery rights against someone else covered by the policy form (for example, a landlord when named as an additional insured), a business firm that either owns or is owned by the insured, or a tenant of the insured (subrogation against a tenant is prohibited by law in some states).

[DA06042]

Other Common Conditions

In addition to the Commercial Property Conditions, several other conditions commonly appear in commercial property coverage forms. Many are drawn from the ISO Building and Personal Property Coverage Form, the principal form for insuring buildings and business personal property in a commercial package policy.

Valuation

For an insurer to determine the amount of a loss, the policy must specify a valuation basis for the type of property insured. Commercial property coverage forms typically use one of three valuation approaches:

Actual cash value (ACV)

Cost to replace property with new property of like kind and quality less depreciation.

- The standard valuation approach in many commercial property forms is **actual cash value (ACV)**. Replacement cost is determined at the time and location of the loss. Thus, depreciation is subtracted from the current replacement cost, not the original cost. Depreciation is based on the property's remaining useful physical life rather than the amounts charged as depreciation in the insured's accounting records. Many states adhere to the broad evidence rule in determining ACV in that every indicator of value must be considered.

- When a commercial property form covers on a **replacement cost basis**, the insured can replace the damaged property with a new item, and the insurer will pay the loss based on replacement cost at the time and place of loss, even if the damaged property was many years old.

- Selling price is a valuation method used in commercial property coverage forms to value stock that has been sold but not delivered at its selling price, less any discounts or unincurred expenses. This valuation method is often added to manufacturers' commercial property policies by endorsement to apply to finished goods that have not yet been sold.

Replacement cost

The cost to repair or replace property using new materials of like kind and quality with no deduction for depreciation.

Coinsurance

Underinsurance is a serious problem for both insurers and insureds. To obtain adequate premiums based on the insurance rates used, insurers seek to obtain premiums based on an amount of insurance that is 80 to 100 percent of the property's full value. This goal is referred to as "insurance to value." Without some mechanism to enforce insurance to value, many insureds would purchase much lower amounts of insurance in the belief that the chance of a large loss is so remote that purchasing higher limits is unnecessary. Because most losses are partial, insureds would recover in full on most of their losses. However, if insurers set rates on the assumption that insureds carry insurance to value, they would not collect sufficient premium.

The coinsurance condition addresses this issue. The insured agrees to carry insurance at least equal to a specified percentage of the covered property's value. If the policy is written for ACV, the covered property's value is its ACV. If the policy is written for replacement cost, the covered property's value is its replacement cost.

The coinsurance percentage most commonly used is 80 percent. Coinsurance percentages of 90 and 100 percent are also available in exchange for a reduced premium rate.

The effect of this condition is to penalize (by means of a lower recovery on the loss) an insured who does not insure to at least the specified percentage of value, the penalty being proportional to the amount of underinsurance. If less than the specified amount of insurance is carried, the amount of loss payable (not to exceed the applicable limit of insurance) is calculated as shown in the exhibit.

The coinsurance formula explains how the amount payable is determined if the coinsurance requirement has not been met, and can be expressed as:

$$\left(\frac{\text{Limit of insurance}}{\text{Value of covered property} \times \text{Coinsurance percentage}}\right) \times \text{Amount of covered loss} - \text{Deductible}$$

Insurance students often remember this formula as "did over should times loss," which can be written as shown:

$$\left(\frac{\text{Did}}{\text{Should}} \times \text{Loss} \right) - \text{Deductible} = \text{Amount of loss payable}$$

"Did" is the amount of insurance carried. "Should" is the minimum amount that should have been carried to meet the coinsurance requirement.

Some policy forms, including those of the American Association of Insurance Services (AAIS), call for subtracting the deductible before applying the coinsurance penalty. This difference is important because subtracting the deductible from the loss before multiplying results in a slightly higher recovery.

The property value used in applying the coinsurance formula is that which existed at the time of the loss, not at the time the insurance commenced. The coinsurance formula is applied separately to each specifically insured type of property as illustrated in the example. See the exhibit "Coinsurance Applied to Different Types of Property."

Coinsurance Applied to Different Types of Property

Sarah operates a restaurant in a building she owns. The building is specifically insured for $1 million, and her business personal property is insured for $2 million. The insurable value of each item is $2.5 million. A covered loss resulted in $400,000 damage to the building and $400,000 damage to her business personal property. The coinsurance formula is applied separately to each item, and Sarah is subject to a coinsurance penalty on the building loss. If Sarah had $2.5 million in insurance on her personal property, which would exceed an 80 percent coinsurance requirement on that item, she would still incur the coinsurance penalty on the building coverage.

[DA06043]

The Coinsurance condition applies to the total of all covered property only when one limit of insurance applies to two or more separate types of property.

The ISO commercial property policy forms contain coinsurance examples of underinsurance and adequate insurance. Even when insurance meets coinsurance requirements, the amount paid for a loss cannot exceed policy limits.

When higher than 80 percent coinsurance applies, the rate is reduced. With 90 percent coinsurance on building or contents insurance, the 80 percent coinsurance rate is typically reduced by 5 percent. With 100 percent coinsurance, the 80 percent coinsurance rate is typically reduced by 10 percent.

Therefore, an insured who agrees to 100 percent coinsurance pays a premium rate that is 10 percent lower than what the rate would have been for 80 percent coinsurance. When a higher coinsurance percentage applies, however, the insured must purchase more insurance to avoid coinsurance penalties. See the exhibit "80 Percent Versus 100 Percent Coinsurance: A Rating Illustration."

---

80 Percent Versus 100 Percent Coinsurance: A Rating Illustration

Joe's business personal property has an actual cash value of $1,000,000. If Joe insures with 80 percent coinsurance, he will have to carry at least $800,000 of insurance to avoid a coinsurance penalty. With a limit of $800,000 and a rate of $0.50 per $100 of insurance, the premium would be calculated as shown:

$$\$800,000 \times \frac{\$0.50}{\$100} = \$4,000.$$

If, instead, Joe insured for $1,000,000 with 100 percent coinsurance, the rate would (assuming a 10 percent reduction for 100 percent coinsurance) be reduced to $0.45 and the premium would be calculated as shown:

$$\$1,000,000, \times \frac{\$0.45}{\$100} = \$4,500.$$

Although Joe would pay an extra $500 in premium with 100 percent coinsurance, he would have an additional $200,000 in coverage. (An additional $200,000 in coverage at the 80 percent coinsurance rate would cost $1,000.)

Thus, if Joe wants to insure his property for its full value, he should use 100 percent coinsurance and receive the 10 percent discount—as long as he is confident that he can maintain an amount of insurance that is equal to the property's full value.

[DA02876]

Many commercial property policies are not subject to coinsurance. In policies that contain a coinsurance condition, coinsurance can often be suspended by the agreed value method. For example, businessowners policies usually do not contain a coinsurance condition. However, when issuing policies written without coinsurance or on an agreed value basis, an insurer must still determine that the amount of insurance carried satisfies the insurer's insurance-to-value requirements, or the insurer may not receive an adequate premium.

Insured's Duties in the Event of Loss

Commercial property policies typically impose a number of duties on the insured in the event that a potentially covered loss occurs. These are usually considered to be conditions precedent; the insured must comply with these requirements before the insurer is obligated to make any payment. There is a general requirement that the insured must cooperate with the insurer in the investigation and settlement of the claim. See the exhibit "Insured's Duties in the Event of Loss."

Insured's Duties in the Event of Loss

Condition	Insured's Duties
Notice of Loss	Prompt notice of loss. Written notice is not required.
Police Report	If a law might have been broken, the police must be notified. For example, if theft is a covered cause of loss, theft losses must be reported to the police. Some policies contain exceptions for employee theft or dishonesty.
Protection of Property Against Further Loss	All reasonable steps must be taken to protect the property from further loss, such as temporary covering over a damaged roof or removal of contents from the building to a safe location.
Inventory and Inspection	A complete Inventory of damaged and undamaged goods, including quantities, costs, values, and amount of loss claimed, may be required. The insured must allow the insurer to inspect the property and examine the records documenting the loss.
Proof of Loss	The insurer may require insureds to sign a sworn proof of loss containing information requested by the insurer.
Examination Under Oath	Any insured may be required to submit to questioning under oath concerning the claim. Usually any refusal will void coverage.

[DA06044]

Appraisal

If the insurer and the insured disagree about the value of covered property or the amount of a covered loss, the appraisal condition allows either party to demand an appraisal. The condition states that each party will select a competent and impartial appraiser and that the two appraisers will select an umpire. A decision agreed to by any two of the three appraisers is binding on the insurer and the insured.

Loss Payment

The insurer usually has the option of either paying the value of the lost or damaged property or paying for repair or replacement. Payment by the insurer is limited to the insured's financial interest in the property. This condition also addresses "party walls," which are walls that separate adjoining properties that are owned by different parties and in which each of the owners has property rights, such as townhouses. The insurer will pay a proportion of the loss to the party wall based on the owner's respective interests.

Recovered Property

If either the insured or the insurer recovers any insured property after the loss settlement, the other party must be notified. The insured may demand return of the recovered property. In that event, the insured must refund the amount paid by the insurer for the loss, and the insurer would provide applicable coverage for repairs and recovery expenses.

Vacancy

If the building in which the loss occurs has been vacant for sixty consecutive days before the loss, the insurer is not obligated to pay for loss caused by vandalism, sprinkler leakage, building glass breakage, water damage, theft, or attempted theft. For all other covered perils, loss recovery is reduced by 15 percent.

Buildings under construction or renovation are not considered vacant. The vacancy condition can be eliminated during a specified time period for an additional premium by adding the Vacancy Permit endorsement (CP 04 50).

Mortgageholders

The Mortgageholders condition applies to covered loss to buildings or structures only. The insurer agrees to pay mortgageholders to the extent of their financial interests in the property and agrees to pay them "in their order of precedence, as interests may appear." Thus, if a property has a first mortgage and a second mortgage, the insurer will pay the holder of the first mortgage first and the holder of the second mortgage second.

The condition states that the insurer will pay covered claims to the mortgageholder even though the insurer has denied the insured's claim because of the insured's acts (such as arson) or because the insured has failed to comply with policy conditions. To obtain coverage in those situations, the mortgageholder must meet several requirements:

- The mortgageholder must pay any premiums due to the insurer.
- The mortgageholder must submit a proof of loss within sixty days of the insurer's request.
- The insurer must be notified of any change in ownership, occupancy, or substantial change in risk known to the mortgageholder.

If the insurer cancels the policy for nonpayment of premium, it must give written notice of cancellation to the mortgageholder at least ten days before the effective date of cancellation. If the insurer cancels the policy for any other reason, it must give the mortgageholder thirty days' notice. If the insurer elects not to renew the policy, it must give the mortgageholder ten days' notice. These time limits are often amended to comply with state law.

Loss Payees

Loss payees other than mortgageholders, such as the owner of equipment leased to the insured or the insured's landlord, can be named on the policy declarations page. However, these payees do not automatically receive the added protection granted to mortgagees under the Mortgageholders condition.

The rights that loss payees receive are described in the Loss Payable Provisions endorsement (CP 12 18). Although the CLM does not require using the endorsement, attaching it to the policy clarifies the loss payee's rights. The endorsement includes space to describe the property in which the loss payee has an interest and indicates which of four sets of provisions applies:

- Loss Payable Clause does not provide any right to the loss payee other than the right to have payment of any loss made jointly to the loss payee and the insured.
- Lender's Payable Clause provides that a loss payee whose interest in the insured property is established by written agreements, such as bills of lading or financing statements, receives protection similar to that provided by the Mortgageholders condition.
- The Contract of Sale Clause provides that a purchaser or seller has the right to have payment of any loss made jointly to the loss payee and the named insured as their interests may appear.
- The Building Owner Loss Payable Clause provides that the owner of a building in which the insured is a tenant can be covered as a loss payee. The insurer further agrees to adjust losses to the described building with the building owner who is shown as loss payee.

Any loss payment made to the loss payee will satisfy the insured's claims against the insurer for the owner's property. The insurer also agrees to adjust losses to tenants' improvements and betterments directly with the insured, unless the lease provides otherwise.

SUMMARY

Organizations use risk management programs to prevent or reduce property losses by applying a six-step risk management process. In this process, they identify and analyze four categories of loss exposures: property, liability, personnel, and net income. They examine the feasibility of various risk management techniques, and then they select from among appropriate risk management techniques and implement their selections. Finally, they monitor the results and revise the risk management program as needed.

In applying their risk management program, organizations use risk control and risk financing techniques. Risk control measures are designed to address the links in the chain of events and the convergence of unrelated events that cause losses. Their use depends on the nature of the particular peril and the hazards being addressed. Causes of property losses include fire; burglary, robbery, and employee theft; explosion; windstorm; flood; and earthquake. Risk control measures can be developed for each. Many organizations use the purchase of insurance as their risk financing technique.

A basic distinction in the format of a commercial insurance policy is whether the policy is a multiline or monoline policy. Another basic distinction is whether the policy is a standard form or a nonstandard from. Beyond these basic distinctions, three common formats for commercial insurance policies are the commercial package policy, the businessowners policy, and the output policy.

The Common Policy Conditions form is attached to every CPP or monoline policy written subject to ISO Commercial Lines Manual rules. The form contains these conditions: Cancellation; Changes; Examination of Your Books and Records; Inspections and Surveys; Premiums; and Transfer of Your Rights and Duties Under This Policy.

The Commercial Property Conditions form and other common policy conditions place significant qualifications on the coverage provided by commercial property insurance policies.

ASSIGNMENT NOTE

1. These forms are not "manuscript forms" in the sense of being individually written. The brokers alter their own computer-stored forms to meet an insured's specific requirements.

Building and Personal Property Coverage Form

Educational Objectives

After learning the content of this assignment, you should be able to:

▷ Describe the types of property covered by the Building and Personal Property Coverage Form (BPP) and where such property is covered.

▷ Identify the types of property not covered by the Building and Personal Property Coverage Form (BPP).

▷ Describe each of the additional coverages included in the Building and Personal Property Coverage Form.

▷ Describe each of the coverage extensions in the Building and Personal Property Coverage Form.

▷ Summarize the following conditions of the BPP:

• Limits of Insurance

• Deductible

• Valuation

▷ Explain how each of the following optional coverages described in the BPP modifies the basic coverage of the BPP:

• Agreed Value

• Inflation Guard

• Replacement Cost

• Extension of Replacement Cost to Personal Property of Others

▷ Determine whether, and for what amount, the Building and Personal Property Coverage Form covers a described loss.

Building and Personal Property Coverage Form

2

BPP COVERED PROPERTY

The Building and Personal Property Coverage Form is the most commonly used commercial property coverage form in the commercial package policy program of Insurance Services Office, Inc. (ISO).

The Building and Personal Property Coverage Form (BPP) can be used to cover any combination of three broad categories of property:

- Building
- Your Business Personal Property
- Personal Property of Others

Throughout the BPP and all other ISO forms, the words "you," "your," and "yours" refer to the person or organization shown in the policy declarations as the named insured. Coverage in any of these categories applies only when the declarations show a limit of insurance for that category.

The distinction between real property and personal property is important to understanding property covered by the BPP. Real property consists of land, all structures permanently attached to the land, and whatever is growing on the land. Thus, a building and property permanently attached to it are real property. Personal property consists of all tangible property (property with physical form and characteristics) other than real property. Therefore, the primary characteristic of personal property is that it is not permanently attached to real property.

Building

When the insured wants building coverage, a description of each insured building or structure is ordinarily entered in the declarations. This description includes each building's location, construction, and occupancy. Usually, the covered building is owned by the insured. However, a lessee might insure a leased building when the terms of the lease require that. In addition to the specific description of the insured building(s) inserted in the declarations, the BPP contains a general definition of what property is covered as part of the building. The building definition is quoted in the exhibit. See the exhibit "BPP Building Definition."

The building definition is essential in identifying covered property associated with covered buildings or structures described in the declarations. The

BPP Building Definition

Building, meaning the building or structure described in the Declarations, including:

(1) Completed additions;

(2) Fixtures, including outdoor fixtures;

(3) Permanently installed:

    (a) Machinery and

    (b) Equipment;

(4) Personal property owned by you that is used to maintain or service the building or structure or its premises, including:

    (a) Fire-extinguishing equipment;

    (b) Outdoor furniture;

    (c) Floor coverings; and

    (d) Appliances used for refrigerating, ventilating, cooking, dishwashing or laundering

(5) If not covered by other insurance:

    (a) Additions under construction, alterations and repairs to the building or structure;

    (b) Materials, equipment, supplies and temporary structures, on or within 100 feet of the described premises, used for making additions, alterations or repairs to the building or structure.

Includes copyrighted material of Insurance Service Office, Inc., used with its permission. Copyright, ISO Properties, Inc., 2007. [DA02860]

Fixture

Any personal property affixed to real property in such a way as to become part of the real property.

building definition is not restricted to a structure with four walls and a roof. It can be any structure, such as a three-story parking garage with no walls, if it is described in the declarations. The definition clarifies that a described building includes **fixtures** as well as permanently installed machinery and equipment. The building definition is not limited to real property. Certain types of personal property are included. For example, personal property owned by the insured and used to maintain or service the building or structure or premises is covered. The building definition lists examples of such property—including outdoor furniture; floor coverings; and refrigerating, ventilating, cooking, dishwashing, and laundering equipment—but the definition does not limit coverage to those articles.

It also covers unlisted articles such as lawn mowers, snowblowers, and window-washing and floor-cleaning equipment. The inclusion of these types of personal property in the building definition can eliminate the need for a landlord to purchase an additional amount of insurance under Your Business Personal Property.

However, furniture and other household personal property owned by a landlord and provided in a furnished apartment or room are not covered, because they are not used to service or maintain the building. A landlord can insure furnishings inside rooms or apartments under Your Business Personal Property. If a building is owner-occupied, coverage for personal property articles included in the building definition overlaps with Your Business Personal Property.

In the event of a covered loss to such articles, the insured could make a claim under either coverage. For example, if the policy provides broader coverage on the building (perhaps the building is covered for replacement cost and the contents are covered for actual cash value), the owner-occupant insured could make claim for these articles under the BPP's building coverage. Alternatively, if the damage to the building exceeded the limit of insurance on the building, some articles could be covered as Your Business Personal Property.

Your Business Personal Property

Your Business Personal Property includes seven specific categories:

1. Furniture and fixtures
2. Machinery and equipment
3. "Stock"
4. All other personal property owned by you and used in your business
5. Labor, materials or services furnished or arranged by you on personal property of others
6. Your use interest as a tenant in improvements or betterments
7. Leased personal property that you have a contractual responsibility to insure, unless otherwise provided for under Personal Property of Others

Coverage can apply to all of these categories or can be restricted to one or more of them by specifying the extent of coverage in the declarations or in an endorsement titled Your Business Personal Property—Separation of Coverage (CP 19 10). For example, if the declarations showed a limit of insurance for only "stock, furniture and fixtures," the policy would cover none of the other categories of personal property. However, most policies show an amount of insurance for Your Business Personal Property and thus cover all seven categories of business personal property.

Categories 1 through 4 of Your Business Personal Property deal with property owned by the named insured, but categories 5 through 7 involve certain types of property owned by others. It may seem strange that a coverage agreement titled Your Business Personal Property would cover some types of property belonging to others—especially because the BPP contains a separate agreement titled Personal Property of Others.

This inconsistency is comparable to the building definition's inclusion of some types of personal property. Its purpose is to cover incidental loss exposures

2.6 Commercial Property Risk Management and Insurance

commonly associated with the main exposure insured, thereby reducing the need for the insured to purchase coverage under an additional coverage agreement.

Categories 1 Through 4—Property Owned by the Insured

Categories 1 through 4 encompass all personal property owned by the named insured and used in the named insured's business. Of the various words used in the first four categories, only "stock" is defined in the BPP. The definition states that "stock" means merchandise held in storage or for sale, raw materials, and in-process or finished goods. It also includes supplies used to pack or ship stock. The term "fixtures," in the context of business personal property coverage, is generally interpreted to encompass not all fixtures (as under the building definition) but only those fixtures that are removable by a tenant, generally called "trade fixtures." **Trade fixtures** are therefore distinct from tenants' improvements and betterments, which the tenants may not remove. Category 4 clarifies that Your Business Personal Property includes all personal property owned by the named insured and used in the named insured's business, even though the property might not qualify under categories 1 through 3.

For example, objects of art displayed in an office building, even if they were deemed not to qualify as "furniture" under category 1, would nevertheless be covered under category 4 if they were owned by the insured and used in the insured's business. However, out-of-season personal clothing that an insured stores in a closet in his or her office because of lack of space at home would not qualify as personal property used in the insured's business.

Labor, Materials, or Services Furnished on Property of Others

Category 5 includes the insured's work on personal property of others. This clarifies that the BPP will cover labor and materials the insured has put into customers' property, if the property is destroyed by an insured peril while still on the insured's premises. For example, a machinery repair shop has coverage for both the parts the shop has installed in a customer's equipment and the labor expended in repairing the equipment.

The coverage applies only to the extent of the insured's own costs; it does not cover any other part of the customers' property. Complete coverage for customers' property can be arranged under Personal Property of Others. In addition, a BPP coverage extension provides up to $2,500 for property of others at each insured location. Category 5 also does not cover the insured's anticipated profit on the work performed.

Trade fixtures
Fixtures and equipment that may be attached to a building during a tenant's occupancy, with the intention that they be removed when the tenant leaves.

Leased Personal Property

To facilitate discussion, category 7, leased property, is described before category 6, improvements and betterments. Leased personal property that the insured is required by contract to insure is covered as part of Your Business Personal Property unless otherwise covered under Personal Property of Others.

Many organizations lease, rather than buy, computers, photocopiers, telephone systems, various types of specialized equipment, and many other kinds of property. Your Business Personal Property includes leased property only if the lease requires the insured to insure the leased property. The category does not include property of others held, but not leased, by the insured, even if the insured has agreed to insure the property.

Improvements and Betterments

This category covers a tenant's use interest in **improvements and betterments** that the tenant has added to the landlord's building and has acquired at its own expense. Examples of tenants' improvements and betterments are the partitions, cabinets, and acoustic ceilings that a group of physicians have installed in their rented office.

> **Improvements and betterments**
>
> Alterations or additions made to the building at the expense of an insured who does not own the building and who cannot legally remove them.

Although a tenant may have made or paid for improvements and betterments, they ordinarily become the landlord's property as soon as they are attached to the building, and the tenant cannot legally remove them without the landlord's consent. Nevertheless, the tenant has an insurable "use interest" in the improvements and betterments for the remainder of the rental period or lease.

By including coverage for improvements and betterments in Your Business Personal Property, the BPP enables a tenant who does not otherwise need building coverage to insure its use interest in such property under the same coverage agreement that covers the tenant's business personal property.

The question often arises whether an item is a trade fixture or an improvement and betterment. Ideally, such questions are settled in the lease agreement, but often they are not. Fixtures are part of the realty and are the building owner's property. Trade fixtures, however, are characterized by the tenant's right (or obligation) to remove them when the tenant vacates the premises. Trade fixtures may include counters, machinery, and appliances. The exhibit contains excerpts from a lease dealing with the classification of trade fixtures.

Whether an item is a trade fixture or an improvement and betterment cannot always be established by looking at it—not even by examining the apparent firmness of its attachment to the structure. Many cases are determined by trade customs. Thus, for example, walk-in freezers and refrigerators in a restaurant and the stage machinery in a theater may be completely built in and firmly attached to the structure. However, by custom they are trade fixtures subject to removal by the tenant and not building improvements that become the property of the building owner. See the exhibit "Valuation Basis for Trade Fixtures and Improvement and Betterments Coverage."

> ## Valuation Basis for Trade Fixtures and Improvement and Betterments Coverage
>
> The BPP covers a tenant's trade fixtures under "furniture and fixtures," the first category of Your Business Personal Property; a tenant's improvements and betterments are covered under the sixth category of Your Business Personal Property. Although both trade fixtures and improvements and betterments are covered, the valuation basis in the event of a loss differs, which makes the distinction important.
>
> Trade fixtures are valued at actual cash value (ACV) or replacement cost, depending on which option applies. Improvements and betterments can sometimes be valued on a pro rata basis that equals neither ACV nor replacement cost.

[DA05958]

Another question about the definition of improvements and betterments concerns the status of maintenance performed by the tenant, such as painting or minor repairs. One viewpoint holds that improvements and betterments must be more substantial, such as a new store front, partitions, acoustical insulation, elevators, floor coverings, and central air-conditioning systems. Another viewpoint holds that anything a tenant does that upgrades the building or structure and cannot be removed qualifies as improvements and betterments. Under the second theory, painting done by the tenant would be covered as an improvement and betterment. Local usage differs, and the exact facts in any particular case would have to be considered.[1]

If a tenant has a significant exposure in this area—for example, the tenant is responsible for all repairs to the building under the terms of a long-term lease—coverage should be clarified with the underwriter when the policy is issued.

Under the BPP, a landlord's interest in any improvements and betterments is insured by the landlord's building coverage. The amount of building insurance carried by the landlord should therefore reflect the value of any improvements and betterments that tenants have added to the structure. Because the landlord and the tenant have simultaneous but separate insurable interests in the same property, each may buy insurance. The most common arrangement is for the landlord to carry insurance on the building, including the landlord's interest in the improvements and betterments, while the tenant insures its use interest in the same property. Consequently, the BPP and most other commercial property forms provide automatic coverage on a tenant's interest in improvements and betterments when the tenant buys personal property coverage. See the exhibit "Alternatives to Landlord and Tenant Insuring Improvements Separately."

Personal Property of Others

Your Business Personal Property includes some types of property of others. Moreover, a coverage extension automatically provides up to $2,500 per

Alternatives to Landlord and Tenant Insuring Improvements Separately

Landlords and tenants often insure their interests in improvements and betterments under separate commercial property policies. However, other alternatives are available. One alternative is for the owner to be named as an additional insured or as a loss payee under the tenant's policy. This approach has drawbacks, however. When owner and tenant are jointly insured, the acts of one may affect the coverage of the other. For example, contracts are voidable in the event of fraud by an insured. Another problem is that the first named insured has the right to cancel the policy, so that the first named insured may have more control over the coverage than others.

A second alternative is for the lease to require one party to make repairs in the event of damage. In that way, the other party is protected to the extent the obligor (the party with the obligation) can fulfill its duty. A common arrangement to ensure the financial ability to make repairs is to require that the obligor carry adequate insurance on the property. One premium, in effect, pays for protection of both parties. To reduce the amount of insurance needed to satisfy coinsurance requirements, the other party can exclude the improvements and betterments from its insurance coverage. However, the possibility remains that the coverage might be voided by acts of the insured party.

[DA05959]

location for property of others in the insured's care, custody, or control. If the insured wants a higher limit of insurance on personal property of others, it can be provided through the BPP's Personal Property of Others agreement.

This agreement insures personal property of others only while it is: (1) in the named insured's care, custody, or control and (2) located in or on the building described in the declarations or in the open (or in a vehicle) within 100 feet of the building or structure or within 100 feet of the described premises, whichever distance is greater. Payment for Personal Property of Others is made to the owner of the property, not to the insured. The coverage pays regardless of whether the insured is legally liable for the loss.

Personal Property of Others coverage is ordinarily bought by insureds that have care, custody, or control of their customers' property in a **commercial bailment**. Cleaners and shoe repairers are obvious examples of commercial bailees. In addition, many manufacturing and processing firms work, at least some of the time, on property that belongs to their customers. Other firms, such as furriers and warehouse operators, store property of others either as an accommodation or for a fee. See the exhibit "Examples of Coverage Combinations Under the BPP."

Commercial bailment
The temporary possession by one party (the bailee) of personal property of another party (the bailor) for a specific purpose beneficial to both parties.

Where Coverage Applies

With only a few exceptions, the BPP restricts coverage to property located at the locations described in the declarations. Under the Building definition, materials, equipment, supplies, and temporary structures used for making

Examples of Coverage Combinations Under the BPP

Named Insured	Worldwide Realty, Inc.	Sue Brown d/b/a Sue's Leather Restoring	Smith and Jones, LLP, law firm	Book Publishers and Fulfillment Services
Property Loss Exposure	Owner of building rented to: • Sue's Leather Restoring • Smith and Jones, LLP	• Her own business personal property • Property of others in her care, custody, and control	$500,000 spent on improvements and betterments for installing ornate wood paneling, glass conference room walls, and interior partitions	• Owns the building next to Worldwide Realty's building • Uses its building as a distribution center for books it has published • Uses building to distribute books of other publishers in its care, custody, and control
BPP Coverage Purchased	Building	• Your Business Personal Property • Personal Property of Others	Your Business Personal Property	• Building • Your Business Personal Property • Personal Property of Others

[DA05961]

additions, alterations, or repairs to an insured building or structure are covered while located on or within 100 feet of the described premises. Under Your Business Personal Property and Personal Property of Others, the property is covered while located in or on the building or structure described in the declarations or in the open (or in a vehicle) within 100 feet of the building or structure or within 100 feet of the described premises, whichever distance is greater. "Within 100 feet of the premises" is ordinarily interpreted to mean within 100 feet of the nearest boundary of the land considered to be part of the insured premises.

If, for example, the declarations describe the insured premises as 1234 Main Street, the premises include both the building and the lot at that address. Thus, if business personal property belonging to the insured is located 20 feet from the insured's land but 200 feet away from the insured's building, the property is within 100 feet of the insured's premises and is therefore covered.

In contrast, if the policy describes the location as 1234 Main Street, Suite 1403, it is generally held that the coverage applies only within suite 1403 and that the 100-foot extension is calculated from the perimeter of suite 1403, not from the perimeter of the entire premises at 1234 Main Street. Business personal property located more than 100 feet from the premises (Suite 1403) would nevertheless be covered if it was located within 100 feet of the *building*

at 1234 Main Street. Only if the business personal property was located more than 100 feet from both the premises and the building would it not be covered because of its location.

Two coverage extensions provide some additional coverage for property away from the described premises. The Property Off-Premises extension provides $10,000 of coverage at other locations within the policy territory, which consists of the United States of America (including its territories and possessions), Puerto Rico, and Canada. The Newly Acquired or Constructed Property extension covers property at locations within the policy territory that the insured acquires after the policy's inception.

BPP PROPERTY NOT COVERED

The Building and Personal Property Coverage Form (BPP) contains an extensive list of property not covered.

The property items are initially excluded either to reduce the amount of insurance needed to satisfy the Coinsurance condition (such as the exclusion of foundations or pilings and underground pipes and flues) or because the type of property (such as bridges, piers, wharves, and docks) requires careful underwriting.

Automatically including coverage for the excluded items could substantially increase the amount of insurance needed. However, the policy can be amended to provide coverage for these items, and the insured should weigh the need for coverage carefully.

For purposes of this discussion, these are the categories of excluded items:

- Buildings and other real property
- Plants and outdoor property
- Other personal property

According to the ISO *Commercial Lines Manual* (CLM), any of the items listed as Property Not Covered, other than land, water, and contraband, can be insured either by endorsement to a BPP or in other coverage parts or policies.

Buildings and Other Real Property Exclusions

Many excluded items are primarily building property or other types of real property. These exclusions reaffirm that building coverage applies only to buildings or structures as defined by the BPP's building definition. These are excluded items:

- Land
- Water
- Bridges

- Roadways, walks, patios, and other paved surfaces
- Retaining walls that are not a part of a building
- Bulkheads, pilings, piers, wharves, and docks
- The cost of excavations, grading, back filling, or filling
- Foundations below the lowest basement floor or, if there is no basement, the surface of the ground
- Underground pipes, flues, and drains

Land and water would not appear to be covered in the first place because the BPP building definition does not list them. However, some court decisions in pollution claims have granted coverage for the cost of restoring polluted land and water under building policies. To prevent similar decisions, insurers now specifically exclude land and water. A BPP additional coverage provides limited coverage for removing pollutants from land or water.

Even though the probability of loss to items such as excavations, foundations below ground, and underground pipes is very low, some insurance practitioners think that this coverage should usually be added back. Damage to these items because of perils such as explosion, flood, or earthquake is possible and can be serious. The Additional Covered Property endorsement (CP 14 10) can be used to cover the excluded items. Even without the endorsement, foundations are covered, except for those that are below the basement or, if there is no basement, below the surface of the ground. Likewise, pipes, flues, and drains are covered property, except when they are underground.

Plants and Outdoor Property Exclusions

A second category of excluded property consists of these items:

- Outdoor grain, hay, straw, and other crops
- Outdoor radio or television antennas, including satellite dishes, their lead-in wiring, masts, and towers
- Outdoor fences
- Outdoor trees, shrubs, and plants unless they are "stock" or part of a vegetated roof

The BPP defines stock as "merchandise held in storage or for sale, raw materials and in-process or finished goods including supplies used in their packing or shipping."

Some of these items would generally not be considered part of a building but are excluded to reaffirm that real property is not covered unless included in the BPP building definition. Other items are so susceptible to some causes of loss that coverage would cost more than most insureds are willing to pay. For example, outdoor trees are frequently damaged by wind, as are fences and radio and television antennas. Limited coverage is provided for some of these items under BPP coverage extensions. All of these items are insurable either by endorsement to a BPP or in other coverage parts or policies.

Other Personal Property

Several additional types of personal property are not covered. With the exception of contraband, all of these additional types of excluded personal property are insurable under other insurance forms.

Money, Securities, and Similar Property

Insurers generally prefer to cover money, securities, and similar property under commercial crime or inland marine forms, which are usually subject to specialized underwriting. The items in this category that are specifically excluded in the BPP are "accounts, bills, currency, food stamps or other evidences of debt, money, notes or securities." The exclusion also clarifies that lottery tickets held for sale are not securities and are therefore covered property.

Electronic Data and Valuable Papers

The loss exposures involved in electronic data processing have created coverage problems for insurers. Coverage in property policies is generally limited to physical loss or damage. Has there been physical damage when computer files are erased or corrupted by a computer virus? What about customer credit card information stolen by a hacker, or a loss of computer system functioning because of a power failure? Most insurers do not believe that events of these types cause physical damage. Court decisions have been mixed. One lower court ruled that, in view of the widespread use of computers and other electronic equipment, physical damage includes computers' loss of functionality.[2]

To clarify and reinforce insurers' positions on this issue with regard to the cost to research, replace, or restore valuable papers and electronic data, the BPP contains these exclusions:

- Electronic data—The BPP defines "electronic data" broadly to include information, facts, or computer programs used with electronically controlled equipment. The BPP excludes all electronic data, subject to three exceptions: "stock" of prepackaged software; and data covered under the Electronic Data additional coverage; and electronic data that are integrated in and operates or controls the building's elevator, lighting, heating, ventilation, air conditioning, or security system. Thus, a retail store that sells prepackaged software or a manufacturer that produces it would be insured for a covered loss to such software that qualifies as stock. The Electronic Data additional coverage provides up to $2,500 per policy year for certain losses of electronic data. Regarding the third exception, electronic data that are integrated in and control a building's security system, for example, is covered property and is not subject to the $2,500 limitation.

- Cost to replace or restore information on valuable papers and records—The BPP also excludes the cost to replace or restore information on valuable papers and records, including those that exist as electronic data. Valuable papers and records include, but are not limited to, proprietary information, books of account, deeds, manuscripts, abstracts, drawings, and card index systems. The Valuable Papers and Records coverage extension provides limited coverage for valuable papers and records other than electronic data.

Vehicles, Watercraft, Aircraft

Most loss exposures arising out of the ownership, maintenance, or use of automobiles, watercraft, and aircraft are ordinarily insured under specialized forms. Accordingly, the BPP excludes loss of or damage to vehicles or self-propelled machines, including aircraft or watercraft, if they are either licensed for use on public roads or principally operated away from the described premises. However, the exclusion does not apply to these items:

- Vehicles or self-propelled machines or autos that the named insured manufactures, processes, or warehouses.
- Vehicles or self-propelled machines, other than autos, that the named insured holds for sale. (Automobiles held for sale are specifically excluded.)
- Rowboats or canoes out of the water at the described premises.
- Trailers, but only to the extent they are covered under the Non-owned Detached Trailers coverage extension.

Because of these exceptions, the BPP covers loss of or damage to such items as lawn tractors held for sale by a garden shop, a forklift used in a factory, an unlicensed truck used to move goods around a yard, and a motorized cart provided for handicapped visitors at a museum. Despite these exceptions, the BPP still excludes most autos, watercraft, and aircraft that the insured might use, as well as self-propelled machines used primarily away from the insured premises, such as a contractor's bulldozer.

Coverage can be added by endorsement for vehicles otherwise excluded. Although most insureds cover their cars and trucks under auto insurance, insureds with a large fleet of owned autos often retain the on-road physical damage exposure. When its autos are on the road, the organization can absorb the relatively small probable maximum loss of one or two vehicles in an accident. However, at night, the concentration of vehicles at a parking or garaging location may increase the loss exposure beyond the firm's desired retention level, so it may choose to insure the garaging exposure under its BPP.

When the BPP or similar form is extended to cover the insured's auto fleet, the resulting coverage is not a complete substitute for auto physical damage coverage. The BPP coverage applies only while the autos are on or within 100 feet of the insured's premises, and the causes of loss are limited to those covered by the causes of loss form attached to the policy. None of the commercial property causes of loss forms provides as broad a scope of coverage as auto collision and comprehensive physical damage insurance.

Animals

The BPP specifically excludes animals. However, the exclusion does not apply to animals owned by the named insured and held for sale or owned by others and boarded by the insured. A pet store's stock of animals, for example, would be covered. Other animal owners may need farm, livestock, or animal mortality policies.

Property More Specifically Described in Another Form

Property more specifically described under the same policy or another policy is covered under the BPP only for any excess over the amount due from the other insurance, whether or not it is collectible. The meaning of "property more specifically described" is illustrated by these comparisons:

- "Stock" is a more specific description than "your personal property."
- "Electronic data processing equipment" is a more specific description than "machinery and equipment."
- "Bulldozer ID# 266402" is a more specific description than "motorized land vehicle."

Property is often more specifically described in another form or endorsement contained in the same policy. For example, computers could be covered under the BPP as Your Business Personal Property and in an attached inland marine coverage form covering "electronic data processing equipment." A similar situation can arise if the computer is insured under a separate inland marine policy. In the case of computers, the inland marine coverage is more specific and therefore pays first; the BPP covers any remaining loss, if the cause of loss is covered.

Airborne or Waterborne Personal Property

The BPP excludes personal property while airborne or waterborne. Various forms of inland and ocean insurance can be used to insure property while being transported by air or water. The BPP excludes contraband or property in the course of illegal transportation or trade. Contraband is probably not covered even if a policy does not specifically exclude it.

BPP ADDITIONAL COVERAGES

The Building and Personal Property Coverage Form, also referred to as the BPP, includes an additional coverages section that provides insurance for certain consequences of property losses that would not otherwise be covered.

The six additional coverages are these:

- Debris Removal
- Preservation of Property

- Fire Department Service Charge
- Pollutant Cleanup and Removal
- Increased Cost of Construction
- Electronic Data

Debris Removal

Following a loss, large amounts of debris may remain on the premises, and the cost of removing the debris may be substantial.

Until the 2012 editions of Insurance Services Office, Inc. (ISO) commercial property forms came into use, beginning in 2013, the Debris Removal additional coverage covered only the cost of removing debris of covered property when such debris resulted from a covered cause of loss during the policy period.

The additional coverage would not, for example, pay to remove the debris resulting from a flood if flood was not a covered cause of loss, nor would it pay to remove debris of the insured's licensed automobiles, because automobiles are not covered property.

Likewise, when a windstorm blew debris from a neighboring building (not covered property) onto the described premises, the Debris Removal additional coverage did not cover the cost to remove it , and this left the insured with uninsured debris-removal expenses.

In response to this problem, one of ISO's revisions in the 2012 edition of the BPP was to broaden the Debris Removal additional coverage to include "other debris that is on the described premises," thus covering the cost to remove debris of property that does not qualify as covered property, as long as the debris results from a covered cause of loss.

The Debris Removal additional coverage, as revised, does not apply to the cost to take any of these actions:

- Remove debris of the insured's own property that is not covered by the BPP, or property in the insured's possession that is not covered property.
- Remove debris of property owned by or leased to the landlord of the building where the described premises are located. However, this exclusion does not apply if the insured has contractually agreed to insure the property and it is insured under the insured's policy.
- Remove property that is Property Not Covered under the BPP, such as automobiles held for sale.
- Remove property of others of a type that would not be Covered Property. If, for example, the debris of a licensed truck was blown onto the insured's premises by a windstorm, the cost to remove this debris would not be covered.
- Remove mud or earth from the grounds of the described premises.

- Extract pollutants (as defined in the form) from land or water.
- Remove or restore polluted land or water.

Under the Debris Removal provision, the most that the insurer will pay for such debris removal is 25 percent of the sum of the direct loss payment plus the deductible amount. Because this amount may not be sufficient in some cases, an additional $25,000 limit per location ($10,000 in the pre-2012 editions of the BPP) is provided if the direct loss plus debris removal expense exceeds the limits of insurance or the debris removal expense exceeds the 25 percent limitation of direct losses.

The $25,000 additional limit (or $10,000 additional limit in earlier forms) can be increased by endorsement to afford protection when a small direct loss causes a large debris removal expense or when the direct damage payment for a total loss exhausts the coverage limit.

The Debris Removal additional coverage may include the cost to clean up pollution at the insured's premises caused by an insured peril, depending on the circumstances. For example, if "Building" is shown as covered property, the cost to clean up debris from a fire that causes the release of toxic chemicals onto the floor of the insured's building would be covered.

However, the Debris Removal provision does not apply to costs for cleanup or removal of pollutants from land or water at the described premises. Limited coverage for these costs is available under the provisions of the Pollutant Cleanup and Removal additional coverage. No coverage is provided for cleanup of off-premises pollution even when it results from a covered loss.

The additional coverage states that covered debris removal expenses will be paid only if they are reported to the insurer in writing within 180 days after the direct physical loss or damage. See the exhibit "Examples of Debris Removal Losses."

Preservation of Property

It is sometimes necessary to move the covered property to another location to protect it. The Preservation of Property additional coverage extends the policy to protect covered property while it is being moved and for up to thirty days at the new location.

This coverage is broader than the normal coverage under the policy. It protects against "any direct physical loss or damage" and is not limited to either the covered causes of loss or locations stipulated in the coverage form.

The protection provided under this additional coverage is subject to the limits of insurance stated in the declarations. Consequently, the additional coverage provides no protection if the applicable limit of insurance is exhausted by payment for the physical loss.

Examples of Debris Removal Losses

Each of the following examples involves a BPP with a limit of $500,000 on the insured's building and a $1,000 deductible.

Example 1—Debris removal is less than 25 percent of the sum of loss payment plus deductible.

Amount of loss: $10,000 damage to building, $2,000 debris removal

Insured collects:

$10,000	for building damage
+ 2,000	for debris removal
$12,000	
− 1,000	deductible
$11,000	

Example 2—Debris removal is greater than 25 percent of the sum of loss payment plus deductible.

Amount of loss: $36,000 damage to building, $22,000 debris removal

Insured collects:

$36,000	for building damage
− 1,000	deductible
$35,000	amount insurer pays for direct physical loss
+ 22,000	for debris removal*
$57,000	

*The insured collects $22,000 for the debris removal. The coverage for debris removal is limited to 25 percent of the sum of the insurer's payment for physical loss plus the deductible ($9,000, calculated as 0.25 × [$35,000 + $1,000 deductible]) plus $13,000 of the $25,000 additional limit of insurance for debris removal.

Example 3—Building loss exceeds the amount of insurance.

Loss: $505,000 damage to building, $60,000 debris removal

Insured collects:

$500,000	for building damage (limit of insurance)
+ 25,000	for debris removal (additional limit of insurance)
$525,000	

In Example 3, the insurer's payment is not reduced by the deductible. The deductible is subtracted from the amount of the loss (not from the limit), and the remainder exceeds the limit of insurance. Therefore, the insurer pays the full building limit.

[DA02469]

Fire Department Service Charge

In some localities, the fire department may make a charge for its services in controlling or extinguishing a fire. The Fire Department Service Charge additional coverage pays fire department charges up to $1,000 for service at each location shown in the declarations, unless a higher limit is listed for a location.

The applicable limit for this additional coverage is payable separately from any other limit(s) of insurance shown in the declarations and is not subject to any deductible. To be payable, fire department service charges must be required by local ordinance or assumed by agreement prior to loss.

Pollutant Cleanup and Removal

The Pollutant Cleanup and Removal additional coverage provides limited coverage for the cleanup and removal of pollutants from land or water at the described premises. The BPP defines "pollutant" as:

> ...any solid, liquid, gaseous or thermal irritant or contaminant, including smoke, vapor, soot, fumes, acids, alkalis, chemicals and waste. Waste includes materials to be recycled, reconditioned or reclaimed. [3]

This additional coverage pays the insured's expenses to extract pollutants from land or water at the described premises if the release, discharge, dispersal, seepage, migration, or escape of the pollutants is the result of a covered cause of loss that occurs during the policy period. These expenses must be reported in writing within 180 days after the loss.

An aggregate limit of $10,000 per location applies to all such expenses that occur during each separate twelve- month period. The limit can be increased, but the few insurers that are willing to increase the limit rarely provide coverage for more than $25,000 or $50,000 per policy year.

Increased Cost of Construction

An Ordinance or Law exclusion excludes the increased cost to comply with ordinances or laws regulating the repair, rebuilding, or replacement of covered buildings.

The Increased Cost of Construction additional coverage provides a small amount of insurance to cover this loss exposure. The amount of insurance is equal to 5 percent of the amount of insurance or $10,000, whichever is less.

It is paid in addition to the policy limit. This additional coverage applies only if the replacement cost option has been selected.

No coverage applies to these items:

- Loss to any undamaged portion of the building that an ordinance or law does not permit to remain in use
- The cost to demolish the undamaged portion of the structure and remove its debris

Coverage for these excluded items, as well as higher limits for the increased cost to repair or reconstruct, can be provided by the Ordinance or Law Coverage Endorsement.

Electronic Data

Because of business' growing dependence on electronic data and the widespread belief that the exposure could better be treated by other forms of insurance, the BPP now contains an electronic data exclusion and the Electronic Data additional coverage. The aggregate limit of coverage is $2,500 (or a higher limit if shown in the declarations) per policy year regardless of the number of occurrences or locations covered. All electronic data damage is deemed to have been sustained in the policy year that an occurrence began, even if the damage continues or results in additional loss or damage in a subsequent policy year.

This additional coverage does not apply to the named insured's stock of prepackaged software or electronic data that are integrated in and operate or control the building's elevator, lighting, security, and climate control systems. The reason for this exclusion is that these same items are covered property because they are specifically excepted from the Property Not Covered section of the BPP.

Thus, they are covered up to the regular policy limits and are not subject to the low limit that ordinarily applies to the Electronic Data additional coverage. Protection of electronic data against a broader array of perils and for higher limits is available in inland marine and commercial crime insurance policies.

BPP COVERAGE EXTENSIONS

The Building and Personal Property Coverage Form, also referred to as the BPP, includes seven coverage extensions that apply only if certain conditions are met.

The BPP coverage extensions apply only if at least 80 percent coinsurance or a value reporting period symbol is shown in the declarations. The amounts payable under the coverage extensions are additional amounts of insurance and are not subject to the limits of insurance stated in the declarations.

These are the seven BPP coverage extensions:

- Newly Acquired or Constructed Property
- Personal Effects and Property of Others
- Valuable Papers and Records (Other Than Electronic Data)
- Property Off-Premises
- Outdoor Property
- Non-Owned Detached Trailers
- Business Personal Property Temporarily in Portable Storage Units

Newly Acquired or Constructed Property

If the policy covers a building, the Newly Acquired or Constructed Property extension provides automatic coverage for a new building being constructed at the premises described in the declarations.

Automatic coverage is also provided for newly acquired buildings at other locations, provided the purpose of the newly acquired building is similar to the use of the building described in the declarations or the newly acquired building will be used as a warehouse. The maximum amount of coverage is $250,000 at each building.

If the policy covers business personal property, the extension also provides automatic coverage for these:

- Business personal property at any newly acquired location other than fairs, trade shows, or exhibitions
- Business personal property located at newly constructed or acquired buildings at the location described in the declarations

The limit for the business personal property extension is $100,000 at each building. The extension does not apply to personal property of others temporarily in the named insured's possession in the course of installing or performing work on the property or in the course of the insured's manufacturing or wholesaling activities.

The coverage for buildings and business personal property provided by this extension is temporary. It terminates automatically at the earliest of three dates:

- The expiration date of the policy
- Thirty days after the acquisition of the new location or the start of construction of the new building
- The date the insured notifies the insurer of the new location or new building

The premium for the coverage is calculated from the date of acquisition or start of construction.

Personal Effects and Property of Others

The Personal Effects and Property of Others extension provides a limited amount of coverage for personal effects (such as a coat or jewelry) owned by an individual insured or a partner, a member, an officer, a manager, or an employee of the insured while on the premises described in the declarations. Personal effects are not covered for loss by theft.

The extension also covers property of others in the care, custody, or control of the insured. However, the limit on all property covered by this extension (personal effects and property of others) is $2,500 at each described location.

If the value of property of others is greater, insurance can be purchased on such property by showing a limit of insurance for personal property of others, as described previously, or by purchasing inland marine bailee coverage.

Valuable Papers and Records (Other Than Electronic Data)

Valuable papers and records (such as records of accounts receivable, mailing lists, legal documents, medical records, specifications, and drawings) are covered as business personal property, but only for the cost of blank records plus the labor to transcribe or copy duplicate information. This extension provides $2,500 of coverage for the cost of researching or reconstructing the lost information, but it does not apply to electronic data; previous versions of the BPP forms did cover the cost of reconstructing electronic data.

Coverage is limited to "specified perils" if the insured carries Special Form coverage, and to the perils covered by the Broad Form or Basic Form if the insured carries them. An insured can obtain additional limits on valuable papers and records coverage by entering a higher limit in the declarations or by using an inland marine form, which can provide broader coverage.

Property Off-Premises

The Property Off-Premises extension provides up to $10,000 in coverage for covered property while it is away from the described premises. In addition to property temporarily at locations that the insured does not own, lease, or operate, the extension covers property in storage at a location leased after the inception of the current policy and property at any fair, trade show, or exhibition.

This extension does not apply to property in or on a vehicle or in the custody of the insured's salespersons unless the property in custody is at a fair, trade show, or exhibition.

Outdoor Property

The Outdoor Property extension covers loss to outdoor fences; radio and television antennas (including satellite dishes); and trees, shrubs, and plants (other than those that are "stock" or part of a vegetated roof).

Unlike the other coverage extensions, the Outdoor Property extension has its own list of covered causes of loss. It covers only loss by fire, lightning, aircraft, riot or civil commotion, or explosion. (A mnemonic device useful for remembering these perils is "FLARE.")

Some of the more likely causes of loss to outdoor property—windstorm, vehicles, and vandalism—are not covered.

The limit of coverage is $1,000, including debris removal expense. However, not more than $250 may be applied to any one tree, shrub, or plant.

These limits apply regardless of the types or number of items lost or damaged in one occurrence. An insured can obtain coverage for higher limits and broader perils on outdoor property by adding a description and limit to the policy declarations as a separate item.

The coverage provided under the Outdoor Property extension for trees, shrubs, and plants includes removal of the debris of trees, shrubs, and plants from the described premises that are the property of others. However, this coverage extension does not apply to trees, shrubs, and plants owned by the landlord of an insured tenant.

Non-Owned Detached Trailers

Insureds frequently lease trailers to expand office space or to provide additional storage or work areas at their own premises. The leases usually require that the lessee provide insurance for the trailer while it is leased.

The Non-Owned Detached Trailers extension permits the insured to extend "your business personal property" to include such trailers. The trailer must be used in the insured's business and be in the insured's care, custody, or control at the described premises. Moreover, the insured must have a contractual responsibility to pay for loss or damage to the trailer.

The coverage does not apply while the trailer is attached to any motor vehicle or motorized conveyance, whether or not it is in motion. Nor does it apply during hitching or unhitching operations or when a trailer becomes accidentally unhitched from a motor vehicle or conveyance.

The limit of liability for this extension is $5,000 unless a higher limit is shown in the declarations, and the coverage is excess over any other insurance covering the trailer. An insured can obtain increased limits on such trailers by adding a description and limit to the policy declarations or by covering the property under an inland marine form.

Business Personal Property Temporarily in Portable Storage Units

This coverage extension provides temporary insurance for business personal property while stored in a portable storage unit, which could include either a unit specifically designed for this purpose or a detached trailer or semitrailer. For the contents of the unit to be covered, the unit must be located within 100 feet of the building or structure described in the declarations or within 100 feet of the described premises, whichever distance is greater.

The coverage is truly limited to temporary storage: coverage ends ninety days after the property is placed in the unit. Moreover, the coverage does not apply if the unit has been in use at the described premises for more than ninety days. Unless a higher limit is shown in the declarations, $10,000 is the most that the insurer will pay for business personal property under this extension, regardless of the number of units in use.

BPP CONDITIONS

The BPP is subject to the Common Policy Conditions and the Commercial Property Conditions. The BPP also contains several conditions, some of which are unique to the BPP form.

The conditions by which coverage is provided by the BPP include these:

- Limits of Insurance
- Deductible
- Valuation

Limits of Insurance

The BPP states that the most the insurer will pay in any one occurrence is the applicable limit of insurance shown in the policy declarations. Except for the additional coverages for pollution cleanup and removal and electronic data, none of the BPP coverages are subject to an aggregate limit capping the amount recoverable under that coverage each policy year.

Although the BPP limits apply separately to each occurrence, the BPP does not define the term "occurrence." See the exhibit "What is an Occurrence?."

The 2007 edition of the BPP limits recovery for outdoor signs, whether or not they are attached to a building, to $2,500 per sign in any one occurrence. Higher limits for outdoor signs can be provided by the Outdoor Signs endorsement (CP 14 40) or an inland marine form. (Previous editions of the BPP had lower limits on outdoor signs, and signs not attached to buildings were covered for only limited perils.)

Several of the BPP additional coverages are subject to per-occurrence limits, including the Debris Removal, Fire Department Service Charge, and Increased Cost of Construction coverages. Additionally, each of the Coverage Extensions in the BPP form is subject to a per-occurrence limit.

Deductible

Under CLM rules, the standard BPP deductible is $500, and rate credits are allowed for deductibles higher than $500. Generally, deductibles higher than $10,000 are typically imposed by insurers as an underwriting tool rather than requested by insureds. The savings in premium is seldom enough to make higher deductibles attractive to insureds.

What is an Occurrence?

The BPP and many other commercial property forms do not define the term "occurrence." An exception is earthquake forms, which define occurrence because of the problem posed by aftershocks. Liability insurance policies also generally include a definition of occurrence. Insureds usually benefit from a broad interpretation of occurrence because deductibles generally apply per occurrence. This example illustrates two approaches to defining and interpreting "occurrence."

A Midwest landlord owns four apartment buildings within a city block of one another and insures them under a BPP with a $1.5 million limit of insurance on each building and a $5,000 deductible per occurrence. A tornado strikes the city and destroys all four buildings within minutes. One of two approaches could be taken to determine application of the deductible, depending on the jurisdiction's definition and interpretation of "occurrence":

- The first interpretation considers the cause of the loss. Because all four building losses resulted from one cause (the tornado that struck the area), the loss of the four buildings could be viewed as one occurrence. Under this interpretation, the $5,000 deductible would apply once for all four buildings; therefore, $5,000 would be deducted from the total loss before any damages were paid.

- Another interpretation considers the effect of the cause of loss. Because four different buildings were damaged, a single loss occurrence can apply to each building. Therefore, this case would constitute four occurrences, despite only one cause of loss. The $5,000 deductible would be applied to each building that was damaged, resulting in a $20,000 deduction from the total loss before any damages were paid.

[DA05948]

The insurer is not obligated to pay anything to the insured unless the loss exceeds the applicable deductible. The limit of insurance then applies to the adjusted amount of loss in excess of the deductible. In colloquial terms, the deductible comes off the loss, not off the limit of insurance. For example, payment under a policy with a $100,000 limit and a $1,000 deductible in each of these losses would be as shown (assuming no coinsurance penalty applied):

- $500 loss: No payment (loss is less than the deductible)
- $100,000 loss: $99,000 payment ($100,000 – $1,000 deductible)
- $110,000 loss: $100,000 payment ($110,000 – $1,000 deductible exceeds the limit of insurance)

The BPP states that when an occurrence involves loss to two or more items of covered property that are insured for separate limits, the losses cannot be combined in determining the application of the deductible. For example, the insurer would make no payment for fire damage of $800 to a building and $400 to business personal property under a policy with a $1,000 deductible that had separate building and business personal property limits.

This provision could pose a problem for insureds with larger deductibles and numerous separately insured items. An insured with a policy covering ten items for separate limits and subject to a $5,000 deductible would receive no payment if each item sustained $3,000 of damage in a windstorm. In effect, the insured would incur a $30,000 deductible.

The application of the deductible to separately scheduled items underscores a potential advantage of blanket coverage. (With blanket insurance, a single limit of insurance applies to two or more items of covered property.) It can be argued that each group of blanketed property is one item with one limit of insurance and therefore the provision regarding loss to separately insured items would not come into play.

Based on that reasoning, if the ten items were insured on a blanket basis, subject to one limit, the insured would collect $25,000 if each of the ten items sustained $3,000 damage. Because insureds usually choose $500 or $1,000 deductibles and losses seldom involve more than a few items, the provision regarding loss to separately insured items will not cause serious economic injury in most cases.

Returning to the example of a schedule policy covering ten items for separate limits, if one of the items sustained damage in excess of the deductible, say $6,000, the insurer would pay $1,000 for that item, after subtracting the $5,000 deductible. Then, because the BPP states that the deductible applies only once per occurrence, the insurer would pay $27,000 for the damage to the other nine items. A blanket policy produces the same result when the loss to one item exceeds the deductible.

Valuation

Three different valuation approaches are actual cash value (ACV), replacement cost, and selling price. The standard valuation provision for most property covered by the BPP is ACV. The ACV approach can be changed to replacement cost valuation by activating the Replacement Cost optional coverage. Regardless of whether the optional coverage is activated, the categories of property that follow are subject to special valuation provisions.

Small Building Losses

If the limit of building insurance satisfies the Coinsurance condition and the cost to repair or replace damaged building property is $2,500 or less, the insurer will pay the full cost of repair or replacement without any deduction for depreciation. Because the term "building" means more than just the structure, this valuation provision also applies to any items included in the building definition except for these, which the valuation provision specifically excludes:

- Awnings or floor coverings
- Appliances for refrigerating, ventilating, cooking, dishwashing, or laundering
- Outdoor equipment or furniture

Stocks Sold But Not Delivered

Stock that has been sold but not delivered is valued at selling price less any unincurred discounts or expenses.

Safety Glass

Many communities require the use of safety glazing materials, rather than ordinary plate glass, when replacing glass in doors, shower stalls, and similar places where people are exposed to injury by broken glass. If glass breakage is covered, the insurer will pay the increased cost for the required safety glazing.

Tenants' Improvements and Betterments

The BPP specifies the different ways of determining the amount a tenant can recover for loss to improvements and betterments in which the tenant has a use interest. (When the insured is the building owner, as opposed to a tenant in the building, improvements and betterments are covered as part of the building and therefore subject to whatever valuation basis—ACV or replacement cost—applies to the building coverage.)

When the tenant promptly repairs or replaces improvements or betterments, the tenant's insurer pays the ACV—or replacement cost, if that option has been chosen—of the improvements or betterments. If the tenant does not repair or replace the improvements or betterments promptly, the tenant's insurer pays a pro rata portion of their original cost.

For example, suppose improvements costing $100,000 were installed on June 1, 2004, and that the insured's lease was due to expire on June 1, 2014. On June 1, 2009, the improvements were destroyed, and not replaced. The tenant had invested $100,000, expecting to use the improvements for ten years (2004 to 2014). However, only five of those ten years had passed at the time of the loss. Because five-tenths (one-half) of the original cost had been "used up" at the time of the loss, the insurer paid one-half of the original $100,000 cost, or $50,000, to cover the loss of the tenant's remaining use interest.

If others pay for the repairs (for example the owner or general lessee), the tenant's insurance pays nothing.

BPP: OPTIONAL COVERAGES

The Optional Coverages section of the BPP contains provisions for four optional coverages:

- Agreed Value
- Inflation Guard
- Replacement Cost
- Extension of Replacement Cost to Personal Property of Others

The optional coverages apply only when an appropriate notation is made on the declarations page. Agreed Value, Inflation Guard, and Replacement Cost may be used for buildings only, personal property only, or both buildings and personal property.

Agreed Value

Agreed Value optional coverage

Optional coverage that suspends the Coinsurance condition if the insured carries the amount of insurance agreed to by the insurer and insured.

To activate the **Agreed Value optional coverage**, an amount is entered under the Agreed Value heading in the declarations for each category of property (building, personal property, or both) to which the option applies. This option enables the insured to remove the uncertainty as to whether the amount of insurance carried complies with the Coinsurance condition. With the option in force, the insurer and the insured have agreed in advance that the amount stated in the declarations—the agreed value—is adequate for coinsurance purposes. Because most losses are partial, insureds are often tempted to underinsure, knowing they will not suffer a coinsurance penalty when the agreed value option is in effect. Therefore, insurers underwrite agreed value carefully, requiring proof of value before providing agreed value coverage. At the very least, the insured ordinarily must submit a signed statement of values. Insurance Services Office, Inc. (ISO) Form CP 16 15, Statement of Values, can be used for this purpose.

The BPP Coinsurance condition does not apply to property insured under the agreed value option. However, it is replaced by a provision that, while not called coinsurance, is the practical equivalent of 100 percent coinsurance based on the agreed value. The agreed value option provides that if the limit of insurance equals or exceeds the agreed value stated in the declarations, losses will be paid in full up to the limit of insurance. If the limit of insurance is less than the agreed value, the amount of loss payment is calculated by this equation:

$$\text{Loss payment} = \left(\frac{\text{Limit of insurance}}{\text{Agreed value}} \times \text{Loss} \right) - \text{Deductible}$$

Coverage under this option extends until the agreed value expiration date shown on the declarations or the expiration date of the policy, whichever occurs first. If the coverage option is not renewed, the Coinsurance condition is reinstated.

Inflation Guard

Inflation Guard optional coverage is coverage for the effects of inflation that automatically increases the limit of insurance by the percentage of annual increase shown in the declarations. This percentage is applied on a pro rata basis, from the date the limit of insurance became effective to the date of the loss, before the loss payment is computed. The percentage of annual increase is shown separately for buildings and personal property.

Replacement Cost

The **Replacement Cost optional coverage** replaces the phrase "actual cash value" with "replacement cost" in the BPP Valuation condition. As a result, the insurer is obligated to pay the cost to replace the damaged or destroyed property with new property of like kind and quality without any deduction for depreciation or obsolescence.

The insurer is not obligated to pay replacement cost until the property has been repaired or replaced, and then only if such repair or replacement is completed in a reasonable time. If repair or replacement is not completed in a reasonable time, the loss payment is based on the actual cash value (ACV) at the time of loss.

The insured may make a claim on the basis of ACV, with the difference between ACV and replacement cost to be paid upon completion of repair or reconstruction. The insurer must be notified within 180 days after the occurrence of loss that a claim will be made for replacement cost.

If the replacement cost option is activated, the Coinsurance condition continues to apply, but with one important difference. The amount of insurance required by the Coinsurance condition is calculated by multiplying replacement cost by the coinsurance percentage if the claim is made on a replacement cost basis. If the insured makes a claim on an ACV basis, coinsurance is also calculated on an ACV basis.

If the replacement cost option is selected, tenants' improvements and betterments are also valued at replacement cost if the tenant actually repairs or replaces them, at its own cost, as soon as reasonably possible after the loss.

The replacement cost option does not apply to property of others; contents of a residence; manuscripts; or works of art, antiques, or rare articles. It also does not apply to "stock" unless the declarations indicate that the replacement cost option includes stock. The BPP defines stock to mean merchandise, raw materials, goods in process, and finished goods.

Inflation Guard optional coverage
Coverage for the effects of inflation that automatically increases the limit of insurance by the percentage of annual increase shown in the declarations.

Replacement Cost optional coverage
Coverage for losses to most types of property on a replacement cost basis (with no deduction for depreciation or obsolescence) instead of on an actual cash value basis.

Extension of Replacement Cost to Personal Property of Others

Insureds frequently lease photocopiers, computers, phone systems, and other equipment. These leases or agreements may make the insured responsible for the replacement cost of these items in the event they are damaged. To cover this loss exposure, insureds who have selected the replacement cost option may also elect to have the personal property of others valued at replacement cost. In such cases, the amount of the loss is calculated according to the written agreement between the insured and the owner of the property, but it cannot exceed the replacement cost of the property or the applicable limit of insurance.

COMMERCIAL PROPERTY CLAIM CASE

Businesses most frequently manage their property damage risk through the purchase of insurance. Therefore, when a loss occurs, the insured relies on an insurance professional to advise what damages are covered and how much will be paid.

This case helps the insurance professional to apply the coverage found under the Building and Personal Property Coverage Form (also referred to as the BPP) to a given set of facts.

Case Facts

Given the facts of this case, will the commercial building and personal property loss be covered? If so, will all the items claimed be covered and what amounts will be paid?

Josh Jones is the owner of J's Smalltown Hardware Store at 135 Main Street, Smalltown, United States. Josh is the fourth-generation owner of the business. The store has grown from one small storefront to half the city block. As the business grew into adjoining space, walls were taken down or large doorways were created. During the Depression, the owners bought the building behind the store, which was subsequently torn down to add a seasonal outdoor sales area and additional customer parking. In this area, there are two wooden deck platforms where merchandise is displayed, surrounded by a four-foot iron fence.

The main sales area is located on the first floor. The business uses the second floor mainly for office space and some storage. Over the decades, a vast collection of hardware odds and ends has accumulated on the third floor. Customers who are now remodeling the older homes in town spend hours on the third floor looking for just the right vintage items for their own projects.

On June 5, 20XX, a tornado struck half a mile to the north of J's. The store sustained considerable damage. The winds tore away a corner of the flat roof, allowing torrential rains to enter the building. The vast collection of hardware items on the third floor was soaked, packaging was ruined, and many items were too wet to salvage. The water also soaked the main office area on the second floor, destroying the computer as well as the printer. There was also minor water damage to the main floor sales area.

Due to the high winds, many items in the seasonal outdoor area became airborne and were damaged when they struck the ground or other items. There was considerable damage, with merchandise scattered throughout the entire area.

Josh promptly notified his insurance company of the loss and with the help of his staff, completed a list of damages. See the exhibit "Damage Estimate."

Josh has a commercial package policy that includes a BPP and the Causes of Loss—Speacial Form covering the hardware store that applies on the date of this loss. The policy does not contain any endorsements; however, the insured has elected the replacement cost option for the building and for owned personal property. This option is indicated on the declarations page. Personal Property of Others coverage is provided on an actual cash value (ACV) basis. See the exhibit "Coverage Facts."

Case Analysis Tools

To determine whether Josh's policy will cover losses due to the windstorm, the insurer's claims representative, Kathy, will first need to review the information on the policy declarations page. The declarations page identifies who is covered, which locations are covered, the policy period, the coverage provided, limits of liability, and any deductibles that apply.

It is important to have a copy of the BPP, the Causes of Loss—Special Form, and any applicable endorsements. In this case, there are no endorsements. The BPP describes the types of property that are and are not covered, and any additional coverages or coverage extensions that may apply.

Determination of Coverage

To determine whether the policy issued to J's Hardware covers this loss, Kathy will first examine the declarations page. The declarations page indicates J's Smalltown Hardware Store as the insured and the property location is listed as 135 Main Street, Smalltown, U.S. The date of loss falls within the policy period shown.

The next step is to determine whether the loss has triggered coverage under the BPP's insuring agreement. For this windstorm loss, Kathy reviews Section A. If coverage is triggered, the insurer agrees to make payment.

Because wind is a covered cause of loss, coverage for direct physical damage is triggered under the BPP (See Section A, "Coverage" of the BPP). Kathy must

Damage Estimate

Item	Description	Amount
Wind and water damage to building	Repairs to roof, first-floor ceiling, second-floor office area, and third-floor storage area.	$86,400
Personal property	Damage to merchandise on display in first-floor sales area and in storage.	7,500
Office furniture and supplies	Desks, chairs, and other related items in office.	3,500
Leased computer equipment	Requesting the required lease payment as the equipment cannot be repaired.	3,000
Pollution clean up	Items were driven by wind and then struck bags of fertilizer, pesticides, and weed killer, spilling their contents. These contents were then forced by the rain into an unpaved area behind the building containing a pond. Authorities required the run-off to be cleaned up.	12,985
Two pick-up trucks with broken windshields	Damage to two trucks used for deliveries and on-premises snow removal.	1,200
Lawnmowers in stock	Eight lawnmowers being held for sale and stored outside sustained major damage and cannot be sold. (J's cost $500 each, retail price $899 each).	7,192
Customers' lawnmowers	Three lawnmowers stored outside awaiting repair sustained damage (value to replace: $899, $698, and $1,096).	2,693
Collection of old hardware	Value difficult to determine, but has a declared value of $3500 for state business property tax purposes, which may be low. The listed amount is an estimate, given that a number of items would be considered antiques.	7,645
Iron fence around outdoor sales area	Damaged beyond repair.	2,200
Pine straw	100 bales held for sale outside of the building (J's cost $2.25 each, retail price $4.95).	495
Total		$134,810

[DA05964]

Coverage Facts

Policy form	Building and Personal Property Coverage Form
Policy dates	01-15-20x0 to 01-15-20x1
Insured	J's Smalltown Hardware Store
Address	135 Main Street Smalltown, USA
Mortgage Holder	None
Building	$800,000 (Replacement cost)
Your Business Personal Property	$1,000,000 (Replacement cost)
Personal Property of Others	$25,000 (ACV)
Deductible	$1,000
Endorsements	None
Building Description	• Three-story masonry veneer built in 1890 with additions in 1927 and 1956—21,000 total square footage • Fire district—Cook Township, Protection Class 7, flat roof type
Occupancy	• Hardware store—Retail sales, service, and delivery of hardware items, lawnmowers, trimmers, blowers, snow blowers, home garden items, plants, and hardscape, including fertilizers and pesticides • Office area on second floor with some storage; storage on third floor

[DA05965]

next determine if the damaged property is covered. The insured is making claim for three types of property: the building in which J's business is located, personal property owned by J's, and customers' property.

Kathy reviews A.1., Covered Property in the BPP and notes that for coverage to apply there must be a limit shown for that property type on the declarations sheet. The BPP lists three types of covered property: Building, Your Business Personal Property, and Personal Property of Others. The declarations page shows limits for each of these property types.

Kathy determines that the building damage falls within the policy description. The damage to the iron fence around the outdoor sales area appears to fall within the description of a.(2) "Fixtures, including outdoor fixtures," but this will have to be analyzed further.

BPP - Section A.1.a. - Covered Property - Building

1. Covered Property

Covered Property, as used in this Coverage Part, means the type of property described in this section, A.1., and limited in A.2., Property Not Covered, if a Limit Of Insurance is shown in the Declarations for that type of property.

a. Building, meaning the building or structure described in the Declarations, including:

(1) Completed additions;

(2) Fixtures, including outdoor fixtures;

(3) Permanently installed:

(a) Machinery and

(b) Equipment;

(4) Personal property owned by you that is used to maintain or service the building or structure or its premises, including:

(a) Fire-extinguishing equipment;

(b) Outdoor furniture;

(c) Floor coverings; and

(d) Appliances used for refrigerating, ventilating, cooking, dishwashing or laundering;

(5) If not covered by other insurance:

(a) Additions under construction, alterations and repairs to the building or structure;

(b) Materials, equipment, supplies and temporary structures, on or within 100 feet of the described premises, used for making additions, alterations or repairs to the building or structure. [4]

Kathy further determines that the eight lawnmowers held for sale, the collection of old hardware on the third floor, office furniture and supplies on the second floor, merchandise on the first floor, and the straw bales fall within personal property coverage. The leased computers would qualify under b.(7) if the lease agreement requires J's to be responsible for insuring them. Kathy reviews the lease provided by J's and finds this to be required.

BPP - Section A.1.b. - Covered Property- Business Personal Property

b. Your Business Personal Property consists of the following property located in or on the building or structure described in the Declarations or in the open (or in a vehicle) within 100 feet of the building or structure or within 100 feet of the premises described in the Declarations, whichever distance is greater:

(1) Furniture and fixtures;

(2) Machinery and equipment;

(3) "Stock";

(4) All other personal property owned by you and used in your business;

(5) Labor, materials or services furnished or arranged by you on personal property of others;

(6) Your use interest as tenant in improvements and betterments. Improvements and betterments are fixtures, alterations, installations or additions:

(a) Made a part of the building or structure you occupy but do not own; and

(b) You acquired or made at your expense but cannot legally remove;

(7) Leased personal property for which you have a contractual responsibility to insure, unless otherwise provided for under Personal Property Of Others.[5]

Kathy also notes that if J's had done any work on the three lawnmowers owned by the customers that J's would have coverage for their labor or materials. Josh is contacted to confirm this and he states that they had not yet done any work on the customers' lawnmowers that were damaged. The three customers' lawnmowers would be covered under Personal Property of Others (see Section A.1.c., "Personal Property of Others" of the BPP). This section provides coverage for property of others in the insured's care, custody, or control while in the open within 100 feet of the building or structure or within 100 feet of the described premises. Payment will be made to the owner of the property and not to the insured. Kathy contacts J's to acquire the needed contact information for each customer.

Kathy must now check the "Property Not Covered" section A.2. of the BPP to determine if any items might be excluded from coverage. Item p. excludes any vehicles that are used on public roads; therefore, the windshield damage for the two vehicles will not be covered under the property policy. Item q. excludes grain, hay, or straw while outside of the building, which means that there is also no coverage for the pine straw bales. This item also excludes fences but indicates "all except as provided in the Coverage Extensions." Kathy must first review that section of the policy before making a decision on coverage for the fence around the outside sales area.

Kathy then examines Section A.4., "Additional Coverages." Item d. provides coverage for pollution clean-up and removal. Therefore, the cost of cleaning up the fertilizer and pesticides that seeped into the pond is covered.

BPP - Section A.4.d. - Additional Coverages - Pollution Clean-up and Removal

d. Pollutant Clean-up And Removal

We will pay your expense to extract "pollutants" from land or water at the described premises if the discharge, dispersal, seepage, migration, release or escape of the "pollutants" is caused by or results from a Covered Cause of Loss that occurs during the policy period. The expenses will be paid only if they are reported to us in writing within 180 days of the date on which the Covered Cause of Loss occurs.

This Additional Coverage does not apply to costs to test for, monitor or assess the existence, concentration or effects of "pollutants". But we will pay for testing which is performed in the course of extracting the "pollutants" from the land or water.

The most we will pay under this Additional Coverage for each described premises is $10,000 for the sum of all covered expenses arising out of Covered Causes of Loss occurring during each separate 12-month period of this policy.[6]

Kathy has not resolved the coverage issue concerning the outdoor fence and reviews the Coverage Extensions section of the policy. Item e. provides coverage for outdoor property, including fences, but this coverage is limited to certain covered causes of loss. As wind is not listed as a covered cause of loss, the fence is not covered under this policy.

BPP - Section A.5.e. - Coverage Extensions - Outdoor Property

e. Outdoor Property

You may extend the insurance provided by this Coverage Form to apply to your outdoor fences, radio and television antennas (including satellite dishes), trees, shrubs and plants (other than trees, shrubs or plants which are "stock" or are part of a vegetated roof), including debris removal expense, caused by or resulting from any of the following causes of loss if they are Covered Causes of Loss:

(1) Fire;

(2) Lightning;

(3) Explosion;

(4) Riot or Civil Commotion; or

(5) Aircraft.

The most we will pay for loss or damage under this Extension is $1,000, but not more than $250 for any one tree, shrub or plant. These limits apply to any one occurrence, regardless of the types or number of items lost or damaged in that occurrence.[7]

Kathy must next determine whether the insureds comply with all policy conditions. J's promptly reported the claims and has fully cooperated in the claims investigation as required under Duties in the Event of Loss or Damage. J's building was not vacant at the time of the loss and the value of the covered property meets the policy coinsurance provision and is within the policy limits. Therefore, the insured complies with all policy conditions.

Determination of Amounts Payable

Having completed the policy analysis for coverage, Kathy now determines the amounts payable under the policy. Because Josh has selected the replacement cost option for the building and owned personal property, there will be no depreciation or actual cash value (ACV) calculations necessary on these items. This option does not apply to personal property of others, so the customers' lawnmowers will be adjusted on an ACV basis.

A property expert has reviewed the damage to the premises and states that the repair estimates are appropriate, so the $86,400 damage to the building and the $7,500 damage to personal property of the insured will be covered on a replacement cost basis. This expert also went through the damaged items on the third floor with Josh. They decided which items could still be held for sale and which could not. Based on this review, the expert established a loss value of $3,425. The office furniture on the second floor is also covered in full for $3,500, as is the leased computer for $3,000.

The Additional Coverages for Pollution Clean-Up is limited to $10,000, which is the amount that will be paid for the fertilizer and pesticides that seeped into the pond.

Kathy knows that the eight lawnmowers are covered property but is uncertain of the amount payable under the policy. The policy states that the insured's loss payment will not be more than its financial interest in the covered property (see Section A.4.d., "Loss Payment" in the BPP). This means that the lawnmowers will be paid at J's cost of $500 each and not at the retail price of $899. The total amount paid will be $4,000.

The payment for the three customers' lawnmowers that were awaiting repairs will be settled directly with each owner on an ACV basis. A depreciation factor of 60 percent will be applied to the loss amount.

These amounts are all within the policy limits of $800,000 for Building, $1,000,000 for Your Business Personal Property, and $25,000 for Personal Property of Others. See the exhibit "Correct Answers."

Correct Answers

Items	Claimed	Coverage Limits Issues	Amount Payable
Repairs to building	$86,400	$1,000 deductible	$85,400
Personal Property	7,500	None	7,500
Pollution Clean-Up	12,985	$10,000 limit in item "d"—Additional Coverages	10,000
Damage to trucks	1,200	Not covered	0
Lawnmowers in stock	7,192	Limited to insured's financial interest	4,000
Customers' lawnmowers	2,693	Paid to individual owners at ACV.	1,616
Old hardware	7,645	Appraised value	3,425
Iron fence around outside sales area	2,200.	Not covered	0
Office furniture and supplies	3,500	None	3,500
Computer equipment	3,000	None	3,000
Pine straw bales	495	Not Covered	0
Total	$134,810		$118,441

[DA05967]

SUMMARY

The Building and Personal Property Coverage Form (BPP) includes separate coverage categories for Building, Your Business Personal Property, and Personal Property of Others.

The BPP contains an extensive list of property not covered. The three general categories of excluded items are buildings and other real property; plants and outdoor property; and other personal property.

Several of the excluded items are types of real property (such as land, roadways, and foundations below the lowest basement floor). Another category of excluded items includes plants and other types of outdoor property, such as antennas and fences.

Other types of excluded property include money, securities, and electronic data. Almost all of the excluded items can be covered by endorsement to the BPP or by another policy.

The BPP contains additional coverages that provide limited coverage for these exposures:

- Debris removal
- Preservation of property
- Fire department service charges
- Pollutant cleanup and removal
- Increased cost of construction
- Electronic data

The BPP contains coverage extensions that provide limited coverage for these exposures:

- Newly acquired or constructed property
- Personal effects and property of others
- The cost to reconstruct information on destroyed records, other than electronic data
- Property while off the insured premises
- Certain types of outdoor property
- Nonowned detached trailers
- Business personal property temporarily in portable storage units

The BPP is subject to the Common Policy Conditions and the Commercial Property Conditions. The BPP also contains several conditions, including BPP conditions that are unique to this form.

The BPP contains four optional coverages: Agreed Value, Inflation Guard, Replacement Cost, and Extension of Replacement Cost to Personal Property of Others. Optional Coverages only apply when an appropriate notation is made on the declarations page.

To respond to an insured's inquires concerning coverages and amounts payable on actual and potential losses properly, an insurance professional should acquire the applicable coverage forms and endorsements and verify the information on the declarations sheet with the facts of the loss.

ASSIGNMENT NOTES

1. Paul I. Thomas and Prentiss B. Reed, Sr., *Adjustment of Property Losses*, 4th ed. (New York: McGraw-Hill Book Company, 1977), pp. 202–203.

2. American Guarantee & Liability Insurance Company v. Ingram Micro, Inc., 2000 WL 726789 (D.Ariz.).

3. Includes copyrighted material of Insurance Services Office, Inc., with its permission. Copyright, Insurance Services Office, Inc., 2011.

4. Includes copyrighted material of Insurance Services Office, Inc., with its permission. Copyright, Insurance Services Office, Inc., 2011.

5. Includes copyrighted material of Insurance Services Office, Inc., with its permission. Copyright, Insurance Services Office, Inc., 2011.

6. Includes copyrighted material of Insurance Services Office, Inc., with its permission. Copyright, Insurance Services Office, Inc., 2011.

7. Includes copyrighted material of Insurance Services Office, Inc., with its permission. Copyright, Insurance Services Office, Inc., 2011.

Causes of Loss Forms

Educational Objectives

After learning the content of this assignment, you should be able to:

▷ Summarize the provisions that define the covered causes of loss and the additional coverages of the Causes of Loss—Basic Form and the Causes of Loss—Broad Form.

▷ Summarize the exclusions in the Causes of Loss—Basic Form and the Causes of Loss—Broad Form.

▷ Determine whether the cause of a described loss is a Covered Cause of Loss under the Causes of Loss—Special Form.

▷ Determine whether one or more of these forms cover a described loss:

- Causes of Loss—Basic Form
- Causes of Loss—Broad Form
- Causes of Loss—Special Form

Causes of Loss Forms

3

CAUSES OF LOSS—BASIC AND BROAD FORMS

Three causes of loss forms are available for designating the perils covered by the Building and Personal Property Coverage Form (BPP) and other commercial property coverage forms developed by Insurance Services Office, Inc. (ISO). The causes of loss forms provide three progressive levels of coverage.

The **Causes of Loss—Basic Form** (CP 10 10) covers fire and other specified causes of loss, while the **Causes of Loss—Broad Form** (CP 10 20) covers the same specified causes of loss as the Basic Form, plus a few others. A third causes of loss form is the Special Form (CP 10 30).

The Causes of Loss—Basic Form and the Causes of Loss—Broad Form are very similar. Both forms specify the causes of loss they cover, subject to several exclusions. If one of the covered causes of loss damages covered property, the loss is covered unless any of the form's exclusions applies. The difference between the two forms is that the Broad Form covers a few more causes of loss than does the Basic Form. The policy language is identical for the perils that both forms cover. See the exhibit "Important Phrases."

Perils Covered by the Basic and Broad Forms

The Basic Form and the Broad Form specifically define only some of the covered perils. The perils defined in the Basic Form are aircraft or vehicles, vandalism, sprinkler leakage, sinkhole collapse, and volcanic action. See the exhibit "Basic Versus Broad Form."

Of the three perils added by the Broad Form, only one—water damage—is defined. When a peril is not defined in the form, common usage, as exemplified by dictionary definitions, prevails unless statutes or courts have defined the term. Whether or not they are defined, all the covered perils, with the exceptions of fire and lightning, are subject to provisions that impose some conditions or limitations on coverage.

Fire

Protection against fire loss was the motivation for forming the first insurance companies in the United States. Fire has always been a relatively common cause of loss, and, unlike some other insured perils, fire can completely destroy a building and its contents. Despite the advances in fire safety technology, fire is still a frequent and often severe cause of property loss.

Causes of Loss—
Basic Form

Form that covers fire, lightning, explosion, windstorm, hail, smoke, aircraft, vehicles, riot, civil commotion, vandalism, sprinkler leakage, sinkhole collapse, and volcanic action.

Causes of Loss—
Broad Form

Form that covers basic form perils plus falling objects; weight of snow, ice, or sleet; water damage; and (as additional coverage) collapse caused by certain perils.

Important Phrases

When any of the causes of loss forms is combined with a coverage form, the causes of loss form is linked by the Coverage provision in the coverage form. In the Building and Personal Property Form (BPP) and many other forms, the Coverage provision indicates that a loss must be a "direct physical loss," and it must be "caused by or resulting from any Covered Cause of Loss." The policy declarations page lists the applicable causes of loss form(s). The phrase "direct physical loss" usually means actual, perceptible damage to, or disappearance of, the covered property. The word "direct" also implies that consequential losses are not covered even when they are caused by covered physical damage. For a loss to be covered, a covered cause of loss must be the proximate cause of the loss. The proximate cause does not have to be the immediate cause of the loss but rather is the cause that sets in motion an unbroken chain of events producing the loss. Nevertheless, the proximate cause must be closely related in time and distance to the loss.

Because of the doctrine of proximate cause, the Basic Form and the Broad Form provide more coverage than is first apparent. For example, an insured with premises on the second floor of a high-rise building whose coverage includes fire as a cause of loss will be covered for water damage to its property resulting from attempts to fight a fire on the tenth floor of the building even though water damage is not a covered peril in the insured's policy. Fire was the proximate cause of the loss.

When the chain of events leading to a loss includes both covered and excluded causes of loss, determining whether loss has been caused by a covered cause of loss can be difficult. In the absence of any specific contractual provision, the most general rule is that once a covered peril has occurred, all subsequent damage is also covered, even when an excluded peril has meanwhile intervened, unless the policy clearly states otherwise. This rule has been modified by the anti-concurrent cause language incorporated into many forms; consequently, proximate cause is an area in which the advice of coverage counsel may be needed in complex cases.

[DA05988]

Although the Basic Form and the Broad Form list fire as a covered peril without any further description, courts have generally held that a fire must involve a flame or glow and rapid oxidation. The flame or glow requirement may not be met when a substance merely smokes because of a buildup of heat but does not actually flame or glow. Courts have also interpreted fire to mean hostile fire, not friendly fire. Hostile fire is a fire that becomes uncontrollable or breaks out from where it was intended to be. A friendly fire is one that remains inside its intended receptacle.

For example, a fire in a fireplace or an incinerator is a friendly fire. If an employee of the insured accidentally puts covered property into an incinerator, the resulting loss of the covered property is not covered if the fire peril is interpreted to include only hostile fire. However, if an ember flies out of a fireplace onto a carpet and sets it on fire, the fire is considered hostile, and the resulting loss is covered under the fire peril.

Basic Versus Broad Form

Both Forms Cover

Fire

Lightning

Explosion

Windstorm or hail

Smoke

Aircraft or vehicles

Riot or civil commotion

Vandalism

Sprinkler leakage

Sinkhole collapse

Volcanic action

Fungus (provided as an additional coverage)

Broad Form Also Covers

Falling objects

Weight of snow, ice, sleet

Water damage

Collapse (provided as an additional coverage)

[DA03510]

In addition to covering loss of property actually burned by fire, the fire peril covers heat and smoke damage resulting from a fire, as well as water damage resulting from attempts to put out the fire. The fire peril also covers other damage to covered property proximately caused by a fire—for example, when firefighters break out windows and knock down doors in the course of extinguishing a fire.

Lightning

Like fire, lightning is listed as a covered peril without further description. Lightning is an electrical discharge from cloud to cloud, between a cloud and the earth, or from earth to a cloud, as opposed to artificially generated electrical currents. To clarify the distinction, the form excludes loss or damage caused by artificially generated electrical current.

If, for example, a surge in voltage damaged a computer, the lightning peril would cover the loss if the surge was caused by lightning, but not if the surge was caused by excessive voltage generated by the utility company.

Explosion

A typical dictionary definition of explosion is "a large-scale, rapid, or spectacular expansion or bursting out or forth" (*Merriam-Webster's Collegiate*

Dictionary, 11th ed.). The explosion peril specifically excludes rupture or bursting because of expansion or swelling of the contents of any building or structure caused by or resulting from water. If, for example, excess moisture in a grain storage silo or elevator causes a sudden expansion and collapse of the structure, the cause of loss will not be covered as an explosion.

The explosion peril also states that "rupture, bursting or operation of pressure relief devices"[1] is not an explosion. This provision refers to the damage that might ensue from the operation of safety valves on steam boilers, hot-water tanks, air tanks, and so forth, which intentionally release excess pressure to avoid damage to the vessel to which the safety valve is attached.

Most furnaces are operated by the combustion of fossil fuels (such as coal, fuel oil, or natural gas), which are burned in a combustion chamber, or "firebox." Explosion of the fuel or gases—called combustion explosion or furnace explosion—is specifically included in the explosion peril.

All three causes of loss forms exclude explosion of steam boilers, steam pipes, steam engines, or steam turbines owned or leased by the insured or operated under the insured's control. This exclusion contains an exception clarifying that loss by fire or combustion explosion that results from an excluded steam boiler explosion is covered. Because steam vessels contain steam under high pressure, they pose a severe explosion risk that insurers underwrite and insure separately under equipment breakdown insurance.

Windstorm or Hail

The perils of windstorm and hail are combined in most property insurance policies that insure against these perils. Generally speaking, a windstorm is a wind of unusual strength that has produced general damage in an area at a particular time. Hurricanes and tornadoes are both windstorms. Less violent windstorms also can cause property damage.

While the Basic Form and the Broad Form do not define windstorm and hail, the forms describe what is not included within those perils. The windstorm or hail peril provides no coverage for losses caused by (1) frost or cold weather or (2) ice (other than hail), snow, or sleet—whether driven by wind or not.

The windstorm or hail peril also does not cover damage to the interior of the building or to its contents caused by rain, snow, sand, or dust unless the force of wind or hail first causes external damage to an insured structure through which the rain, snow, sand, or dust enters. For example, damage caused by rain that a windstorm blows through an open window, roof vents, or cracks is not covered. But if the windstorm breaks a window and wind-blown rain enters the structure through the broken window, the policy will cover the resulting water damage.

Windstorm or hail also excludes loss or damage by hail to lawns, trees, shrubs, or plants that are part of a vegetated roof. Significantly, loss or damage to the same items by windstorm is covered.

Although the windstorm peril covers windstorm damage caused by a hurricane, the causes of loss forms contain a Water exclusion that applies to damage caused by surface water or overflow from a body of water, whether wind-driven or not. When covered property is damaged by a windstorm that involves both wind damage and flooding, the direct damage caused by the windstorm is covered.

Determining how much damage resulted from the windstorm and how much resulted from excluded water damage can be a challenging task for the claim adjuster, as evidenced by the extensive litigation stemming from insurers' claim settlements to insureds whose property was destroyed by wind and wind-driven flooding accompanying Hurricane Katrina in 2005.

Smoke

The smoke peril is limited to smoke causing sudden and accidental loss or damage. Moreover, smoke from agricultural smudging or industrial operations is excluded. Agricultural smudging is the burning of oil to generate smoke that can protect crops, such as citrus fruit, against frost damage. No other restrictions apply to the peril. The smoke causing a covered loss may originate on or off the insured's premises. The fire peril covers smoke from a hostile fire, because the proximate cause of the loss is fire. Hence, the value of the smoke peril is that it extends coverage to smoke resulting from friendly fires, such as smoke from a fireplace or furnace.

An example of a loss covered by the smoke peril is an oil-burner puff-back. A puff-back is caused by incomplete combustion of the fuel in an oil-fired heating system. It can spread sooty, oily smoke throughout a building, resulting in substantial damage and cleanup expense.

The smoke peril also covers damage caused by smoke when there is insufficient flame or glow for the event to qualify as fire (such as smoldering oily rags).

Aircraft or Vehicles

The aircraft or vehicles peril includes "only physical contact of an aircraft, a spacecraft, a self-propelled missile, a vehicle or an object thrown up by a vehicle with the described property or with the building or structure containing the described property."

The form does not define the words "vehicle" and "aircraft." Dictionary definitions of "vehicle" are ordinarily broad. For example, *Webster's New World Dictionary* (2nd ed.) defines vehicle as "any device or contrivance for carrying or conveying persons or objects, including land conveyances, vessels, aircraft and spacecraft." An insured would have a strong argument that the vehicle peril could include damage from contact with such objects as a boat, a horse-drawn carriage, or another type of conveyance that might not, at first glance, be thought of as a "vehicle."

The aircraft or vehicles peril requires physical contact, which can preclude coverage in some circumstances. The physical contact requirement is presumably not met if, for example, a covered building is damaged by vibrations from heavily loaded logging trucks running on an adjacent road. But the aircraft or vehicles peril specifically includes loss or damage caused by objects that fall from aircraft, or caused by "an object thrown up by a vehicle." An example of the latter type of object is a wheel that comes off a vehicle at high speed and strikes the insured's building.

The aircraft or vehicles peril excludes damage caused by vehicles owned by the named insured or operated in the course of the named insured's business. If, for example, a truck owned by the named insured is backed into the named insured's loading dock at an excessive speed, the aircraft or vehicles peril does not cover the resulting damage to the loading dock.

Riot or Civil Commotion

Riot has statutory definitions that vary by state. A general-purpose definition of riot, from *Black's Law Dictionary* (8th ed.), is "an assemblage of three or more persons in a public place for the purpose of accomplishing by concerted action—and in a turbulent and disorderly manner—a common purpose." The same source defines civil commotion as "a public uprising by a large number of people who, acting together, cause harm to people or property." Civil commotion and riot are similar, and the two terms include most incidents of civil unrest. The riot or civil commotion peril specifically includes acts of striking employees while occupying the described premises.

Looting frequently accompanies riots or civil disorders and has been the cause of some costly disasters in U.S. history. Civil disorders in Los Angeles in 1992 resulted in over $1 billion in insured losses. Although theft is not a named peril in the Basic Form, the riot or civil commotion peril specifically includes "looting occurring at the time and place of a riot or civil commotion." Thus, the riot or civil commotion peril covers theft of covered property if it qualifies as looting during a riot or civil commotion. See the exhibit "Fire and Extended Coverage."

Fire and Extended Coverage

The insured perils of fire, lightning, explosion, windstorm, hail, smoke, aircraft, vehicles, riot, and civil commotion were, until the 1980s, sold as a package called "fire and extended coverage" or "fire and EC." More specifically, this package consisted of the 1943 Standard Fire Policy and the Extended Coverage Endorsement. Insurance professionals still need to know what fire and extended coverage includes because some leases, mortgages, condominium offering plans, and other agreements still contain outdated language requiring the lessee, mortgagor, condominium association, or other party to the contract to obtain fire and extended coverage on the property. Any one of the three ISO causes of loss forms exceeds, in almost all respects, the coverages included in the fire and extended coverage forms.

[DA03511]

Vandalism

The Basic Form and the Broad Form define vandalism as "willful and malicious damage to, or destruction of, the described property." Thus, both intent ("willful") and motive ("malicious") must be established for a loss to be considered vandalism. Vandalism, in contrast to riot and civil commotion, may involve only one person.

In the pre-2000 editions of the ISO causes of loss forms, the vandalism peril excluded damage "to glass (other than glass building blocks) that is part of a building, structure, or an outside sign." Post-2000 editions of the ISO causes of loss forms omitted the limitations on glass coverage.

The use of higher deductibles made it possible for glass to be treated like any other covered property because policy deductibles eliminate claims for minor glass breakage. Building glass broken by vandals is covered as a building loss. Glass that is personal property (such as a glass display case) is covered as business personal property. The loss in any case is subject to the deductible. Underwriters can address claim frequency problems by increasing the deductible.

The vandalism peril excludes loss caused by theft, other than building damage caused by the forcible entry or exit of burglars. Coverage for theft of property can be purchased under the Special Form or commercial crime forms. See the exhibit "Separate Glass Coverage Forms."

Sprinkler Leakage

Both the Basic Form and the Broad Form state that sprinkler leakage includes leakage or discharge of any substance from an automatic sprinkler system. Therefore, the peril includes not only the discharge of water but also accidental discharge from a system containing any other extinguishing agents, such as carbon dioxide or dry chemical powder, as well as antifreeze solution, which is used to prevent freezing of the liquid in sprinkler pipes. "Automatic sprinkler system" is broadly defined in the form to include components such as sprinkler heads, piping, tanks, pumps, and standpipes.

The definition of sprinkler leakage also includes the collapse of automatic sprinkler system tanks. System tanks are sometimes located in separate water towers or underground, but tanks can also be located on the roof of a building. The collapse of such a tank and the dispersal of the water that it contains can cause extensive damage.

If the policy covers the building, the sprinkler leakage peril also covers the cost to repair or replace damaged parts of the sprinkler system if the damage results in sprinkler leakage or is caused by freezing. The insurer will also pay for tearing out and replacing any part of the building to make these repairs.

Property protected by an automatic sprinkler system receives a significant rate reduction. When allowing such a discount, insurers want to be sure that the protection is maintained. Accordingly, the insurer may attach to the policy

Separate Glass Coverage Forms

After removing the glass breakage exclusion from the vandalism peril in its commercial property forms, ISO withdrew its Glass Coverage Form. However, separate glass coverage continues to be available from insurers that have filed their own forms and from insurers that use the Glass Coverage Part of the American Association of Insurance Services (AAIS). Separate glass forms provide very broad coverage. The AAIS Glass Coverage Part covers loss caused by breakage, rupture, or fracture that penetrates the inside and outside surfaces of the glass; or sudden and accidental or malicious application of chemical or caustic substance to the glass. Glass forms have few exclusions. The AAIS form contains just three: Fire, War, and Nuclear Hazard.

The need for separate glass forms will continue. The ISO causes of loss forms exclude loss caused by flood or earthquake. Even when an insured carries flood or earthquake coverage, those perils are subject to substantial deductibles. Separate glass forms do not exclude flood or earthquake.

More importantly, many leases for retail stores make the tenant responsible for repairing glass breakage and often require the tenant to carry glass insurance. A typical lease reads as follows: "Tenant shall also pay the premiums for and keep in full force and effect, plate glass insurance at the demised premises, naming the tenant and landlord as insured."

There is an ISO endorsement that enables tenants to buy building glass coverage to satisfy a landlord's request for such coverage. The Building Glass—Tenant's Policy endorsement (CP 14 70) covers the building glass described in the endorsement's schedule against the causes of loss (Basic, Broad, or Special, as well as any related endorsements) indicated in the schedule, up to the limit of insurance stated in the schedule.

[DA03512]

the Protective Safeguards endorsement (IL 04 15), which states that fire coverage is automatically suspended if the insured knows that the sprinkler system is not operational and fails to notify the insurer.

Sinkhole Collapse

The Basic Form and the Broad Form define sinkhole collapse as "loss or damage caused by the sudden sinking or collapse of land into underground empty spaces created by the action of water on limestone or dolomite." Dolomite is a rock heavier than but similar to limestone. The peril covers damage to covered property, such as buildings and business personal property, resulting from sinkhole collapse. Damage to the land on which the building is situated is not covered because land is not covered property under the BPP. The sinkhole collapse peril specifically excludes the cost of filling sinkholes.

Because the sinkhole collapse peril refers to "empty spaces created by the action of water on limestone or dolomite," it does not cover mine subsidence (collapse of land into an underground mine). To reinforce this point, the sinkhole collapse peril specifically excludes loss caused by the sinking or collapse of land into man-made underground cavities. In several states with a history of mining, insurers are required to offer a mine subsidence coverage endorsement.

Volcanic Action

The volcanic action peril was added to commercial property forms after the eruption of Mount St. Helens in 1980, the first volcanic eruption in the contiguous forty-eight states since 1914.

Both the Basic Form and the Broad Form define volcanic action:

> Volcanic Action, meaning direct loss or damage resulting from the eruption of a volcano when the loss or damage is caused by:
>
> a. Airborne volcanic blast or airborne shock waves;
>
> b. Ash, dust or particulate matter; or
>
> c. Lava flow.[2]

The volcanic action peril does not cover costs to remove volcanic debris unless the debris has caused physical loss or damage.

Volcanic action is distinct from volcanic eruption. The Earth Movement exclusion found in all three causes of loss forms specifically excludes coverage for "volcanic eruption, explosion or effusion" but by exception allows coverage for resulting damage caused by volcanic action, as defined, or by fire. The fire peril covers fire damage resulting from a volcano. Earthquake and volcanic eruption can be insured by endorsement.

Volcanic action and volcanic eruption do not encompass all causes of loss connected with volcanoes. In the Mount St. Helens eruption, much of the damage resulted from floods caused by melting snow, displacement of mountain lake water by mudflows, and heavy rains caused by condensation of steam from the eruption. Flooding and mudflows are not covered under the Basic, Broad, or Special Form. Flood insurance can be provided in various ways.

The limits and deductibles of the BPP apply separately to each occurrence. Sometimes it is questioned whether successive eruptions of a volcano are one occurrence or multiple occurrences—subject to one set of limits and deductibles or several. However, the volcanic action peril settles this question by stating that all volcanic eruptions that occur within any 168-hour period (seven consecutive days) will be considered a single occurrence.

Additional Perils Covered by Broad Form

In addition to the perils covered by both the Basic Form and the Broad Form, the Broad Form covers three perils:

- Falling objects
- Weight of snow, ice, or sleet
- Water damage

The Broad Form also provides an additional coverage for collapse.

Falling Objects

A falling object (not defined in the form) can be anything that falls, such as a branch falling from a tree, an entire tree itself, or a rock. The peril excludes damage to personal property in the open. It also excludes damage to the interior of a building or structure, or property inside a building or structure, unless the falling object first damages the roof or an outside wall. If, for example, a heavy object fell from an overhead conveyor inside a factory building, the falling objects peril would not cover the resulting loss to either the object itself or any property damaged by the falling object.

Weight of Snow, Ice, or Sleet

All damage caused by the weight of snow, ice, or sleet is covered except for damage to personal property outside of buildings or structures and damage to lawns, trees, shrubs, or plants that are part of a vegetated roof. The buildup of snow, ice, or sleet on a building's roof can exert great force on the structure, causing roof collapse or other structural damage. Flat roofs are especially susceptible to damage by weight of snow, ice, or sleet. This peril has caused many severe building and contents losses over the years.

The covered peril does not refer to rain or other water. Damage resulting from the weight of rain or other water is therefore not covered by this peril, but the Additional Coverage—Collapse covers building collapse resulting from the weight of rain that collects on a roof.

Water Damage

This peril might be more appropriately titled "limited water damage" because it does not cover loss caused by flooding, surface water, and other sources of water excluded by the causes of loss forms. The water damage peril covers damage caused by accidental discharge or leakage of water or steam as the direct result of the breaking apart or cracking of a plumbing, heating, air conditioning, or other system or appliance located on the described premises. Because sprinkler leakage is covered as a separate peril, it is excluded from coverage under the water damage peril.

If the building or structure containing the system or appliance is covered property, the insurer also agrees to pay the cost to tear out and replace any part of the building or structure to repair damage to the system or appliance, but the cost to repair the defect that caused the loss is excluded.

The peril also excludes water damage from these causes:

- Discharge or leakage from roof drains, gutters, downspouts, or similar fixtures or equipment.

- Discharge or leakage from a sump or related equipment or parts, including overflow caused by sump pump failure or excessive volume of water.

- Continuous or repeated seepage or leakage of water or steam from an insured system (including the presence or condensation of humidity, moisture, or vapor) occurring over a period of more than fourteen days.

- The gradual seepage of water through a floor or inside a wall. An example of a loss from this peril is rotting of flooring or structural members.

- Freezing of plumbing, unless "you" (the insured) (1) "do your best" to maintain heat in the building or (2) shut off the water supply and drain the equipment if heat is not maintained. The purpose of this exclusion is to cover freezing losses only if the insured has taken reasonable preventive measures.

Basic and Broad Form Additional Coverages

The Basic Form and the Broad Form cover certain types of losses through "additional coverages" rather than through covered causes of loss. The Basic Form and the Broad Form both contain an additional coverage for loss resulting from fungus, wet rot, dry rot, or bacteria, and the Broad Form also contains an additional coverage for loss resulting from the abrupt collapse of a building or personal property inside a building.

The losses insured by these additional coverages are difficult to insure, and insuring them through additional coverages, rather than as covered causes of loss, allows the form to impose the conditions that insurers believe are necessary.

Additional Coverage—Fungus

The Basic Form and the Broad Form both exclude loss resulting from fungus, wet rot, dry rot, and bacteria. To reinforce the exclusion and provide limited coverage for this exposure, the forms contain an additional coverage titled Limited Coverage for Fungus, Wet Rot, Dry Rot and Bacteria.

Each form defines "fungus" to mean any type or form of fungus, including mold or mildew, and any mycotoxins, spores, scents, or by-products produced or released by fungi. For convenience, the term fungus as used here also includes wet rot, dry rot, and bacteria unless the context indicates otherwise.

The most that the insurer will pay for fungus damage to property, including the costs of necessary tearing out and replacement of property and of testing for the presence of fungus after damaged property has been repaired or replaced, is $15,000 per annual policy period. Although the *Commercial Lines Manual* (CLM) includes increased limits factors, an insurer may not be willing to offer significantly higher limits of insurance.

The $15,000 limit is the most the insurer will pay even if the fungus resulting from a particular loss continues or recurs in a later policy period.

Coverage applies only when the fungus is the result of one or more covered causes of loss that occur during the policy period. The additional coverage does not apply to losses resulting from fire and lightning, because the fungus exclusion does not exclude fungus resulting from fire and lightning. Furthermore, coverage does not apply unless all reasonable means are used to save and preserve the property from further damage at the time of and after the occurrence.

The additional coverage does not apply to lawns, trees, shrubs, or plants that are part of a vegetated roof. For example, if plants on a vegetated roof were killed by a fungus, the additional coverage would not pay for the loss.

Additional Coverage—Collapse

Property policies once included "collapse" as a covered peril. Since 1983, collapse has been treated as an additional coverage. Under the Additional Coverage—Collapse in the Broad Form, the insurer agrees to pay for loss or damage caused by the abrupt collapse of a building or any part of a building, or the abrupt collapse of personal property inside a building.

The form states that "abrupt collapse means an abrupt falling down or caving in of a building or any part of a building with the result that the building or part of the building cannot be occupied for its intended purpose." Moreover, the Additional Coverage—Collapse does not apply to buildings under certain described circumstances:

> a. A building or any part of a building that is in danger of falling down or caving in;
>
> b. A part of a building that is standing, even if it has separated from another part of the building; or
>
> c. A building that is standing or any part of a building that is standing, even if it shows evidence of cracking, bulging, sagging, bending, leaning, settling, shrinkage or expansion.[3]

Collapse coverage applies only if the collapse is caused by one or more of these perils:

- Any cause of loss covered by the Broad Form
- Hidden building decay (unless known to the insured before the collapse)
- Hidden insect or vermin damage (unless known to the insured before the collapse)
- Weight of people or personal property

- Weight of rain that collects on a roof
- Use of defective materials or methods in construction, remodeling, or renovation if the abrupt collapse occurs during the course of construction, remodeling, or renovation

When defective materials or construction methods contribute to the abrupt collapse of a completed building, such collapse is covered as long as the collapse is caused in part by one of the Broad Form perils or one of the perils applicable to Additional Coverage—Collapse.

The policy definition of collapse is important only for perils other than those already covered by the causes of loss form in which the collapse coverage is provided. For example, if a fire (a covered peril) damages a support beam, causing a partition wall to bulge, the damage to the wall would be covered as fire damage (fire is the proximate cause). However, if the beam sagged because of hidden decay and that situation caused the bulge in the partition wall, there would be no coverage under the Additional Coverage—Collapse. Bulging does not constitute collapse, and hidden decay is not an otherwise-covered peril.

CAUSES OF LOSS—BASIC AND BROAD FORM EXCLUSIONS

In addition to the limitations and exclusions contained in their descriptions of covered perils, the Causes of Loss—Basic Form and the Causes of Loss—Broad Form contain several exclusions.

The Basic Form (CP 10 10 10 12) and the Broad Form (CP 10 20 10 12) each have a separate section of exclusions, which contains three parts:

- A group of eight exclusions with lead-in wording that contains anti-concurrent causation language
- A group of four additional exclusions that does not contain anti-concurrent causation language
- A group of "special exclusions" that apply only to certain coverage forms other than the Building and Personal Property Coverage Form (BPP) (such as for business income and extra expense coverage, which are discussed in another section)

Anti-Concurrent Causation Language

The exclusions in the first two groups, which relate to anti-concurrent causation language and apply to any commercial property coverage form, are itemized in the exhibit.

In addition to having anti-concurrent causation language, the exclusions in the first group are specific about whether the involvement of a covered peril in the chain of loss causation will result in coverage. Some exclusions eliminate coverage for loss stemming from a covered cause resulting from an excluded cause. See the exhibit "Basic and Broad Form Exclusions."

Basic and Broad Form Exclusions

Exclusions Subject to Anti-Concurrent Causation Language

Ordinance or Law

Earth Movement

Governmental Action

Nuclear Hazard

Utility Services

War and Military Action

Water

"Fungus", Wet Rot, Dry Rot and Bacteria

Exclusions Not Subject to Anti-Concurrent Causation Language

Artificially Generated Electrical Energy

Explosion of Steam Boilers

Mechanical Breakdown

Neglect

[DA03513]

For example, the War and Military Action exclusion eliminates coverage for a building fire caused by an act of war, even though fire is a covered cause of loss. In contrast, some of the exclusions make an exception for fire and, in some cases, other perils that ensue from the excluded cause. For instance, the Earth Movement exclusion states that fire or explosion loss resulting from an earthquake is covered.

The lead-in paragraph to the first group of exclusions, in response to concurrent causation claims, states that these exclusions apply to loss or damage caused directly or indirectly by any of the excluded causes, "regardless of any other cause or event that contributes concurrently or in any sequence to the loss." This provision is often referred to as "anti-concurrent causation wording" and is aimed at counteracting the legal doctrine of concurrent causation, which holds that if a property loss can be attributed to two causes—one excluded by the policy and one covered—the policy covers the loss.

The exclusions in the second group are not subject to the concurrent causation lead-in language. Their lead-in language simply states that the insurer "will not pay for loss or damage resulting from" any of the excluded perils. See the exhibit "Concurrent Causation."

Concurrent Causation

The concurrent causation doctrine holds that a loss is covered when caused by two or more independent, concurrent perils only if one of the perils is covered—even if the other peril or perils are clearly excluded. Adopting this doctrine, a court found that damage resulting when heavy rains broke through flood-control facilities and inundated parts of Palm Desert, California, was covered under an "all-risks" property policy because the negligent construction of the flood control structures was an independent, concurrent cause that was not specifically excluded.

In response, insurers revised the lead-in to the exclusions in their property policies to emphasize that certain exclusions apply even if another cause is involved in the loss. Additionally, they deleted "all" from "all-risks" in the insuring agreement of the Special Form to avoid coverage that was broader than intended, and they eliminated collapse as a cause of loss, but added the Additional Coverage—Collapse to cover collapse resulting from specified perils.

[DA05992]

Ordinance or Law

Most municipalities and states have ordinances or laws regulating building construction. Buildings already standing when such regulations are adopted are usually permitted to continue to be used and occupied even though they do not conform to the current building code or law. However, when a non-conforming building is severely damaged, the regulations typically provide that it may be rebuilt only if it is made to conform to current requirements.

Such building laws increase potential loss severity. Following a loss in which the law prohibits repair of the damaged building, the insured loses the value of the undamaged portion of the building and also incurs the expense of demolishing the undamaged portion and removing its debris.

If it is more expensive to construct a conforming building as a replacement than it would be to construct a building identical to the original one, the insured can also incur increased construction costs.

Ordinances and laws can increase the cost of repairs in other ways, even if demolition is not required. Building codes are constantly updated, and a building's reconstruction may require additional features not included in the original building, such as additional fire exits; a fire-resistant roof; wiring, heating, or plumbing systems that comply with the current code; a sprinkler system; or an elevator. These upgrades do not require demolition of the building and are frequently required whenever any repairs or new construction occurs.

Basic premium rates do not anticipate ordinance or law exposures that exceed those covered by the Increased Cost of Construction additional coverage of the BPP. Therefore, the causes of loss forms contain an Ordinance or Law exclusion, which excludes loss resulting from this cause:

The enforcement of or compliance with any ordinance or law:

(1) Regulating the construction, use or repair of any property; or

(2) Requiring the tearing down of any property, including the cost of removing its debris.[4]

The courts have not uniformly applied this exclusion. When the building is physically but not legally repairable (because of an ordinance or a law), some courts have denied the insured recovery for the undamaged portion of the building.

In other cases, courts have allowed the insured to collect for a total loss. In states with valued policy laws (which require the insurer to pay the full policy limit in the event of a total loss), courts have rejected the exclusion and treated the building as a constructive total loss.

However, when the ordinance or law permits the building to be repaired but imposes requirements that increase the cost of repairs, the exclusion has generally been applied to eliminate payment for the increased cost.

The ordinance or law exposure is insurable. However, not every insured needs the coverage, and underwriters want to be able to evaluate the loss exposure before accepting it. The BPP provides limited coverage for this exposure under the Increased Cost of Construction additional coverage. Higher limits and broader coverage can be provided by the Ordinance or Law Coverage endorsement.

Earth Movement

The causes of loss forms exclude earthquake and other types of earth movement because such losses are difficult to insure, for several reasons. The geographic areas most likely to have severe earthquakes are somewhat limited, resulting in a poor spread of risk.

No one has discovered how to accurately forecast earthquake loss frequency and severity, making it difficult to establish a rating system that reflects loss potential. And perhaps most significantly, earthquakes can cause catastrophic loss; a single earthquake and its aftershocks affect many separate buildings and their contents.

The 1994 earthquake centered in Northridge, California, damaged thousands of buildings and caused insured property damage estimated at $23.7 billion (in 2012 dollars), making it the fifth most costly disaster ever for U.S. insurers.[5] The magnitude of the Northridge earthquake was 6.7 on the Richter scale, in comparison with the 7.8 magnitude of the San Francisco earthquake of 1906. This means that the level of ground shaking in the Northridge earthquake was about ten times less than that of the San Francisco earthquake. If an earthquake of 7.8 magnitude were to occur in a large U.S. city today, the resulting losses could be several times those of the Northridge earthquake.

The Earth Movement exclusion in the ISO causes of loss forms eliminates coverage not only for earthquakes but also for any other type of earth movement, as well as for volcanic eruption, explosion, and effusion. This is the exclusion's wording:

> (1) Earthquake, including tremors and aftershocks and any earth sinking, rising or shifting related to such event;
>
> (2) Landslide, including any earth sinking, rising or shifting relating to such event;
>
> (3) Mine subsidence, meaning subsidence of a man-made mine, whether or not mining activity has ceased;
>
> (4) Earth sinking (other than sinkhole collapse), rising or shifting including soil conditions which cause settling, cracking or other disarrangement of foundations or other parts of realty. Soil conditions include contraction, expansion, freezing, thawing, erosion, improperly compacted soil and the action of water under the ground surface.
>
> But if Earth Movement, as described in b.(1) through (4) above, results in fire or explosion, we will pay for the loss or damage caused by that fire or explosion.
>
> (5) Volcanic eruption, explosion or effusion. But if volcanic eruption, explosion or effusion results in fire or Volcanic Action, we will pay for the loss or damage caused by that fire or Volcanic Action.
>
> This exclusion applies regardless of whether any of the above, in Paragraphs (1) through (5), is caused by an act of nature or is otherwise caused.[6]

The exceptions to the exclusion are important aspects of commercial property coverage. Fire following earthquake can be a major source of loss, especially in metropolitan areas. Broader coverage for loss caused by earthquake or volcanic eruption is available under an ISO endorsement and also under other forms.

Governmental Action

In some situations, police, firefighters, or other government officials must confiscate or otherwise take control of an insured's property to protect the common good of the community. For example, a governmental agency might confiscate contaminated property.

Because insurers do not intend to cover loss resulting from such actions, the causes of loss forms contain a Governmental Action exclusion, which excludes any "seizure or destruction of property by order of governmental authority." However, the insurer agrees to pay for loss or damage caused by or resulting from acts of destruction ordered by governmental authority at the time of a fire to prevent its spread.

Nuclear Hazard

The Nuclear Hazard exclusion excludes loss or damage caused by "nuclear reaction or radiation, or radioactive contamination, however caused."

However, if loss or damage by fire results from the excluded events, the insurer agrees to pay for the resulting loss or damage.

For example, if a nuclear reactor should go out of control and cause a fire, the fire damage would be covered, although the damage caused by the nuclear reaction—apart from the ensuing fire—would not be covered. If a fire causes the release of radioactive particles, contamination damage from them is not covered.

Insurance for nuclear power plants in the U.S. is available from American Nuclear Insurers. Users of radioactive isotopes for medical, industrial, or research purposes can purchase radioactive contamination coverage by endorsement to their commercial property insurance.

Utility Services

The Utility Services exclusion eliminates coverage for loss caused by the failure of power, communication, water, or other utility service supplied to the described location, in either of these circumstances:

- The failure originates away from the described location.
- The failure originates at the described location, but only if the failure involves equipment used to supply the utility service to the described location from a source off the described location.

As an illustration of how the exclusion might apply, assume that a fire at a public generating station caused a power failure that in turn caused spoilage of refrigerated food at the insured's store. The exclusion would eliminate coverage for the spoilage loss even though the power failure was caused by fire, an insured peril. The exclusion would also apply if the power failure was caused by high winds downing a power transmission line on the described location.

The exclusion states that failure of any utility service includes lack of sufficient capacity and reduction in supply. The exclusion applies also to loss or damage caused by power surge if the surge would not have occurred but for an event causing a failure of power. However, if the utility failure or power surge results in a covered cause of loss, the insurer will pay for the loss or damage caused by the covered cause of loss.

For example, loss of natural gas or electrical service might shut down a building's heating system. If the loss of heat occurs during cold weather and causes water pipes to freeze and burst, with resulting water damage to covered property, the Broad Form (or the Special Form) would cover the resulting water damage loss.

Coverage for losses resulting from loss of utility services because of damage by an insured peril can be insured under various endorsements.

War and Military Action

Most property insurance policies exclude loss caused by war and other hostilities because losses caused by war are potentially catastrophic and cannot be estimated with any certainty. Although war risk insurance is widely available on ocean vessels, aircraft, and ocean and air cargo, war risk coverage on land-based property is generally unavailable except in special circumstances.

The War and Military Action exclusion eliminates coverage for loss caused by insurrections, civil wars, and undeclared wars, as well as by formally declared wars. Although the riots that have wracked many large cities have sometimes been referred to as insurrections or rebellions, not since the U.S. Civil War has there been the usurping of governmental power in the U.S. that would be necessary to trigger this exclusion. Similarly, many officials and commentators characterized the September 11, 2001, terrorist attacks as acts of war. Nevertheless, no insurer invoked its war exclusion to deny coverage.

Unlike some other exclusions, the War and Military Action exclusion contains no exception for ensuing fire. Fires resulting from war are not covered because of the potential for catastrophic loss. For example, some of the fires that resulted from bombing raids in World War II destroyed entire cities. See the exhibit "What Is 'War'?."

What Is 'War'?

In Pan American World Airways, Inc. v. Aetna Casualty & Surety Company, 505 F.2d 989 (2d Circuit 1974), the Second Circuit Court of Appeals held that when members of a political activist group from Jordan hijacked an aircraft and destroyed it after forcing the pilot to land in Egypt, the resulting loss to the aircraft was not excluded as war damage by the "all-risks" policies covering the aircraft.

The court stated that "cases have established that war is a course of hostility engaged in by entities that have at least significant attributes of sovereignty; under international law, war is waged by states or state-like entities . . . and includes only hostilities carried on by entities that constitute governments at least de facto in character." The court concluded that a group must have at least some attributes of sovereignty before its activities can properly be defined as war.

In Holiday Inns, Inc. v. Aetna Insurance Company, 571 F. Supp. 1460 (S.D.N.Y 1983), the U.S. District Court in New York, quoting extensively and approvingly from the Pan American case, declined to apply the war risks exclusion to a claim for damage to a hotel that was shelled during battles in Beirut, Lebanon.

Source: Susan Massmann, "War Risk Exclusion Legal History Outlined," National Underwriter (Property & Casualty/ Risk & Benefits Management ed.), September 24, 2001, pp. 40, 45. Used with permission of the National Underwriter Co., Erlanger, Kentucky. Adapted from the Fire, Casualty, and Surety Bulletins (FC&S), Copyright 2002, The National Underwriter Co. [DA03518]

Water

Hurricanes, heavy rain, the run-off from melting snow, and collapsing dams can all cause widespread flooding and catastrophic losses.

Flood damage to mobile property, because it is not fixed in location and can often be moved to a safer location, can often be covered under standard policies. For example, auto physical damage insurance and many inland marine forms cover loss caused by flood.

Although widespread flooding can cause numerous claims amounting to substantial sums in total under auto and inland marine policies, insurers can cope with these exposures through reinsurance.

The Water exclusion precludes coverage for flood-type losses and is therefore commonly referred to as the flood exclusion. However, the exclusion applies to many sources of water damage other than floods. Water that backs up or overflows from sewers or drains may not be the result of flooding, and the same may be true of underground water that flows or seeps into a building. Coverage for either of those events is nevertheless excluded.

In 1992, dozens of buildings in downtown Chicago were shut down when water from the Chicago River surged into an unused tunnel and inundated the buildings' basement mechanical equipment. Many commercial property insurers denied coverage to insureds whose policies contained this exclusion, but the National Flood Insurance Program ruled that the occurrence did not constitute a flood.

Specifically, the exclusion eliminates coverage for loss from these causes:

(1) Flood, surface water, waves (including tidal wave and tsunami), tides, tidal water, overflow of any body of water, or their spray from any of these, all whether or not driven by wind (including storm surge);

(2) Mudslide or mudflow;

(3) Water that backs up or overflows or is otherwise discharged from a sewer, drain, sump, sump pump or related equipment;

(4) Water under the ground surface pressing on, or flowing or seeping through:

(a) Foundations, walls, floors or paved surfaces;

(b) Basements, whether paved or not; or

(c) Doors, windows or other openings.

(5) Waterborne material carried or otherwise moved by any of the water referred to in Paragraph (1), (3) or (4), or material carried or otherwise moved by mudslide or mudflow.

This exclusion applies regardless of whether any of the above, in Paragraphs (1) through (5), is caused by an act of nature or is otherwise caused. An example of a situation where a dam, levee, seawall or other boundary or containment system fails in whole or in part, for any reason, to contain the water.

But if any of the above, in Paragraphs (1) through (5), results in fire, explosion or sprinkler leakage, we will pay for the loss or damage caused by that fire, explosion or sprinkler leakage (if sprinkler leakage is a Covered Cause of Loss).[7]

This exclusion does not eliminate coverage for all water damage. Water damage resulting from efforts to extinguish a hostile fire is covered under the fire peril because fire is the proximate cause of the water damage. Sprinkler leakage is also covered because it is a covered peril in all three causes of loss forms. Moreover, the Broad Form specifically includes a water damage peril. However, that peril covers damage caused by water that accidentally discharges from an on-premises plumbing system or appliance that cracks or breaks apart, whereas the Water exclusion deals with water from other sources.

Fungus, Wet Rot, Dry Rot, and Bacteria

Given adequate moisture, mold spores secrete enzymes that digest cellulose-based materials. As a result, drywall, wallpaper, paneling, hardwood flooring, insulation, carpeting, siding, paint, decking, and wooden framing are all susceptible to mold-induced damage. Mold generally develops within enclosed cavities of structures, and property damage arising from mold is usually discovered only after structural components have been removed. Consequently, ascertaining the date when a mold loss occurred can be problematic.

Because of the problems involved in insuring mold damage, insurers have chosen to exclude most coverage for mold under standard property and liability forms. The causes of loss forms exclude loss or damage resulting from fungus, wet rot, dry rot, or bacteria. Fungus is defined to include mold, mildew, and any by-products produced or released by fungi. However, the exclusion does not apply if the fungus, wet rot, dry rot, or bacteria results from fire or lightning. (More specifically, the exclusion does not apply if the mold results from the insured property becoming saturated by water used to extinguish a fire.)

An additional coverage in the causes of loss forms provides limited coverage for loss resulting from fungus, wet rot, dry rot, and bacteria. Some insurers are willing to provide broader coverage and higher limits for mold losses after separately underwriting the insured's exposure to such losses.

Four Additional Basic and Broad Form Exclusions

Four additional basic and broad form exclusions do not contain anti-concurrent causation language:

- Artificially generated electrical energy
- Explosion of steam boilers
- Mechanical breakdown
- Neglect

Artificially Generated Electrical Energy

Both the Basic Form and the Broad Form contain this exclusion:

> Artificially generated electrical, magnetic, or electromagnetic energy that damages, disturbs, disrupts or otherwise interferes with any:
>
> (1) Electrical or electronic wire, device, appliance, system or network; or
>
> (2) Device, appliance, system or network utilizing cellular or satellite technology.[8]

However, damage by an ensuing fire loss is covered. Damage to electrical or electronic components caused by lightning is covered under both forms and is not affected by this exclusion because lightning is naturally, not artificially, generated.

Explosion of Steam Boilers

Both the Basic Form and the Broad Form exclude damage caused by or resulting from explosion of "steam boilers, steam pipes, steam engines or steam turbines owned or leased by you, or operated under your control."

The exclusion does not apply to combustion explosion or resulting loss by fire. An important nuance of this exclusion is that it does not apply to steam boiler explosions when the boiler or other steam equipment is not owned or leased by the insured or operated under the insured's control.

Thus, for example, a tenant's commercial property policy would cover damage to the tenant's personal property resulting from the explosion of a steam boiler in the landlord's building that the tenant did not own, operate, or control. In most cases, the tenant's insurer, after paying the tenant's loss, would pursue a subrogation recovery against the landlord as long as the tenant had not waived its recovery rights against the landlord.

Mechanical Breakdown

Both the Basic Form and the Broad Form exclude loss or damage caused by or resulting from mechanical breakdown, including rupture or bursting caused by centrifugal force. However, the exclusion states that the insurer will pay for resulting loss or damage by a covered cause of loss. Thus, for example, both forms would cover a fire that resulted from friction caused by the mechanical breakdown of a production machine.

Physical damage and resulting business interruption caused by the excluded perils of electrical disturbance, steam boiler explosion, and mechanical breakdown can be insured under an equipment breakdown policy.

Neglect

The Basic Form and the Broad Form exclude loss or damage caused by or resulting from an insured's neglect to use all reasonable means to save and preserve the property from further damage at and after the time of loss.

Insureds sometimes believe, mistakenly, that they should do nothing after a loss until the insurer has had an opportunity to inspect the loss. In reality, the insured is obligated to protect the property from further loss.

For example, if a fire damages the roof on the insured's building and the insured fails to make temporary repairs with reasonable speed, the insurer may decline to pay for preventable damage that occurs when a rainstorm follows the loss.

Other Exclusions in the Basic Form

The Basic Form contains two additional exclusions. These exclusions reinforce the fact that the Basic Form does not cover the types of damage covered by the Broad Form's water damage peril.

However, the exclusions contain exceptions to clarify that breakage of plumbing systems and appliances and resulting water damage are covered if caused by a covered cause of loss. If, for example, a water pipe bursts because of a natural gas explosion (a covered cause of loss), the damage to the pipe and the resulting water damage to other insured property are covered. However, if the water pipe bursts because of freezing, wear and tear, or some other peril that is not covered, the Basic Form provides no coverage.

Limitation on Loss of Animals

A Limitation provision in both the Basic Form and the Broad Form states that the insurer will pay for loss of animals only if they are killed or their destruction is made necessary. This limited coverage applies only to animals that the BPP includes as covered property—that is, animals boarded or held as stock for sale.

For example, an insured pet store is covered for death or necessary destruction of animals being held for sale, if the death or necessary destruction results from a covered cause of loss. The pet store owner is not covered for veterinary care of living animals even though the care was necessitated by a covered peril.

CAUSES OF LOSS—SPECIAL FORM

Because it is the broadest option for covered causes of loss, the Insurance Services Office, Inc. (ISO) commercial property policy's Causes of Loss—Special Form is the most frequently selected of the three causes of loss forms.

The Causes of Loss—Special Form (CP 10 30) states that it covers "direct physical loss unless the loss is excluded or limited in this policy," instead of listing the perils covered. Moreover, the loss or damage must be accidental and unforeseen by the insured in order to be covered. The Special Form is designed to cover any loss that would be covered by the Basic and Broad

Forms. In addition, the Special Form covers perils that are not specified in the Basic and Broad Forms.

The Special Form offers these advantages to the insured:

- Certain causes of loss that are omitted or excluded under the Broad Form are not excluded—and are therefore covered—under the Special Form. Most significantly, the Special Form covers theft of covered property under a wide variety of circumstances, subject to some exclusions and limitations. The Basic and Broad Forms cover theft by looting at the time of a riot or civil commotion, but in no other circumstances.

- By covering direct physical losses other than those that are specifically excluded, the Special Form covers losses that the insured might not have anticipated.

- The Special Form shifts the "burden of proof" from the insured to the insurer. Under a named perils form, such as the Basic or Broad Form, the insured must prove that the loss was caused by a covered cause. Under the Special Form, an accidental loss to covered property is presumed to be covered unless the insurer can prove that it was caused by an excluded peril.

Exclusions and Limitations

The Special Form contains most of the exclusions of the Basic and Broad Forms, including many (but not all) of the limitations expressed in the descriptions of the basic and broad covered causes of loss. In those instances in which the Special Form does not contain an exclusion or a limitation equivalent to any of those contained in the Basic and Broad Forms, it provides broader coverage, as in these examples:

- The vehicle peril in both the Basic and Broad Forms excludes loss or damage caused by or resulting from vehicles owned by the named insured or operated in the course of the named insured's business. The Special Form, in contrast, does not contain such an exclusion. For example, the Special Form covers loss or damage to an insured building when an employee accidentally drives a truck owned by the insured into the building's garage wall.

- The windstorm peril in the Basic and Broad Forms excludes damage to the interior of a building by rain, snow, sleet, ice, sand, or dust, unless the roof or walls of the building are first damaged by a Covered Cause of Loss. The Special Form contains the same exclusion, but with an additional exception—the Special Form exclusion does not apply if loss results from the melting of ice, sleet, or snow on the building or structure. Therefore, unlike the Basic and Broad Forms, the Special Form covers water damage that occurs when water backs up under roof shingles because roof gutters are clogged with ice, a phenomenon known as ice damming.

Exclusions and Limitations Unique to the Special Form

Because the Special Form covers more causes of loss than the Broad Form, it contains some exclusions and limitations that are not needed in the Broad Form. The Special Form covers any risks of loss other than those that are specifically excluded. Thus, many difficult-to-insure perils that are not covered under the Basic and Broad Forms (because they are not named as covered causes of loss in those forms) must be specifically excluded in the Special Form. Examples of perils that the Special Form specifically excludes are these:

- Wear and tear
- Rust, corrosion, decay, deterioration, or hidden or latent defect
- Smog
- Settling, cracking, shrinking, or expansion
- Infestations and waste products of insects, birds, rodents, or other animals
- Mechanical breakdown
- Dampness or dryness of atmosphere, changes or extremes in temperatures, or marring or scratching (applicable to personal property only)

However, the insurer will pay losses caused by a "specified cause of loss" that results from the excluded peril. The Special Form defines "specified causes of loss" to include all of the causes of loss insured under the Broad Form. However, if one of these excluded causes of loss results in a "specified cause of loss," the insurer will pay for the loss caused by the resulting "specified cause of loss."

The Special Form also excludes loss caused by these:

- Weather conditions that contribute to other excluded causes of loss. If, for example, covered property is damaged by flood waters that were driven in part by high winds, the flood damage will not be covered even though windstorm is not otherwise excluded.
- Acts or decisions, including the failure to act or decide, of any person, group, organization, or governmental body. Thus, for example, if flooding occurs because municipal authorities fail to take proper flood control measures, the flood exclusion cannot be overcome by the insured's claim that the municipality's failure to act was the cause of the loss.
- Faulty or inadequate planning, zoning, surveying, siting, design, specifications, workmanship, repair, construction, renovation, remodeling, grading, compaction, materials, or maintenance.

If one of these excluded causes of loss results in a Covered Cause of Loss, the insurer will pay the loss resulting from the covered cause. For example, the failure of a city's fire department to take necessary measures might allow a fire to spread and burn down several row houses adjoining the insured's building. Even though the fire department's failure to act contributed to the destruction of the adjoining row houses, they were destroyed by fire, a Covered Cause of Loss. Thus, fire damage to the insured's building would be covered.

The Loss or Damage to Products exclusion eliminates coverage for damage to merchandise, goods, or other products resulting from production errors, such as adding wrong ingredients or measuring ingredients incorrectly. Many insurers believe that damage to products resulting from errors in the production process is a business risk that should not be insurable under commercial property policies. However, the exclusion specifically does not apply to loss or damage caused by a Covered Cause of Loss that results from an error or omission in the production process. If, for example, an error in the production process results in an explosion, the explosion damage will be covered.

Another noteworthy exclusion that is unique to the Special Form eliminates coverage for the release, discharge, or dispersal of pollutants. However, the exclusion does not apply to any release of pollutants caused by any of the specified causes of loss, nor does it apply to glass damaged by chemicals applied to the glass.

Loss to these kinds of property is covered only if it is caused by specified causes of loss:

- Valuable papers and records
- Animals, and then only in the event of their death
- Fragile articles if broken, such as glassware, statuary, marble, chinaware, and porcelain (but not including building glass and containers of property held for sale)
- Builders' machinery and equipment owned or held by the insured unless on or within 100 feet of the described premises

Another exclusion unique to the Special Form concerns trees, shrubs, plants, and lawns that are part of a vegetated roof. Covered property under the Building and Personal Property Coverage Form (BPP) includes trees, shrubs, plants, and lawns that are part of a vegetated roof.

Consequently, the BPP covers such items without application of the per item and per occurrence limits and the restricted specified perils that apply to other trees, shrubs, and plants under the BPP's Outdoor Property coverage extension. However, the Special Form excludes these causes of loss to trees, shrubs, plants, or lawns that are part of a vegetated roof:

1. Dampness or dryness of atmosphere or of soil supporting the vegetation;
2. Changes in or extremes of temperature;
3. Disease;
4. Frost or hail; or
5. Rain, snow, ice or sleet[9]

The excluded perils are either commercially uninsurable or would require a significant additional premium to insure. It is noteworthy that the Special Form covers trees, shrubs, plants, and lawns that are part of a vegetated roof against loss by windstorm as well as any other causes of loss that are not specifically excluded.

Theft-Related Exclusions and Limitations

The Special Form does not contain an absolute exclusion of theft, and thus it covers any theft of covered property that is not specifically excluded. Several theft-related exclusions and limitations define the scope of theft coverage under the Special Form.

The Special Form excludes dishonest or criminal acts (including theft) of the insured or of partners, members, officers, managers, directors, or employees of the insured, but the exclusion does not apply to acts of destruction by employees. For example, if Fred vandalizes his employer's property in response to being demoted, the vandalism damage is covered. If, however, Fred steals money from his employer, this dishonest act is subject to the exclusion. Losses resulting from the excluded types of dishonest acts can be covered under separate crime coverage forms.

The Special Form also excludes the voluntary surrendering of property as the result of a fraudulent scheme or trickery. If, for example, a thief posing as an honest customer tricks the insured's salesperson into voluntarily allowing the thief to remove merchandise from the insured's store, the resulting theft loss will not be covered. Similarly, the Special Form excludes loss of property transferred outside the described premises on the basis of unauthorized instructions.

Loss by theft of construction materials not attached as part of the building is excluded unless the materials are held for sale by the named insured. Moreover, the Special Form excludes loss of property that is simply missing without explanation or that is evidenced only by an inventory shortage.

The Special Form imposes special limits on theft loss of certain kinds of property that are especially attractive to thieves, such as furs, jewelry, precious metals, and tickets. Such property can be insured for higher limits under separate crime or inland marine forms.

A theft exclusion endorsement can be attached to the policy to eliminate theft coverage entirely when the underwriter feels that the risk is unacceptable or when the insured wants to reduce the policy premium.

Additional Coverages and Coverage Extensions

The Special Form includes the same additional coverages for collapse and fungus as the Broad Form. It also contains three coverage extensions that insure certain losses not otherwise covered.

The Property in Transit extension provides up to $5,000 of additional protection for loss to the insured's property in transit. The property must be in or on a motor vehicle owned, leased, or operated by the insured and cannot be in the custody of the insured's sales personnel. It covers only those losses that occur within the coverage territory.

The transit extension does not provide special form coverage. The perils insured against are fire, lightning, explosion, windstorm, hail, riot, civil commotion, vandalism, upset or overturn of the conveying vehicle, collision of the conveying vehicle with another vehicle or an object other than the roadbed, and theft. The coverage for theft is limited to theft of an entire bale, case, or package by forced entry into a securely locked body or compartment of the vehicle, evidenced by marks of the forced entry.

Because the transit extension has a low coverage limit and restricted covered perils, insureds who have property in transit should consider covering such property under an inland marine or ocean marine policy.

The Water Damage, Other Liquids, Powder or Molten Material Damage extension covers the cost to tear out and replace any part of a building necessary to repair an appliance or a system from which water or another liquid—or even powder fire-extinguishing agents or molten materials—has escaped. The extension does not pay for the repair of any defect that resulted in the leakage. It does pay for repairs to fire extinguishing equipment if the damage results in the discharge of any substance from an automatic fire protection system or is directly caused by freezing.

The Glass extension covers the expenses of installing temporary glass plates or boarding up openings when repair or replacement of damaged glass has been delayed. The insurer will also pay for the cost to clear obstructions (but not window displays) that prevent replacement of the glass. While the Basic, Broad, and Special Forms all insure glass breakage by a Covered Cause of Loss, only the Special Form includes this Glass coverage extension.

Apply Your Knowledge

A soft-drink producer is insured under the Building and Personal Property Coverage Form, also referred to as the BPP, with Special Form coverage. A mistake during the production process for one of its diet sodas causes too much artificial sweetener to be added to a large quantity of the beverage, forcing the soft drink producer to dispose of the entire batch. Would the cause of this loss be covered under the soft-drink producer's Special Form?

Feedback: No, the cause of the loss would not be covered under the soft-drink producer's Special Form, because the Loss or Damage to Products exclusion eliminates coverage for damage to merchandise, goods, or other products resulting from production errors, such as adding wrong ingredients or measuring ingredients incorrectly.

An office building is insured under the BPP with Special Form coverage. Firefighters' efforts to extinguish a fire caused extensive water damage to the insured building. In addition, several windows were broken by the intense heat of the fire. Would the cause of these losses be covered under the Special Form? Additionally, would the Special Form cover the cost of boarding up the windows?

Feedback: Yes, the Special Form would cover the cause of this loss, which was fire, because the Special Form does not exclude fire or any of the consequences of the fire.

DETERMINING WHAT IS COVERED BY THE COMMERCIAL PROPERTY CAUSES OF LOSS FORMS

To best meet the needs of their commercial property insurance clients, insurance professionals must understand the coverages provided by the various causes of loss forms. Only then can they recommend the form or forms that best address each client's loss exposures.

Different causes of loss forms provide different coverages. To determine whether one or more of the Basic, Broad, and Special causes of loss forms would cover a particular loss, insurance professionals need to do four things:

• Understand the coverage provided under each insuring agreement

• Determine whether any exclusions apply that would preclude coverage

• Ascertain whether other policy provisions eliminate or limit the coverage provided

• Determine whether any optional coverages (endorsements) affect coverage

Case Facts

Anita is the office manager at International Giftware, an import company. As part of an overall commercial package policy, the commercial property coverage for the warehouse is under a Building and Personal Property Coverage Form, also referred to as the BPP, with Basic Form causes of loss coverage. Last winter, during an uncharacteristically cold weekend, the newly installed heating system in the company's warehouse malfunctioned. Employees returned to the warehouse on Monday to discover that several plumbing pipes had frozen and burst, causing water damage to the warehouse and its contents. Anita called the company's insurance broker to report the claim, only to discover that the policy did not cover the water damage loss.

Additionally, the staff noticed that, in a small addition under construction at the back of the warehouse, some installed copper piping had been stolen. The insurer denied coverage for the theft, as well.

International Giftware's broker, Jorge, has come into Anita's office to discuss International's insurance renewal. Anita wants to ensure that International's policy will cover any similar losses in the future. What can Jorge do to provide the coverages that Anita requests?

Case Analysis Tools and Information

Jorge will need copies of all three causes of loss forms—Basic, Broad, and Special. The specific areas that he will need to review with Anita are the insuring agreements, the exclusions, and any optional overages (endorsements), if applicable. If he can show her the applicable sections of each insurance policy wording, he can demonstrate which form or forms would provide the required coverages.

Case Analysis Steps

Jorge will complete these steps in his coverage review with Anita:

- Review the covered causes of loss in the Basic and Broad Forms
- Examine the exclusions in the Broad Form to determine whether any apply
- Review the insuring agreement in the Special Form
- Examine the exclusions, limitations, additional overages, and extensions in the Special Form, as well as any endorsements, to determine whether any apply
- Make coverage recommendations

Review Basic and Broad Form Causes of Loss

Jorge begins by explaining to Anita that both the Basic and Broad Forms are named perils forms, covering only those causes of loss specifically described in the policy. In contrast, the Special Form covers all causes of loss not specifically excluded. See the exhibit "Perils Insured Against—Basic and Broad Forms."

A review of the Basic Form reveals that water damage is not listed among the covered causes of loss, explaining why International's claim in the previous winter was not covered. However, when Jorge turns to the Broad Form, Anita sees that water damage is included as a covered cause of loss. Anita then reads the description of the water damage peril:

Water Damage

a. Water Damage, meaning accidental discharge or leakage of water or steam as the direct result of the breaking apart or cracking of a plumbing, heating, air conditioning or other system or appliance, that is located on the described premises and contains water or steam.

However, Water Damage does not include:

(1) Discharge or leakage from:

(a) An Automatic Sprinkler System;

(b) A sump or related equipment and parts, including overflow due to sump pump failure or excessive volume of water; or

Perils Insured Against—Basic and Broad Forms

Peril	Causes of Loss—Basic Form	Causes of Loss—Broad Form
Fire	X	X
Lightning	X	X
Explosion	X	X
Windstorm or hail	X	X
Smoke	X	X
Aircraft or vehicles	X	X
Riot or civil commotion	X	X
Vandalism	X	X
Sprinkler leakage	X	X
Sinkhole collapse	X	X
Volcanic action	X	X
Falling objects		X
Weight of ice or snow		X
Water damage		X

[DA06028]

(c) Roof drains, gutters, downspouts or similar fixtures or equipment;

(2) The cost to repair any defect that caused the loss or damage;

(3) Loss or damage caused by or resulting from continuous or repeated seepage or leakage of water, or the presence or condensation of humidity, moisture or vapor, that occurs over a period of 14 days or more; or

(4) Loss or damage caused by or resulting from freezing, unless:

(a) You do your best to maintain heat in the building or structure; or

(b) You drain the equipment and shut off the water supply if the heat is not maintained.

b. If coverage applies subject to a. above, and the building or structure containing the system or appliance is Covered Property, we will also pay the cost to tear out and replace any part of the building or structure to repair damage to the system or appliance from which the water or steam escapes. But we will not pay the cost to repair any defect that caused the loss or damage [10]

Jorge draws Anita's attention to the two sections of the coverage description that he has highlighted. The first confirms that the accidental water leak from a plumbing system is covered. The second indicates that water damage losses caused by freezing may not be covered under certain circumstances.

However, this limitation would not have applied to International's previous loss because the company had made every effort to maintain heat in the building. In fact, the newly installed heating system's malfunctioning had caused the loss.

Examine Broad Form Exclusions

Jorge next turns to the Broad Form exclusions. He explains to Anita that checking for applicable exclusions is always essential before confirming specific coverage. Anita quickly scans the exclusions and finds one titled "Water." However, Jorge explains that, while this exclusion applies to flood and similar types of events, it does not apply to leakage from plumbing systems.

> g. Water
>
> (1) Flood, surface water, waves (including tidal wave and tsunami), tides, tidal water, overflow of any body of water, or spray from any of these, all whether or not driven by wind (including storm surge);
>
> (2) Mudslide or mudflow;
>
> (3) Water that backs up or overflows or is otherwise discharged from a sewer, drain, sump, sump pump or related equipment;
>
> (4) Water under the ground surface pressing on, or flowing or seeping through:
>
> (a) Foundations, walls, floors or paved surfaces;
>
> (b) Basements, whether paved or not; or
>
> (c) Doors, windows or other openings;
>
> or
>
> (5) Waterborne material carried or otherwise moved by any of the water referred to in Paragraph (1), (3) or (4), or material carried or otherwise moved by mudslide or mudflow.
>
> This exclusion applies regardless of whether any of the above, in Paragraphs (1) through (5), is caused by an act of nature or is otherwise caused. An example of a situation to which this exclusion applies is the situation where a dam, levee, seawall or other boundary or containment system contain the water.

But if any of the above, in Paragraphs (1) through (5), results in fire, explosion or sprinkler leakage, we will pay for the loss or damage caused by that fire, explosion or sprinkler leakage (if sprinkler leakage is a Covered Cause of Loss).[11]

Jorge and Anita review the remaining exclusions and confirm that none precludes coverage for water leakage from a plumbing system caused by freezing. Anita is pleased to learn that, by upgrading from the Basic Form to the Broad Form, International would have coverage for this type of occurrence in the future.

Anita and Jorge next consider whether the Broad Form would have covered the theft of copper piping that had been installed in the addition under construction. Because theft is not listed as a covered cause of loss in the Broad Form, the theft loss would not have been covered.

The only instance in which the Basic Form and the Broad Form cover theft of covered property is "looting occurring at the time and place of a riot or civil commotion," as stated in the Riot or Civil Commotion description that appears in both forms.

Review the Special Form Causes of Loss

Next, Jorge turns to the insuring agreement of the Special Form. He reminds Anita that the Special Form covers direct physical loss unless the loss is excluded or limited in the policy.

The form generally provides broader coverage than either the Basic Form or the Broad Form. He also points out that the insuring agreement indicates that they will need to review the Exclusions and Limitations Sections of the Special Form to confirm what coverage this form would have provided for International's losses.

Review the Special Form Exclusions and Limitations

Anita tells Jorge that she would like to review the Special Form exclusions and limitations for herself. Once she makes a tentative coverage determination, Jorge can confirm whether she has done so correctly. Jorge agrees to this approach.

Anita first reviews the exclusions and immediately finds one related to leakage from a sprinkler system. However, she recognizes that it is worded in the same way as the coverage description in the Broad Form.

The exclusion applies only if the insured has not maintained heat in the building or drained and shut off the system. Given the circumstances of International's previous loss, this exclusion would not apply. Anita finds no other exclusions that would apply to the water damage loss.

> g. Water, other liquids, powder or molten material that leaks or flows from plumbing, heating, air conditioning or other equipment (except fire protective systems) caused by or resulting from freezing, unless:
>
> (1) You do your best to maintain heat in the building or structure; or
>
> (2) You drain the equipment and shut off the supply if the heat is not maintained.[12]

Next, Anita turns to the Limitations Section. She reads carefully through each of the limitations and the special limits included in the section. She is confident that none of them would have applied to International's water damage loss.

She determines that the loss would have been covered under both the Broad Form and the Special Form. Jorge confirms that provided International had complied with its obligations under the policy, the water damage loss would have been covered.

Anita and Jorge next review the BPP and the Special Form to determine whether the theft of copper piping would have been covered if the Special Form had applied to International's BPP. Because the copper piping was attached to the described building when the loss occurred, the piping qualifies as covered property, and no exclusion or limitation in the Special Form would eliminate coverage for the theft of that property.

If the piping had not been attached to the building when the loss occurred, it would have been excluded by the Special Form's limitation applicable to "building materials and supplies not attached as part of the building or structure, caused by or resulting from theft."

Make a Coverage Recommendation

Based on their analyses of the three policy forms, Jorge and Anita have determined that the Special Form would provide the coverages that Anita wanted. However, Jorge points out that the Special Form will also cover a variety of other losses not covered by the Broad Form. For example, if a maintenance employee were to spill paint on the carpet in the office, the Special Form would cover that loss because it does not exclude that type of loss.

Jorge reminds Anita that an organization's loss exposures are not limited to those types of losses they have faced in the past. The Special Form would protect International from a wider range of unanticipated future losses, and he recommends that Anita seriously consider purchasing Special Form coverage. He offers to provide a quote for adding the Special Form for Anita to review, and she agrees. He also recommends that the company take greater precautions in securing building materials such as the copper piping that was stolen. See the exhibit "Correct Answer."

Correct Answer

After analyzing the insuring agreements, exclusions, and other policy provisions of the Basic, Broad, and Special causes of loss forms, as well as any endorsements, Jorge and Anita determined that both the Broad Form and the Special Form would have provided coverage for International's previous water damage loss that resulted from frozen pipes, but only the Special Form would have covered the theft loss. By upgrading the company's coverage from Basic Form to Special Form, Anita can be assured that, if the same types of losses occur in the future, the company will be fully covered.

[DA06029]

SUMMARY

The Causes of Loss—Basic Form covers fire and other specified causes of loss, while the Causes of Loss—Broad Form covers the same specified causes of loss as the Basic Form, plus a few others.

In addition to the limitations and exclusions contained in the Basic and Broad Form descriptions of covered perils, both forms have a separate section of exclusions, which contains three parts:

- A group of eight exclusions with lead-in wording that contains anti-concurrent causation language
- A group of four additional exclusions that does not contain anti-concurrent causation language
- A group of "special exclusions" that apply only to certain coverage forms other than the BPP

The most frequently selected of the three causes of loss forms, the Causes of Loss—Special Form is designed to cover any loss that would be covered by the Basic and Broad Forms. In addition, the Special Form provides coverages not found in the Basic and Broad Forms.

The Special Form offers several advantages to the insured, including coverage for certain causes of loss that are omitted or excluded under the Broad Form, coverage for losses the insured might not have anticipated, and the placement of the "burden of proof" on the insurer as opposed to the insured.

By reviewing and analyzing the insuring agreement, exclusions, limitations, and other policy provisions in the Basic, Broad, and Special causes of loss forms, insurance professionals and insureds can determine whether a particular type of loss is covered. Water damage resulting from frozen plumbing pipes would be covered under the Broad and Special Forms, but not the Basic Form. The Special Form would also cover theft of building materials attached to the building.

ASSIGNMENT NOTES

1. This quotation and, unless indicated otherwise, all other quotations in the Causes of Loss—Basic and Broad Forms section are from the Causes of Loss—Basic Form (CP 10 10 10 12), Causes of Loss—Broad Form (CP 10 20 10 12), or Causes of Loss—Special Form (CP 10 30 10 12) of Insurance Services Office, Inc. Includes copyrighted material of Insurance Services Office, Inc., with its permission. Copyright, Insurance Services Office, Inc., 2011.

2. Includes copyrighted material of Insurance Services Office, Inc. with its permission. Copyright, Insurance Services Office, Inc., 2011.

3. Includes copyrighted material of Insurance Services Office, Inc. with its permission. Copyright, Insurance Services Office, Inc., 2011.

4. Includes copyrighted material of Insurance Services Office, Inc. with its permission. Copyright, Insurance Services Office, 2011.

5. Insurance Information Institute, Insurance Fact Book 2014, pp. 144, 155–156.

6. Includes copyrighted material of Insurance Services Office, Inc. with its permission. Copyright, Insurance Services Office, 2011.

7. Includes copyrighted material of Insurance Services Office, Inc. with its permission. Copyright, Insurance Services Office, 2011.

8. Includes copyrighted material of Insurance Services Office, Inc. with its permission. Copyright, Insurance Services Office, 2011.

9. Includes copyrighted material of Insurance Services Office, Inc., with its permission. Copyright, Insurance Services Office, Inc., 2011.

10. Includes copyrighted material of Insurance Services Office, Inc. with its permission. Copyright, Insurance Services Office, Inc., 2011.

11. Includes copyrighted material of Insurance Services Office, Inc. with its permission. Copyright, Insurance Services Office, Inc., 2011.

12. Includes copyrighted material of Insurance Services Office, Inc. with its permission. Copyright, Insurance Services Office, Inc., 2011.

Direct Your Learning ▶▶

Other Commercial Property Coverage Options

Educational Objectives

After learning the content of this assignment, you should be able to:

▷ Describe the operation of blanket insurance and its advantages over specific insurance.

▷ Describe the purpose and operation of each of the following forms for insuring business personal property that is subject to fluctuation in value:

- Peak Season Limit of Insurance endorsement
- Value Reporting Form

▷ Identify the international property loss exposures that are covered, and those that are not covered, by the following endorsements:

- Business Personal Property—Limited International Coverage
- Property in Process of Manufacture by Others—Limited International Coverage

▷ Explain how each of the following endorsements modifies a commercial property coverage form:

- Additional Covered Property
- Specified Business Personal Property Temporarily Away From Premises
- Manufacturers' Consequential Loss Assumption
- Brands and Labels
- Increased Cost of Loss and Related Expenses for Green Upgrades
- Increase in Rebuilding Expenses Following Disaster

4

▷ Explain how each of the following endorsements modifies the causes of loss covered by commercial property coverage forms:

- Ordinance or Law Coverage
- Utility Services—Direct Damage
- Spoilage Coverage
- Radioactive Contamination
- Discharge from Sewer, Drain or Sump (Not Flood-Related)
- Theft of Building Materials and Supplies (Other Than Builders Risk)
- Equipment Breakdown Cause of Loss

▷ Describe the purpose and operation of each of the following endorsements for modifying the valuation methods or provisions affecting the amounts payable in commercial property coverage forms:

- Manufacturer's Selling Price (Finished "Stock" Only)
- Functional Building Valuation
- Functional Personal Property Valuation (Other Than "Stock")
- Limitations on Coverage for Roof Surfacing

▷ Given a case regarding a particular organization's loss exposures, recommend appropriate commercial property coverage options.

Other Commercial Property Coverage Options

BLANKET INSURANCE

The basic method of insuring buildings and personal property is to schedule a specific amount of insurance in the declarations for each building and a specific amount of insurance for personal property at each location. This approach is called **specific insurance**. An example of how specific insurance might be indicated in the declarations of a commercial property policy is:

- $1,000,000 on the building at 123 Main St., Des Moines, IA
- $800,000 on your business personal property at 123 Main St., Des Moines, IA

The alternative to specific insurance is **blanket insurance**, which is insurance that covers either of the following with one limit of insurance:

- One type of property in one or more separately rated buildings
- Two or more types of property in one or more separately rated buildings

Operation of Blanket Insurance

No special endorsement is required to effect blanket insurance. The word "blanket" is simply added to the statement of coverage in the declarations. If the property previously described was insured on a blanket basis, the statement of coverage in the declarations might read:

$1,800,000 blanket on the building and your business personal property at 123 Main St., Des Moines, IA

Property at different locations can also be covered on a blanket basis. In that case, coverage can apply to one or more types of property at more than one location, as in these examples:

$5,000,000 blanket on buildings and your business personal property at:

- 760 Walnut St., Cincinnati, OH
- 987 Third St., Cincinnati, OH
- 12 Elm St., Fort Thomas, KY

Specific insurance
Insurance that covers each building for a specific limit of insurance and personal property at each building for a specific limit of insurance.

Blanket insurance
Insurance that covers either of the following with one limit of insurance: (1) one type of property in one or more separately rated buildings or (2) two or more types of property in one or more separately rated buildings.

or $7,500,000 blanket on buildings at:

- 78 Broadway, Malvern, PA
- 971 Tenth St., Philadelphia, PA
- 88 Highland Rd., Pottstown, PA

Before they will provide blanket coverage, most underwriters require that the insured file a statement of values that separately shows the insurable value for the building and contents at each location. This helps the underwriter to evaluate the adequacy of the requested amount of insurance and to calculate the rate to be charged. (Blanket rates are calculated as a weighted average using the rates and amounts of insurance at each location.)

Coinsurance Requirement for Blanket Insurance

Blanket insurance may involve an additional cost. The minimum coinsurance clause is 90 percent, but the rates are the same as for 80 percent coinsurance. The insured with blanket insurance must insure to 90 percent of value to avoid a coinsurance penalty but does not receive the 5 percent discount that applies to specific insurance with a 90 percent coinsurance requirement. Thus, to meet coinsurance requirements, the insured with blanket insurance must buy more insurance than otherwise would be required.

Advantages of Blanket Insurance

Despite the additional premium, blanket insurance entails several advantages for an insured. Consider the example of Contemporary Furniture, Inc. (CFI), which owns and operates furniture stores at two locations. Assume that the value of CFI's business personal property in each store is $1,000,000 at the inception of the policy. To comply with the 80 percent coinsurance requirement, CFI might purchase specific insurance with a limit of $800,000 on its business personal property at each location. In that event, if a loss exceeds $800,000, CFI will be uninsured for the portion in excess of $800,000. If CFI had purchased a blanket policy with a limit of $1,800,000 (90 percent of $2,000,000), it would be fully insured for the loss at any one location up to $1,800,000 as long as the total amount of insurance satisfied the coinsurance requirement.

Now suppose that at the time of the loss the value of CFI's property at one store has increased to $1,200,000 and the value of the property at the other store has decreased to $800,000. If the amount of insurance has not been adjusted, a total loss at the first store would leave CFI with a $400,000 uninsured loss if CFI had specific insurance, even though the total amount of insurance was adequate. With blanket insurance, CFI's $1,200,000 loss would have been paid in full. CFI's large uninsured loss (without blanket insurance) might be reduced by the Newly Acquired or Constructed Property coverage extension. That extension would provide coverage for up to $100,000 on property that CFI had acquired within the thirty-day period before the loss.

Additional debris removal coverage is another advantage of blanket insurance. Even if CFI had purchased insurance equal to 100 percent of its insurable value on a specific basis ($1,000,000 at each location), a total loss at either location would leave only the $10,000 additional coverage for debris removal. If only one location was involved in the loss, blanket insurance could cover the loss, including debris removal, in full.

Furthermore, CFI may not know the exact insurable value at each location. With specific insurance, CFI would either have to purchase a higher amount of insurance to provide a cushion against error in estimating insurable values or risk an uninsured loss. With blanket insurance, assuming the two locations are not likely to be damaged by the same occurrence (such as a hurricane that devastates a wide area), the minimum amount of insurance needed to comply with coinsurance requirements would be sufficient to fully protect CFI's property.

Combining the Agreed Value Option With Blanket Insurance

Most risk management professionals regard the combination of the Agreed Value option with blanket insurance as the preferred method to provide property insurance. The Agreed Value option avoids any coinsurance penalty, and if separate locations are involved that are not subject to the same loss, the danger of underinsurance is greatly reduced.

Underwriters are often reluctant to offer blanket coverage, particularly when combined with the Agreed Value option, because ascertaining that the insured is carrying insurance to value is difficult, and a large blanket limit may expose the insurer to unanticipated catastrophe exposure.

The recent introduction of margin clauses has reduced underwriters' concerns about blanket insurance (and made it less attractive to insureds). A margin clause provides that the insured's recovery is limited, in any event, to not more than a specified percentage above the values filed with the insurer. The percentage is typically between 15 and 50 percent. Thus, if the sum of the building and contents listed in the statement of values is $2,000,000 and the policy specifies a margin of 20 percent, the most that the insured could collect for any one loss at that location is $2,400,000. Without a margin clause, an insured could theoretically collect the entire blanket limit for a loss at one location.

FLUCTUATING PERSONAL PROPERTY VALUES

Fluctuating personal property values pose an insurance problem for many businesses—especially those with widely varying inventory levels. For some businesses, values fluctuate in predictable cycles, but for other businesses, external and other factors may cause inventory fluctuations with no predictable pattern.

The term "fluctuating values" refers to values that rise and fall over time. For some businesses, values fluctuate in predictable cycles. A toy store, for example, may predictably double its inventory during the months preceding Christmas, with inventory values declining rapidly just before Christmas and stabilizing for the next nine months.

Similarly, a seasonal business such as a nursery can be expected to have higher inventory values in spring and summer than in fall and winter. Other businesses may experience inventory fluctuations with no predictable pattern.

The insurable value of a lumberyard's inventory, for example, may be affected by external factors such as the number of houses being built in the area or rapid changes in the price of material. Whatever the cause of the fluctuation, an insured usually wants insurance to adjust to the circumstances and provide economical protection year-round, rather than pay excess premiums (for unneeded coverage) or have too little coverage (to avoid paying excess premiums).

The usual approach of a single, fixed amount of insurance, with premiums based on that policy limit, is unsatisfactory for fluctuating inventories.

Two amendments to commercial property coverage forms provide more efficient ways to meet an insured's needs in these coverage situations: the Peak Season Limit of Insurance endorsement and the Value Reporting Form.

Peak Season Endorsement

Peak Season Limit of Insurance endorsement

Endorsement that covers the fluctuating values of business personal property by providing differing amounts of insurance for certain time periods during the policy period.

The **Peak Season Limit of Insurance endorsement** (CP 12 30) provides differing amounts of insurance for selected time periods during the policy term, as indicated by specific dates shown in the endorsement.

For example, a swimsuit manufacturer is covered under a Business and Personal Property Coverage Form (BPP) providing $3 million of coverage on business personal property with a peak season endorsement increasing coverage to $4 million from February 1 through May 31, the time when its inventories increase to meet summertime demand. This would have exactly the same effect as endorsing the policy on February 1 to increase the coverage and endorsing it again on May 31 to reduce the coverage.

The peak season endorsement eliminates the need for these extra transactions and avoids the risk that the insured may overlook the need to increase its insurance.

Usually, the Peak Season Limit of Insurance endorsement is attached when the policy is issued—although it may be added mid-term—and a pro rata increased premium is charged for the period during which the limit is increased.

☑ Reality Check

Peak Season Endorsement Considerations

The peak season endorsement is well suited for organizations whose business personal property values fluctuate in predictable patterns. In fact, "other than a possible coinsurance consideration, this endorsement has none of the penalties or surcharges associated with value reporting forms."

There is a significant challenge, however, in accurately predicting when and for how long property values will peak. For example, a lumber supplier has a higher supply of inventory on hand during the summer months when construction is most active. The supplier uses a peak season endorsement to raise its coverage during the summer months. However, the supplier read forecasts that new housing construction in the local area was going to rise sharply in late spring. This would cause a great increase in demand for building materials such as lumber. Consequently, the supplier increased its inventory level early but forgot to also increase its policy limit. When a fire occurred in its warehouse, which was almost filled to capacity, the supplier was underinsured and assessed a coinsurance penalty.

"Peak Season Coverage," www.roughnotes.com/pfm/200/..%5C100%5C130_0612.htm (accessed April 13, 2010) [DA05978]

Value Reporting Form

The **Value Reporting Form** (CP 13 10) provides another way to avoid the costs of overinsuring or underinsuring business personal property. Briefly, it works this way:

A limit of insurance is set high enough to cover the insured's maximum expected values at any time during the policy period. The insured reports values to the insurer at periodic intervals specified in the form. As long as the insured reports property values accurately and on time, the insurer will pay the full amount of any loss that occurs (subject to the policy limit), even if the values on hand at the time of the loss are greater than those last reported to the insurer.

At the end of the policy period, the insurer computes the average values that were exposed to loss and uses that average to determine the premium. Thus, the final premium is based not on the policy limit but on the values reported by the insured as exposed to loss.

Major features of the Value Reporting Form include these:

- Reporting requirement
- Limit of insurance
- Penalties

Value Reporting Form

A commercial property form that bases the insured's premium for business personal property on the values that the insured reports to the insurer periodically during the policy period.

- Provisional premium
- Treatment of specific (nonreporting) insurance

Reporting Requirement

The insured must give the insurer periodic reports of dollar values covered by the policy. The time period for which the reports of value are due is referred to as a reporting period. Five reporting period options are available. These are the options and code letters used to indicate them:

- DR—daily values reported monthly

- WR—values as of the last day of the week reported monthly

- MR—values as of the last day of the month reported monthly

- QR—values as of the last day of the month reported quarterly

- PR—values as of the last day of the month reported at the end of the policy year

MR, monthly reporting of monthly values on the last day of the month, is the most commonly used alternative.

The applicable code letters (DR, WR, and so forth) appear in the commercial property declarations in place of a coinsurance percentage. The insured must file the required report within thirty days after the end of each reporting period. The thirty-day requirement applies to the renewal, by the same insurer, of a policy previously written with a reporting form. For coverage that was not previously written with a reporting form by the insurer, the insured has sixty days from the end of the reporting period to file the first report on all except the quarterly report basis. Different rules apply to quarterly reports, as described in the form.

Limit of Insurance

Usually, a specific limit of insurance applies to property at each location. The insurer's obligation is limited by this maximum amount per location unless coverage is written on a blanket basis, in which event the blanket limit can apply at any one location.

The insured is required to report the value (using the valuation basis specified in the policy) of all covered property on hand as of each report date. If $250,000 worth of property is on hand and the limit of insurance is $150,000, then the insured must still report $250,000. Because the premium is based on the reported values, the insured must also pay a premium based on $250,000. However, coverage is still capped by the $150,000 limit of insurance. If such a situation occurs, the insured should increase the policy limit or purchase specific insurance to cover the additional $100,000 of value.

The Report of Values (CP 13 60) that is used to report property values to the insurer prominently displays this notice of this potential problem: "The values you report do not change your limits of insurance. If values exceed or come close to your limits of insurance, contact your agent or broker. You may need additional insurance."[1]

For the Value Reporting Form to work properly—and for the insurer to collect adequate premiums—the insurer must have information that accurately reflects the values exposed to loss. Accordingly, the form imposes penalties for failure to submit reports on time and for inaccurate reports.

Penalty for Failure to Submit Required Reports on Time

If at the time of loss the first required report of values is due, but has not been received, the insurer will pay no more than 75 percent of the amount that would otherwise have been paid. For example, assume that the insured had made no reports of value at the time that a loss occurred under these circumstances:

Limit of insurance   = $100,000

Reporting period   =   MR (monthly values reported monthly)

Policy inception   =   January 1

Date of loss   =   April 12

Amount of loss   = $40,000

Because the first report was due but had not been received at the time of the loss, the insured would collect only 75 percent of the amount that the insurer would otherwise have paid. Thus, ignoring any deductible, the insurer would pay $30,000 instead of the full $40,000 loss.

If at the time a loss occurs the insured has failed to submit any required report after the first required report has been made, the insurer will pay no more than the values last reported for the location at which the loss occurred. This provision can result in a serious penalty for an organization whose values at the loss location are higher than they were at the time of the last report. However, it has no effect on an organization whose values at the loss location are the same or lower than they were at the last report date.

This loss example illustrates the provision:

Limit of insurance   = $100,000 (single location)

Reporting period   =   MR (monthly values reported monthly)

Value last reported   = $60,000 (first report; accurate)

Policy inception   =   January 1

Date of loss   =   June 20 (second report was overdue)

Amount of loss   = $70,000

Because the second report was overdue at the time of the loss, the insurer would pay no more than the value last reported for that location; thus, disregarding any deductible, the insurer would pay only $60,000, leaving the insured with a $10,000 uninsured loss. Had the loss been $60,000 or less, no penalty would have applied.

Penalty for Inaccurate Reports

The Value Reporting Form replaces the Coinsurance condition of the BPP with a Full Reporting provision, which stipulates that if the last report showed less than the full value of covered property at the affected location on the report date, then the insurer would pay claims according to this formula:

$$\text{Insurer's payment (not to exceed limit)} = \left(\frac{\text{Value reported}}{\text{Actual value}} \times \text{Loss} \right) - \text{Deductible.}$$

To understand the consequences of underreporting values, assume that a loss occurs under these circumstances, and the insurer's claim representative investigating the loss has discovered that the actual value at the time of the last report was greater than the value reported:

Limit of insurance	=	$2,000,000 (single location)
Value last reported	=	$1,000,000
Actual value at time of report	=	$1,500,000
Amount of loss	=	$600,000
Deductible	=	$1,000

The insurer's payment would be calculated as shown:

$$\left(\frac{\$1,000,000}{\$1,500,000} \times \$600,000 \right) - \$1,000 = \$399,000.$$

In this case, the insured's inaccurate reporting resulted in an uninsured loss that was $200,000 greater than it would have been if the insured had made an accurate report. The potential severity of the penalty for inaccurate reports should deter anyone who is aware of it from trying to save on premiums by intentionally underreporting values.

Unfortunately, many insureds do not understand the consequences of inaccurate (or late) reports until after they have suffered a loss.

As long as reports are accurate and made on time, the penalties described do not apply; the insurer will pay the full amount of any loss (up to the limit of insurance), even if it exceeds the amount last reported. See the exhibit "Insured Underreported Values."

Insured Underreported Values

A&R Supply Company, a wholesaler that deals in seasonal products, insures its business personal property under a BPP to which a Value Reporting Form has been attached. The amount of insurance is $5 million with a $1,000 deductible. Reports of values are due monthly. The inception date of the policy was January 1.

On the following November 10 of the policy year, A&R suffered a business personal property loss of $240,000 caused by an insured peril. The actual value of A&R's business personal property at the time of its last report, which was made on time, was $4 million. However, the value stated on that report was $3.2 million. At the time of the loss, A&R's business personal property had a value of $3.5 million.

Question: What amount would A&R's insurer pay for the described loss?

Answer: A&R's last report of values, although made on time, showed less than the full value of covered property on the report date. Thus, the amount payable by the insurer is calculated using the method described in the Full Reporting provision: the insured will be able to collect only that proportion of the loss that the amount last reported bears to the actual value of covered property when the last report was made. The calculation is as shown:

$$\left(\frac{\$3,200,000}{\$4,000,000} \times \$240,000\right) - \$1,000 = \$191,000.$$

[DA03535]

Provisional Premium

Like most other types of property insurance, the Value Reporting Form carries a limit of insurance that is the most the insurer will pay for a loss. However, unlike most other property insurance limits, the limit of insurance for property subject to the Value Reporting Form is usually set for an amount that is higher than the maximum value expected at any one time during the policy term.

Because the limit usually exceeds the exposure, the initial premium, called the provisional premium, is not based on the full limit of insurance. The provisional premium is typically 75 percent of the annual premium that would be required to purchase nonreporting coverage with the same limit. Ordinarily, the provisional premium must be paid at the beginning of the policy period. The earned premium for the entire policy period depends on the average values reported during the policy term. At the end of the policy period, an additional premium may be due or a refund may be owed to the insured. Refunds and additional premiums are calculated on a pro rata basis.

Specific Insurance

Reporting form insurance may be combined with other, nonreporting insurance covering the same property. This other insurance is then referred to as specific insurance. The terminology is confusing because "specific" is also used as the opposite of "blanket."

The Value Reporting Form defines specific insurance as:

> . . . other insurance that:
>
> a. Covers the same Covered Property to which this endorsement applies; and
>
> b. Is not subject to the same plan, terms, conditions and provisions as this insurance, including this endorsement.[2]

Coverage on property subject to the Value Reporting Form is excess over the total of (1) the amount due from specific insurance plus (2) the amount of any deductible applying to the specific insurance.

If the specific insurance is written with no coinsurance, the specific coverage pays the loss up to its policy limit, and the reporting insurance pays the balance, less any applicable deductible.

If the specific insurance has a coinsurance requirement, the reporting form coverage is not counted when determining whether the coinsurance requirement has been met.

The insured and the insurer must be alert to any change in specific coverage. In particular, when any specific coverage expires, the change must be noted in the next report. See the exhibit "Value Reporting Advantages and Disadvantages."

Value Reporting Advantages and Disadvantages

Advantages:	Disadvantages:
• Ideal way to insure property values that fluctuate substantially. Insured can get the effect of full coverage without paying for more insurance than necessary, resulting in a savings in premium.	• If the insured reports its property values late and a claim occurs, the claim payment is reduced. • If the insured's report of values is too low—either intentionally to save premium or unintentionally—and a claim occurs, the claim payment is reduced. • The savings in premium may not justify the cost to generate the reports. • If the value of the property exceeds the policy limit, the insured pays the premium on the full value, but the coverage remains the same at the policy limit.

[DA05979]

LIMITED INTERNATIONAL COVERAGE ENDORSEMENTS

At one time, most businesses domiciled in the United States did not have to concern themselves with foreign exposures because they seldom had any foreign operations. Now, even relatively small firms do business around the world.

The commercial property coverage part is designed to cover property at designated premises with only limited extensions of coverage away from those premises, but never outside the coverage territory (the U.S., its territories and possessions, Puerto Rico, and Canada). To meet some of the coverage needs of firms with exposures outside that territory, ISO's commercial property program includes four limited international coverage endorsements.

Two of these endorsements, covering direct physical loss to an insured's business personal property in a foreign coverage territory, are discussed here. The other two endorsements cover business income and extra expense.

Business Personal Property—Limited International Coverage

An insured may send a salesperson on a business trip to Europe to call on prospective customers and to show them samples of the insured's products, or the insured may have a booth at a trade show in Mexico to exhibit its merchandise. Once the insured's property is outside the coverage territory, the commercial property policy will not cover it.

The Business Personal Property—Limited International Coverage endorsement (CP 04 32) provides a partial solution to this problem. This endorsement extends the insured's business personal property coverage to include certain property in, or en route to or from, a foreign coverage territory. The endorsement schedule provides a blank space to list a specific foreign territory or a box to select all foreign territories.

For coverage under this endorsement to apply, the property must meet these criteria:

- Temporarily in the foreign coverage territory specified in the schedule
- Used in the insured's business in the foreign coverage territory
- Located at a business location the insured owns, operates, or leases; or in the care, custody, or control of the insured or its authorized representative

The endorsement schedule provides blanks to indicate the time limit, in weeks or months, for coverage applying to each trip. The trip begins when the property leaves the described premises and ends when the property returns to those premises or when the policy expires (if sooner). The endorsement schedule shows the limit of insurance, the applicable causes of loss form, and any coverage endorsements that apply to the endorsement.

The endorsement excludes property exported to or held for sale in the foreign coverage territory. The endorsement also excludes property in the care, custody, or control of a common or contract carrier or bailee unless the carrier or bailee is at the same time transporting the insured or its authorized representative.

Coverage is extended to include the insured's business personal property used during personal travel to communicate with the described premises, such as cell phones or laptop computers used to send e-mail.

The loss settlement provision provides that losses are valued in U.S. currency and are based on values and costs in the area of the described premises where the insured's business personal property is permanently located.

Property in Process of Manufacture by Others— Limited International Coverage

"Offshoring" by U.S. manufacturers—that is, contracting with foreign manufacturers— has grown substantially in recent years.

For example, clothing manufacturers send piece goods to Central America to have them sewn into garments, and electronic hardware producers use manufacturing facilities in Asia. Although large companies often establish and run their own facilities in foreign countries, smaller companies often contract with foreign manufacturers without acquiring any ownership interest in them.

To meet insureds' needs for coverage of property being manufactured by these foreign companies, ISO has developed an endorsement titled Property in Process of Manufacture by Others—Limited International Coverage (CP 04 33).

The endorsement extends the insured's business personal property coverage to include raw materials and in-process goods while being manufactured in a foreign coverage territory at a location not owned, operated, or leased to the insured. Coverage continues while these goods are temporarily stored awaiting transport at any location in the foreign coverage territory other than a location owned, operated, or leased by the insured.

The schedule for the endorsement shows all the same items as the schedule for the Business Personal Property—Limited International Coverage endorsement, other than the each-trip time limitation, which does not apply to the Property in Process of Manufacture by Others endorsement.

The foreign coverage territory in the Property in Process of Manufacture by Others endorsement excludes any territory where sanction or embargo prohibits the transactions covered in the endorsement. The foreign coverage territory also excludes any territory where insurance law prohibits the insurer from providing this coverage. Many foreign countries require that property coverage be placed with domestic insurers and prohibit placing coverage with nonadmitted insurers.

The endorsement does not cover merchandise held for sale, property in transit, or property while in the care, custody, or control of a carrier or bailee hired to transport the property. The loss settlement provision is the same as in the Business Personal Property—Limited International Coverage endorsement.

Both of the endorsements are appropriately titled Limited International Coverage. Here is a summary of some of their limitations:

- The Business Personal Property endorsement does not cover property shipments by a carrier other than the one transporting the insured or its authorized representative.
- The Business Personal Property endorsement does not cover shipments while within the standard coverage territory.
- The Property in Process of Manufacture by Others endorsement does not cover property in transit or held by carriers or bailees.
- The Property in Process of Manufacture by Others endorsement does not cover property at premises owned, operated, or leased by the insured.
- Both endorsements base valuation on domestic costs even if property is replaced overseas.
- Neither endorsement covers merchandise held for sale.

Furthermore, neither endorsement provides any coverage for property permanently outside the regular coverage territory (the U.S., its territories or possessions, Puerto Rico, or Canada) other than property in the process of manufacture. For example, neither endorsement would cover furniture, fixtures, and supplies and goods for sale at an office or a store operated by the insured in England. When insureds want coverage for the exposures excluded by the ISO endorsements, they can obtain independently developed foreign coverage policies.

Independently developed foreign coverage policies can insure property and business income exposures for property at foreign locations as well as provide general liability, workers compensation, and crime coverages that the insured may need. Inland and ocean marine insurance can cover transit and storage exposures, including many not covered by the endorsements. See the exhibit "Foreign Coverage Policies."

Foreign Coverage Policies

For firms with significant foreign property exposures, several options are offered by insurers that either do business on a worldwide basis or are part of an international network.

Foreign-issued local policies—Where required by local law or by the insured's preference, these insurers can arrange to have a foreign policy issued by an affiliated insurer admitted to do business in the local country or through other insurers that are members of an overseas network of insurers. The required coverage is often not as broad as that offered by U.S. insurers and, in many cases, broader coverage is not available from admitted insurers in the foreign country.

Foreign master policy—This type of policy is issued in the U.S. It provides nonadmitted property coverage for the insured's foreign exposures. It can be written on an excess basis ("difference in limits") over the limits of any foreign-issued local policies. It can also be written covering exposures not written in the foreign-issued local policies ("difference in conditions"). This option enables the insured to achieve uniformity in coverage worldwide despite the differences in coverages that result from the requirement in many countries that property insurance be placed with local insurers. In most cases, the insurer providing the master policy can also provide the required admitted coverage through its affiliates. A master policy approach is usually a more cost-effective method than attempting to buy broader coverage in each foreign country, even when such coverage is available.

[DA03538]

COMMERCIAL PROPERTY ENDORSEMENTS

In addition to the optional coverages contained in the Building and Personal Property Coverage Form, also referred to as the BPP, many other coverage options are available for commercial property coverage forms by endorsement.

Endorsements for adding coverage options to the BPP and to other commercial property coverage forms include these:

- Additional Covered Property (CP 14 10)
- Specified Business Personal Property Temporarily Away From Premises (CP 04 04)
- Manufacturers' Consequential Loss Assumption (CP 99 02)
- Brands and Labels (CP 04 01)
- Increased Cost of Loss and Related Expenses for Green Upgrades (CP 04 02)
- Increase in Rebuilding Expenses Following Disaster (CP 04 09)

Additional Covered Property

Almost all the items of property that are excluded in the BPP can be insured. More specialized coverages are the best alternative for certain types of property, such as crime coverage forms for money and securities. However, coverage for many types of excluded property can easily be added to the BPP using the Additional Covered Property endorsement.

An earlier edition of this endorsement included both a printed list of items that could be added and blank space for listing other combinations. The current edition of the endorsement provides only blank space for inserting the additional property to be covered. A list of the items that were included in the earlier edition of the endorsement is shown in the exhibit. All of those items can be insured under the current endorsement by inserting the necessary wording in the endorsement. See the exhibit "Additional Covered Property."

Additional Covered Property

Examples of items that can be included as additional covered property are these:

- The cost of excavation, grading, backfilling or filling
- Foundations of buildings, structures, machinery or boilers if their foundations are below:
  - (1) The lowest basement floor; or
  - (2) The surface of the ground, if there is no basement.
- Underground pipes, flues, or drains
- Pilings, piers, wharves or docks
- Fences outside of buildings
- Retaining walls that are not part of the building
- Bridges, roadways, walks, patios or other paved surfaces
- Vehicles or self-propelled machines the insured does not manufacture, process, or warehouse (including aircraft or watercraft) that:
  - (1) Are licensed for use on public roads; or
  - (2) Are operated principally away from the described premises
- Animals

Includes copyrighted material of Insurance Services Office, Inc., with its permission. Copyright, Insurance Services Office, Inc., 2011. [DA03539]

For the most part, such requests to add the excluded items should pose no problem for insurers; in many cases, the excluded items present a lower risk of loss than the other property insured. The amount of insurance carried should be increased to reflect the value of the additional items covered.

Sometimes the excluded property is of a type that requires more specialized underwriting and loss control—bridges, piers, and wharves, for example.

Specified Business Personal Property Temporarily Away From Premises

The Specified Business Personal Property Temporarily Away From Premises endorsement covers business personal property such as electronic devices carried by the named insured's employees while away from the described premises but within the regular coverage territory of the United States, its territories or possessions, Puerto Rico, or Canada. The endorsement provides coverage that is more flexible in some respects than the Property Off-Premises extension found in the BPP and in other commercial property coverage forms.

The endorsement covers the types or items of property scheduled in the endorsement for up to the each occurrence limit shown, which could be more or less than the $10,000 limit that applies to the Property Off-Premises extension. If the damaged or lost property is subject to a special limitation in the coverage form to which it is attached, the endorsement will pay no more than the limitation amount, even if the endorsement's limit is for a higher amount.

To be covered by the endorsement, the scheduled property must be temporarily away from the described premises in the course of the named insured's daily business activities, and in the care, custody, or control of the named insured or an employee of the named insured.

The endorsement does not cover property in the care, custody, or control of a common or contract carrier or a bailee for hire, nor is any property covered while airborne or waterborne. Thus, the endorsement is not a substitute for annual transit or ocean cargo insurance. The endorsement also does not cover samples of the insured's products unless such property is located at a fair, a trade show, or an exhibition.

If theft is a covered cause of loss in the insured's policy, the endorsement covers theft from a land motor vehicle only if there are visible marks of forced entry into a securely locked body or compartment of the vehicle.

Broader coverage for property away from the described premises is available under commercial inland marine forms. However, the commercial property endorsement may be a convenient solution for some insureds with uncomplicated off-premises exposures.

Manufacturers' Consequential Loss Assumption

If stock in the process of manufacture is damaged or destroyed, the physical loss can decrease the value of other stock that is undamaged. Clothing manufacturers are particularly exposed to this type of loss. If a front, or any other part of an unassembled garment, is destroyed or damaged, the remaining parts will have little more than scrap value unless the missing part can be replaced.

Other manufacturers also face this exposure. Whenever parts of the end product cannot be recombined with other parts to produce a finished product, a consequential loss can occur. The Manufacturers' Consequential Loss Assumption endorsement provides coverage for this type of situation. See the exhibit "Other Consequential Loss Assumption Provisions."

Other Consequential Loss Assumption Provisions

Consequential loss assumption provisions that are broader than those of the Insurance Services Office, Inc. (ISO) endorsement are available in independently filed commercial property forms and in inland marine coverage forms.

Broader coverage might be needed, for example, by a garment manufacturer that sells to large buyers such as department stores and discount chains. Large buyers normally want a full range of colors, styles, and sizes when they place an order. They will not accept, for instance, a shipment of dresses with no size 10s. Therefore, destruction of part of a lot—here, the size 10s—may substantially reduce the value of the undamaged items. The ISO endorsement will not cover consequential loss to items that have already been completed (that is, are not in the course of manufacture) when the physical loss to the size 10s occurs.

One independently filed form provides that if a full lot or range of sizes or colors is broken because of a covered loss to some of the articles, the insurer will pay for the reduction in value of the remaining undamaged articles. For this coverage to apply, the insured must customarily sell the articles in lots or ranges of sizes or colors, and the insured must be unable, despite a good-faith effort, to reassemble the lots or ranges from the remaining undamaged articles or from any other source.

[DA03547]

Brands and Labels

After an insurer pays for loss to covered property, it has the right to take any salvage, such as smoke-damaged merchandise. This can pose a problem for an insured that bases its marketing appeal on a brand-name reputation for high quality. The salvaged material might be saleable but not meet the insured's quality standards.

To help protect the reputation of the insured's goods when the insurer takes any part of the property as salvage, the Brands and Labels endorsement permits the insured to take these actions:

Stamp "salvage" on the merchandise or its containers, if the stamp will not physically damage the merchandise; or

Remove the brands or labels, if doing so will not physically damage the merchandise. You must relabel the merchandise or its containers to comply with the law.[3]

The endorsement also states that the insurer will cover, within the limit of insurance, the costs incurred by the insured in taking the measures just described.

Some independently filed policies have broader brands and labels clauses. In some cases, the insured has virtually full control over the sale of salvaged brand-label merchandise.

Green Upgrades

If the insured wishes to replace damaged property with more environmentally friendly materials following a covered loss, the Increased Cost of Loss and Related Expenses for Green Upgrades endorsement can be used to accomplish this. There are three coverages available under this endorsement.

The first coverage provides an additional limit of insurance to cover the increased cost of replacing damaged property with more environmentally sound materials or methods. For example, when reconstructing an office building following a covered loss, the insured may decide to use rapidly renewable wood flooring materials and low-emitting paints and adhesives. The cost of these environmentally conscious materials may be higher than traditional building materials. This increased cost will be covered by this endorsement up to the limit shown on the schedule.

The second coverage provides an additional amount for expenses related to green updates. These include waste reduction and recycling expenses, design and engineering fees, certification fees and related equipment testing costs, as well as expenses for building air-out and related air testing.

The third coverage applies only if business income or extra expense coverage is included in the policy. This coverage extends the period of restoration for any increased construction time resulting from the use of green upgrades. The extension period lasts for thirty days or the number of days shown in the schedule, whichever is greater.

The endorsement includes a schedule that indicates maximum amounts for building and personal property, an increased cost of loss percentage, a coverage amount for related expenses, and the number of days covered for the extended period of restoration.

Increase in Rebuilding Expenses Following Disaster

The endorsement for Increase in Rebuilding Expenses Following Disaster covers the higher costs incurred as a result of labor and materials being in short supply after a widespread disaster and the total cost of repair or replacement exceeding the limit of insurance. Noteworthy features of the endorsement include these:

- The building(s) to be covered must be identified in the endorsement's schedule.
- Coverage applies to damage resulting from an event declared to be a disaster, including damage resulting from an event that occurs close in time to the disaster. The operative language in the endorsement, "in close

temporal proximity to the event," is not defined in the endorsement and is therefore open to legal interpretation.

- The maximum amount of additional coverage is determined by applying a specific percentage to the Limit of Insurance, or to the value of the building when coverage is written on a blanket basis.

- The coverage can also be applied to debris removal expenses and, if the policy includes Ordinance Or Law Coverage C, the costs to comply with building codes.

- A separate amount of coverage applies to buildings covered under the policy's extension for newly acquired or constructed buildings, based on the highest percentage listed in the Schedule and the applicable limit of insurance for a newly acquired or constructed building.

- Coverage applies on an annual aggregate basis.

- Coverage is reduced by expenses paid by any business income or extra expense coverage included in the policy.

ENDORSEMENTS FOR MODIFYING COMMERCIAL PROPERTY CAUSES OF LOSS

Insurance Services Office, Inc. (ISO) offers several coverage options that modify the commercial property causes of loss forms.

Several endorsements are available for covering losses that would otherwise be excluded under the commercial property causes of loss forms. These are some of the endorsements:

- Ordinance or Law Coverage (CP 04 05)
- Utility Services—Direct Damage (CP 04 17)
- Spoilage Coverage (CP 04 40)
- Radioactive Contamination (CP 10 37)
- Discharge From Sewer, Drain or Sump (CP 10 38)
- Theft of Building Materials and Supplies (CP 10 44)
- Equipment Breakdown Cause of Loss (CP 10 46)

Ordinance or Law Coverage

The requirements imposed by ordinances or laws governing restoration of damaged buildings can substantially increase an insured's loss. The Ordinance or Law exclusion in all three causes of loss forms eliminates coverage for such losses other than the limited amount provided by the Building and Personal Property Coverage Form, also referred to as the BPP, additional coverage for increased cost of construction.

Ordinance or Law
Coverage endorsement
Endorsement that covers three
types of losses resulting from
the enforcement of building
ordinances or laws: (1) the
value of the undamaged
portion of a building that must
be demolished, (2) the cost
to demolish the building's
undamaged portion and
remove its debris, and (3) the
increased cost to rebuild the
property.

More substantial insurance for this exposure can be added by the **Ordinance or Law Coverage endorsement** (CP 04 05), which provides three coverages:

- Coverage A covers the reduction in value of the undamaged portion of the building that must be demolished to comply with an ordinance or a law.
- Coverage B covers the cost to demolish the undamaged portion of the structure and remove its debris.
- Coverage C covers the increased cost to repair or reconstruct damaged property, or to reconstruct or remodel undamaged portions of the property, in conformity with the minimum requirements of an ordinance or a law.

The Coinsurance condition does not apply to Coverages B and C. Coverage A can be arranged on either an actual cash value or a replacement cost basis.

If coverage is on a replacement cost basis and the building is replaced, Coverage A will pay the lowest of these amounts:

- The amount the insured actually spends
- What it would have cost to restore a building comparable to the original building
- The limit of insurance applicable to the building

Coverage C is available only if the Replacement Cost optional coverage has been activated. Under Coverage C, the property must be repaired or replaced as soon as reasonably possible after the loss.

The insurer is not obligated to pay increased construction costs unless the reconstruction is made within two years, although the period may be extended at the insurer's option. The two-year limitation can be problematic in certain situations.

For example, many properties remained unrepaired more than two years after they were damaged in Hurricane Katrina. The replacement building may be on the same premises or elsewhere, but it must be intended for occupancy similar to the damaged premises unless such occupancy is no longer permitted.

The ordinance or law must be in force at the time of the loss. Often, a catastrophic loss will demonstrate the need to update building ordinance standards. Even if the insured is compelled to comply with upgraded standards introduced after a loss occurs, the Ordinance or Law Coverage endorsement will not apply to the costs of complying with upgrades enacted after the loss.

In addition, none of the three coverages will pay for (1) loss resulting from an ordinance or a law that the insured failed to comply with if compliance was required before the loss; (2) costs associated with any ordinance or law that requires the insured in any way to respond to or assess the effects of pollutants; or (3) loss resulting from an ordinance or a law requiring the insured to respond in any way to fungus, wet or dry rot, or bacteria.

If the building is damaged by two perils, one covered and the other not covered (for example, damage by wind and flood under a policy that does not cover flood), and the building damage in its entirety triggers the requirement to comply with a building ordinance or law, the policy will pay a part of the cost of the upgrade.

The part covered is equal to that proportion that the loss caused by the covered peril bears to the total loss. However, if the damage by the covered peril alone would have required compliance, the policy will pay the full cost covered by the policy.

If the ordinance or law is triggered solely by the damage done by the peril that is not covered, the policy will not pay any part of the cost of the upgrade.

Coverage A becomes part of the building coverage, so no additional amount of insurance is needed. However, the building rate is increased to recognize the increase in exposure.

Separate amounts of insurance can be shown for Coverages B and C for each building, or Coverages B and C can be combined for a single limit on each building. Combined coverage is preferable because the insured will have greater flexibility in the event of a loss.

Coverage C also applies to the increased cost of repair or reconstruction of these items that the BPP ordinarily excludes: excavations, grading, backfilling, and filling; foundations; pilings; and underground pipes, flues, and drains. The exclusion of these items in the BPP is deleted, but only with respect to the coverage provided by Coverage C of the Ordinance or Law Coverage endorsement.

Utility Services Coverage

Coverage for physical losses excluded by the Utility Services exclusion can be provided through the **Utility Services—Direct Damage endorsement.**

The endorsement extends coverage to include damage to property described in the endorsement schedule, caused by the interruption of service to the described premises. The interruption must result from damage by a covered peril to any of these types of property:

Utility Services—Direct Damage endorsement

A commercial property endorsement that covers damage to covered property caused by the interruption of utility services (water, communications, or power) to the insured premises.

- Water-supply property
- Communication-supply property (including overhead transmission lines)
- Communication-supply property (not including overhead transmission lines)
- Power-supply property (including overhead transmission lines)
- Power-supply property (not including overhead transmission lines)

The insured can select coverage for any or all of the foregoing properties subject to the insurer's acceptance of coverage. (Many insurers are reluctant to cover overhead transmission lines.) The insured's choices as to covered properties, supply properties covered, amounts of insurance, and causes of loss forms applicable are indicated in the endorsement's schedule.

The endorsement excludes loss of or damage to electronic data. If the policy shows a limit of insurance for this endorsement, it is a sublimit and does not increase the total amount of insurance. If no limit is shown, the coverage is subject to the applicable limit of insurance on the covered property.

Spoilage Coverage

Spoilage Coverage endorsement

Endorsement that covers damage to perishable stock due to power outages; on-premises breakdown; or contamination of the insured's refrigerating, cooling, or humidity control equipment.

Power or equipment failure can cause spoilage of perishable stock such as food or cut flowers. Although spoilage losses can be covered under the Utility Services—Direct Damage endorsement, they can also be covered by the **Spoilage Coverage endorsement.**

Coverage under the Utility Services—Direct Damage endorsement applies only if the loss of power is caused by damage to power-supply services by an insured peril. The Spoilage Coverage endorsement provides broader coverage.

It not only covers spoilage resulting from power outages, but it also covers spoilage resulting from change in temperature or humidity caused by mechanical breakdown or mechanical failure of refrigerating, cooling, or humidity-control apparatus or equipment on the described premises.

Mechanical breakdown also includes loss caused by contamination when the contaminant is the refrigerant used in cooling equipment. Power-outage coverage applies whether the outage originates on or off the premises, with no requirement that the outage be caused by another insured peril. However, the power outage must be caused by conditions beyond the insured's control.

The insured can select coverage for mechanical breakdown, power outage, or both. Coinsurance does not apply to coverage provided by the endorsement. The Agreed Value, Inflation Guard, and Replacement Cost optional coverages, if selected by the insured, do not apply to the coverage provided by the endorsement.

The *Commercial Lines Manual* (CLM) once imposed a $50,000 per-location maximum limit of insurance for the Spoilage Coverage endorsement. The CLM no longer imposes any maximum limit for this endorsement, making it suitable for insureds with spoilage loss exposures exceeding $50,000, assuming the insurer is willing to provide higher limits.

Radioactive Contamination endorsement

A commercial property endorsement for organizations that have a radioactive contamination exposure on their premises, other than a nuclear reactor or fuel for a nuclear reactor; covers physical loss to covered property caused by sudden and accidental radioactive contamination.

Radioactive Contamination

The **Radioactive Contamination endorsement** is available to meet the needs of organizations that have a radioactive contamination exposure on their premises, other than a nuclear reactor or fuel for a nuclear reactor. (Facilities with nuclear reactors are insured only under nuclear energy policies available from specialized underwriting pools.)

Hospitals, medical clinics, and educational and research institutions frequently use radioactive materials. Some manufacturers, contractors, and engineers may also use radioactive materials, typically in measuring devices.

The endorsement provides some coverage that the Nuclear Hazard exclusion would otherwise eliminate. The endorsement covers "radioactive contamination," defined as "direct physical loss or damage caused by sudden and accidental radioactive contamination, including resultant radiation damage to the described property." [4]

Two coverage alternatives are possible—the first treats radioactive contamination as a consequence of another covered cause of loss; the second, as a freestanding cause of loss.

Neither coverage applies if the described premises contain a nuclear reactor or new or used nuclear fuel. Losses arising from radioactive material off premises are also excluded.

Discharge from Sewer, Drain or Sump (Not Flood-Related)

This endorsement covers, with respect to the premises described in the endorsement's schedule, direct physical loss to covered property caused by the discharge of water or waterborne material from a sewer, drain, or sump on the described premises. However, the discharge is not covered if it results from flood or flood-related conditions. References to flood in the endorsement include surface water, waves, tidal water, and overflow of any body of water, including storm surge.

The Discharge Limit for Property Damage shown in the schedule is the most that the insurer will pay under the endorsement for the total of all covered loss and expense. This limit is part of, not in addition to, the limit of insurance applicable to the covered property, business income, or extra expense.

If a Discharge Limit for Business Interruption is shown in the schedule, the endorsement will also cover business income loss and/or extra expenses resulting from direct physical loss covered by the endorsement, in accordance with the terms of the business income and/or extra expense coverage form included in the insured's policy.

The schedule also allows the insurer to activate an Annual Aggregate Limitation, which states that the applicable Discharge Limit is an annual aggregate rather than an each occurrence limit. An insurer might exercise this limitation when there is a likelihood that the insured will have multiple covered occurrences during the policy period. The Annual Aggregate Limitation exhausts coverage for the remainder of the twelve-month policy period once the insurer has paid losses equaling the limit.

The endorsement excludes coverage when the discharge results from the insured's failure to perform routine maintenance or necessary repairs to keep the drain lines and related equipment free of obstruction and in working condition. The endorsement also excludes sump pump failure resulting from power failure unless the policy is endorsed to cover power failure at the described premises. Another exclusion states that the insurer will not cover the cost to repair or replace a sewer, drain, sump, sump pump, or related parts.

Theft of Building Materials and Supplies (Other Than Builders Risk)

Insureds who are making additions, alterations, or repairs to their buildings may temporarily store building materials and supplies on or adjacent to their premises. Although the Causes of Loss—Special Form covers theft of covered property, it specifically excludes theft of building materials and supplies not attached as part of the building or structure (unless the materials or supplies are held for sale by the insured).

The Theft of Building Materials and Supplies (Other Than Builders Risk) endorsement provides a way to cover building supplies under a commercial property coverage form other than the ISO Builders Risk Coverage Form, which has its own endorsement for covering theft of building materials (Builders Risk—Theft of Building Materials, Fixtures, Machinery, Equipment [CP 11 21]).

Two basic conditions of the Theft of Building Materials and Supplies (Other Than Builders Risk) endorsement are that the described premises must be subject to the Causes of Loss—Special Form (the only commercial property causes of loss form that covers theft) and the theft coverage provided by the Special Form must not be excluded. If these two conditions are met, the insurer will pay for loss by theft of building materials and supplies located on or within 100 feet of the described premises, as long as the materials are intended to become a permanent part of the building or structure described in the schedule.

The endorsement states that theft as covered under the endorsement does not include losses that would fall within any of these exclusions in the Causes of Loss—Special Form:

- Dishonest or criminal acts
- Voluntary parting
- Inventory shortage or no physical evidence

Equipment Breakdown Cause of Loss

Most commercial property coverage forms exclude equipment breakdown and related causes of loss. If the insured wants to obtain equipment breakdown coverage, one option is to buy an equipment breakdown coverage form that is separate from the commercial property coverage part. A simpler option is to add the Equipment Breakdown Cause of Loss endorsement to a commercial property coverage part.

This endorsement, which can only be used with the Causes of Loss—Special Form, adds "breakdown" of "covered equipment" as a covered cause of loss under the Special Form and states that all terms and conditions of the Special Form apply to breakdown of covered equipment except as stated otherwise in the endorsement.

The endorsement contains long definitions of breakdown and covered property, which are very similar to the definitions of these terms in ISO's Equipment Breakdown Protection Coverage Form, thus providing comparable coverage. In summary, the "breakdown" definition includes failure of pressure or vacuum equipment, mechanical failure, and electrical failure.

The definition of "covered equipment" includes equipment operated under internal pressure or vacuum; electrical or mechanical equipment used to generate, transmit, or utilize energy; communication equipment; and computer equipment. Both definitions are subject to several exceptions.

The endorsement removes or reduces multiple exclusions and limitations in the Special Form. For example, exclusions for mechanical breakdown and breakdown caused by electromagnetic energy or exploding steam boilers do not apply.

Exclusions for wear and tear, rust, and hidden defects are still applicable, but if a breakdown occurs that is caused by one of these perils, the insurer will pay for the resulting loss or damage.

The endorsement also excludes loss or damage to covered equipment while undergoing a pressure or electrical test. However, the insurer will pay for loss or damage caused by resulting fire or explosion.

Because adding this endorsement results in equipment breakdown being a covered cause of loss, any business income and extra expense coverage subject to the Causes of Loss—Special Form in the same policy is triggered if equipment breakdown at the described premises results in suspension of the insured's operations.

A sublimit on the limit of insurance provided by this endorsement applies when the loss is caused by ammonia contamination or a hazardous substance. The sublimit is 10 percent of the limit of insurance applicable to the covered equipment or $25,000, whichever is less.

The Suspension condition allows any representative of the insurer to immediately suspend the coverage provided by this endorsement if the covered equipment is found to be in, or exposed to, a dangerous condition.

ENDORSEMENTS FOR MODIFYING VALUATION METHODS

Various coverage options are available to modify commercial property coverage forms and causes of loss forms to meet an insured's particular needs.

Various valuation methods apply to property covered under the Building and Personal Property Coverage Form, also referred to as the BPP, including the optional coverages for replacement cost coverage. By endorsement, other valuation methods can be applied to property covered by the BPP or other commercial property coverage forms.

The endorsements include these:

- Manufacturer's Selling Price (CP 99 30)
- Functional Building Valuation (CP 04 38)
- Functional Personal Property Valuation (CP 04 39)
- Limitations on Coverage for Roof Resurfacing (CP 10 36)

Manufacturer's Selling Price

Manufacturer's Selling Price (Finished "Stock" Only) endorsement

A commercial property endorsement that values finished stock manufactured by the insured at selling price, less any discounts and expenses that the insured otherwise would have had.

The BPP valuation provision values stock that has been sold but not delivered at selling price, less any discounts and expenses that the insured otherwise would have had. The **Manufacturer's Selling Price (Finished "Stock" Only) endorsement** applies the same approach to the value of finished stock manufactured by the insured—whether or not it has been sold.

This endorsement is important for a manufacturer that wants protection against loss of business income from an insured peril, because destruction of finished stock can reduce income and increase expenses. Business income insurance excludes loss resulting from the destruction of finished goods.

The Manufacturer's Selling Price endorsement, because it compensates the insured for the profit that the insured would have made on the finished goods had no loss occurred, pays the part of the business income loss that business income insurance excludes. Some insurers offer selling price valuation for retailers and wholesalers as well as manufacturers.

Great care is needed in underwriting such coverage. Selling price clauses for nonmanufacturers can duplicate the coverage provided by business income insurance.

While insurers in such situations argue that the insured cannot collect twice for the same loss, insureds counter that the coverages (for which they have paid separate premiums) are different: one is a valuation basis for current inventory, and the other is coverage for the interruption of operations.

The resulting confusion has generated a number of lawsuits, in which courts have generally agreed with insurers that collecting under both coverages would amount to double recovery.[5] Unless the nonmanufacturing insured does not carry business income coverage, it is better to restrict selling price coverage to policies covering manufacturers or to goods that have been sold but not delivered.

Functional Building Valuation

Many buildings have a replacement cost that far exceeds their market value. A typical example is an older building that was constructed using designs, materials, and techniques that are now prohibitively expensive for most organizations. Insuring such buildings on either an actual cash value or a replacement cost basis can be problematic if the building could be repaired or replaced for much less using contemporary building techniques and materials.

The **Functional Building Valuation endorsement** addresses this problem by providing modified replacement cost coverage. For a total loss, the endorsement covers the cost to repair or replace the building with a less costly building that is functionally equivalent to the original one. For a partial loss, the insurer's payment for the damaged portion's repair or replacement is calculated on the basis of using less costly material, if available, in the architectural style that existed before the loss.

Lower cost but functionally equivalent replacement can also apply to a partial loss. For example, three-coat, wood-lathe plaster walls, common in older construction but rare today, could be replaced with plasterboard construction to serve the same purpose at a much lower cost. The loss payment cannot, in any event, exceed the amount of insurance or the amount necessarily spent to repair the damaged building with less costly material, if available.

The Functional Building Valuation endorsement also deletes the BPP Coinsurance condition. Therefore, the insured and the insurer, when using the endorsement, should determine the cost to replace the building with a functionally equivalent structure and should set the amount of insurance accordingly.

If the insured fails to contract for repairs within 180 days after the loss occurs or otherwise chooses not to make a claim based on the cost to repair or replace, the endorsement sets the maximum that the insured can collect at the lowest of these amounts:

* The limit of insurance shown in the endorsement
* The market value of the damaged building, exclusive of the land value, at the time of the loss
* The cost to repair or replace the building on the same site with less costly material in the same architectural style, less an allowance for physical deterioration and depreciation

The endorsement defines "market value" as "the price which the property might be expected to realize if offered for sale in a fair market."

Functional Building Valuation endorsement

A commercial property endorsement that provides modified replacement cost coverage on buildings; may be appropriate when insuring a building with a replacement cost far in excess of its market value.

The Functional Building Valuation endorsement automatically includes ordinance or law coverage, subject to the regular limit of insurance on the building. Ordinance or law coverage insures against additional costs resulting from actions the insured must take to comply with current building codes or laws.

Ordinance or law coverage is also available under a separate endorsement. The endorsement is unnecessary for a policy that includes the Functional Replacement Cost endorsement.

The buildings the endorsement is likely to cover often lack many of the items required by current building codes; a loss might result in a substantial upgrading of the building. In addition, a relatively small amount of damage might trigger a large expenditure to comply with current building codes. Thus, in some cases, an underwriter may be unwilling to provide functional building valuation as configured with ordinance or law coverage.

Functional Personal Property Valuation

The Functional Personal Property Valuation (Other Than Stock) endorsement is available for providing functional valuation on personal property other than stock.

The endorsement might be useful when insuring older machinery or equipment that is no longer available, such as a machine that has been superseded by a newer, more efficient, less expensive model. An example of such equipment is an old computer system that cost more when purchased than a new system that has several times the capacity of the old one. Any personal property covered by the endorsement must be described in the schedule.

As long as the insured contracts for repair or replacement of covered property within 180 days of loss by a covered peril, the insurer will pay the smallest of these amounts:

- The applicable limit of insurance
- The cost to replace, on the same site, the damaged item with the most closely equivalent property available
- The amount necessarily spent to repair or replace the property

If the insured makes no claim for repair or replacement, the insurer's liability is limited to the smallest of these amounts:

- The applicable limit of insurance
- The market value of the property at the time of loss
- The amount it would cost to repair or replace the damaged property with material of like kind and quality, less an allowance for physical deterioration and depreciation

The Functional Personal Property Valuation endorsement also deletes the Coinsurance condition of the form to which it is attached.

Limitations on Coverage for Roof Surfacing

When a building is insured under the BPP or another commercial property form with the Replacement Cost optional coverage in effect, replacement cost valuation is applicable to all covered building property, including the building's roof surfacing.

If the roof is damaged by a covered cause of loss, the insurer may be obligated to pay the full cost of replacing the roof surfacing, even if it is worn out and close to the end of its useful life. Consequently, the insurer's claim payment can be far in excess of the roof's actual cash value (ACV) immediately before the loss occurred, and the insured receives a substantial betterment.

The Limitations on Coverage for Roof Surfacing endorsement enables an insurer to change the valuation of roof surfacing from replacement cost to ACV for any building identified in the endorsement schedule. In this way, the insurer will be able to deduct accumulated depreciation or deterioration of the roof surfacing when determining the amount of loss payable for roof damage resulting from a covered cause of loss.

By adding an appropriate notation to the schedule, the insurer can also exclude cosmetic damage to roof surfacing caused by wind and/or hail. Damage to roof surfacing is considered cosmetic if, despite marring, pitting, or other superficial damage, the roof continues to function as a barrier from the elements to the same extent it did before the covered loss.

The Insurance Services Office, Inc. (ISO) *Commercial Lines Manual* (CLM) rule for this endorsement calls for a small premium reduction for each of these limitations.

CASE STUDY: COMMERCIAL PROPERTY COVERAGE OPTIONS

It is important to understand the coverage provided by the commercial property forms developed by Insurance Services Office, Inc. (ISO), such as the Building and Personal Property Coverage Form (BPP), and the causes of loss forms that are used with these coverage forms. It is also important to understand the additional coverage options that can be provided by adding endorsements.

Insurance professionals must develop skills to determine the appropriate coverage for business owners' commercial insurance needs. Once they have a basic understanding of the commercial property coverage forms, it is important to understand the coverage options provided by various endorsements. Applying that understanding to the facts of a case develops the ability to assist organizations with the appropriate insurance options for their loss exposures.

Insurance professionals need to understand how endorsements can modify commercial property coverage for an organization's unique loss exposures.

Case Facts

Too Cool Clothing operates a small garment factory in downtown Los Angeles. Too Cool is an upscale, trendy brand currently experiencing a great deal of media "buzz." The owners, Li and Mai, who belong to several environmental preservation groups, recently upgraded their factory with solar panels to provide electricity.

Li attends a celebrity fashion show in Hollywood, where Max, another designer and manufacturer of trendy clothing, described a fire at his factory. One of his employees forgot to turn off a toaster oven. It caught nearby newspapers on fire, and the fire quickly spread to the trash and kitchen cabinets. Many garments that were ready for shipment were heavily damaged by smoke. Max's insurance policy covered the damage to the garments; however, his insurer took the garments as salvage to be sold. Max did not have coverage for the expense of overtime for his garment workers, who were frantically working to replace the damaged garments and to remove the labels before the insurer took the damaged garments as salvage. Max worked for two days straight to remove the labels himself, and he missed an important premiere as a result. However, he believed he had to remove the labels to prevent his brand from being associated with damaged goods sold at "fire sale" prices.

Li and Mai decide to meet with their insurance broker. They want to be sure they have appropriate insurance coverage after their "green" upgrades and after learning of Max's fire loss. Now that Too Cool is experiencing successful growth, they want to review their coverage. Their broker, Julio, meets with them at the factory.

What endorsement(s) would Julio be likely to recommend for Too Cool's BPP policy?

Case Analysis Tools and Information

Julio reviews Too Cool's BPP and these potential endorsements:

- Increased Cost of Loss and Related Expenses for Green Upgrades endorsement (CP 04 02 09 09)
- Brands and Labels Endorsement (CP 04 01 10 00)
- Manufacturers' Consequential Loss Assumption endorsement (CP 99 02 07 88)

Case Analysis Steps

Julio first looks at the loss exposure from the recent addition of the solar panels. If Too Cool experienced damage to the factory from a covered cause of loss, the BPP would pay for repair and replacement with standard building materials, not with the upgrades. Julio therefore recommends adding an

Increased Cost of Loss and Related Expenses for Green Upgrades endorsement that will list coverage for the solar panels in the endorsement's schedule.

After discussing Max's fire loss with Li and Mai, Julio recommends a Brands and Labels endorsement for Too Cool. Now that Too Cool has become an upscale, trendy brand, Li and Mai would not want the label to be associated with damaged goods sold by their insurer as salvage in the event of a covered loss. The Brands and Labels endorsement provides coverage for the expense of removing labels if this type of loss should occur at Too Cool's factory.

In touring the factory, Julio observes that the front and back panels for some sequined shirts are manufactured separately. The backs of the shirts have designs that are silk-screened onto the fabric in one part of the plant, while the fronts of the shirts have the sequins sewn onto the fabric in another part of the plant. The fronts and backs of the shirts are then sewn together in yet another area of the factory. If there were a fire or another covered loss in one part of the factory, it is possible that either the fronts or the backs of the shirts would be damaged. However, a loss to either part of the shirts would also result in a loss to the undamaged part because the fabric could not be exactly matched to replace the damaged portion. Julio recommends a Manufacturers' Consequential Loss Assumption endorsement to cover this type of situation.

Coverage Recommendations

Julio recommends a total of three endorsements to Too Cool's owners that should provide coverage that will give them enhanced protection in the event of a loss similar to the fire and subsequent damage that occurred at the factory of their fellow designer, Max. The three recommended endorsements are: the Increased Cost of Loss and Related Expenses for Green Upgrades endorsement (CP 04 02), the Brands and Labels Endorsement (CP 04 01), and the Manufacturers' Consequential Loss Assumption endorsement (CP 99 02).

This solution might not be the only viable one. Other solutions could be exercised if justified by the analysis. In addition, specific circumstances and organizational needs or goals may enter into the evaluation, making an alternative action a better option. See the exhibit "Recommendations for Commercial Property Coverage Options Case Study."

Recommendations for Commercial Property Coverage Options Case Study

Loss Exposure	Endorsement
Solar Panels	Increased Cost of Loss and Related Expenses for Green Upgrades endorsement
Brand reputation if labeled merchandise is sold as salvage	Brands and Labels endorsement
Loss of undamaged garment parts because of damage to other parts of the garment	Manufacturers' Consequential Loss Assumption endorsement

[DA06047]

SUMMARY

The basic approach to insuring buildings and personal property is called specific insurance, in which a limit is shown for each covered building and for personal property at each building. An alternative to specific insurance is blanket insurance, which covers one type of property in more than one separately rated building or two or more types of property in one or more separately rated buildings under a single limit of insurance.

Fluctuating Inventory values can be addressed through the Peak Season Limit of Insurance endorsement or the Value Reporting Form. The peak season endorsement provides different amounts of insurance for specified time periods. The Value Reporting Form bases premiums on the actual values exposed to loss and reported to the insurer at regular intervals.

Other endorsements for modifying the BPP include two international coverage endorsements that provide limited insurance for the insured's property while outside the policy's regular coverage territory.

Endorsements for modifying the BPP and other commercial property coverage forms include these:

- Additional Covered Property, which provides a way to cover various types of otherwise- excluded property
- Specified Business Personal Property Temporarily Away From Premises, which covers business personal property while away from the described premises but within the regular coverage territory
- Manufacturers' Consequential Loss Assumption, which covers the decrease in value of undamaged stock in the course of manufacture caused by physical damage to other stock in the course of manufacture
- Brands and Labels, which permits the insured to remove the labels or stamp "salvage" on its damaged goods if the insurer takes the goods as salvage after a covered loss

- Increased Cost of Loss and Related Expenses for Green Upgrades, which provides additional amounts for green upgrades and related expenses as well as an extended number of days for the period of restoration required because of the use of green upgrades
- Increase in Rebuilding Expenses Following Disaster, which covers the additional costs incurred to rebuild a building because of labor and materials being in short supply, and at a higher price, after a widespread disaster

Endorsements for modifying the commercial property causes of loss forms include these:

- Ordinance or Law Coverage
- Utility Services—Direct Damage
- Spoilage Coverage
- Radioactive Contamination
- Discharge from Sewer, Drain or Sump (Not Flood-Related)
- Theft of Building Materials and Supplies (Other Than Builders Risk)
- Equipment Breakdown Cause of Loss

In addition to the valuation provisions contained in the BPP, optional valuation methods can be provided by certain endorsements, including Manufacturer's Selling Price (Finished "Stock" Only), Functional Building Valuation, Functional Personal Property Valuation (Other Than "Stock"), and Limitations on Coverage for Roof Surfacing.

Each organization has unique loss exposures. It is important for insurance professionals to understand how to modify standard package coverage forms to provide effective risk transfer to meet the needs of different types of organizations.

ASSIGNMENT NOTES

1. Includes copyrighted material of Insurance Services Office, Inc., with its permission. Copyright, Insurance Services Office, Inc., 1999.
2. Includes copyrighted material of Insurance Services Office, Inc., with its permission. Copyright, ISO Properties, Inc., 2001.
3. Includes copyrighted material of Insurance Services Office, Inc., with its permission. Copyright, Insurance Services Office, Inc., 2011.
4. Includes copyrighted material of Insurance Services Office, Inc., with its permission. Copyright, Insurance Services Office, Inc., 1999.
5. For example, see J&R Electronics Inc. v. One Beacon Insurance Company, N.Y.A.D. 1 Dept., 2006. The court wrote, "When calculating plaintiff's actual loss of business income as provided under the Business Interruption clause of the insurance policy, defendant [the insurer] properly deducted a payment already made to plaintiff for its damaged merchandise at the selling price. Plaintiff would otherwise have received a double recovery for these goods."

5

Other Commercial Property Coverage Forms

After learning the content of this assignment, you should be able to:

▷ Describe the characteristics of condominiums, cooperative corporations, and planned unit developments and the considerations involved in insuring them.

▷ Describe the purpose and provisions of the Condominium Association Coverage Form.

▷ Describe the purpose and provisions of the Condominium Commercial Unit-Owners Coverage Form and the Condominium Commercial Unit-Owners Optional Coverages endorsement.

▷ Describe the purpose and provisions of the Builders Risk Coverage Form and these endorsements:

- Builders Risk Renovations
- Builders Risk—Collapse During Construction
- Builders Risk—Theft of Building Materials, Fixtures, Machinery, Equipment

▷ Describe the purpose and provisions of the Standard Property Policy.

▷ Describe the purpose and provisions of the Legal Liability Coverage Form.

▷ Describe the leasehold interest loss exposure and the provisions of the Leasehold Interest Coverage Form.

▷ Given a scenario, explain whether any of the following forms would cover a described loss:

- Condominium Association Coverage Form
- Condominium Commercial Unit-Owners Coverage Form
- Builders Risk Coverage Form

5

- Standard Property Policy
- Legal Liability Coverage Form
- Leasehold Interest Coverage Form

Other Commercial Property Coverage Forms

CONDOMINIUMS

In addition to the Building and Personal Property Coverage Form (BPP), other commercial property coverage forms are available from Insurance Services Office, Inc. (ISO) for covering special situations and exposures. This section describes the characteristics of condominium buildings and contents that need to be insured.

Because condominium ownership interests differ from other ownership interests, specially designed forms are used to insure condominium buildings and contents. This section covers these topics:

- Basic concepts of this type of ownership
- Enabling statutes and documents
- Bare-walls, single-entity, and all-in concepts
- Other forms of combined ownership
- Condominium insurance requirements

Basic Concepts

A **condominium** is a real estate development consisting of a group of units, such as apartments, attached or detached homes, offices, and so forth, along with the land on which they sit.

A **condominium unit** is the portion of a condominium owned solely by the unit owner. It can be thought of as the "box of air" enclosed by the unfinished surfaces of perimeter walls, floors, and ceilings.

Property of any kind within the condominium unit, except (1) common building elements and (2) pipes, wires, conduits, and other utilities specified in easements, is considered to be solely owned by the unit owner.

In addition, the unit owner may be the sole owner of some property normally considered as "building" (such as a wall) that is located within the unit but is not a common building element or building utility.

Although the air space within each unit is owned by the unit owner, title to all remaining real and personal property, referred to as the "common elements," is held by the condominium association. The **condominium association** manages the condominium and owns the common elements.[1]

Condominium

A real estate development consisting of a group of units, in which the air space within the boundaries of each unit is owned by the unit owner, and all remaining real and personal property is owned jointly by all the unit owners.

Condominium unit

The portion of a condominium owned solely by a unit owner.

Condominium association

An entity composed of the unit owners in a condominium to manage the condominium and to own the common elements.

Common elements

Areas of a condominium that are jointly owned by all unit owners, including the land on which the buildings are located.

The **common elements** that are jointly owned by all unit owners generally include the foundations; exterior walls; interior walls except those contained within individual units; structural columns and beams; roofs; corridors; lobbies; stairs; parking and storage areas; central power, light, heating, and air conditioning systems; and often other property items such as grounds, swimming pools, tennis courts, and other amenities.

Some of these items may be located within, or may pass through, the unit owner's "box of air." The condominium association agreement designates what is considered part of the condominium unit and what is considered to be a common element.

Enabling Statutes and Documents

Before arranging condominium insurance coverage, producers, underwriters, and persons with risk management responsibility for condominiums should be familiar with enabling statutes as well as the condominium association agreement.

All fifty states, Puerto Rico, and the District of Columbia have enabling statutes for condominiums. These laws can vary substantially by jurisdiction. Many of the laws include provisions relating to ownership interests and the purchase of insurance.

Along with enabling statutes, the other essential document for evaluating the exposures of any particular condominium association or unit owner is the **condominium association agreement**, also referred to as the master deed or declarations.

Condominium association agreement

A document that describes what each condominium unit owner has purchased and clarifies the rights and responsibilities of the unit owners and the association.

This document is usually prepared by attorneys for the developer who first established the condominium association, describes what each unit owner has purchased, and clarifies the rights and responsibilities of the unit owners and the association.

The agreement describes the land, the building, and the common elements and identifies each individual unit. It establishes a method of collecting and paying for such common expenses as maintenance, upkeep of common areas, and insurance.

Greater detail on the governance and operation of the association is usually set out in bylaws. The bylaws describe the duties and powers of the directors and officers of the association and often include, among other details, the minimum amounts of insurance coverage to be purchased by the association.

The agreement also specifies the governing procedures, the powers of the association, and the procedures for modifying the agreement and the bylaws.

Under condominium statutes or agreements, the condominium association is usually obligated to maintain insurance for the unit owners' benefit. Unit owners are also permitted to purchase insurance at their own expense for their own benefit. Such insurance is usually excess over the association's insurance. See the exhibit "An Example of Condominium Insurance Requirements."

An Example of Condominium Insurance Requirements

Here is an example of wording excerpted from a condominium agreement:

The Board of Managers shall maintain fire insurance with extended coverage insuring the buildings containing the units (including all units and the bathroom and kitchen fixtures initially installed therein by the sponsor, but not including carpeting furnished by the sponsor, or furniture, furnishings or other personal property supplied or installed by the unit owners or tenants of unit owners), together with all service machinery contained therein and covering the interest of the condominium, the Board of Managers and all unit owners and their mortgagees, as their respective interests may appear, in an amount equal to the full replacement value of the buildings (exclusive of foundations) without deduction for depreciation. . . [provisions concerning mortgagee clause and loss payment to trustee omitted].

All policies of physical damage insurance shall contain waivers of subrogation and of any defense based on co-insurance or of invalidity arising from acts of the insured and of the pro rata reduction of liability, and shall provide that such policies may not be cancelled or substantially modified without at least ten days' written notice to all the insureds, including mortgagees of units. . . [provision for sending duplicate originals to mortgagees and certificates to unit owners omitted].

The Board of Managers shall also maintain, to the extent obtainable, (1) fidelity insurance covering all officers and employees of the Condominium and of the managing agent who handle Condominium funds; (2) public liability insurance. . . [wording dealing with liability insurance omitted].

The cost of all such insurance shall be paid by the Board of Managers and shall be borne by all unit owners as part of the common charges.

The fire insurance to be maintained on the building at the time construction is completed shall be $7,000,000. Until the first meeting of the Board of Managers elected by the Unit Owners, the public liability insurance will be in a limit of $1,000,000 covering all claims for bodily injury or property damage in respect of any one occurrence. The Board of Managers shall review such limits annually.

Unit owners shall not be prohibited from carrying other insurance for their own benefit provided such policies contain waivers of subrogation and further provided that the liability of the carriers issuing insurance procured by the Board of Managers shall not be affected or diminished by reason of any Unit Owner's insurance.

This wording, like that of many condominium agreements, refers to "extended coverage" and omits many coverages that insurance professionals consider to be important for condominiums: special causes of loss form, earthquake, flood, business income, personal injury liability, umbrella liability, directors and officers liability, and workers compensation, to name a few. The board of managers is authorized to purchase such other coverages; they will need competent advice to protect the condominium properly.

[DA05271]

Condominium agreements are individually drafted and can vary in important ways. Therefore, in addition to having a working knowledge of the condominium law in the jurisdiction, those responsible for arranging insurance for a condominium association should also review the applicable the condominium association agreement.

Bare-Walls, Single-Entity, and All-In Concepts

An important issue in assessing condominium loss exposures involves the dividing line between the unit owners' property interests and the association's interests. Three general approaches appearing in condominium statutes and agreements are the bare-walls concept, the single-entity concept, and the all-in concept.

Bare-Walls Concept

Bare-walls concept

A concept of condominium ownership in which the association has no ownership interest within the bare walls of each unit.

Under the **bare-walls concept**, the association has no ownership interest within the unit's bare walls. All paint and wall coverings, carpet and floor coverings, drapes, cabinets, appliances, nonload-bearing interior walls, interior doors, plumbing, and electrical fixtures are considered to be owned by the individual unit owner, but the association may be required to insure these elements for the benefit of the individual unit owners (by statute, declarations, or bylaws). In that event, the association's insurable interest in the unit owner's property is that of a trustee.

Single-Entity Concept

Single-entity concept (original specifications coverage)

A concept of condominium ownership in which the association is considered to be the owner of all property contained in the unit as sold to the original purchaser or replacements of such property if the replacements are of like kind and quality.

Under the **single-entity concept**, also known as original specifications coverage, the condominium association is considered to be the owner of all property contained in the unit as sold to the original purchaser or replacements of such property if the replacements are of like kind and quality. Normally, at the time of sale, carpets, cabinets, electrical fixtures, and appliances have been installed. Consequently, the association would be responsible for insuring those items.

All-In Concept

All-in concept (additional installations coverage)

A concept of condominium ownership that is similar to the single-entity concept except that the all-in concept includes improvements made by the unit owner, not just the original installations or replacements of like kind and quality.

The **all-in concept**, also called additional installations coverage, is similar to the single-entity concept but includes improvements made by the unit owner, not just the original installations or replacements of like kind and quality. For example, the unit may originally have contained plastic-laminate kitchen counters that the unit owner replaced with more expensive granite counters, or the original construction may have included wood floors that the unit owner replaced with marble. If the condominium association's policy is written on a single-entity basis, the insurer's liability in the event of damage by a covered peril would be based on plastic-laminate counters or wood floors. A policy written on an all-in basis would call for valuation of the loss (and the amount of insurance required) based on granite counters or marble floors.

Some condominium agreements require that the unit owner pay any additional premium attributed to the increased value of improvements made by that unit owner.

Arranging the Appropriate Coverage

Some states have condominium statutes that specify the basis of coverage required. In states without such statutes, the condominium association agreement, the master deed, or the declaration may specify the basis of coverage required. In practice, these documents are often not clear about how to insure all items exposed to loss. When there is doubt, the problem can be addressed by having the association obtain insurance with the broadest possible description of covered property, with a policy limit set accordingly.

However, if unit owners adopt a similar strategy and insure as broadly as possible, they may be obtaining expensive and unnecessary duplicate coverage. A better solution is for the association to agree with its insurer on the extent of coverage provided under the association's policy and to communicate that information to the unit owners so that they can tailor their insurance accordingly.

The problem is not merely one of describing covered property. More difficult is the problem of measuring insurable values (versus market value) and purchasing appropriate amounts of insurance.

It can be especially difficult for the directors of a condominium association to value items located within the various units under the all-in concept if the unit owners have modified their units. Inaccurate evaluation of property items exposed to loss could leave a commercial unit owner or a condominium association with a coinsurance penalty following a partial loss, or with inadequate coverage to pay for a substantial loss.

The Agreed Value optional coverage can eliminate the possibility of a coinsurance penalty, and, for condominiums with separate buildings spread over several acres, blanket insurance can reduce the possibility of inadequate coverage for a substantial loss.

Other Forms of Combined Ownership

Two additional forms of combined ownership of real property by the occupants—cooperative corporations and planned unit developments—are similar to condominiums. The exhibit summarizes the distinguishing characteristics of cooperative corporations and planned unit developments. See the exhibit "Comparison of Condominiums, Cooperatives, and Planned Unit Developments."

Comparison of Condominiums, Cooperatives, and Planned Unit Developments

	Condominium Unit Owners	Cooperative Shareholders	Planned Unit Development Homeowners
Own an identifiable portion of the property?	Yes	No	Yes
Own common elements jointly with others?	Yes	No*	Yes
Own stock in the corporation that owns the property?	No	Yes	No
Have "fee simple" title to their unit?	No	No	Yes
Insurance requirements are usually spelled out in the governing agreements or bylaws?	Yes	Yes	Yes

*Shareholders do not directly own corporate property.

[DA03554]

Cooperative Corporations

Cooperative corporation

A form of real property ownership in which the real property is owned by a corporation whose shareholders are the tenants of the property.

In a **cooperative corporation**, the real property is owned solely by a corporation rather than jointly by unit owners. However, the tenants of the property own the corporation's stock.

Unlike condominium unit owners, the shareholder-tenants of a cooperative corporation do not own the "box of air" contained within their units. Nevertheless, the proprietary lease that gives occupancy rights to the shareholder- tenants often makes each shareholder-tenant responsible for the maintenance and repair of all fixtures and appliances within the leased unit.

Some agreements even adopt the bare-walls approach. The lease or the cooperative agreement may make the cooperative corporation responsible for insuring fixtures and appliances within the leased units, or this responsibility may be left to the shareholder-tenants. Again, only examination of the pertinent documents—the cooperative agreement, the proprietary lease, and real-property law of the state involved—can ensure proper arrangement of the insurance.

Most insurers use the same forms to insure condominiums and cooperatives. Careful drafting would suggest that the policy be endorsed to indicate that "cooperative corporation" be substituted for "condominium" wherever the policy reads "condominium."

Planned Unit Developments

A **planned unit development (PUD)**, also referred to as a homeowners' association, resembles individual home ownership more than it does a condominium or a cooperative corporation.

In a PUD, the occupants have exclusive ownership of their own units in exactly the same way that individual homeowners own their property. However, a PUD differs from individual home ownership in that a PUD occupant owns only the land that the structure occupies and sometimes a small portion of the surrounding land.

The surrounding land, including lawns, ponds, private roads, swimming pools, tennis courts, recreational or service buildings, and the like, is owned in common by a homeowners' association composed of all the unit owners.

No standard insurance requirements exist for PUDs. In some cases, each unit owner is required to insure his or her own unit, and the association is responsible only for the insurance on the commonly owned property.

In other cases, the homeowners' association has the duty to insure all real property, whether owned by the association or by an individual unit owner. As with condominiums and cooperatives, only examination of the pertinent documents can indicate how the insurance should be arranged.

When the association is responsible for insuring all the real property, insurers often use condominium association forms. Associations sometimes have difficulty in obtaining coverage when only the common property is to be insured by the association, because the policy's liability coverage will then apply to high-risk liability exposures such as swimming pool accidents, accidents on private roads, assault and battery in public areas, and the like, with little property coverage to balance the account.

> **Planned unit development (homeowners association)**
> A real estate development in which each occupant has exclusive ownership of its own unit and the land that the structure occupies and a homeowners' association composed of all the unit owners jointly owns the surrounding land and structures.

Condominium Insurance Requirements

Ideally, the applicable statute or the condominium agreement is clear enough to indicate what insurance the association should carry. However, this is not always the case. Those responsible for managing the insurance for a condominium association should bring the questions concerning insurance coverage to the attention of the governing board for resolution. In some cases, a legal opinion about what coverages are required or an amendment of the agreement by action of the entire membership may be advisable.

The insurance needs of a condominium association are similar to the building insurance needs of a building owner/landlord, and the needs of a condominium unit owner are similar to the personal property insurance needs of a tenant.

Two ISO commercial property forms have been designed especially for condominium property exposures:

- Condominium Association Coverage Form
- Condominium Commercial Unit-Owners Coverage Form

Like the BPP, each of these forms must be combined with a causes of loss form and other component documents to form a monoline policy or a commercial package policy. The condominium commercial property forms resemble the BPP in many ways, and much of their language is identical to that of the BPP, but the condominium forms do have some distinctive features.

CONDOMINIUM ASSOCIATION COVERAGE FORM

An insurance professional must understand the unique policy language used in the Condominium Association Coverage Form to competently meet the needs of a condominium association.

The Condominium Association Coverage Form (CP 00 17) is designed to insure the building and business personal property loss exposures of condominium associations. Like the Building and Personal Property Coverage Form, also referred to as the BPP, the Condominium Association Coverage Form can cover property in three categories:

- Building
- Your Business Personal Property
- Personal Property of Others

Each category is covered only if a limit of insurance for that category is shown in the declarations. The Condominium Association Coverage Form provides the same additional coverages and coverage extensions as the BPP.

Building

Although the building coverage of the Condominium Association Coverage Form closely resembles the building coverage of the BPP, they differ in their treatment of fixtures, improvements, alterations, and appliances contained within individual units (including, but not limited to, those used for refrigerating, ventilating, cooking, dishwashing, laundering, and housekeeping).

In the Condominium Association Coverage Form, building coverage applies to these items only if the condominium association agreement requires the association to insure them. Otherwise, such property items are not included in the association's building coverage.

This provision underscores the importance of examining the condominium association agreement when establishing insurance requirements. The agreement affects the amount of insurance required to comply with the Coinsurance condition as well as the coverage to be carried by the unit owner.

Following a loss, insurance adjusters frequently ask for a copy of the condominium agreement and bylaws to determine how the coverage applies. However, it is advantageous to resolve ambiguities before any loss occurs.

Because of the ambiguities present in most of the insurance requirements stated in condominium association agreements, some independently developed forms do not tie coverage to the agreement, using instead bare-walls, single-entity, or all-in approaches to coverage. Insurance Services Office, Inc. (ISO) has prepared state-specific endorsements that tailor the policy to the applicable laws.

Your Business Personal Property

A condominium association might need insurance to cover personal property that does not already fall within the scope of building coverage. For example, many condominiums have community clubhouses, recreation halls, health clubs, and so forth. The furnishings and equipment of these facilities can be covered as business personal property.

The Condominium Association Coverage Form clarifies the distinction between personal property insured by the association and that insured by individual unit owners:

- The Condominium Association Coverage Form covers business personal property that is owned by the association or that is indivisibly owned by all unit owners.

- The Condominium Association Coverage Form does not cover business personal property that is individually owned by a unit owner.

Personal Property of Others

The Condominium Association Coverage Form's coverage for personal property of others is the same as that of the BPP. If 80 percent or higher coinsurance is in effect, the form automatically includes a coverage extension for property of others up to $2,500 at each described location. If this extension is not adequate, the insured can buy an additional amount of insurance under the Personal Property of Others coverage agreement.

This coverage may have special significance if individual unit owners allow their personal property to be used in the building's common areas for decorative purposes or for specific building maintenance and repair projects. Subject to other policy terms, the Condominium Association Coverage Form would cover such items under the coverage extension or under Personal Property of Others (if a limit for this coverage is shown in the declarations). See the exhibit "Categories of Property Coverage in the Condominium Association Coverage Form."

Categories of Property Coverage in the Condominium Association Coverage Form

Building	• Coverage closely resembles that of the BPP.
	• Coverage applies to property contained within individual units, such as fixtures, improvements, alterations, and appliances, only if the condominium association agreement requires the association to insure them.
	• Some independently filed forms do not tie coverage to the agreement, instead using bare-walls, single-entity, or all-in approaches to coverage.
Your Business Personal Property	• Coverage applies to personal property that does not already fall within the scope of building coverage (for example, furnishings and equipment of community clubhouses, recreation halls, and health clubs).
	• Coverage does not apply to business personal property individually owned by a unit owner.
Personal Property of Others	• Coverage is the same as the BPP.
	• If 80 percent or higher coinsurance is in effect, the form automatically includes a coverage extension for property of others up to $2,500 at each described location.
	• Additional insurance can be added under Personal Property of Others coverage agreement.

[DA05969]

Conditions

There are several important differences between the Condominium Association Coverage Form conditions and the BPP's conditions, which include these:

• Loss Payment—The Loss Payment condition contains an additional clause stating that if the association has designated an insurance trustee, then the insurer may pay covered claims to the designated insurance trustee. The condominium's board of trustees generally serves in this capacity, receiving all loss proceeds in trust for the individual unit owners. The board then acts on all unit owners' behalf. Sometimes, however, a financial institution serves as trustee. Designating an insurance trustee can avoid unnecessary complications in the event of a loss because some insurers believe that, otherwise, the names of all the unit owners and their mortgagees must appear on a loss draft.

- Unit-Owner's Insurance—The Unit-Owner's Insurance condition states that the association's policy is primary if a unit owner also has coverage applying to the same property.
- Waiver of Rights of Recovery—In the Waiver of Rights of Recovery condition, the insurer agrees not to subrogate against any unit owner.

Most of the other conditions of the Condominium Association Coverage Form are the same as those of the BPP. See the exhibit "Condominium Additional Provisions Endorsement."

Condominium Additional Provisions Endorsement

Act or Omission	No act or omission by any unit owner will void the policy or bar recovery unless the unit owner acts on behalf of the association.
Expanded Waiver of Right of Recovery	Rights of recovery are waived, beyond the condition in the coverage form, to include members of unit owners' households and members of the board of directors when acting within the scope of their duties.
Notice of Cancellation or Nonrenewal	The insurer will provide at least thirty days' written notice to the first named insured of policy cancellation or nonrenewal.
Additional Protection for Mortgageholders	The insurer will give thirty days' advance notice of cancellation or nonrenewal to each of the mortgageholders. If the condominium is terminated, the insurer will pay covered loss to buildings or structures to each mortgageholder shown in the declarations in their order of precedence.

[DA05970]

The Condominium Additional Provisions endorsement (CP 01 07), a mandatory policy amendment in several states, includes provisions to meet special needs. Independently developed condominium association forms often include some of these provisions. The provisions shown in the exhibit are from the ISO endorsement.

CONDOMINIUM COMMERCIAL UNIT-OWNERS COVERAGE FORM

Many condominiums are residential, and others are used for offices, stores, or other commercial occupancies. Unit owners in residential condominiums can insure their units with a homeowners form, such as the HO-6 policy. Separate forms are available for insuring unit owners in commercial condominiums.

One form used for insuring commercial unit owners of condominiums is the Insurance Services Office, Inc. (ISO) **Condominium Commercial Unit-Owners Coverage Form** (CP 00 18), which is designed to insure business personal property and building improvements and betterments of unit owners. The form can be analyzed in terms of which property is covered and how to coordinate its coverage with the coverage provided by the condominium association.

The Condominium Commercial Unit-Owners Optional Coverages endorsement (CP 04 18) is often attached to the Condominium Commercial Unit-Owners Coverage Form. This endorsement contains two optional coverages referred to as **loss assessment coverage** and **miscellaneous real property coverage**.

Covered Property

A condominium unit owner generally has no need for full building insurance in its own name, so the form includes coverage only for Your Business Personal Property and Personal Property of Others.

These coverages are, in most ways, the same as in the Business and Personal Property Coverage Form, also referred to as the BPP. However, Your Business Personal Property in the Condominium Commercial Unit-Owners Coverage Form includes fixtures, improvements, and alterations that are part of the building and owned by the unit owner.

In the BPP, Your Business Personal Property includes improvements and alterations only to the extent of a tenant's use interest in them, because the tenant does not own improvements and betterments. A unit owner, however, can actually own fixtures, improvements, and alterations to the unit.

Coordination With Association Coverage

The Condominium Commercial Unit-Owners Coverage Form contains an exclusion that coordinates the unit owner's coverage with the condominium association's coverage. Fixtures, improvements, alterations, and appliances (such as those used for refrigerating, cooking, and so on) are not covered by the unit owner's policy if the condominium association agreement requires the association to insure such property.

If the agreement requires the association to insure such property but the association fails to do so, the unit owner's form still does not apply. Another policy provision makes unit-owners coverage excess over the coverage of any association insurance covering the same property.

Condominium Commercial Unit-Owners Coverage Form
Form that covers business personal property and building property exposures of commercial (nonresidential) condominium units.

Loss assessment coverage
Coverage for a commercial condominium unit-owner's share of any assessment made by the association against all unit owners because of physical loss to condominium property caused by a covered cause of loss.

Miscellaneous real property coverage
Coverage for real property (such as a storage shed or garage building) that pertains only to the named insured's condominium unit or real property that the named insured has a duty to insure according to the condominium association agreement.

Optional Coverages

The Condominium Commercial Unit-Owners Optional Coverages endorsement contains provisions for two optional coverages often needed by condominium unit owners: loss assessment coverage and miscellaneous real property coverage. The insured can select either or both of these optional coverages.

Loss Assessment Coverage

Typically, condominium associations have the right to assess all unit owners for uninsured losses that the association incurs.

Under the optional loss assessment coverage, the insurer agrees to pay the unit owner's share of any assessment charged to all unit owners by the condominium association when the assessment is made as a result of direct physical loss or damage caused by an insured peril to property in which each unit owner has an undivided interest.

The coverage allows payment for each assessment up to the limit of insurance shown in the endorsement, subject to the deductible shown in the endorsement. However, if the assessment is a result of a deductible in the insurance purchased by the condominium association, the insurer's payment is limited to $1,000 unless a higher amount is shown in the endorsement's schedule. Coverage is provided by the policy in force when the assessment is made, not when the loss occurred.

Miscellaneous Real Property Coverage

The Condominium Commercial Unit-Owners Coverage Form normally covers only personal property, fixtures, improvements, and alterations.

The optional miscellaneous real property coverage extends the form to include condominium property not included under Your Business Personal Property under either of these situations:

- The condominium property pertains to the named insured's condominium unit only.
- The named insured has a duty to insure the condominium property according to the condominium association agreement.

If the condominium association has other insurance covering the same property, the unit owners' insurance is excess coverage.

Various situations, such as these, may suggest a need for miscellaneous real property coverage:

- A storage building erected by a unit owner for use in the unit owner's business operations
- A separate garage structure owned by the association but used solely by the unit owner, who is therefore required to insure the garage
- An attached addition to the external walls, such as a balcony, that benefits only the unit owner and that the unit owner thus is required to insure

BUILDERS RISK COVERAGE FORM

The Insurance Services Office, Inc. (ISO) Builders Risk Coverage Form (CP 00 20) can be used to insure buildings under construction. Although this form is similar to the Building and Personal Property Coverage Form, also referred to as the BPP, there are significant differences.

Although builders risk policies that provide broader coverage can be obtained under independently developed inland marine forms, the ISO Builders Risk Coverage Form (BRCF) is typically used for smaller projects and by producers who may not have access to the more specialized inland marine markets.

The Builders Risk Exposure

Buildings under construction present several unique exposures:

- The insured property's value increases as the work progresses.
- The variety of interests involved, such as owners, contractors, and subcontractors.
- The increased hazards posed by buildings under construction.

Buildings under construction face special hazards. Because securing a construction site can be difficult, building materials are susceptible to loss by theft. Materials that have not yet been installed are easily stolen, and some burglars also can remove items that have been installed, such as appliances, lighting fixtures, and copper pipes. Moreover, because fire protection (sprinkler systems, standpipes, and so on) may not be fully installed or operational and fire walls may not be in place at various stages in the construction, builders' risks can be especially susceptible to fire damage. Temporary heating devices may add a risk of explosion. Collapse and windstorm damage are also more likely during construction. These hazards may require special policy treatment and are reflected in the premium rates.

Eligible Property and Insureds

Under *Commercial Lines Manual* (CLM) rules, the BRCF may be used to insure any building in the course of construction, including buildings such as farm buildings and dwellings that will not be eligible for coverage under the BPP when construction is completed.

The BRCF may be used to insure the interests of the building owner, the contractor, or the owner and the contractor jointly, as their interests may appear. When appropriate, subcontractors' interests may be excluded or specifically insured by endorsement.

In some cases, the insured may want to exclude the work being performed by a separate contractor or subcontractor (for example, when the subcontractor is responsible for any damage to the work and carries its own insurance). ISO endorsements are available to handle such situations.

The BRCF may also be used for insuring additions or alterations to existing buildings. The Builders Risk Renovations endorsement (CP 11 13) excludes the value of the existing property, covering only the renovations under construction. The endorsement includes space to add the name of a loss payee. This addition might be necessary when other parties, such as contractors or lenders with an insurable interest in the renovation, require coverage. During the course of construction, the value of the renovations should be excluded from the BPP or another insurance form covering existing property.

Covered Property

The BRCF covers the building or structure being built, building materials and supplies intended to become a permanent part of the building, and temporary structures such as scaffolding and forms. See the exhibit "Covered Property Under ISO Builders Risk Coverage Form."

Coverage also applies to personal property (for example, uninstalled windows, doors, sinks, and furnaces) if it is intended to be permanently located in or on the building or structure described in the declarations or within 100 feet of its premises. This restriction eliminates coverage, for example, for building materials and supplies while in transit to the work site or in storage at other locations. If the insured is exposed to loss of property in transit to the site and wishes to insure the exposure, separate transit insurance is needed.

When the Causes of Loss—Special Form is attached to the BRCF, the insured receives $5,000 in coverage for property in transit on the insured's own vehicles. Shipments of materials by common carrier are often undertaken at the purchaser's risk, and the common carrier's liability is frequently limited. The ISO BRCF does not cover this exposure. Inland marine builders risk policies usually provide more extensive coverage for property in transit.

The Property Not Covered section of the BRCF is brief. The only excluded types of property are land or water and these types of property when outside of buildings: lawns, trees, shrubs, or plants (other than those that are part of a vegetated roof); antennas; and signs not attached to the building. Foundations are specifically covered. The BPP excludes many parts of a building or structure, such as underground pipes, flues, or drains. The absence of an exclusion

---

Covered Property Under ISO Builders Risk Coverage Form

1. **Covered Property**

   Covered Property, as used in this Coverage Part, means the type of property described in this section, **A.1.**, and limited in **A.2.**, Property Not Covered, if a Limit Of Insurance is shown in the Declarations for that type of property.

   Building Under Construction, meaning the building or structure described in the Declarations while in the course of construction, including:

   a. Foundations;

   b. The following property:

   (1) Fixtures and machinery;

   (2) Equipment used to service the building; and

   (3) Your building materials and supplies used for construction;

   provided such property is intended to be permanently located in or on the building or structure described in the Declarations or within 100 feet of its premises.

   c. If not covered by other insurance, temporary structures built or assembled on site, including cribbing, scaffolding and construction forms.

of these items in the BRCF means that coverage is provided if such items are intended to be part of the described building or structure; unlike the BPP, no specific endorsement is needed to include such items in the BRCF.

Additional Coverages

The BRCF contains four of the six additional coverages of the BPP—debris removal, preservation of property, fire department service charges, and pollutant cleanup and removal. The BRCF does not provide the additional coverages, as in the BPP, for increased cost of construction or electronic data, or any of the BPP coverage extensions. Instead, the BRCF contains two coverage extensions:

- The Building Materials and Supplies of Others extension provides up to $5,000 at each described location to cover building materials and supplies owned by others, such as building materials brought by a subcontractor onto the work site. The materials and supplies must be in the named insured's care, custody, or control; located in or on the building or within 100 feet of its premises; and intended to become a permanent part of the building. In some cases, the insured may be required to insure materials and supplies owned by others. When the value of such property exceeds the limit of the extension, a higher limit can be specified in the declarations if the insured is required to provide coverage.

- The Sod, Trees, Shrubs, and Plants extension covers landscaping outside of buildings on the described premises. This extension, similar to the Outdoor Property coverage extension of the BPP, is offered for only five causes of loss (fire, lightning, aircraft, riot/civil commotion, and explosion). Coverage is limited to $1,000 in any one loss and to $250 for any one tree, shrub, or plant.

Covered Causes of Loss

Like the BPP, the BRCF must be combined with an ISO causes of loss form (Basic Form, Broad Form, or Special Form), plus any necessary endorsements, to be a complete policy.

The Broad Form and the Special Form cover collapse of a building resulting from certain named perils, including "use of defective materials or methods in construction, remodeling or renovation if the collapse occurs during the course of the construction, remodeling or renovation." The BRCF specifically excludes collapse caused by this peril, which leaves a serious loss exposure uninsured. Collapse of a building insured under the BRCF can be covered by adding the Builders Risk—Collapse During Construction endorsement (CP 11 20).

The endorsement, in return for an additional premium, reinstates the coverage previously described, and it extends the coverage to cover collapse (during the course of construction, remodeling, or renovation) caused by faulty design, plans, specifications, or workmanship. Because collapse during construction can result in a catastrophic loss, this endorsement is an important addition to the policy.

Theft is a frequent problem at building construction sites. Before doors, windows, and burglar alarm systems are installed in the building, thieves may be able to enter the building easily. Materials that have not yet been installed are easily stolen, and some burglars will also remove items that have been installed, such as appliances, lighting fixtures, and copper pipes. Even after doors and windows have been installed, an unoccupied, unguarded, unlighted building is still highly attractive to thieves. Many risk control measures can be taken, including fences, security patrols, and exterior lighting.

The Basic Form and the Broad Form do not cover theft. The Special Form covers theft, subject to various exclusions. One of these exclusions eliminates coverage for loss of "building materials and supplies not attached as part of the building or structure." Thus, even when it includes the Special Form, the BRCF does not cover theft of uninstalled building materials.

Coverage for this exposure can be added with the Builders Risk—Theft of Building Materials, Fixtures, Machinery, Equipment endorsement (CP 11 21). Coverage does not apply while construction is not in progress unless security personnel are on duty. The endorsement includes space to insert a sublimit for this coverage as well as a separate deductible that can differ from the deductible for other losses. The endorsement excludes dishonest or criminal acts committed by the named insured; any of the named insured's partners, members, officers, managers, employees (including temporary employees and leased workers), directors, trustees, or authorized representatives; contractors or subcontractors or their employees; or anyone else to whom the property is entrusted for any purpose.

The Special Form exclusions of voluntary parting, missing property, and inventory shortage are repeated in endorsement CP 11 21 because the endorsement could also be used with the Basic Form or the Broad Form, neither of which contains these exclusions. Underwriters will generally require robust risk control measures before granting this coverage. With such protection in place, insureds often decide to retain this exposure.

Completed Value Approach

The BRCF is designed to be issued, at policy inception, for an amount of insurance equal to the building's full completed value. This method of providing builders risk coverage is referred to as the completed value approach.

One of the builders risk rules in the *CLM* requires that the inception date of a builders risk policy be no later than the date construction starts above the level of the lowest basement floor or, if there is no basement, the date construction starts. This rule helps the insurer earn an adequate premium for the risk assumed. In the absence of this rule, insureds who are willing to retain the risk themselves for the first few weeks or months of a building project (when covered property's value is low) could select a later inception date to reduce the earned policy premium. To earn an adequate premium, the insurer must earn premium over the project's duration.

This rule does not preclude the insured from selecting a policy inception date earlier than the date construction starts above the level of the lowest basement floor. Some building projects include extensive foundation work below the basement floor, and the BRCF covers foundations. If the insured wishes to insure the foundation work before construction begins above the basement floor, the inception date can be set at an earlier date. Some insureds may take the cautious approach of placing coverage as soon as construction starts to avoid any uninsured exposure. Also, a builders risk policy will often be required for a mortgage closing even though no construction above the basement level has commenced. Complying with the request is generally easier than negotiating an exception.

Although completed value builders risk policies are issued for a minimum term of one year, the insured receives a refund of the unearned premium if the project is completed in less than a year.

Need for Adequate Insurance

The Need for Adequate Insurance condition is, in effect, a 100 percent coinsurance clause in which the amount of insurance that should be carried is based on the value of the building on the date it will be completed. The formula is as shown:

$$\text{Amount payable} = \left(\frac{\text{Limit of insurance}}{\text{Completed value}} \times \text{Loss} \right) - \text{Deductible}.$$

No underinsurance penalty is involved if, at the time of the loss, the limit of insurance equals or exceeds the building's completed value. The value of all permanent fixtures and decorations that constitute a part of the building should be included in setting the completed value.

Although insuring to the completed value might appear to be simple, the completed value of a building is not necessarily firmly fixed before construction begins. Changes in design, increases in labor or material costs, or errors in calculating completed value can result in a potential penalty for underinsurance if a loss occurs.

To avoid this problem, the insured should review the builders risk limit whenever changes occur that will increase the building's completed value. The Agreed Value optional coverage of the BPP is not available with the BRCF. If the policy limit is increased at some point in the policy period, *CLM* rules call for the additional premium to be calculated from the time of policy inception, regardless of when the increase becomes effective.

Valuation

The BRCF contains a standard valuation condition that provides coverage on the basis of actual cash value. Because the actual cash value and the replacement cost of a building under construction are typically the same, the BRCF does not contain optional replacement cost coverage provisions.

Builders Risk Reporting Form

Another method, less commonly used, is to write builders risk coverage on a value reporting basis. By adding the Builders Risk Reporting Form endorsement (CP 11 05), the BRCF can be changed to a value reporting basis.

The endorsement requires the insured to report to the insurer the actual cash value of covered property as of a specified date each month during the policy period. The insurer charges an initial premium and adjusts the premium during the policy period based on the values reported by the insured.

As with the Value Reporting Form used with the BPP, potentially serious penalties apply if reports are late or inaccurate. Given the administrative burden of preparing and submitting timely and accurate reports and the potential penalties for late or inaccurate reports, most insureds prefer their builders risk policies to apply on a completed value basis.

When Coverage Ceases

The BRCF is intended to cover buildings during the course of construction only. When the work is completed, another policy, such as the BPP or a homeowners policy, is needed. The BRCF therefore contains an explicit condition of when coverage ceases.

Unless the insurer agrees otherwise, coverage ceases sixty days after an insured building is occupied, in whole or in part, or is put to its intended use. Even if the building is not occupied or put to use—for example, if the building remains vacant while the owner tries to sell it—coverage ceases ninety days after the construction is completed.

Coverage ceases immediately when any of these events occur:

- The named insured's interest in the property ceases.
- The property is accepted by the purchaser.
- The named insured abandons the project with no intention of completing it.

Obviously, coverage also ceases when the policy expires or is canceled. Despite the apparent precision of these policy provisions, the date and time at which one of these conditions occurs are sometimes difficult to determine.

STANDARD PROPERTY POLICY

Commercial properties that do not meet the underwriting criteria of the standard insurance market still need insurance coverage. Residual markets use special policy forms to write property insurance for these loss exposures.

**Standard Property
Policy (SPP)**

A commercial property policy form for covering buildings and business personal property on restricted terms.

The **Standard Property Policy (SPP)**, which covers buildings and business personal property on restricted terms, is designed for insuring "distressed risks," properties with unfavorable attributes that have made them unacceptable in the standard insurance market. Thus, the SPP could be used by Fair Access to Insurance Requirements (FAIR) plans, which function as the residual markets for property insurance in many states, or by insurers that specialize in insuring distressed property risks.

The SPP (CP 00 99) is a self-contained monoline policy containing all necessary policy provisions in a single document. Only a completed declarations page is needed to complete the contract. As a result, the SPP cannot be a part of a package policy. Any additional coverages, such as general liability coverage, must be obtained separately.

In most respects, property coverage under the SPP is similar to that under the Building and Personal Property Coverage Form, also referred to as the BPP.

It can also be endorsed to cover condominium associations, condominium unit owners, or builders risks. However, some differences exist between the SPP and the BPP with the Causes of Loss—Basic Form. See the exhibit "Comparison of SPP and BPP."

Comparison of SPP and BPP

Standard Property Policy	BPP With Basic Perils
Policy is self-contained. Form includes: • Common policy conditions • Commercial property conditions • Causes of loss (and exclusions)	Separate forms must be attached to provide these.
Coverage may be purchased separately for the following incremental groupings of causes of loss: • Fire, lightning, and explosion (mandatory) • Windstorm and hail (may be excluded); smoke, aircraft, or vehicles; riot or civil commotion; sinkhole collapse; volcanic action • Vandalism and/or sprinkler leakage	All perils included automatically in basic causes of loss form, with options to exclude: • Windstorm and hail • Vandalism • Sprinkler leakage
Coverage extensions apply only in state where described premises are located.	Coverage territory is the United States and Canada.
No coverage for buildings vacant or unoccupied after: • 30 days for vandalism • 60 days for any other peril Vacancy definition is not significant, because the exclusion applies to vacant or unoccupied buildings.	Unlimited unoccupancy permitted. After 60 days' vacancy, no coverage for vandalism or sprinkler leakage, and amount recoverable for other perils reduced by 15%. Vacancy defined as less than 31% of square footage occupied.
No replacement cost coverage.	$2,500 replacement cost coverage built in for building losses if coinsurance is complied with. Full replacement cost coverage is optional.
Coverage is suspended during any increase in hazard.	No such condition.
No optional coverages	Optional coverages available in form for inflation guard, agreed value, and replacement cost.

Adapted from ISO handout at Commercial Lines Seminar, 1986. [DA03559]

Covered Property

The declarations indicate what limits of insurance, if any, apply to buildings, business personal property, and property of others. The additional coverages and coverage extensions are the same as those of the BPP, except that the coverage extensions apply only to property located in the same state as the described premises.

Coverage applies on an actual cash value basis. The SPP does not offer any options for replacement cost coverage, inflation guard, or agreed value.

Covered Perils

Considering the fact that the SPP is used to insure distressed property risks, flexibility in limiting the covered perils is an important feature of the policy. All the perils covered by the Basic Form are available in the SPP, but the insurer can restrict the covered perils to these combinations:

- Fire, lightning, and explosion. (All are mandatory.)
- Windstorm, hail, smoke, aircraft, vehicles, riot, civil commotion, sinkhole collapse, and volcanic action can be added by making an appropriate entry in the declarations (and windstorm and hail can be omitted from this combination).
- Vandalism and sprinkler leakage can also be triggered by marking the declarations page accordingly.

Conditions

The SPP contains three conditions that result in more restrictive coverage than under the BPP:

- Vacancy and unoccupancy—Under the SPP, the insurer will not pay for loss or damage by any peril if the building has been vacant or unoccupied for more than sixty days. After thirty days of vacancy or unoccupancy, coverage for vandalism ceases. "Vacancy" is defined to mean that the building contains no contents pertaining to the operations or activities customary to the building's occupancy. The SPP does not make the 31 percent building occupancy distinction that the BPP does, and the SPP does not have different definitions of vacancy for owners and tenants. A building with some occupancy, but less than 31 percent, would not be considered vacant under the SPP. Thus, coverage would not be excluded for certain losses or reduced 15 percent for the remainder, as would be the case under the BPP when the condition has existed for more than sixty days. However, the SPP provides no coverage if a building is unoccupied, but not vacant, for more than sixty days, whereas the BPP imposes no penalty at all for unoccupancy.
- Increase in hazard—Coverage is suspended during any period in which the hazard has been increased by means within the named insured's

knowledge and control. This clause, which was a provision of the Standard Fire Policy, is not included in the BPP.

- Cancellation—The insurer may cancel the policy by providing only five days' advance notice to the insured. This difference from the BPP is not significant because most state laws require longer notification periods.

LEGAL LIABILITY COVERAGE FORM

The Legal Liability Coverage Form provides a flexible solution for enterprises that want to insure their potential liability for damage to buildings or personal property of others in their care, custody, or control.

Developed by Insurance Services Office, Inc. (ISO), the **Legal Liability Coverage Form** (CP 00 40) differs from other commercial property forms, such as the Building and Personal Property Coverage Form, also referred to as the BPP, in that it provides liability coverage on buildings or personal property of others in the insured's care, custody, or control. The reason a liability form is included in ISO's commercial property program is that fire is the major cause of property loss for which the insured could be held liable. When this type of coverage was first developed, many insurers had separate property and liability underwriting departments, and the property underwriters had the expertise needed to evaluate the fire and other property perils involved in this liability loss exposure.

The BPP includes coverage for personal property of others regardless of whether the insured is legally liable to pay for the loss. Because the Legal Liability Coverage Form covers losses only if the insured is legally liable, the rate charged for that form is lower than the usual commercial property contents or building rate.

> **Legal Liability Coverage Form**
>
> A commercial property coverage form that provides legal liability coverage on buildings or personal property of others in the insured's care, custody, or control.

Insuring Agreement

The insurer agrees to pay those sums that the named insured becomes legally obligated to pay as damages because of direct physical loss or damage, including loss of use, to covered property caused by accident and arising out of any covered cause of loss. The covered causes of loss are determined by whichever causes of loss form is applicable.

The fact that loss of use is covered means that the insurer will pay for time element losses that the owner of the property incurs as a result of the physical damage. Such time element losses include loss of income or extra expenses incurred for rental of replacement property. Coverage for loss of use is an important advantage of the Legal Liability Coverage Form. The BPP can be arranged to cover direct damage to property of others regardless of fault, but it does not cover claims for loss of use of the damaged property.

The insurer agrees to pay related defense costs and make other supplementary payments in addition to the limit of insurance. No deductible applies to the Legal Liability Coverage Form.

Exclusions

An applicable causes of loss form, shown in the declarations, expresses the covered causes of loss, exclusions, and limitations for the Legal Liability Coverage Form.

Each causes of loss form contains an exclusion that applies only to the Legal Liability Coverage Form and eliminates coverage for damages that the insured is legally liable to pay solely by reason of the insured's assumption of liability in a contract or an agreement. The test for applying this exclusion is answering the question, "Would the insured have been liable in the absence of the assumption of liability?" If so, the exclusion does not apply, even though the insured has assumed liability.

All of the other exclusions of the causes of loss forms apply to the Legal Liability Coverage Form, except these:

- Ordinance or Law
- Governmental Action
- Nuclear Hazard
- Utility Services
- War and Military Action

The Nuclear Hazard exclusion is replaced with an exclusion of defense costs and payment of damages for all loss resulting from nuclear reaction or radiation or radioactive contamination, however caused.

Legal Liability Coverage Form Versus CGL Coverage

The Commercial General Liability (CGL) Coverage Form excludes coverage for damage to property of others in the insured's care, custody, or control.

However, by exception to its exclusions, the CGL form provides limited coverage for liability arising out of damage to that part of a building rented to or temporarily used by the insured. This coverage, generally referred to as either "fire legal liability" or "damage to premises rented to you," covers liability for fire damage to the part of the building occupied by the insured. ISO rules call for a minimum limit of $100,000 for this coverage, which can be increased for an additional premium.

The CGL form also provides coverage for damage, by perils other than fire, to premises (and their contents) rented to the named insured for no longer than seven consecutive days, for the same limit that applies to fire legal liability coverage.

A major advantage of the Legal Liability Coverage Form is the broader range of perils that can be insured when the property is rented for longer than seven consecutive days. Also, fire legal liability coverage applies only to real property, whereas the Legal Liability Coverage Form can apply to both real and personal property.

Premium Rates

The rate for the Legal Liability Coverage Form is lower than the rate for direct property insurance because the insurer is obligated to pay only when the insured is liable for the damage. The legal liability rate that an insurer charges for real property is generally 25 percent of the 80 percent coinsurance building rate that would otherwise apply, and the legal liability rate for personal property is generally 50 percent of the 80 percent coinsurance contents rate. For example, if the 80 percent coinsurance contents rate is $0.20 per $100 of coverage, the legal liability rate for personal property at the same location would be $0.10 per $100. See the exhibit "Using the Legal Liability Coverage Form."

Using the Legal Liability Coverage Form

Premier Injection Molding, Inc. (PIM) does contract plastic-injection molding for manufacturers of plastic products using molds supplied by its customers. Because the molds are often reused, PIM stores them in its warehouse. PIM is concerned about insurance coverage for the molds.

PIM has considered a number of risk management approaches. It could include the molds in its BPP as property of others, but PIM does not know the value of the molds—some of them are never used again. It could return the molds to the customer, but storing the molds creates goodwill and encourages repeat business. It could contractually limit its responsibility for the molds in its agreements with customers, but one can never be certain that a court will enforce an exculpatory agreement. PIM could also purchase legal liability coverage.

PIM has decided on a combination of techniques. First, PIM modified its agreement to provide that it is responsible for the molds only if the damage is the result of its negligence and that its maximum liability is $100 for each mold unless the owner declares, and pays for, a higher valuation. Second, PIM purchased insurance under the Legal Liability Coverage Form to cover its liability as limited in its contract and to protect it in the event a court invalidates the agreement.

[DA03560]

Additional Insureds

These types of entities cannot be added to the Legal Liability Coverage Form as additional insureds:

- Tenants, lessees, concessionaires, or exhibitors, in policies covering general lessees, managers, or operators of premises
- Contractors or subcontractors, in policies covering tenants or lessees of premises

All other additional insureds may be added without charge, except for general lessees, managers or operators of the premises, and employees other than executive officers and partners. An additional premium charge of 25 percent applies when anyone in those classifications is named as an additional insured.

Insurance to Value

The Legal Liability Coverage Form has no coinsurance condition. This omission is appropriate because the insured frequently does not know the value of property of others in its care, custody, or control.

Nonetheless, insurance buyers and advisers should carefully estimate the severity of the exposure when establishing insurance limits. The maximum possible loss that could be sustained under this form would include loss of all covered property of others in the insured's care, custody, or control—including damages for loss of use—that might be sustained in a single loss.

The Legal Liability Coverage Form can be used to cover the insured's liability for damage to building property in the insured's care, custody, or control. If the insured occupies the entire building, the limit of insurance should reflect the building's full value, including projected damages for loss of use.

If a tenant occupies only a portion of the building, the limit should reflect the value of that portion only (plus loss of use). Damage to portions of the building not in the insured's care, custody, or control, if caused by the insured's negligence, would normally be covered by the insured's CGL insurance.

LEASEHOLD INTEREST COVERAGE FORM

An insurance professional should know how to help an insured lessee become aware of leasehold interest exposures and the coverages that are available to protect the insured who chooses to not retain the risk.

The **Leasehold Interest Coverage Form** (CP 00 60) insures a tenant's financial losses resulting from the cancellation of the tenant's lease because of damage to the premises by a covered cause of loss. The amount of insurance is automatically reduced each month during the life of the lease.

Many leases of premises allow the lessor (landlord) to terminate the lease if (1) the building or premises are damaged by fire or other perils to a stipulated

Leasehold Interest Coverage Form

A commercial property coverage form for insuring a tenant's financial losses resulting from the cancellation of the tenant's lease because of damage to the premises by a covered cause of loss.

percentage of the value of the building or premises (for example, 25 percent) or (2) the amount of time required to repair or replace the damaged property exceeds a stipulated period.

If the lease does not address the issue, the laws in many states provide for cancellation of a lease when more than 50 percent of the property is damaged and cannot be occupied.

Examples of Loss Exposure

Cancellation of a lease may cause a lessee (tenant) to suffer a financial loss in any of these circumstances:

- The lessee has a lease at a rental rate much lower than the current rental value of comparable premises. If, as is likely, the lessee would be unable to obtain as favorable a lease upon cancellation, the loss would be the additional cost to rent equivalent premises for the duration of the current lease.

- The lessee has sublet the premises to another at a profit. The loss would be the loss of the profit margin for the duration of the lease.

- The lessee paid a bonus to acquire the lease. The loss would be the unamortized value of the bonus. If, for example, the bonus was $50,000 for a five-year lease and the lease was canceled with three years remaining on the lease, the unamortized value would be three-fifths of the $50,000, or $30,000.

- The lessee has paid advance rent that is not recoverable under the terms of the lease in the event of cancellation. The loss would be the unused value of the advance rent.

- The lessee has installed improvements and betterments. The tenant's use value of the improvements and betterments would be lost as a result of the cancellation of the lease. This exposure is distinct from the improvements and betterments exposure covered by the Building and Personal Property Coverage Form, also referred to as the BPP. The BPP exposure involves physical damage to the improvements by a covered cause of loss. In a contract, a leasehold interest loss involving improvements and betterments is caused by cancellation of the lease because of damage by an insured peril at the insured premises; the improvements and betterments themselves need not be damaged at all.

Characteristics of the Coverage Form

The Leasehold Interest Coverage Form covers the total amount of net leasehold interest of the insured for the unexpired period of the lease. The amount of insurance is automatically reduced during the life of the lease.

The covered causes of loss for the Leasehold Interest Coverage Form are identified in the applicable causes of loss form that the insured has selected.

In addition to their standard exclusions and limitations, each causes of loss form contains two special, exclusion-related provisions that apply only to the Leasehold Interest Coverage Form.

- The first provision states that the Ordinance or Law exclusion does not apply to leasehold interest coverage. For example, coverage is provided even if the lease is canceled because a local ordinance prevents the owner from rebuilding.
- The second provision is an exclusion of loss caused by the named insured's canceling the lease; the suspension, lapse, or cancellation of any license; or any other consequential loss.

The Vacancy condition of the Leasehold Interest Coverage Form differs substantially from the BPP Vacancy condition. Vacancy, with respect to leasehold interest coverage, exists when the unit or suite rented or leased to the tenant does not contain enough business personal property to enable the tenant to conduct customary operations. Buildings under construction or renovation are not considered vacant.

With the exception of premises that the insured has entered into an agreement to sublease, the insurer will not pay for any leasehold interest loss that occurs when the premises are vacant. This is apparently the case even if the premises are vacant for one day.

Why Leasehold Interest Is Seldom Insured

Although leasehold interest insurance fills a need for some insureds, such insurance is seldom bought, perhaps because many risk managers and producers are unaware it exists. Even when risk managers are aware of the leasehold interest exposure, they may choose to retain it because it is a relatively small exposure for most tenants.

Also, some insurers include nominal amounts of lease cancellation coverage in their commercial property policies. This fringe coverage provides at least some protection and can serve as an impetus for the risk manager and producer to discuss the needed amount of coverage.

Another reason the Leasehold Interest Coverage Form is not used is that lessees find it difficult to conceptualize the exposure even when it is brought to their attention. If, in an area where rents have risen sharply, the lessee considers the potential gain it could realize by subletting the premises to another firm at the market rate, the lessee may be able to see that the cancellation of a long-term lease can also pose a substantial loss exposure.

Or, a lessee that has installed extensive improvements and betterments might find it easier to understand the financial exposure to loss and the desirability of insuring the exposure. The loss of a firm's investment in improvements and betterments is more easily demonstrated. Accounting rules require that the cost of improvements and betterments be carried on a firm's books as assets and with the amount amortized over the length of the lease.

Insurance advisers can encourage the use of leasehold interest coverage by asking the insured's financial officer the amount of unamortized improvements and betterments and reviewing the firm's leases to determine the potential loss resulting from lease cancellation.

CASE STUDY: OTHER COMMERCIAL PROPERTY COVERAGE FORMS

It is important to understand other commercial property coverage forms in comparison with the Building and Personal Property Coverage Form (BPP) to determine which policy would provide coverage for the loss exposures of an organization. The other coverage forms available include these:

- Condominium Association Coverage Form
- Condominium Commercial Unit-Owners Coverage Form
- Builders Risk Coverage Form
- Standard Property Policy
- Legal Liability Coverage Form
- Leasehold Interest Coverage Form

Commercial property forms developed by Insurance Services Office, Inc. (ISO) are designed to be used with one of three causes of loss forms:

- Causes of Loss—Basic Form
- Causes of Loss—Broad Form
- Causes of Loss—Special Form

The Building and Personal Property Coverage Form (BPP) is not appropriate for every organization's insurance needs. It is important for insurance professionals to be aware of the coverage provided by other commercial property coverage forms and how to determine coverage when an insured organization experiences a loss.

An analysis of a specific loss scenario will assist insurance professionals in understanding the types of coverage provided by specialized property coverage forms. The case study is also an opportunity to determine whether there is coverage, and the extent of that coverage, in the context of a specific loss scenario.

Case Facts

J&J Construction Company is a family-owned business that builds houses and small commercial structures. The company employs a three-person crew of carpenters for general construction and hires licensed contractors for plumbing, electrical, and air conditioning work. On June 10, J&J is nearing completion of construction on a house near the Gulf Coast. The company has advertised the house for sale, but it has not yet found a buyer.

The remaining work involves finish carpentry to the interior, installation of certain fixtures, and exterior landscaping. The kitchen appliances and the fixtures in the first-floor bathroom have been installed. Installation of the master bathroom fixtures, which were purchased by J&J, is not yet complete. Mike's Plumbing Company is the contractor working on the installation of the bathroom fixtures. Shrubs and a palm tree, purchased by J&J from a local nursery, are on site. J&J has scheduled a landscaping company to plant them on June 13.

On June 11, a hurricane strikes with winds of 115 miles per hour. The wind from the hurricane damages a section of the tile roof above the master bedroom suite. Although J&J used a foam adhesive that is stronger than mortar for the tile roof, according to standards for construction in hurricane-prone areas, the gable roof on the master suite had increased vulnerability to wind damage. There is also damage to one exterior wall of the master bedroom suite, starting at the roof juncture and extending to the floor of the second story.

The fixtures in the master bathroom are propelled out of the building through the opening created in the wall by the force of the wind. The fixtures break when they strike the ground. The palm tree is knocked over, but it survives the storm. The shrubbery, however, is destroyed. The exterior lights along the walkway are damaged.

Would one of these specialized commercial property coverage forms provide coverage for this hypothetical loss?

- Condominium Association Coverage Form
- Condominium Commercial Unit-Owners Coverage Form
- Builders Risk Coverage Form
- Standard Property Policy
- Legal Liability Coverage Form
- Leasehold Interest Coverage Form

Case Analysis Tools and Information

To determine whether any of the specialized commercial property coverage forms would provide coverage for this loss, it is necessary to understand the purpose of each of these coverage forms. See the exhibit "Other Commercial Property Coverage Forms."

ISO commercial property forms are designed to be used with one of three causes of loss forms. It is important to understand the causes of loss covered by each of these forms. See the exhibit "Causes of Loss Forms."

Other Commercial Property Coverage Forms

Coverage Form	Purpose
Condominium Association Coverage Form	To insure the building and business personal property loss exposures of condominium associations
Condominium Commercial Unit-Owners Coverage Form	To insure business personal property and building improvements and betterments of unit owners in condominiums used for offices, stores, or other commercial occupancies
Builders Risk Coverage Form	To cover buildings or structures during the course of construction
Standard Property Policy	To insure "distressed risks" on restricted coverage terms
Legal Liability Coverage Form	To provide liability coverage on buildings or personal property of others in the insured's care, custody, or control
Leasehold Interest Coverage Form	To insure a tenant's financial losses resulting from the cancellation of the tenant's lease because of damage to the premises by a covered cause of loss

[DA05984]

Case Analysis Steps

Analysis to determine if one of the specialized commercial property coverage forms would provide coverage for the named insured's described loss would employ these four steps:

1. Compare the purpose of the various coverage forms to determine if one of them applies to the organization engaged in the type of business on the premises described in the scenario
2. Determine if the loss was caused by a covered cause of loss
3. Determine if the property that was damaged or lost is covered
4. Determine if there are any conditions, extensions, exclusions, or endorsements that affect coverage

This analysis involves study of the coverage forms as well as the causes of loss forms. See the exhibit "Coverage Analysis Method."

Causes of Loss Forms

Causes Of Loss Form	Causes Of Loss Covered
Basic Form	Fire, lightning, explosion, windstorm or hail, smoke, aircraft or vehicles, riot or civil commotion, vandalism, sprinkler-leakage, sinkhole collapse, volcanic action, fungus (provided as an additional coverage)
Broad Form	• All causes of loss covered by Basic Form • Also covers falling objects; weight of snow, ice, and sleet; water damage; collapse (provided as an additional coverage)
Special Form	• All causes of loss covered by Broad Form • Also covers all causes of loss that are not excluded • Broadest coverage of the three forms

[DA05985]

Coverage Analysis Method

1.	Coverage Form	• Review policy form • Determine if the organization's described business activity at the time of loss is covered • Determine if the property and insured are eligible for coverage
2.	Covered Cause of Loss	• Review the causes of loss form listed in the policy declarations • Determine if the cause of loss is covered
3.	Covered Property	Determine if the property that is lost or damaged is covered
4.	Conditions, Extensions, Exclusions, or Endorsements	Determine if there are any conditions, extensions, exclusions, or endorsements in the policy that would expand or limit coverage for the loss

[DA05986]

Coverage Form

The first step determines if one of the other commercial property coverage forms would cover the type of loss described in the scenario.

An analysis indicates that the Builders Risk Coverage Form is designed to cover the special loss exposures of buildings under construction. The coverage provided by the BPP for new buildings while they are under construction is limited and is intended only as incidental protection. The other commercial property coverage forms are designed to insure different types of risks. The Builders Risk Coverage Form would cover the business risk in the described loss scenario—a house under construction. J&J Construction Co. as the named insured, and the location of the house under construction as the insured premises, would be eligible for coverage under the Builders Risk Coverage Form.

Covered Cause of Loss

The next step is to determine if the described loss was caused by a covered cause of loss.

All of the commercial property coverage forms require a causes of loss form, named in the declarations, to form a complete policy.

Review of the three types of causes of loss forms indicates that windstorm is a covered cause of loss in all three forms. Wind is the cause of the loss in the described loss scenario, and this cause of loss would be covered by any causes of loss form that would be used with the Builders Risk Coverage Form.

Covered Property

The third step is to determine if the damaged property is covered property under the commercial property coverage form.

The Builders Risk Coverage Form covers the building or structure being built, building materials and supplies intended to become a permanent part of the building, and temporary structures such as scaffolding and forms. Coverage also applies to personal property, such as uninstalled windows, doors, sinks, and furnaces, if they are intended to be permanently located in or on the building or structure described in the declarations or within 100 feet of its premises. However, there is no coverage for building materials and supplies while in transit to the work site or in storage at other locations. See the exhibit "Covered Property in Builders Risk Coverage Form."

The damage to the roof and wall of the house constitutes damage to the building under construction, and this is covered by the Builders Risk Coverage Form as outlined in the policy section on covered property.

The bathroom fixtures, although they are to be installed by Mike's Plumbing Company, were purchased by J&J Construction. They are intended to be permanently located in the building, and thus they are covered property.

Covered Property in Builders Risk Coverage Form

BUILDERS RISK COVERAGE FORM

Various provisions in this policy restrict coverage. Read the entire policy carefully to determine rights, duties and what is and is not covered.

Throughout this policy the words "you" and "your" refer to the Named Insured shown in the Declarations. The words "we", "us" and "our" refer to the Company providing this insurance.

Other words and phrases that appear in quotation marks have special meaning. Refer to Section G., Definitions.

A. Coverage

We will pay for direct physical loss of or damage to Covered Property at the premises described in the Declarations caused by or resulting from any Covered Cause of Loss.

1. Covered Property

Covered Property, as used in this Coverage Part, means the type of property described in this section, A.1., and limited in A.2., Property Not Covered, if a Limit of Insurance is shown in the Declarations for that type of property.

Building Under Construction, meaning the building or structure described in the Declarations while in the course of construction, including:

a. Foundations;

b. The following property:

(1) Fixtures and machinery;

(2) Equipment used to service the building; and

(3) Your building materials and supplies used for construction;

provided such property is intended to be permanently located in or on the building or structure described in the Declarations or within 100 feet of its premises;

c. If not covered by other insurance, temporary structures built or assembled on site, including cribbing, scaffolding and construction forms.

2. Property Not Covered

Covered Property does not include:

a. Land (including land on which the property is located) or water;

b. The following property when outside of buildings:

(1) Lawns, trees, shrubs or plants;

(2) Radio or television antennas (including satellite dishes) and their lead-in wiring, masts or towers; or

(3) Signs (other than signs attached to buildings).

3. Covered Causes Of Loss

See applicable Causes Of Loss Form as shown in the Declarations.

The shrubbery is not covered because the policy form states that covered property does not include lawns, trees, shrubs, or plants.

The exterior lights are fixtures located on the premises and therefore would be covered.

Conditions, Extensions, Exclusions, or Endorsements

An important condition in the Builders Risk Coverage Form is the condition regarding when coverage ceases.

> 4. When Coverage Ceases
>
> The insurance provided by this Coverage Form will end when one of the following first occurs:
>
> a. This policy expires or is cancelled;
>
> b. The property is accepted by the purchaser;
>
> c. Your interest in the property ceases;
>
> d. You abandon the construction with no intention to complete it;
>
> e. Unless we specify otherwise in writing:
>
> (1) 90 days after construction is complete; or
>
> (2) 60 days after any building described in the Declarations is:
>
> (a) Occupied in whole or in part; or
>
> (b) Put to its intended use.[2]

Construction is not yet complete on this house. Therefore, coverage would not have ceased.

The Builders Risk Coverage Form can be extended to provide coverage for loss or damage to sod, trees, shrubs, and plants outside of buildings on the described premises. However, this extension only covers five causes of loss, including fire, lightning, explosion, riot or civil commotion, or aircraft, with a limit of $1,000, and no more than $250 for any one tree, shrub, or plant. The cause of loss in the described loss scenario— wind—would not be covered by this extension.

The Builders Risk Coverage Form can also be extended to cover property owned by others in the care, custody, and control of the insured and intended to become a permanent part of the building up to $5,000 for each described premises (this limit can be extended by specifying a higher limit in the declarations). This extension is not applicable to the loss scenario described.

There are no exclusions applicable to this loss scenario.

This solution might not be the only viable solution. Other solutions could be exercised if justified by the analysis. In addition, specific circumstances and organizational needs or goals may enter into the evaluation, making an alternative action a better option. See the exhibit "Correct Answer to Case Study on Other Commercial Property Coverage Forms."

Correct Answer to Case Study on Other Commercial Property Coverage Forms

The Builders Risk Coverage Form, designed to cover buildings or structures during the course of construction, would provide coverage in the described loss scenario.

The cause of loss—wind—would be covered with any of the three causes of loss forms that could be used with the Builders Risk Coverage Form.

These items, damaged or destroyed in the loss, would be covered:

- Roof
- Wall
- Bathroom fixtures
- Exterior lighting fixtures

The damaged shrubbery would not be covered.

There are no conditions, extensions, or exclusions in the Builders Risk Coverage Form that restrict or extend coverage in this loss scenario.

[DA05987]

SUMMARY

Condominiums have special insurance needs because multiple owners have an interest in condominium property. Other forms of combined ownership include cooperative corporations and planned unit developments.

The Condominium Association Coverage Form is designed to insure the building and business personal property loss exposures of condominium associations. Although it resembles the BPP in many ways, the Condominium Association Coverage Form has important differences from the BPP.

Its building coverage applies to fixtures and appliances within individual units only if the association is required to insure them, and Your Business Personal Property coverage does not insure property individually owned by any unit owner. However, the association can optionally cover unit owners' personal property (being used, for example, in a common area) under Personal Property of Others. Noteworthy differences are also contained in the Loss Payment, Unit-Owner's Insurance, and Waiver of Rights of Recovery conditions.

The Condominium Commercial Unit-Owners Coverage Form has two issues that must be resolved when applying coverage: what property is covered and how to coordinate that coverage with the condominium association's coverage. The Condominium Commercial Unit-Owners Optional Coverages endorsement contains provisions for two optional coverages often needed by condominium unit owners: loss assessment coverage and miscellaneous real property coverage.

Buildings under construction present several unique exposures. The BRCF can be used to insure any building in the course of construction. The BRCF covers the building or structure being built, building materials and supplies intended to become a permanent part of the building, and temporary structures such as scaffolding. The BRCF also contains the debris removal, preservation of property, fire department service charge, and pollutant cleanup additional coverages of the BPP. Also like the BPP, the BRCF must be combined with an ISO causes of loss form (Basic Form, Broad Form, or Special Form), plus any necessary endorsements, to be a complete policy. The BRCF is designed to be issued, at policy inception, for an amount of insurance equal to the building's full completed value. Because the BRCF is intended to cover buildings during the course of construction only, it contains a condition that explicitly states when coverage ceases.

The SPP is a commercial property policy form that covers buildings and business personal property on restricted terms. Because the SPP is used to insure distressed property risks, flexibility in limiting the covered perils is an important feature of the policy. The SPP's conditions relating to vacancy and unoccupancy, increase in hazard, and cancellation result in more restrictive coverage than under the BPP.

The Legal Liability Coverage Form can be used to cover the named insured's liability for damage, including resulting loss of use, to buildings or personal property in the insured's care, custody, or control. An exclusion in the ISO causes of loss forms eliminates coverage under this form for damages that the insured is legally liable to pay solely by reason of the insured's assumption of liability in a contract or an agreement. The premium rate for the Legal Liability Coverage Form is lower than the rate for direct property insurance because the insurer is obligated to pay only when the insured is liable for the damage. Several types of entities, such as tenants and contractors, cannot be added to the Legal Liability Coverage Form as additional insureds. The Legal Liability Coverage Form has no coinsurance condition.

The Leasehold Interest Coverage Form insures a tenant's financial losses resulting from the cancellation of the tenant's lease because of damage to the premises by a covered cause of loss. It is helpful to use examples when trying to explain how a leasehold exposure could occur. The causes of loss forms contain two special, exclusion-related provisions that apply only to the Leasehold Interest Coverage Form.

The insurer will not pay for any leasehold interest loss that occurs when the premises are vacant. Leasehold interest insurance is seldom bought, perhaps because many risk managers and producers are unaware the coverage exists or because lessees choose to retain the relatively small loss exposure or are unaware of the exposure.

It is important for insurance professionals to understand how other commercial property coverage forms can provide coverage for the loss exposures of organizations. It is also important to understand how to determine coverage when an organization experiences a loss.

ASSIGNMENT NOTES

1. A condominium's governing documents usually provide for the election of officers and a board of directors to oversee operation of the condominium. The board of directors has broad powers including, usually, the obligation or right to place insurance. Many boards retain managing agents to handle daily operations, but ultimate authority resides with the board.

2. Includes copyrighted material of Insurance Services Office, Inc., with its permission. Copyright. ISO Properties, Inc., 2007.

Direct Your Learning ▶▶

6

Flood, Earthquake, and Specialty Forms

Educational Objectives

After learning the content of this assignment, you should be able to:

▷ Describe the National Flood Insurance Program (NFIP) in these terms:

- Eligibility for the program
- Maximum amounts of insurance available
- Coverages provided by the National Flood Insurance Program General Property Form and the Residential Condominium Building Association Policy

▷ Summarize the provisions of the Flood Coverage Endorsement.

▷ Summarize the provisions of the Earthquake and Volcanic Eruption Coverage Endorsements.

▷ Summarize the provisions typically contained in difference in conditions (DIC) policies and DIC-type endorsements, as well as the advantages and disadvantages of DIC coverage.

▷ Describe the loss exposures insured by the following:

- Output policies
- Insurance for highly protected risks (HPRs)
- Layered property insurance programs

▷ Given a case, recommend the commercial property specialty form(s) and endorsement(s) that will provide the appropriate insurance coverage for a described organization.

Flood, Earthquake, and Specialty Forms

6

NATIONAL FLOOD INSURANCE PROGRAM

The United States Congress acknowledged insurers' inability to offer flood coverage at a price that consumers were willing to pay by creating the National Flood Insurance Program (NFIP).

The Mitigation Directorate of the Federal Emergency Management Agency (FEMA) administers the NFIP. Policies may be obtained directly through FEMA, or through an insurer that participates in the NFIP **"Write Your Own"** program (WYO). Rates, which the NFIP establishes, do not vary among insurers. Under the WYO program, participating insurers issue and service NFIP policies in exchange for a percentage of the premium and a fee for claim adjustment services. WYO insurers write the vast majority of NFIP policies.

The NFIP sets eligibility requirements, coverage limits, and coverages under its General Property Form and the Residential Condominium Building Association Policy.

Write Your Own (WYO)

A program allowing private insurers to write flood insurance under the National Flood Insurance Program (NFIP).

Eligibility

National flood insurance is available to owners of property located in communities that participate in the NFIP. To participate, communities are required to regulate new construction and substantial alterations and improvements of existing structures by adopting and enforcing community floodplain management ordinances.

The NFIP classifies areas with a high risk of flooding as special flood hazard areas (SFHAs), or areas that are determined to have a 1 percent or greater likelihood of flooding in any given year. Federal regulations mandate that federally regulated or insured lenders require flood insurance on properties located in these high-risk areas. Flood Insurance Rate Maps (FIRMs) show boundaries of SFHAs, the various flood zones, and base flood elevations (BFEs). A BFE is the computed elevation to which floodwater is anticipated to rise during the base flood and is shown on both FIRMs and flood profiles. The BFE is the regulatory requirement for the elevation or floodproofing of structures, and the relationship between the BFE and a structure's elevation determines the flood insurance premium. The zone in which a property is located determines flood insurance rates.

Regular program

Second phase of the National Flood Insurance Program in which the community agrees to adopt flood-control and land-use restrictions and in which property owners purchase higher amounts of flood insurance than under the emergency program.

Emergency program

Initial phase of a community's participation in the National Flood Insurance Program in which property owners in flood areas can purchase limited amounts of insurance at subsidized rates.

The NFIP consists of an **emergency program** and a **regular program**. A community that becomes eligible for NFIP participation is placed in the emergency program until the required floodplain management plan and necessary FIRMs are developed. Coverage in the emergency program is offered at subsidized rates. However, maximum limits of insurance are much higher in the regular program.

Maximum Amounts of Insurance Available

In the regular program, the maximum amount of insurance available for nonresidential properties is $500,000 for building coverage and $500,000 for personal property. In the emergency program, the maximum amounts are $100,000 on buildings ($150,000 in Alaska, Hawaii, Guam, and the U.S. Virgin Islands) and $100,000 on contents. Maximum limits apply per building.

To illustrate, in the regular program, an insured with five separate buildings at one location could purchase up to $500,000 in building coverage and up to $500,000 in contents coverage for each building, totaling $5 million of insurance. At the time of loss, however, any unused coverage from one insured building cannot be used to increase limits available to another building.

Residential condominium associations can purchase building coverage up to $250,000, times the number of units in the building. However, contents coverage is limited to a maximum of $100,000 per building. (Homeowners can purchase up to $250,000 per single family dwelling and up to $100,000 in contents coverage under the Dwelling Policy Form. Renters also may purchase flood coverage for contents up to a maximum of $100,000).

General Property Form

The version of the National Flood Insurance Program (NFIP) Standard Flood Insurance Policy that is used for insuring commercial buildings and contents.

Residential Condominium Building Association Policy (RCBAP)

A version of the National Flood Insurance Program (NFIP) Standard Insurance Policy that is used for insuring residential condominium buildings, as well as contents that are owned either by the unit owners in common or by the condominium association solely.

NFIP General Property Form and Residential Condominium Building Association Policy

An NFIP Standard Insurance Policy comes in two forms:

- **General Property Form**
- **Residential Condominium Building Association Policy (RCBAP)**

The General Property Form is used to insure most commercial building and contents risks, such as factories, retail businesses, warehouses, or residential condominium buildings that are not eligible for coverage under the RCBAP.

The General Property Form

The General Property Form covers direct physical loss caused by flood, as defined in the policy, at the premises described on the declarations form.

Flood, as used in the flood insurance policy, means:

1. A general and temporary condition of partial or complete inundation of two or more acres of normally dry land area or of two or more properties (at least one of which is your property) from:

a. Overflow of inland or tidal waters;

b. Unusual and rapid accumulation or runoff of surface waters from any source;

c. Mudflow.

2. Collapse or subsidence of land along the shore of a lake or similar body of water as a result of erosion or undermining caused by waves or currents of water exceeding anticipated cyclical levels that result in a flood as defined in [A.]1.a. above.

Mudflow, used in the definition of flood, is defined as follows:

A river of liquid and flowing mud on the surfaces of normally dry land areas, as when earth is carried by a current of water. Other earth movements, such as landslide, slope failure, or a saturated soil mass moving by liquidity down a slope are not mudflows.[1]

The NFIP General Property Form and standard commercial property coverage forms have some key differences:

- The NFIP General Property Form covers building and contents on an actual cash value (ACV) basis with no option for replacement cost. The NFIP does offer a replacement cost option on residential risks.

- The NFIP General Property Form does not include a **coinsurance** provision.

- The NFIP General Property Form cannot be written on a blanket basis. All buildings must be separately described and insured.

- The NFIP General Property Form excludes loss of use and loss of income. These optional coverages are not available from the NFIP.

- The NFIP General Property Form excludes several types of property, such as property located in, on, or around water; underground structures; and buildings and contents if more than 49 percent of the ACV of the building is below ground, unless the lowest level is above the base flood elevation. The policy also excludes coverage for contents in a basement, with the exception of building service equipment.

Coinsurance
An insurance-to-value provision in many property insurance policies providing that if the property is underinsured, the amount that an insurer will pay for a covered loss is reduced.

The Property Covered section of the policy contains these coverages:

- Coverage A—Building Property
- Coverage B—Personal Property
- Coverage C—Other Coverages
- Coverage D—Increased Cost of Compliance

Coverage A—Building Property provides coverage for building property that is generally more restrictive than coverage offered under a standard commercial property form. The General Property Form also includes a more restrictive definition of a covered building. Under the NFIP policy, a covered building must include two or more outside rigid walls and a secured roof. Under this definition, some buildings that could be insured under the standard commercial property form would not be eligible for coverage under the NFIP General Property Form, such as open-sided parking garages.

In addition to the described building, Coverage A includes coverage for these types of property:

- Additions and extensions attached to the covered building by a rigid exterior wall, a solid load-bearing interior wall, a stairway, an elevated walkway, or a roof
- Specifically listed fixtures, machinery, and equipment
- Materials and supplies to be used for construction, alteration, or repair at the described location (however, these items are only covered if stored in a fully enclosed building)
- A building under construction, alteration, or repair (however, the policy includes significant limitations for buildings not yet walled or roofed)

Coverage B—Personal Property covers either household personal property or other than household personal property, but not both. The "household personal property" category covers "property usual to a living quarters" that belongs to the insured, a member of the household, a domestic worker, or a guest. The second category, "other than household personal property," would be appropriate for most commercial property owners and includes coverage for these items:

- Furniture and fixtures
- Machinery and equipment
- Stock (including merchandise, raw materials, and in-process or finished goods)
- Other personal property owned by the insured and used in the insured's business

Unlike the standard commercial property form, the NFIP General Property Form does not include coverage for property owned by others. Additionally, unlike the standard form, when a General Property Form covers both property and contents, items that may fall under either category (for example, building service equipment, such as stoves and refrigerators) must be insured under the building coverage. The insured would usually have a choice of where to insure such items under the standard form.

The NFIP applies the deductible separately to building and contents coverages even if both are damaged by the same flood loss.

Coverage C—Other Coverages includes three insuring agreements:

- Debris Removal
- Loss Avoidance Measures
- Pollution Damage

The Debris Removal coverage under the General Property Form is significantly different in two ways from the debris removal coverage found under the standard commercial property form:

- The General Property Form includes coverage for removal of debris of other property, not just debris from covered property. This difference recognizes that floodwaters commonly include floating debris.

- The General Property Form does not include the traditional 25 percent sublimit (limiting debris removal coverage to no more than 25 percent of the policy's limits); nor does it include the $10,000 additional coverage provided under the standard commercial property policy. Therefore, under the flood policy, the insured may use the entire policy limit toward debris removal if needed.

Coverage for loss avoidance measures pays for measures to protect property from imminent flood damage, allowing reasonable expenses, up to $1,000, for the cost of sandbags or other supplies to protect the property. The coverage also provides for a separate $1,000 limit applicable towards the cost of moving property to a safer location when flooding is imminent.

Pollution damage coverage pays up to $10,000 for damage to the covered property caused by the discharge, seepage, migration, release, or escape of pollutants because of flood. This coverage does not cover the costs of testing or monitoring pollutants unless required by law.

None of the coverages under Coverage C is subject to a deductible. Nor do these coverages increase the Coverage A or Coverage B limits of liability.

Coverage D— **Increased Cost of Compliance (ICC)** differs from building and ordinance coverage that may be added to standard commercial property policies in that it pays only for compliance costs related to floodplain management. The ICC coverage pays up to $30,000 for activities necessary to comply with state or local floodplain management laws or ordinances that meet NFIP minimum standards. Such activities might include elevation, flood proofing, relocation, or demolition. Coverage D is available only in policies with building Coverage A building coverage. The $30,000 limit is an additional amount of insurance and may increase the amount of coverage. However, the total payment may not exceed the maximum limit allowed under the NFIP (currently $500,000).

For example, ignoring any deductible, if a qualifying insured has a $300,000 Coverage A policy limit and incurs $330,000 worth of building damage and $20,000 in ICC costs, the policy will pay only $320,000. If the insured has a $500,000 policy limit and incurs $500,000 in building damage and $40,000 in ICC expenses, the policy will pay no more than $500,000, the maximum commercial property limit available under the NFIP.

ICC coverage is available only for a building defined as a "repetitive loss structure," meaning a building that meets specific damage that lowers its market value, is covered by the NFIP, has suffered flood damage on at least

Increased Cost of Compliance (ICC)
National Flood Insurance coverage that pays for compliance costs related to floodplain management for qualifying structures.

two occasions within ten years, and is subject to state or community repetitive loss management provisions.

Residential Condominium Building Association Policy

The NFIP's Residential Condominium Building Association Policy (RCBAP), commonly called "REBAP," insures residential condominium associations as well as contents owned by the unit owners in common or by the condominium association. A residential building has at least 75 percent of its floor area occupied for residential purposes. Non-residential condominiums can be insured under the General Property Form.

Coverage under the REBAP is similar to that found in the General Property Form. However, the REBAP differs in three distinct ways:

- A higher limit of insurance may be purchased. The maximum limit of coverage under the REBAP is $250,000 times the number of units. For example, purchasing the maximum building limit, a high-risk condominium building with thirty units could be insured for up to $7,500,000. Because higher limits are available, condominium associations rarely need to seek additional building coverage beyond the NFIP policy. However, the maximum limit on contents is $100,000. Unit owners would be expected to insure their contents under separate policies.

- The NFIP offers replacement cost coverage on building property insured under a REBAP.

- The REBAP includes an 80 percent coinsurance requirement on building property coverage. The building must be insured to at least 80 percent of the building's replacement cost or the maximum amount of insurance available, whichever is less, to avoid a loss payment penalty.

FLOOD COVERAGE ENDORSEMENT

One of the side effects of NFIP flood mapping is the increased availability of commercial flood insurance. Underwriters are better able to assess the flooding hazards of the properties they insure with the result that flood insurance for commercial property located outside of Special Flood Hazard Zones is widely available.

To facilitate writing this coverage, ISO's commercial property program includes a Flood Coverage Endorsement (CP 10 65) for use with the ISO commercial property program. Some insurers offer independently developed flood endorsements.

The ISO endorsement uses essentially the same definition of flood as used in the NFIP flood policies, but the endorsement does not follow the other terms and conditions of the NFIP policies. The ISO Flood Coverage Endorsement is subject to certain provisions and limitations including: limits of insurance, the other insurance condition, exclusions and limitations, property not covered, additional coverage extensions, and coinsurance.

The ISO Flood Coverage Endorsement is part of the commercial property policy to which it is attached and follows that policy's terms and conditions, except when the endorsement states otherwise.

The Flood Coverage Endorsement and NFIP coverage differ in these ways:

- NFIP policies limit the types of structures that can be insured against flood damage, whereas the ISO endorsement can provide coverage for a greater variety of property.
- NFIP policies provide no business income coverage and only very limited extra expense and ordinance or law coverage. The Flood Coverage Endorsement can be attached to a commercial property coverage part providing the full range of commercial property coverages.
- NFIP policies are written primarily on an ACV basis, whereas the ISO endorsement can be written subject to the replacement cost or functional valuation options available under commercial property forms.

Limits of Insurance

One of the most important differences between the flood endorsement and the other coverages in the commercial property coverage part is that the flood endorsement is often subject to a separate limit of insurance that may be substantially lower than the regular policy limit(s).

Because reinsurance for flood losses can be both scarce and expensive, many insurers are willing to provide only $1 million or $2 million of flood insurance. To accommodate those insureds that want higher limits, insurers can purchase facultative reinsurance.

If the insurer is unwilling to provide the higher limits, the insured can obtain higher layers of flood coverage in excess property or difference in conditions (DIC) policies.

Occurrence and Aggregate Limit

The limit shown for flood is the most the insurer will pay in a single occurrence. Additionally, an annual aggregate limit normally applies. The aggregate limit is the most the insurer will pay for all floods within a twelve-month period starting with the beginning of the policy's present annual period. Unless a higher limit is specified, the aggregate limit is equal to the flood occurrence limit.

If a single occurrence of a flood begins during one annual policy period and ends during the following annual policy period, any limit of insurance applicable to the second policy will not be available to cover the loss.

Ensuing Loss

Some losses may raise the question of whether the limits for each coverage are cumulative and can be "stacked." For example, when a flood causes a fire and both perils damage the property, the insured might argue that the flood damage is covered up to the flood limit and the fire damage is covered up to the fire limit, posing the possibility of collecting the sum of the flood limit and the fire limit.

To avoid this interpretation, the endorsement states that, in the event of an ensuing covered loss (such as an explosion or a fire resulting from a flood), the most that the insurer will pay is the limit applicable to fire. The insurer will not pay the sum of the fire and flood limits. In addition, if the damage from the flood is more than the limit of insurance applicable to flood, the payment for the flood loss will be limited to the amount of flood insurance.

Deductible

Knowing the flood zone in which the property is located, as determined from the applicable flood insurance rate map, assists the underwriter in setting the deductible. For properties not located in special hazard zones, insurers sometimes provide flood coverage with a deductible as low as $10,000 or $25,000.

For properties located in special hazard zones, flood coverage, if available, has a higher deductible. The deductible for properties in a special hazard zone could be $100,000 or more; the current trend is to require that the insured carry the maximum available NFIP insurance as primary coverage. From an insured's viewpoint, a fixed deductible is the better choice.

The deductible applicable to the Flood Coverage Endorsement is shown in the policy declarations or the Flood Coverage Schedule. If a flood results in a covered ensuing loss (such as damage by fire or explosion), only the higher deductible (generally, it will be the flood deductible) will apply.

If the flood endorsement applies excess of NFIP coverage, the insurer will not pay any part of the loss attributable to the NFIP policy deductible.

Other Insurance

The flood endorsement provides that coverage under the endorsement is excess over the maximum NFIP limits available whether or not the insured actually has an NFIP policy, unless the insurer waives that requirement. If the NFIP requirement has not been waived, the insurer will pay only that portion of the loss exceeding the maximum amount that could be insured under an NFIP policy, whether collectible or not.

The requirement for NFIP coverage is often waived for property located outside a special hazard zone. For property located within a special hazard zone, the insurer will generally require that the insured carry the maximum available NFIP limits, if it is willing to provide coverage at all. An insured's loss history will be a significant factor.

Any waiver of underlying NFIP coverage is indicated in the Flood Coverage Schedule (CP DS 65). When a waiver applies only to some of the insured's locations, these locations must be specified in the Flood Coverage Schedule.

Like the NFIP Other Insurance condition, the Other Insurance condition in the flood endorsement is important because many insureds have flood coverage under two or more policies.

The Other Insurance condition in the flood endorsement has these effects:

- The endorsement coverage will contribute proportionately with insurance other than NFIP coverage. More specifically, the insurer will pay that proportion of the loss that the insurer's limit bears to the total limits of all applicable flood insurance. If, for example, an insured has a $1 million limit under the flood endorsement from Insurer A plus an additional $2 million of non- NFIP flood insurance from Insurer B, Insurer A will pay one-third of any loss ($1 million/$3 million), up to Insurer A's flood limit.
- The endorsement's coverage is excess over the maximum limit that could have been insured under an NFIP policy.

Because the coverage in an NFIP policy does not apply to many of the items covered by a CPP, the resulting loss apportionment when both NFIP and commercial flood insurance are in force can be complex. See the exhibit "Apportionment of Flood Loss."

Apportionment of Flood Loss

In both examples, the named insured is the owner of an office building that is rented to multiple tenants.

EXAMPLE 1

Coverages Applicable

- NFIP General Property Form—$500,000 limit (the maximum NFIP amount available).
- ISO Commercial Package Policy that includes these:
  - Building and Personal Property Coverage Form—$5 million building limit (replacement cost)
  - Flood Coverage Endorsement—$1 million limit with $25,000 deductible

Flood Loss

- Building damage—$800,000 on a replacement cost basis ($650,000 on an ACV basis).

Claim Settlements

- NFIP policy pays $500,000.
- ISO flood endorsement pays $275,000 (excess of maximum available from NFIP, less deductible).

EXAMPLE 2

Same facts as Example 1 except that NFIP policy limit was only $100,000.

Claim Settlements

- NFIP policy pays $100,000.
- ISO flood endorsement pays $275,000 (excess of maximum available from NFIP, less deductible).

[DA03564]

Exclusions and Limitations

The Flood Coverage Endorsement is subject to all of the exclusions and limitations found in the causes of loss form attached to the policy, subject to these exceptions:

- Any part of the Water exclusion in the causes of loss form that conflicts with the Flood Coverage Endorsement does not apply to the endorsement.
- The Flood Coverage Endorsement covers loss caused by a tsunami (a huge wave caused by an underwater earthquake or volcanic eruption) if it causes the overflow of tidal waters. Earthquake coverage usually excludes damage from a tsunami.

- The Flood Coverage Endorsement does not cover damage to property in the open unless specified in the flood schedule or declarations.

- The Ordinance or Law exclusion applies unless ordinance or law coverage is added by endorsement—either the Ordinance or Law Coverage endorsement (CP 04 05) or a special endorsement that the insurer has developed.

- The Flood Coverage Endorsement does not cover flood damage unless the flood begins more than seventy-two hours after the inception of the endorsement. If the coverage is increased after the inception date, the increase will also not be effective for floods that begin within the first seventy-two hours after the request was made. Additional policy wording clarifies that these provisions do not apply to renewal policies.

- The endorsement does not cover loss caused by the destabilization of land resulting from the accumulation of water in subsurface land areas.

An important point is that the flood endorsement does not cover all of the causes of loss excluded by the Water exclusion found in the commercial property causes of loss forms. The Water exclusion is often referred to as a flood exclusion, but it excludes more than flood, surface water, and mudslide.

For example, the Water exclusion specifically excludes loss caused by water and waterborne material discharged from a sewer, drain, or sump. The Flood Coverage Endorsement excludes the same type of loss unless the discharge results from flood and occurs within seventy-two hours after the flood recedes.

Similarly, the Water exclusion specifically excludes loss caused by underground water that presses on or seeps through foundations, walls, floors, or other structural components. The Flood Coverage Endorsement does not cover loss caused by underground water unless it is associated with a flood.

Property Not Covered

The Property Not Covered section of the Flood Coverage Endorsement differs in several ways from the Property Not Covered section of the BPP (or other commercial property coverage form). Some of the items excluded by NFIP policies are added to the Property Not Covered list for the ISO flood coverage.

However, some types of property that are not covered by either the BPP or an NFIP policy are covered under the ISO flood endorsement because they are not listed under Property Not Covered.

The flood endorsement does not cover these items:

- Property in the open unless specifically listed in the flood coverage schedule or declarations

- Property not eligible for flood insurance pursuant to the Coastal Barrier Resource Act or the Coastal Barrier Improvement Act

- Boat houses and open structures if located on or over a body of water
- Bulkheads, pilings, piers, wharves, docks or retaining walls even if they have been removed from the property not covered list for other causes of loss

The flood endorsement does not exclude (and therefore covers) these items:

- Foundations below the lowest basement floor
- Underground pipes, flues, and drains

Foundations and underground pipes, flues, and drains are covered property under the flood endorsement even if they are not covered for any other perils under the rest of the policy.

Additional Coverages and Coverage Extensions

Of the various additional coverages and coverage extensions in standard commercial property coverage forms, only the debris removal and newly acquired property provisions are modified by the flood endorsement.

All other additional coverages and coverage extensions provided by the commercial property coverage forms attached to the policy apply to the flood endorsement except that the amounts payable under the additional coverages or coverage extensions do not increase the limit of insurance for flood insurance.

This limitation is deemed necessary because the same flood can damage a widespread area, and insurers wish to avoid the pyramiding of limits.

Debris Removal

The flood endorsement covers the insured's expense to remove debris of covered property and other debris resulting from a flood.

The coverage extends to the cost of removing debris from the premises (including both the building and the grounds), not just from covered property as is the case with NFIP policies.

However, the cost of removing deposits of earth or mud from the grounds is not covered. By implication, the cost of removing mud from within the building is covered.

Thus, if trees were uprooted by flooding and deposited on the parking lot at the insured's premises, the flood endorsement would pay the cost to remove them; the cost to remove earth and mud from the parking lot would not be covered.

An NFIP policy would not cover either expense. The flood endorsement also specifically covers the expense to remove debris of covered property that has floated or been hurled off the described premises.

The most that the insurer will pay for debris removal and damage to covered property is the limit for flood insurance that applies to the affected described property.

Newly Acquired or Constructed Property

The flood endorsement limits the coverage extension for newly acquired or constructed property in two respects:

- With regard to flood coverage, the extension does not apply to any building or structure that is not fully enclosed by walls or roof. (A newly acquired structure without walls or roof—such as a building under construction or an open-sided parking structure—could be covered by specifically describing it in the declarations.)

- The limit of insurance for newly acquired or constructed property is changed to 10 percent of the total of all limits of insurance for flood coverage provided by the endorsement, but this additional coverage does not increase the total limit for flood insurance.

Coinsurance

Coinsurance may apply to the flood endorsement in the same manner as specified in the coverage form attached to the policy. Alternatively, coinsurance may be eliminated from the endorsement by electing the no-coinsurance option.

No coinsurance is the more likely choice because the limit for flood insurance is usually lower than the limit applying to other perils. Because coverage extensions in the commercial property coverage forms ordinarily are applicable only when a coinsurance percentage is specified, the flood endorsement eliminates that requirement if the no-coinsurance option is in effect.

EARTHQUAKE AND VOLCANIC ERUPTION ENDORSEMENTS

Earthquake insurance can be hard to obtain and is very expensive in areas with a high probability of severe earthquake damage, principally parts of the West Coast states, including Alaska, and the portions of Arkansas, Illinois, Indiana, Kentucky, Mississippi, and Tennessee that are affected by the New Madrid fault. In other areas, earthquake insurance is generally available but is often overlooked.

Common Earthquake Limits

Insurers, almost without exception, purchase reinsurance to protect against the catastrophic loss potential of earthquakes and floods.

As is true with flood insurance, most insurers can provide low limits of earth-quake coverage, usually from $1 million to $5 million per occurrence. These limits are sufficient to satisfy many insureds for these reasons:

- The insureds are located in areas with low exposure to earthquake and they expect only partial damage
- The insureds underestimate their exposure to earthquake loss
- The insureds are unwilling or unable to purchase higher limits

Two ISO endorsements are available for adding earthquake and volcanic erup-tion as covered perils under a commercial property coverage part:

- CP 10 40, Earthquake and Volcanic Eruption Endorsement
- CP 10 45, Earthquake and Volcanic Eruption Endorsement (Sub-Limit Form)

Both endorsements extend commercial property coverage to include earth-quake and volcanic eruption ("eruption, explosion or effusion of a volcano") as covered causes of loss. Neither form defines the word "earthquake."

However, to clarify the application of the per-occurrence limit and deductible, both forms state that all earthquake shocks or volcanic eruptions occurring within a 168-hour (seven-day) period will be considered a single earthquake or volcanic eruption. Because of this provision, for insurance purposes most aftershocks will be considered part of the original event.

The principal difference between the two endorsements is that CP 10 40, unlike CP 10 45, is subject to the same coinsurance requirement that applies to the rest of the policy, and therefore the limit for endorsement CP 10 40 (which applies to earthquake and volcanic eruption losses) must be the same as the policy limit that applies to other covered perils.

In contrast, CP 10 45 is not subject to coinsurance and thus permits earth-quake and volcanic eruption coverage to be written subject to a sublimit that is lower than the policy limit that applies to other covered perils.

When earthquake coverage is provided on the sublimit form, an addi-tional endorsement, CP DS 06 (Earthquake—Volcanic Eruption Coverage Schedule), can be used to schedule specific or blanket limits for all covered locations and to show the applicable deductibles. The information for CP 10 40 is normally entered on the commercial property Declarations page.

In many ways, the endorsements are identical. See the exhibit "Summary of Differences Between CP 10 40 and CP 10 45."

Exclusions

Both ISO earthquake endorsements are subject to the standard exclusions pertaining to ordinance or law, governmental action, nuclear hazard, utility services, and war and military action.

Summary of Differences Between CP 10 40 and CP 10 45

	Earthquake and Volcanic Eruption Endorsement	Earthquake and Volcanic Eruption Endorsement (Sublimit Form)
	CP 10 40	CP 10 45
Format	Deductibles, limits, and options are shown on the Declarations page.	A separate endorsement is used to show deductibles, specific or blanket limits, and options.
Limit on earthquake loss	Must insure for same limit applicable to other covered perils.	May insure for lower limit than regular policy limit.
Annual aggregate limit	No.	Yes. May be equal to one or two times the occurrence limit.
Deductible for property specifically insured	Percentage of the amount of insurance on the affected property.	Percentage of the value of the affected property.
Coinsurance	Coinsurance applies unless suspended by agreed value option.	No coinsurance.
Stacking limitations in the event of covered ensuing loss, such as fire	Not needed. The limit of insurance is the most that will be paid.	Yes. Payment is limited to the highest limit for either covered peril.

[DA03565]

Loss caused by landslide, mine subsidence, tidal wave, tsunami, flood, mudslide, or mudflow, even if attributable to an earthquake or a volcanic eruption, is excluded. (Some water-related losses can be insured under flood coverage.)

The endorsements also exclude loss caused by an earthquake or a volcanic eruption that begins before the inception of the insurance.

Underground Property

Underground foundations, underground pipes, flues, drains, and similar types of property not normally susceptible to damage by fire or other basic causes of loss are excluded from coverage in the BPP to reduce the amount of insurance needed to meet coinsurance requirements.

Those property items are, however, highly susceptible to earthquake damage. Therefore, when purchasing earthquake coverage, the insured should consider using the Additional Covered Property endorsement to cover such items.

Adding the excluded items insures them against damage by any covered peril, not just earthquake. Appropriate adjustments in policy limits should be made to avoid a coinsurance penalty. Some independently developed earthquake coverage forms automatically add coverage for foundations and underground property.

Masonry Veneer

Masonry veneer (such as brick facing on a frame structure) is particularly vulnerable to earthquake. The earthquake endorsements exclude coverage for loss to masonry veneer unless the veneer is limited to 10 percent or less of the exterior wall area.

Masonry veneer coverage can be added by placing the words "including masonry veneer" in the premises description in the declarations and paying an appropriate additional premium.

Deductibles

The ISO earthquake endorsements both contain a percentage deductible (such as 5 or 10 percent) that replaces the dollar deductible in the BPP or other coverage form to which the endorsement is attached.

The endorsements apply their deductibles differently with respect to specific insurance (other than builders' risk) that is not written on a value reporting form. In CP 10 40 (the coinsurance form), the amount of the deductible is a percentage of the limit of insurance applicable to the property that has sustained loss or damage.

In CP 10 45 (the no-coinsurance, sublimit form), the amount of the deductible is a percentage of the value of the property that has sustained loss or damage.

The two loss examples shown here illustrate this difference. In each case, assume that the insured owns a building with an insurable value of $2,500,000.

- If the building is insured against earthquake under CP 10 40 with an 80 percent coinsurance clause, a limit of $2,000,000, and a 5 percent deductible, the amount payable for a $200,000 earthquake loss will be $200,000 minus a $100,000 deductible (calculated as 5 percent of the $2,000,000 limit).
- If the building is insured against earthquake under CP 10 45 with a sublimit of $1,000,000 and no coinsurance requirement, the amount payable

for a $200,000 earthquake loss will be $200,000 minus a $125,000 deductible (calculated as 5 percent of the $2,500,000 building value).

For specific insurance written on a value reporting form or for any insurance written on a blanket basis, both endorsements call for the deductible percentage to be applied to the value of the property that has sustained loss or damage. Both endorsements specify the same methods for determining the value of the property insured on each coverage basis in accordance with value reporting or blanket basis statement of values requirements.

The earthquake deductible is calculated for, and applied separately to, each item insured. For example, a policy with the sublimit earthquake endorsement covers a building valued at $100,000 and business personal property valued at $50,000 and calls for a 10 percent deductible.

If an earthquake damaged both the building and the business personal property, a $10,000 deductible would apply to the building loss, and a $5,000 deductible would apply to the personal property loss. The earthquake deductibles do not apply to earthquake losses covered by the various ISO coverage forms for business income and/or extra expense. See the exhibit "Deductibles in Independently Developed Earthquake Forms."

Deductibles in Independently Developed Earthquake Forms

In addition to using percentage deductibles, independently developed earthquake coverage forms frequently offer a flat dollar deductible for properties in areas with a low probability of earthquake damage. The deductible is usually larger than the regular policy deductible. For example, a $1,000 deductible might apply to all covered causes of loss other than earthquake, and a $25,000 deductible might apply to the earthquake coverage.

The flat dollar deductible on earthquake loss often applies per occurrence rather than per item, and many insureds prefer that approach. For example, an insured may be willing to accept a $25,000 deductible even on a building that is worth only $250,000 (in effect, a 10-percent-of value deductible). The same insured would be very unhappy with even a 1 percent deductible on properties with a total value of $50 million because that could amount to as much as $500,000 in deductibles if all the properties were damaged.

[DA05939]

Aggregate Limit

Another difference between the two ISO earthquake endorsements is that endorsement CP 10 45 (the sublimit endorsement) contains an aggregate limit, whereas endorsement CP 10 40 (the coinsurance form) does not. In the sublimit endorsement, the aggregate limit is equal to the occurrence limit applicable to earthquake and volcanic eruption.

Thus, the occurrence limit shown is the most that will be paid for any one loss and the most that will be paid, in total, for all covered earthquake and volcanic eruption losses during the policy year. The CLM provides an option, for an additional premium, to increase the aggregate limit to twice the occurrence limit.

Ensuing Loss

Earthquakes frequently cause fires, and such fires can be severe. The bulk of the damage from the San Francisco earthquake of 1906 was caused by the fires that ensued.

The ISO causes of loss forms each cover loss by fire or explosion resulting from an earthquake. To prevent stacking of the regular policy limit and the earthquake limit when an earthquake results in fire or another covered cause of loss, endorsement CP 10 45 (sublimit form) contains a provision titled Ensuing Loss.

This provision states that in the event of ensuing loss caused by another peril that is covered by the policy (such as fire), the most that the policy will pay for the entire loss (for example, all loss caused by earthquake and fire) is the limit for the other covered peril (fire, in this case).

The endorsement specifically states that the insurer will not pay the sum of the two limits. Further, the payment for the damage caused by each peril will be limited to the insurance coverage for that peril.

In the case of endorsement CP 10 40 (coinsurance form), no special wording is needed to distinguish between loss caused by earthquake and loss caused by other covered perils.

The policy limit is the most that will be paid for any one occurrence regardless of how many perils are involved.

Earthquake Sprinkler Leakage Coverage Option

Under both of the earthquake endorsements, the insured can elect to restrict coverage to loss due to sprinkler leakage resulting from earthquake or volcanic eruption. Because sprinkler systems are susceptible to earthquake damage, insureds that do not want or cannot obtain full earthquake coverage might elect this less expensive coverage.

When the insured selects the sprinkler leakage only option, the regular earthquake deductible does not apply. Instead, the deductible is the same one that applies to fire losses.

DIFFERENCE IN CONDITIONS

A source of coverage for flood, earthquake, and possibly other loss exposures not covered under regular commercial property policies is a difference in conditions (DIC) policy. Because DIC policies are often written by nonadmitted insurers or as nonfiled inland marine policies, policy provisions and rates are open to negotiation between the insurer and the insured.

Difference in conditions (DIC) policies can serve a variety of needs. They are available to almost any insured and fill in gaps left by the insured's other property insurance. DIC policies are still used for that purpose; however, with the widespread availability of open perils coverage in commercial property policies, the purposes for buying DIC policies have evolved. For example, DIC policies can be used to cover flood and earthquake loss exposures not covered by commercial property policies, to provide excess limits over underlying flood and earthquake coverages, to cover loss exposures not covered in commercial property policies such as property in transit, or to cover property worldwide. Typical DIC policies have certain common policy provisions. Additionally, DIC policies present both advantages and disadvantages to insureds.

> **Difference in conditions (DIC) policy, or DIC insurance**
> Policy that covers on an "all-risks" basis to fill gaps in the insured's commercial property coverage, especially gaps in flood and earthquake coverage.

Property Covered

The property covered by a DIC policy generally is the same property covered by the insured's other policies: buildings and business personal property. DIC policies often exclude many of the same types of property excluded in other property forms, such as accounts, records, bills, deeds, money, and securities.

Other property that can be readily damaged or stolen may also be excluded, such as jewelry, watches, furs, gems, or fine arts. The exclusions that apply to such types of property vary by insurer and depend on the insured's operations and exposures.

The list of property not covered in DIC policies is generally shorter than in standard commercial property policies. For example, DIC policies often do not exclude foundations and underground piping.

Perils Covered

Most DIC policies provide coverage equivalent to the Causes of Loss—Special Form, but with certain basic perils excluded. Because many DIC policies still contain the "all-risks" wording of older commercial property forms, they are still often called "all-risks" policies.

However, an insured that needs a DIC policy only to cover an unusual or a catastrophic loss exposure can obtain a DIC policy that covers on a named peril(s) basis. Often, the perils covered by a DIC policy are broader than those found in standard policies. For example, collapse coverage is often not limited to the causes of loss that apply in the Insurance Services Office, Inc. (ISO) form.

Earthquake and Flood Coverage

One of the main reasons for buying a DIC policy is to obtain either primary or excess coverage for earthquake and flood losses. DIC policies often limit the insurer's exposure to earthquake or flood loss in the same manner as the ISO earthquake and flood endorsements: limiting coverage to $5 million or less per occurrence and applying substantial deductibles, or requiring the maximum amount of NFIP coverage as underlying insurance.

When covering property in high-risk areas, a DIC policy may cover only a stated percentage (as low as 50 percent) of earthquake or flood loss above the deductible.

Earthquake coverage may be provided under an "all-risks" DIC policy simply by omitting any exclusion of earthquake or other earth movement, subject perhaps to an exclusion of earth movement loss to masonry veneer. This approach provides broader coverage than the ISO earthquake endorsements because coverage is not limited to earthquake and volcanic eruption; damage caused by other types of earth movement (such as landslide, or excavation at adjacent premises that undermines a building's foundation) would be covered unless they were specifically excluded.

Earthquake coverage may also be provided under a DIC policy on a named perils basis. The breadth of coverage for earthquake and other types of earth movement will then depend on the policy's definition of the covered peril.

DIC policies differ in the extent of flood or water damage coverage they provide. In some cases, the definition of flood in DIC policies is broader than that found in commercial property flood endorsements or in NFIP policies. In most cases, however, a DIC policy that provides flood coverage in excess of a commercial property endorsement or an NFIP policy will not "drop down" to cover water damage losses encompassed by the DIC policy's definition of flood but not by the definition of flood in the underlying coverage.

Another method of providing broader water damage coverage under an "all-risks" DIC policy is to limit the water exclusion in the DIC policy to flood as defined by the NFIP. When that is done, the policy will cover many types of water damage that are not included in the NFIP definition of flood.

By endorsement, the insurer then provides coverage for flood, as defined by the NFIP, subject to any special flood restrictions, such as lower limits, higher deductibles, or the requirement that the flood coverage is payable in excess of the maximum amount available from the NFIP. This method is preferable, from the insured's point of view, because the other causes of covered water damage are not subject to the lower limit of insurance and higher deductible applicable to flood losses covered by the endorsement.

In contrast, some DIC policies contain a broad exclusion of water damage, similar to the one found in ISO commercial property forms, adding back only coverage for flood as defined by the NFIP. A policy using this approach does not cover such causes of loss as sewer backup and underground water.

Finally, the flood coverage of some DIC policies falls short of even the NFIP definition. The deficiency in these policies is usually the absence of coverage for mudflow. At the insured's request, underwriters will sometimes broaden the water damage coverage in the more restrictive DIC policies.

Exclusion of Basic Perils

Classifying DIC policies as inland marine can, in those states that treat DIC policies as a nonfiled class of business, exempt them from rate- and form-filing requirements, allowing greater flexibility.

An additional benefit to insurers of classifying their DIC policies as inland marine is the avoidance of increased residual market participation in states that have residual property or windstorm plans based on property, but not inland marine, premiums written.

The Nationwide Marine Definition states that a DIC policy, to be considered inland marine, must exclude fire and the perils covered by the Extended Coverage endorsement: windstorm, hail, smoke, explosion, riot, riot attending a strike or civil commotion, aircraft, and vehicles. Insurers often add vandalism and malicious mischief to the list of excluded perils.

Equipment Breakdown Exposures

DIC policies commonly exclude loss caused by steam boiler explosion or mechanical or electrical breakdown. Thus, the DIC exclusion of these exposures should be coordinated with any equipment breakdown (boiler and machinery) coverage the insured has.

Crime Exposures

For some insureds, a principal reason for choosing a DIC policy is to cover significant theft exposures that are not covered under the insured's commercial property policy. For example, if an underwriter believes that the theft exposure for an otherwise acceptable insured is greater than that contemplated by the rate for the Causes of Loss—Special Form, he or she may attach a theft exclusion endorsement eliminating theft coverage from the insured's commercial property coverage.

To fill the gap, the insured can obtain a DIC policy that specifically covers theft or provides open perils coverage without a theft exclusion. The insurer often applies a substantial theft deductible to eliminate smaller losses, and the limit of insurance for theft may be less than the total exposure. In many cases, the insured will accept a lower theft limit because even a severe burglary or theft loss is not likely to involve the insured's entire stock of merchandise.

General Provisions

Some of the distinguishing features of DIC policies are contained in the general provisions.

Coverage Territory

The basic approach of DIC policies is to cover property located within the United States and Canada. When worldwide coverage is needed, many DIC insurers are willing to provide it.

The principal exposure is normally at the insured's premises, but the insured may need, when transit coverage is included, broad territorial limits if the insured is shipping property to or receiving property from foreign countries.

Valuation

Property can be valued in whatever way is mutually agreeable to the insurer and the insured. Different valuation methods may be used in the same policy.

For example, the DIC policy (like the property insurance it complements) may cover buildings and contents for replacement cost. If the DIC also covers property in transit, the DIC may value such property at invoice cost plus freight and other charges. Other valuation provisions might be used to meet particular needs.

Other Insurance

When DIC policies were originally developed, most insureds had only "fire and extended coverage." DIC policies, designed to cover additional perils but not provide additional limits for perils covered by the fire and extended coverage (EC) policy, excluded these perils. Because the DIC policy contained additional exclusions, the result was that some perils were covered by the fire and EC policy, others by the DIC policy, and still others by neither.

The development and widespread use of open perils coverage has added a fourth classification: perils that are covered by both the commercial property policy and the DIC policy. In such cases, the Other Insurance provisions of both policies are important in determining which policy applies and in what amounts.

The Other Insurance clauses of DIC policies typically provide that the DIC policy will be excess over any other insurance. This type of Other Insurance clause handles the cases in which the DIC policy is intended to provide excess insurance, as is often the case with flood and earthquake coverage, as well as those cases in which a commercial property policy duplicates some aspect of coverage also provided by the DIC policy.

Although the Other Insurance clause may be clearly worded in a DIC policy, problems can arise when the commercial property policy contains the same type of Other Insurance clause as the DIC. In such a case, each policy provides that it is excess to the other. The insurers often settle the conflict of provisions through negotiation. In some cases, the commercial property insurer pays the full amount that would be due under its policy if there were no other insurance, takes an assignment of the insured's rights under the DIC policy, and settles the conflict through arbitration.

If the parties cannot settle their differences and the dispute ends up in court, many courts require the insurers to share the loss on a pro rata basis. Some courts recognize the essentially excess nature of the DIC policy and hold that the DIC policy need not pay until the commercial property coverage is exhausted.

Insurance-to-Value Conditions

DIC policies seldom require coinsurance. The amount of coverage provided by a DIC policy is, in many cases, only a portion of the total insurable values exposed to loss. DIC policies are judgment rated, and the underwriter determines the premium on the basis of exposure to loss, after considering the total values exposed. Thus, as long as the underwriter has evaluated the exposure accurately and has charged an appropriate premium, a coinsurance clause is not needed. Keeping the limit low has the advantage of allowing the insurer to reduce the cost and increase the availability of its reinsurance.

If limits were set equal to total insurable value, an insurer's total exposure—and therefore its costs for reinsurance—would increase substantially. The total exposure might even exceed the limits available in the market. To further reduce their maximum possible loss from catastrophic loss exposures, DIC underwriters sometimes impose an annual aggregate limit on flood and earthquake coverage.

Advantages and Disadvantages of DIC Policies

DIC policies are often an alternative to other policies an insured might choose to solve a particular coverage problem. For example, an insured could obtain flood insurance from the NFIP, from the same insurer that is writing the commercial package policy, or from a separate DIC insurer. In choosing among alternatives, the insured should be aware of the possible advantages and disadvantages of DIC policies.

The possible advantages of a DIC policy to the insured include these:

- DIC insurance can be a cost-effective method of obtaining flood and earthquake coverage.
- DIC policies usually do not require coinsurance.

- DIC forms are often easier to modify to meet the insured's particular needs. Because DIC forms are nonfiled in many states, they often are easier to modify to meet the insured's particular needs.
- DIC forms may offer broader coverage for some perils, and some exclusions may be less restrictive.

DIC policies can also present some disadvantages to the insured (and, in some cases, to the insurer):

- The market for DIC policies is limited, and the terms of coverage that insurers are willing to provide can vary over time.
- The insured and the insurer cannot be as certain of how the provisions will be interpreted by courts as when standard provisions are used because the provisions for DIC policies are not standardized.
- Insurance regulators in many states have not evaluated or approved the policy language, because in such states, DIC policies are written as non-filed inland marine or issued by nonadmitted insurers.
- Minimum premium requirements may make the coverage disproportionately expensive for smaller insureds.
- A DIC policy may take more time to negotiate and prepare than a policy made up of standard forms and endorsements.

DIC-Type Endorsements

Although ISO flood and earthquake endorsements are available, some insurers offer to attach DIC-type endorsements to their commercial property policies. These independently developed endorsements serve some of the same purposes as a DIC policy. DIC-type endorsements do not provide open perils coverage; they are named perils forms, typically covering the perils of earthquake, flood, or other specified perils.

However, in many respects, these endorsements are similar to DIC policies. Like a separate DIC policy, the DIC-type endorsements have these characteristics:

- They do not include coinsurance provisions.
- They generally provide coverage for an amount of insurance less than that carried on the property under the insured's regular commercial property policy.
- They are subject to higher deductibles than the commercial property policies to which they are attached.

DIC-type endorsements provide two advantages compared with separate DIC policies:

- The convenience of one policy
- The avoidance of minimum premiums for the DIC coverage

The disadvantage of these endorsements is that the coverage is often not as broad as that of a separate DIC policy. For example, the endorsements sometimes define flood in NFIP terms and provide no coverage for other types of excluded water damage. Moreover, the amount of insurance provided is often less than an insured wants.

SPECIALTY POLICIES

Several specialty property policies meet the needs of large commercial insureds. These policies usually have broader coverage provisions than standard commercial property forms.

Standard commercial property forms may include exclusions or lack the broad coverage needed by some insureds. These policies are available to provide expanded coverage, improved pricing, and/or additional coverage limits:

- Output policies
- Insurance for highly protected risks (HPRs)
- Layered property insurance programs

Output Policies

An output policy combines all or most of the property coverages a commercial organization needs. Although output policies were originally written only for manufacturers, eligibility has been broadened to include most types of commercial insureds. For example, output policies have recently been developed to meet the needs of medium and large agricultural operations, such as farms, ranches, and wineries, and for construction-related operations.

Output policies provide broader property coverage than standard commercial property forms but do not provide liability coverage. Coverage is typically written to cover risks of direct physical loss other than those specifically excluded, with exclusions being similar to standard commercial property forms. These policies are generally judgment rated rather than manual rated, which provides flexibility in pricing. Some insurers use output policies as part of a package policy. Almost all output policies either omit or suspend coinsurance requirements. This is an extremely important coverage feature for typical output policy insureds.

As with other commercial property forms, output policies cover buildings, other structures, and personal property. There are, however, some differences in how these types of property are covered:

- Buildings and other structures
- Personal property at unspecified locations
- Personal property in transit
- Personal property of others

Buildings and Other Structures

Some output policies express their coverage as "business real property" rather than "buildings," thus covering all real property except that which is specifically excluded. Under output policies, coverage often extends to materials and equipment within 1,000 feet of the described premises rather than 100 feet. Other than this coverage enhancement and a few additional items, output building coverage is not much different from that provided by standard commercial property policies.

Personal Property at Unspecified Locations

One important feature of an output policy is that personal property can be covered anywhere within the policy territory without listing the location in the policy. With a few exceptions, standard commercial property policies cover only personal property at listed locations.

This feature is important for insureds that have multiple locations that frequently change during the policy year. Providing personal property coverage at unspecified locations saves the insurer, producer, and the insured the cost of repeatedly endorsing changes of locations. Additionally, the insured does not have to be concerned about overlooking coverage for a new location. Underwriters need to make a careful evaluation of all covered locations and the potential for new locations before providing this coverage. See the exhibit "Example—Personal Property at Unspecified Locations."

Example—Personal Property at Unspecified Locations

XYZ Communications is a midsize computer specialty company. To increase the use of its products, XYZ established training centers across the U.S. Searching for the best mix of locations, the training department opened and closed locations frequently. The finance department was responsible for reporting new locations, as well as those to be deleted, to the insurance broker. Unfortunately, it was often more than thirty days after the location had been set up before the finance department could notify the broker, and the amount of coverage needed exceeded the automatic limit provided by the policy. Furthermore, the underwriter was burdened with the task of preparing the endorsements for adding and deleting locations that, in total, provided very little additional premium. An output policy provided a workable solution. By setting a limit of insurance that was adequate to cover any one location, the policy provided coverage automatically, and the need for a constant flurry of endorsements was eliminated.

[DA03567]

Personal Property in Transit

A common feature of most output policies is broad transit coverage, including personal property on the insured's vehicles and in the custody of the insured's salespeople. This feature eliminates the need for a separate transit policy and provides more comprehensive coverage than that provided by standard commercial property forms. Most output policies, however, do not provide coverage for overseas transit of exports and imports.

Personal Property of Others

Some output policies provide coverage for personal property of others only if the insured has agreed before the loss to insure it for the benefit of the owner or the insured is legally liable for the damage.

To maintain customer goodwill, insureds often prefer to provide complete coverage for customers' goods even when they are not legally responsible for the damage, and an output policy could be endorsed to meet these needs.

Many output policies also cover property for which the insured is responsible under an installation agreement until the buyer accepts the installation. This feature can eliminate the need for purchasing a separate installation floater.

Other Coverage Options

Additional output policy coverage options that are not ordinarily included in standard commercial property policies are these:

- Auto physical damage coverage—This is an option for those insureds with large fleets of automobiles that are at risk of a loss involving several vehicles at one time (for example, a loss caused by fire in a garage where a large fleet of vehicles is stored or by a hurricane that affects a wide geographic area that damages many of the insured's vehicles even though they were not in a single location). Covering auto physical damage under an output policy with a $5,000 or larger deductible eliminates the insurance cost for smaller losses while providing catastrophe protection.

- Equipment breakdown coverage—Equipment breakdown coverage is another option available under the output policy that enables insurers to provide equipment breakdown coverage in a package policy. Although this coverage is often included in standard package policies, output policies provide the coverage differently. Some insurers provide equipment breakdown coverage by eliminating the commercial property exclusions pertaining to equipment breakdown exposures rather than by adding a separate coverage form. This approach creates more seamless coverage, which can avoid potential coverage gaps.

- Flood and earthquake coverage—Most output policies include an option to add flood and earthquake coverage, reducing or eliminating the need for a difference in conditions (DIC) policy. Backup of sewers and drains is also included as part of the flood coverage extension under some output policies.

Output policies can also often be broadened to provide certain coverages not readily available in standard commercial property policies, such as interruption of websites, damaged or destroyed research and development projects, inventory appraisal and expense, and arson reward.

Insurance for Highly Protected Risks

Highly protected risk (HPR)

A large property whose construction meets high standards of risk mitigation and control characteristics and whose management maintains best practices loss control and risk mitigation techniques for the specific occupancy.

Similar to output policies, **highly protected risks (HPRs)** insurance is generally used only for large property accounts. Insurers that offer HPR insurance provide intensive risk control services that would be too expensive for insurers to provide on smaller accounts. In return for the insured's compliance with the HPR standards, the insurer provides property coverage that is broader than that provided by standard commercial property forms. HPR rates are also considerably lower than the usual commercial property rates. Because a large volume of HPR business is needed to amortize the loss control costs, most HPR insurance is written by a few large insurers with substantial property insurance expertise.

Characteristics of HPR Insurance

Although HPR insurance is often associated with complete automatic sprinkler protection, these are the basic attributes needed for HPR insurance:

- An insured whose managers are determined to control property losses
- An insurer that is able to provide the loss prevention engineering needed to implement a complete protection plan for the insured's property

An organization that does not value risk control for reasons other than premium reduction will probably soon conclude that meeting HPR standards is interfering with its business. Similarly, an insurer without the necessary staffing will probably be unable to underwrite HPR accounts profitably.

Additionally, properties insured under HPR insurance generally have these characteristics:

- Fire-resistive, masonry noncombustible, or heavy timber (mill) construction
- Automatic sprinkler systems and other loss prevention equipment
- Adequate water supply and water pressure
- Adequate public or private fire protection

Property Covered

Most HPR policies define covered property as "real property and personal property" rather than as "building and personal property." The HPR wording includes all property except that which is excluded. The standard Insurance Services Office (ISO) commercial property wording encompasses only the property that meets the policy definitions of "building" and "business personal property."

For example, virtually all HPR policies cover foundations; excavations; and underground pipes, flues, and drains. Many HPR policies also cover items such as bridges, roadways, walks, fences, retaining walls, signs, and radio or television antennas and towers. Another common feature of HPR policies is that they extend coverage to property located within 1,000 feet, rather than 100 feet, of the described locations.

Perils Covered

Most HPR policies provide open perils coverage with fewer exclusions than in the Causes of Loss—Special Form, and many HPR policies still contain "all-risks" wording.

HPR policies usually do not limit coverage for collapse to the named-perils approach used in the ISO Broad and Special causes of loss forms. In contrast, most HPR policies cover such collapse even if it occurs after construction, remodeling, or renovation is completed.

HPR policies usually cover backup of water through sewers or drains, as well as seepage. Damage caused by artificially generated electric current or electric arcing is also usually covered. HPR insurers that have the expertise to provide equipment breakdown insurance often build that coverage into the HPR policy.

Supplementary Coverages

HPR policies usually contain an unintentional errors clause, which provides coverage for properties that have been unintentionally omitted or erroneously described in the listing of covered locations. In some cases, this clause even extends to unintentional failure to include newly acquired properties or erroneous cancellation of coverage on existing properties.

HPR policies also frequently provide more debris removal coverage than standard forms. Typically, HPR forms provide up to $5 million for debris removal or 25 percent of the amount of the loss, whichever is greater. In contrast, the ISO Building and Personal Property Coverage Form provides only 25 percent of the amount of the loss plus $10,000.

HPR forms commonly include demolition and increased cost of construction coverage, consequential damage coverage, and broad coverage for newly acquired property. However, HPR forms often do not include some of the coverage extensions found in ISO forms, such as those covering property in transit, valuable papers and records, and pollutant cleanup and removal. The nominal amounts of insurance provided by these ISO coverage extensions would not be appropriate for the loss exposures covered by HPR policies. If such coverages are needed by the HPR insured, they can usually be added by endorsement for the full amounts required.

Amending the ISO Standard Forms

Standard ISO endorsements are available to match some of the coverages provided by typical HPR policies. Examples of such endorsements include these:

- Ordinance or Law Coverage endorsement (called Demolition and Increased Cost of Construction in some HPR policies)
- Debris Removal Increased Limit of Insurance endorsement
- Additional Covered Property endorsement

Some insurers will also add manuscript endorsements to ISO standard forms to include unintentional errors coverage, backup of sewers or drains, and other coverages.

Layered Property Insurance Programs

When an insured wants high limits of liability insurance, they are usually obtained by purchasing one or more umbrella or excess policies above the insured's primary liability policies. Each separate policy, providing $1 million or more of coverage, is commonly referred to as a "layer." Property insurance, as well as liability insurance, can be written in layers. **Layered property coverage** is not as common, but it can sometimes be a valuable tool, and the basic technique is similar to layering liability insurance.

For example, Insurer A might provide the first $1 million, Insurer B the next $10 million excess of $1 million, and Insurer C $25 million excess of $11 million, for a total of $36 million. In the event of a covered loss, Insurer B's **attachment point** would be $1 million; it would not participate unless the loss is likely to exceed $1 million. Insurer C's attachment point would be $11 million; it would not participate unless the loss is likely to exceed $11 million. In this example, there is only one insurer per layer. In practice, particularly for larger risks, several insurers may each write a portion of a given layer. See the exhibit "Example of Layered Property Insurance."

Generally, the first layer is intended to cover frequency losses, and the upper layers are intended to provide catastrophe coverage. Because only larger insureds purchase layered property coverage, deductibles are usually higher than those used in most standard commercial property policies. In fact, the largest accounts often self-insure the first layer and purchase only excess layers. Deductibles are not used in the second and higher levels because deductibles are intended to eliminate the small losses that should fall within the first layer.

Layered property coverage

Two or more property policies arranged in levels of coverage; the policies in the second or higher levels provide coverage only when the loss exceeds the coverage afforded by the lower-level policies.

Attachment point

The dollar amount above which the reinsurer responds to losses.

Example of Layered Property Insurance

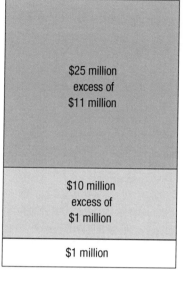

$25 million
excess of
$11 million

Insurer C pays up to $25 million for losses that exceed the $11 million attachment point.

$10 million
excess of
$1 million

Insurer B pays up to $10 million for losses that exceed the $1 million attachment point.

$1 million

Insurer A pays losses up to $1 million.

The insured in this example has a total of $36 million in property coverage provided by Insurers A, B, and C.

[DA03569]

Advantages of Layered Property Insurance

There are four main advantages of layered property insurance:

- Obtaining adequate and flexible limits—Because layered policies do not contain a coinsurance clause, insureds have more flexibility in setting limits for layered policies than they do for standard property policies.

- Pricing considerations—The premium for the primary layer is higher than the premium for a similar amount of insurance written on a coinsurance basis because the primary layer will pay small losses in full (less the deductible) with no participation from the excess insurers. However, for most insureds, the cost for the excess layers should be low because losses seldom penetrate the upper layers. The combined premium of layered policies is often lower than the premium that an insurer would charge for a single policy subject to standard coinsurance rules because the insured may not need to purchase insurance to value.

- Availability of broader coverages—An insured can obtain coverage for perils such as flood and earthquake much more easily in a layered property program than in a standard policy, often eliminating the need for a DIC policy.

- Accessing additional markets—While relatively few insurers are willing to write all of a large property risk for their own account, many insurers are willing to participate in a layered insurance program.

☑ Reality Check

Layered Property Insurance

Joe, a producer for a large broker, is working with a new client on a large account. This client owns and operates ten large shopping malls in several states and has requested quotes for commercial property coverage. This account presents a significant opportunity for Joe's firm and could result in additional business when the general liability and other coverages come up for renewal later in the year. The total property exposure for the client's real property, personal property, and business income is $950 million. The largest total property exposure at any one location is $110 million. The geographic dispersion of the mall locations is such that no two malls are exposed to any one loss.

Joe, however, has concerns about being able to place the coverage due to current hard market conditions and a lack of market capacity, particularly for property coverage. Most of his major property insurers have restricted the amount of coverage they will provide for any one account. After negotiating with the underwriters at these insurers, Joe is able to develop a layered property insurance program and is successful in writing the account for this client.

This program provides $150 million in layered coverage, rather than in a single standard property policy, with a limit of $760 million or more that would be required with a minimum 80 percent coinsurance clause. There are five insurers involved in the program, with the first layer written at $5 million with a $25,000 deductible. Subsequent layers provide the remainder of the $150 million of coverage.

[DA05980]

Disadvantages of Layered Property Insurance

While there are advantages to layered property insurance, the insured should also consider these potential disadvantages:

- Conflicts in wording and interpretation among the various layers can result in coverage disputes among claim representatives responsible for different layers. In one case, the first layer applied to both business income and direct damage, whereas the upper layers covered only direct damage.

When a loss occurred involving both direct damage and business income, a dispute arose about the attachment points for the upper layers.

- If an insurer is unwilling or unable to participate in layered property coverage, it might also be unwilling to provide other coverages (such as general liability or auto liability insurance) that the insured needs. An organization with a layered property program might therefore have difficulty in finding insurers willing to cover its liability exposures that would otherwise be acceptable as part of a package policy.

- Just as the market for layered property coverage can sometimes be extremely competitive, it can also shrink rapidly, making it very difficult and expensive for an insured to place all the desired layers of coverage.

- Minimum premium requirements for each layer may make the cost of layered coverage higher than the cost of a standard policy.

COMMERCIAL PROPERTY SPECIALTY FORMS AND ENDORSEMENTS—CASE STUDY

Standard commercial property forms cover the insurance needs of most customers. There are, however, customers that have unique coverage needs such as flood or earthquake insurance. Commercial property specialty forms are available to meet such coverage needs.

When a commercial property customer needs flood coverage, these specialty forms may be used:

- National Flood Insurance Program (NFIP) coverage
- ISO Flood Coverage endorsement
- Difference in Conditions (DIC) policy coverage
- Output policy

Each form or policy provides different coverage features that must be examined to determine which will best fit the customer's needs.

Case Facts

Jerry and Jeffrey started a business ten years ago designing and assembling computer components for major technology companies. This business was started shortly after they both graduated from college and has grown from 5 employees to almost 200. Because of this growth, the company is moving most of its operations from a suburban office/industrial park location to a new location in the nearest town. It will retain some office space at the original location (Location 1) for billing and other administrative operations with a replacement cost value of $500,000 for personal property.

There are two buildings at the new location (Location 2): a newly renovated three-story former factory building with a replacement cost of $3 million and a one-story storage building with a replacement cost of $750,000. The replacement cost for personal property at Location 2 is $1.5 million for personal property located in the main building and $500,000 for personal property located in the storage building.

These buildings are located in a riverfront area that has recently undergone a lot of redevelopment. Many of the buildings in this area were vacant factories and warehouses, which were once used for the town's booming steel industry. As the steel companies relocated overseas or to other parts of the country or went out of business, the area declined, and most of the buildings were abandoned. Because of the efforts of local and state governments and other organizations, a large amount of reinvestment has occurred in this area, and new businesses have been moving in over the past five years. Most of the older buildings have either been razed and rebuilt or substantially renovated.

Jerry and Jeffrey meet with their insurance agent to develop an insurance program for the new location. Most of the commercial property coverage the company currently carries can be easily revised to cover the new location. One change is the addition of building coverage, as the company had leased its former location and did not require building coverage. The insurance agent has also identified a major new exposure at the new location. Because the new building is located in a riverfront area and is situated a few hundred feet from the water, there is a need for flood coverage. Flood coverage is also required by the bank that holds the mortgage on the property.

What coverage options are available for this flood exposure? Is flood coverage readily available or is it difficult to find? How much additional premium will be charged for this coverage? The insurance agent will be able to answer these questions and provide flood coverage options for the new location.

Case Analysis Tools and Information

To develop coverage options for Jerry and Jeffrey's company, the agent will research the market to determine the availability of flood insurance. Because the agent is local and has several insureds in the same area, he is familiar with how flood insurance can be provided. Different methods exist that vary based on the size and scope of the customer's operations, the customer's coverage needs, and the premium levels that best fit the customer's financial needs.

Case Analysis Steps

After his meeting with Jerry and Jeffrey, the agent puts together a coverage proposal and contacts several of his insurers for quotations. For the flood exposure, the agent develops these options:

- National Flood Insurance Program (NFIP) coverage
- ISO Flood Coverage endorsement

- Difference in Conditions coverage
- Output policy

National Flood Insurance Program

One option for providing flood insurance is the NFIP, which the agent can obtain directly from the Federal Emergency Management Agency (FEMA) or through an insurer participating in the Write Your Own (WYO) program.

The town in which the business is located participates in the NFIP's regular program. The General Property Form, for which factories and warehouses qualify, would be used to cover Jerry and Jeffrey's building and contents.

The maximum amount of insurance available under this program is $500,000 for the building and $500,000 for personal property. Deductibles apply separately to building and to contents, even if both are damaged by the same flood loss.

When reviewing the available options, the agent must consider the differences between the General Property Form and standard commercial property forms. As part of his proposal to Jerry and Jeffrey, he will need to explain these key differences:

- The NFIP General Property Form covers building and contents on an actual cash value (ACV) basis with no option for replacement cost.
- The NFIP General Property Form does not include a coinsurance provision.
- The NFIP General Property Form cannot be written on a blanket basis; all buildings must be separately described and insured.
- Loss of use and loss of income are excluded under the NFIP General Property Form. These optional coverages are not available from the NFIP.
- The NFIP General Property Form excludes several types of property including property located in, on, or around water; underground structures; and buildings and contents if more than 49 percent of the actual cash value of the building is below ground, unless the lowest level is above the base flood elevation. The policy also excludes coverage for contents in a basement, with the exception of building service equipment.

ISO Flood Coverage Endorsement

Another option for providing flood coverage is to add ISO's Flood Coverage endorsement (CP 10 65) to the existing standard commercial property form covering this business. Unlike with the NFIP's General Property Form, a coinsurance percentage would apply, replacement cost coverage may be available, and loss of use and loss of income coverages could be provided. Also with this option, Jerry and Jeffrey could write both locations and all buildings and contents on a blanket basis.

Generally, insurers offer a sublimit for flood rather than providing the entire value of the building or contents. When sublimits are used, the insured usually chooses a no-coinsurance option. In addition, larger deductibles would apply for flood coverage than for other causes of loss included under the standard property forms.

The flood coverage limit is the most an insurer will pay in a single occurrence, and an annual aggregate limit usually applies. This aggregate limit is the most an insurer will pay for all floods within any twelve-month period.

The flood endorsement also excludes some items, such as property in the open unless specifically listed, open structures located over a body of water, and wharves or piers, among others. The agent is not concerned with this provision, as the location currently does not include any property of this type. He will review these provisions with Jerry and Jeffrey in the event that any changes are made to the location in the future.

Difference in Conditions Coverage

Another option to cover the flood exposure is a DIC policy or a DIC endorsement to the standard property policy, if available. DIC coverage can be a cost-effective method of obtaining flood coverage.

Because DIC forms are usually nonfiled and vary from one insurer to another, the agent will have to review the forms carefully to determine what coverage is being provided. This feature of the DIC form does allow the agent to negotiate coverage modifications to meet Jerry and Jeffrey's needs. Some DIC forms provide broad flood coverage, while others are more restrictive. DIC coverage can be written to provide sublimits for flood coverage or can be written in excess of an NFIP General Property Policy or a commercial property endorsement. When coverage is written in excess of other policies, however, the coverage will usually not "drop down" to cover water damage losses covered under the DIC policy's definition of flood but not covered within the definition of flood in the underlying policy.

DIC coverage can be written on a replacement cost basis and generally does not require coinsurance. The other insurance provision usually states that DIC coverage is provided in excess of other insurance.

Output Policy

One final option available to provide flood coverage is to replace the existing standard property coverage with an output policy. Because Jerry and Jeffrey currently carry a commercial package policy, the agent would have to provide a separate policy for all non-property coverages, such as general liability. Coverage for the building would be similar to that provided under the standard property forms. Personal property coverage includes personal property at unspecified locations, personal property in transit, and personal property of others.

The output policy also includes an option to add flood coverage. As with the other options, flood coverage is usually written for lower coverage limits than those provided for other perils, and the flood limit is typically subject to an annual aggregate.

Additional coverage options are also available in the output policy. Two of these may be relevant to Jerry and Jeffery's business:

- Interruption of Web sites, covering losses that result when a server away from an insured location is damaged by a covered peril
- Research and development (R&D) projects, covering the property and investment lost when an R&D project is damaged or destroyed by a covered peril

The business has a very active Web site on which it relies to communicate with customers and to provide information on its products and services. Due to the nature of the operation in designing computer components, it has a large R&D department with many new projects under development.

Coverage Recommendations

After developing several proposals for Jerry and Jeffrey to consider, the agent schedules a meeting to review them.

Proposal 1 is to continue the package policy including the standard commercial property forms on a replacement cost basis with a blanket building limit of $3.75 million for the two buildings at Location 2. The blanket personal property amount for Locations 1 and 2 is $2.5 million. A $1,000 deductible applies to the property coverage.

To cover the flood exposure, an NFIP General Property Policy would be purchased on an ACV basis in the amount of $500,000 for the main building and $450,000 for the storage building at Location 2. Personal property limits would be $500,000 for the main building and $250,000 for the storage building at Location 2. A $500 deductible applies separately to the building and to the personal property. An ISO flood coverage endorsement will be added to the commercial property policy with a sublimit of $2 million. This endorsement is on a replacement cost basis with no coinsurance requirement. Because the location is in a flood zone, the insurer is requiring a $25,000 deductible for the flood coverage endorsement.

Proposal 2 involves a different insurer but covers the same limits as Proposal 1. However, a $2,500 deductible applies. This proposal also includes an NFIP General Property Policy in the same amounts as Proposal 1 but includes a DIC policy in the amount of $1 million on a replacement cost basis, subject to a $50,000 deductible with no coinsurance requirement. This policy applies in excess of the NFIP policy.

Proposal 3 is an output policy providing a blanket building and personal property limit of $6 million on a replacement cost basis subject to a $1,000 deductible for Locations 1 and 2. The output policy includes flood coverage with a sublimit of $1.5 million and a $25,000 deductible. This proposal also includes a package policy covering the personal property at the original location on a replacement cost basis with a $200,000 limit and an 80 percent coinsurance requirement. This property coverage is subject to a $250 deductible. The package policy also includes the general liability and other non-property coverages for this business.

After reviewing the three proposals and considering the premiums, Jerry and Jeffrey choose Proposal 1. This option allows the insureds the opportunity to retain their package policy while providing the highest available limits for flood coverage with a lower deductible than the DIC option. See the exhibit "Correct Answer."

Correct Answer

Insurance Proposals for Jerry and Jeffrey*

Proposal 1—Package policy with ISO flood coverage endorsement and a separate NFIP General Property Policy		
Blanket building limit	$3,750,000	$1,000 deductible applies/ replacement cost basis
Blanket personal property	$2,500,000	
ISO flood coverage endorsement	$2,000,000 sublimit $4,000,000 aggregate limit	$25,000 deductible applies/ replacement cost basis
NFIP General Property Form—Building limit	$500,000 Loc 2/ Bldg 1 $450,000 Loc 2/Bldg 2	$500 deductible applies/ ACV basis
NFIP General Property Form—Personal Property limit	$500,000 Loc 2/ Bldg 1 $250,000 Loc 2/Bldg 2	$500 deductible applies/ ACV basis

*This solution might not be the only viable solution. Other solutions could be exercised if justified by the analysis. In addition, specific circumstances and organizational needs or goals may enter into the evaluation, making an alternative action a better option.

[DA06033]

SUMMARY

The National Flood Insurance Program (NFIP) sets eligibility requirements, coverage limits, and coverages provided by the NFIP General Property Form and the Residential Condominium Building Association Policy.

Flood insurance can also be obtained from commercial insurers by endorsement to their commercial property policies. The ISO Flood Coverage Endorsement uses the NFIP definition of flood and therefore does not cover all the types of loss excluded by the Water exclusion in the ISO causes of loss forms.

Two versions of the ISO Earthquake and Volcanic Eruption Endorsement are available. One endorsement is written for the same limits and coinsurance percentage that apply to the commercial property policy to which it is attached (CP 10 40). The other endorsement (the sublimit form, CP 10 45) can be written for a lower limit without coinsurance and is subject to an annual aggregate limit. Both endorsements are subject to a percentage deductible.

The DIC policy is a means of providing "all-risks" coverage to an insured whose basic property policy covers only named perils. Additionally, DIC policies are also used to fill coverage gaps, cover additional loss exposures, or provide excess coverage limits.

Some of the notable features found in output policies include coverage for personal property at unspecified locations used by the insured, in domestic transit, and belonging to others. Optional coverages include auto physical damage coverage, equipment breakdown coverage, and flood and earthquake. HPR insurance offers very low property insurance rates and is available to large property accounts that comply with stringent property risk control standards. The "layering" technique is used to provide property insurance for insureds with either high total values or a high concentration of values at one location.

Commercial property specialty forms and endorsements can provide solutions for customers with specific insurance needs that may not be fully covered under standard property forms.

ASSIGNMENT NOTE

1. National Flood Insurance Program, Standard Flood Insurance Policy.

Direct Your Learning ▶▶

7

Business Income Insurance

Educational Objectives

After learning the content of this assignment, you should be able to:

▷ Describe the following aspects of the business income loss exposure:

- Measurement of business income loss

- Effect of business interruption on expenses

- Property and perils involved in business income losses

▷ Describe the factors that should be considered in a pre-loss analysis of business income and extra expense loss exposures.

▷ Describe the factors that should be considered when estimating an organization's maximum loss of business income.

▷ Summarize the provisions of the business income and extra expense insuring agreements of the Business Income (and Extra Expense) Coverage Form.

▷ Summarize the provisions of each of the additional coverages, the Newly Acquired Locations coverage extension, and the Extended Period of Indemnity optional coverage in the Business Income (and Extra Expense) Coverage Form.

▷ Summarize each of the following conditions of the Business Income (and Extra Expense) Coverage Form:

- Duties in the Event of Loss

- Loss Determination

- Coinsurance

▷ Describe the operation of each of the alternatives to coinsurance under the Business Income (and Extra Expense) Coverage Form.

▷ Explain how the Extra Expense Coverage Form differs from the Business Income (and Extra Expense) Coverage Form.

7

▷ Describe the operation and potential benefits of each of these business income and extra expense coverage options:

- Blanket business income insurance
- Payroll Limitation or Exclusion endorsement
- Discretionary Payroll Expense endorsement
- Power, Heat, and Refrigeration Deduction endorsement
- Endorsements for dependent property exposures
- Business Income Changes—Educational Institutions endorsement
- Utility Services—Time Element endorsement
- Ordinance or Law—Increased Period of Restoration endorsement
- Food Contamination endorsement

▷ Given a case, determine whether, and for what amount, a described loss would be covered either by the Business Income (and Extra Expense) Coverage Form or the Business Income (Without Extra Expense) Coverage Form.

Business Income Insurance

BUSINESS INCOME LOSS EXPOSURES

Commercial property coverage forms are tailored to insure buildings and personal property against damage by covered perils. However, the loss in value of the property and the expense of restoring it are not the only losses that a business may sustain.

Almost all of a commercial firm's property is acquired because of the income that it will generate or facilitate. This income can be lost when property is damaged or destroyed.

To evaluate the coverage needs an organization faces and determine how business income policy provisions are applied, an insurance practitioner should first understand how business income losses are measured, how a business interruption affects expenses, and the property and perils that business income losses can involve.

Measurement of Business Income Losses

Simply described, **business income insurance** covers the reduction in an organization's income when operations are interrupted by damage to property caused by a covered peril. The exact insurance recovery, of course, is determined by the terms and conditions of the policy. Because the severity of a business income loss is directly related to the length of time required to restore the property, business income coverage is considered a "time element" coverage. It is also called a "business interruption" coverage, because the loss of business income results from the interruption of the insured's business.

Business income losses are measured in terms of **net income**, which is the difference between revenues (such as money received for goods or services) and expenses (such as money paid for merchandise, rent, and insurance). It can be expressed by the formula:

Revenues – Expenses = Net income

Profit is net income that results when revenues exceed expenses. **Net loss** is the net income that results when expenses exceed revenues. For accounting purposes, the amount of a net loss appears in parentheses or is preceded by a minus sign (–).

Business income insurance covers the reduction in a firm's net income caused by accidental property damage. This reduction can be calculated by

Business income insurance

Insurance that covers the reduction in an organization's income when operations are interrupted by damage to property caused by a covered peril.

Net income

The difference between revenues (such as money received for goods or services) and expenses (such as money paid for merchandise, rent, and insurance).

Profit

Net income that results when revenues exceed expenses.

Net loss

Net income that results when expenses exceed revenues.

subtracting the amount of net income that a firm actually earned in a period of interruption from the amount of net income that the firm could reasonably have been expected to earn during the same period.

The following simplified example illustrates these concepts. Locksey Hardware Store suffered a partial fire loss and was closed for three months until the building could be repaired and the personal property replaced. During the three-month interruption, Locksey's revenue was reduced to nil, some ordinary expenses (payroll, electricity, and so on) were temporarily reduced or eliminated, and Locksey incurred some additional expenses (such as overtime labor and express freight on merchandise) to reopen the store as soon as possible. See the exhibit "Locksey's Revenue, Expenses, and Profit."

Locksey's Revenue, Expenses, and Profit

	Expected	Actual
Revenue	$300,000	$ 0
Expenses	240,000	120,000
Net profit (or loss)	$ 60,000	($120,000)

[DA02477]

The "Expected" column shows the revenue, expenses, and profit that Locksey could reasonably have expected during the three-month period, had no business interruption occurred. The "Actual" column shows its actual revenue, expenses, and net loss (indicated by parentheses) during the three-month period of interruption.

Locksey's business income loss is the $180,000 difference between the $60,000 profit it expected and the $120,000 net loss it actually experienced during the period of interruption. Locksey's loss can also be calculated by adding the $60,000 net income it would have earned to the $120,000 expenses that it actually incurred during the period.

For the sake of simplicity, this example assumes that Locksey's revenue returned to its normal level as soon as it reopened, which is seldom the case. In reality, Locksey's business income loss could have continued for several months after the store reopened.

Continuing expenses
Expenses that continue to be incurred during a business interruption.

Noncontinuing expenses
Expenses that will not continue during a business interruption.

Effect of Business Interruption on Expenses

During a business interruption, some of the organization's expenses (called **continuing expenses**) will continue, and other expenses (called **noncontinuing expenses**) will not continue. A business can also incur extra expenses during a business interruption. All changes in expenses must be considered when measuring a business income loss.

Continuing Expenses

If business is interrupted for only a short time, payroll of key employees, debt repayments, taxes, insurance, and many other expenses will continue during the interruption. If a longer interruption of business occurs, many expenses can be reduced or eliminated. Workers can be laid off, taxes are reduced (because of reduced income), and insurance premiums are smaller. It is often difficult to predict which expenses will continue and which will not.

Any reduction in expenses during a business interruption lessens the severity of the resulting business income loss. Nevertheless, continuing expenses can be, and ordinarily are, a significant part of business income losses. If, for example, an organization generates no revenue during a business interruption, its business income loss will be its lost profit for the period of interruption, plus the continuing expenses for that period, plus any extra expenses. In many cases, a company's continuing expenses exceed the profit that the company would have earned during the period.

Extra Expenses

Extra expenses are expenses, in addition to ordinary expenses, that an organization incurs to mitigate the effects of a business interruption. These are examples of extra expenses:

- In order to reopen an assembly line that had been shut down because of an explosion, a factory owner pays the additional costs of overtime labor and overnight air shipment of repair parts.
- After sustaining fire damage to its warehouse, a wholesale distributor rents a similar warehouse and continues its operations within two weeks instead of shutting down entirely for several months.
- To continue classes while an elementary school building is rebuilt following hurricane damage, a school district rents mobile classrooms and situates them on the school's playground.

Extra expense measures often pay for themselves. For example, the extra cost of overtime labor and air freight of needed parts may have been considerably less than the income that would have been lost had such measures not been taken. Such measures actually reduce the business income loss, and most organizations will readily undertake measures that reduce loss.

Some organizations will incur extra expenses even when such expenditures exceed any reduction in the business income loss. For example, after a property loss occurs, a hospital might incur substantial extra expenses to maintain essential services for its patients even though such expenses increase its business income loss. The decision to incur such extra expenses depends on the organization's objectives. For some organizations, maintaining continuous service to customers may be more important than reducing the business income loss.

Extra expenses

Expenses, in addition to ordinary expenses, that an organization incurs to mitigate the effects of a business interruption.

Property and Perils Involved in Business Income Losses

Business income losses typically result from physical damage to the affected organization's own buildings or personal property. However, a tenant's operations can be interrupted by damage to the building in which the tenant is located even though the part of the building the tenant occupies has not been damaged. For example, an explosion that debilitates heating, air conditioning, and ventilating equipment makes offices in sealed high-rise buildings uninhabitable in very hot or very cold weather, even though the offices themselves are not damaged.

In some cases, a physical loss at one location can cause a business interruption elsewhere. For example, a business may have to close because of damage to off-premises property that provides utilities such as electricity, water, or communications. Alternatively, one business may depend on another business as a major customer or as a key supplier. A business may be dependent simply because it is near a key facility or "magnet" property that attracts customers to the site (such as a major department store in a shopping mall). Damage to these kinds of properties could cause a business income loss at a location where no physical damage occurred.

The causes of loss for business income losses associated with property exposures are typically the same as those for physical damage losses. Thus, a fire or a windstorm that damages property may also cause a business income loss. A business income loss can also result when there has been no physical damage to buildings or personal property. For example, the closing of a road or a labor strike can cause a business income loss. However, such risks are generally not insurable. Any number of other events that are not covered by business income insurance can reduce an organization's net income. Prudent organizations use risk management techniques to avoid or lessen business income loss exposures that cannot be transferred by insurance. In order for business income insurance to apply, this must occur: an interruption of operations caused by property damage from a covered peril to property at locations or situations described in the policy resulting in a loss of business income and/or extra expense.

If any of these conditions are not met, there is no coverage under business income coverage.

PRE-LOSS ANALYSIS OF BUSINESS INCOME AND EXTRA EXPENSE EXPOSURES

In addition to analyzing business income and extra expense losses, risk management and insurance professionals are also confronted with a more difficult problem: pre-loss analysis of business income and extra expense exposures to serve as the basis for selection of appropriate risk control and risk financing measures. Insurance professionals should consider several factors when identifying and analyzing business income loss and extra expense exposures.

Key factors for insurance professionals, as well as organizations, to consider are all aspects of an organization's business income and extra expense exposure resulting from an accidental property loss. Not all the causes and occurrences of loss are insurable; an organization must also be aware of its uninsurable exposures.

For example, many firms spend millions of dollars to build brand loyalty. A decrease in brand loyalty is generally uninsurable. Thus, an organization should consider noninsurance techniques—such as duplicate facilities and increased loss prevention—to avoid both insurable and uninsurable business income and extra expense losses.

Events That Could Cause a Business Income Loss

Loss of business income can result from many causes. Enterprise-wide risk management, which considers all the risks that a firm faces, entails treating all exposures, whether they are insurable or not.

One of the most important steps an organization can take to prevent or reduce business income and extra expense losses is to prepare a disaster plan. To do that, the organization must think through the crucial actions necessary in the event of an unexpected emergency and make arrangements for recovery in advance. Research has shown that the key to successful recovery from a disaster is advance planning, not the level of insurance coverage.

From the viewpoint of a firm's bottom line, it does not matter whether a loss of income is caused by a tornado that destroys the firm's facilities or by new competitors. In the context of commercial property insurance, however, business income loss refers to loss of net income resulting from accidental loss of or damage to property, rather than from poor business management, market conditions, competitive forces, or other general business risks.

Loss of business income resulting from the death or disability of key employees is a loss exposure that life insurance and disability insurance can treat.

The property loss or damage that causes an organization to experience a business income loss can occur either on or away from the organization's own premises.

Damage to Property at the Organization's Own Premises

Most insurable business income and extra expense losses result from physical damage to property at the organization's own premises that prevents the organization from operating or that reduces its capacity to operate.

Identifying an organization's direct property loss exposures also reveals potential sources of business income and extra expense loss. Any risk control measure taken to reduce the frequency or severity of direct losses affecting the organization can also reduce the frequency or severity of business income and extra expense losses.

The on-premises business income and extra expense exposure is not limited to a firm's own property. For example, a tenant can suffer a severe business interruption if the building it occupies is destroyed by explosion, even though the tenant does not own the building.

Damage to Property Away From the Organization's Own Premises

An organization can also suffer a business income loss because of physical damage to property at locations not owned or controlled by the organization. This type of loss can result from any of these exposures:

- Loss or damage to the organization's own property off premises
- Dependent property exposures
- Interruption of utility services
- Acts of civil authorities
- Adverse weather

Organization's Own Property Off Premises

An exposure often overlooked involves damage to an organization's own property while off premises, perhaps while in transit or while being stored or worked on at the premises of a bailee.

Dependent Property Exposures

Dependent property exposure

The possibility of incurring business income loss because of physical loss occurring on the premises of an organization that the insured depends on for materials, products, or sales.

An organization can depend on other firms in ways that create a **dependent property exposure**. This exposure is sometimes referred to as a "contingent business income" exposure.

The outsourcing of all or parts of a firm's operations has complicated business income exposures in many ways. Negative consequences of outsourcing include the elimination of a firm's backup facilities. When a firm produced the entire product in its own facilities, it often had a number of plants that were geographically separated. When catastrophe struck one plant, the other locations could often make up the lost production at the damaged plant. In fact, disaster plans were often built around that capacity. Because of outsourcing, this is no longer true for most companies.

Outsourcing has had other adverse effects. Supply chain management—that is, control of a far-flung network of suppliers—is now a common operational function. The large inventories of raw materials and components that once served to cushion the effect of supply interruptions have been eliminated by the "just-in-time" inventory systems that firms have adopted to reduce costs. Using a large network of suppliers or contractors multiplies the chance that a critical part of the process may be shut down; it has also decreased the loss controls that can be applied to those operations.

A dependent property exposure also exists when a supplier or producer is highly dependent on a buyer.

For example, a small manufacturer of auto parts might sell more than half of its output to one auto maker. If a property loss shuts down the auto maker's plant, the supplier will suffer a loss of business income.

Another type of dependency exists for small businesses in or near a shopping mall. Such businesses may depend on customers who are drawn to the mall by a major department or discount store, sometimes referred to as a "leader property" or "magnet store." If a property loss shuts down the magnet store, then the customers shop elsewhere and the small "satellite stores" lose customers and business income even though the satellite stores suffered no physical loss.

An obvious way to control dependency exposures is to lessen the dependency. A manufacturer that is highly dependent on one or two suppliers might increase the number of its suppliers and reduce the amount purchased from any one of them.

The flexibility of business income and extra expense insurance to address dependency exposures allows businesses with dependency exposures to achieve some certainty against risk.

Interruption of Utility Services

Physical damage to power transmission lines or generating stations is another source of business interruption caused by off-premises occurrences. The resulting loss of power or other utilities can shut down almost any organization. See the exhibit "Example of Business Interruption Caused by Damage to Utilities."

Example of Business Interruption Caused by Damage to Utilities

Among the risk management lessons learned after the destruction of the World Trade Center was the potential loss of income that can be caused by communications disruption. One example: A small fire and burglar alarm service company in Westchester County, New York (more than thirty miles from the World Trade Center), lost telephone monitoring capacity to clients in New York City for more than three weeks because of the destruction of the phone company's switching office at 7 World Trade Center. The result was a $100,000 drop in the alarm company's net income, insignificant in the overall calamity, but a serious economic blow to the small firm.

[DA03573]

Acts of Civil Authorities

The Civil Authority additional coverage provides payment for loss of business income and extra expense if access to the insured's premises is prohibited by civil authority because of damage to property at another premises. Damage must be caused by a covered peril. For example, this coverage applies if authorities prohibit access to a shopping center following a fire loss to an adjacent store or if an explosion releases toxic fumes, resulting in an order to evacuate the surrounding area. However, if civil authorities prohibit access because of earthquake damage to other buildings, no coverage applies if the insured's policy does not include earthquake coverage.

Adverse Weather

A windstorm and heavy rain may do little or no damage to a firm's property but may wash away roads and bridges or cover them with debris, making it difficult or impossible for customers, employees, and supplies to reach the premises. This is a frequent problem in areas swept by hurricanes and other tropical storms. Adverse weather may also impede a business's operations even when no damage occurs to property.

For example, heavy rain can cause cancellation or poor attendance at outdoor events that were expected to attract large crowds and generate substantial income.

Time Factors of Business Income Loss

The answer to the question "How much could a business interruption cost?" depends not only on anticipated revenue and expense figures but also on these issues:

- How long business income is reduced (or extra expenses are incurred)
- Seasonal fluctuations in business income

The duration of a business interruption is directly related to the time required to replace damaged property plus the time required to restore the normal level of operations.

Time Required to Replace Damaged Property

In most cases, the time required to resume operations depends on the time needed to repair or reconstruct the building that the business occupies. The most reliable method of estimating the reconstruction time for a building is to obtain an estimate from a reputable contractor. If that is impractical, reference books or services are available for estimating reconstruction times.

Most organizations greatly underestimate the time needed for a complex construction project. The construction timeline shown in the exhibit shows a typical school construction project schedule. See the exhibit "Construction Timeline."

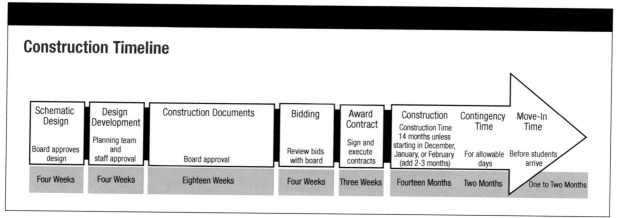

Construction Timeline

Schematic Design	Design Development	Construction Documents	Bidding	Award Contract	Construction	Contingency Time	Move-In Time
Board approves design	Planning team and staff approval	Board approval	Review bids with board	Sign and execute contracts	Construction Time 14 months unless starting in December, January, or February (add 2-3 months)	For allowable days	Before students arrive
Four Weeks	Four Weeks	Eighteen Weeks	Four Weeks	Three Weeks	Fourteen Months	Two Months	One to Two Months

Adapted from Chapter 7 of Gary Hubler, The School Design Primer: A How-To Manual for the 21st Century (Washington, D.C.: National Clearing House for Educational Facilities, 1996). [DA03574]

The amount of time allotted to building design and document preparation for compliance with various zoning and building codes is significant. Organizations often overlook these steps when they estimate the time needed to restore serious damage. In a project involving disputes about zoning or environmental issues, even the time shown in the exhibit might be inadequate.

The enforcement of building or zoning codes can cause considerable delay in rebuilding or repairing an organization's premises before business can be resumed following a loss. The extra cost of complying with these laws is not considered part of the business income and extra expense loss exposure; however, the delay caused by having to meet these requirements must be taken into account when estimating maximum business income and extra expense losses.

When goods in process sustain physical loss, the severity of the resulting business income loss depends on the amount of time required to bring new raw materials to the same stage of production that the destroyed goods had reached before the physical damage occurred.

Construction delays can also be expected in the aftermath of major hurricanes and earthquakes or other events that cause damage over a widespread area. In such instances, transportation and communications are disrupted, and the people and materials needed for repair and replacement are in short supply.

For some firms, the time needed to replace crucial items may be the critical issue. Firms that use highly specialized equipment or depend on overseas manufacturers for parts or repairs can face a period of extended restoration. After identifying crucial items, the risk analyst can evaluate exposures by asking the manufacturer, dealer, or servicer of the particular item how quickly a replacement could be obtained under the worst possible circumstances.

This aspect of the loss exposure is often responsive to risk control. For example, a company might keep spare parts or replacement machinery on hand, or it might enter into contracts with outside firms that can provide prompt emergency repairs.

A company might also consider the availability of replacement parts and emergency repair service as a decision criterion when buying new equipment or machinery.

Other measures that might be effective include storing building and machinery plans off-premises to simplify reconstruction, keeping a current list of capable contractors and suppliers, investigating alternative facilities before any loss occurs, and maintaining duplicate records at a second location for both electronic and other data.

Time Required to Restore Normal Level of Operations

Not all business income losses cease when the damaged property has been restored. In some cases, businesses lose their customers after a long shutdown and must win them back, which can take time.

A shutdown can also lead to loss of customer goodwill and market share. Restoration of building, equipment, and stock will be to no avail if customers do not return. Some types of businesses are more susceptible than others in this regard.

A convenience store in a favorable location might return to its normal level of operations shortly after reopening following a lengthy shutdown. In contrast, a self-storage facility may need many months to locate enough new tenants to restore profitability.

Special circumstances affect schools and colleges, which may lose tuition for an entire academic year or longer if the campus is unusable when students are enrolling or making financial commitments for the school year.

Similarly, a beauty salon's patrons may have transferred their loyalties to other hairdressers during a shutdown, or an office equipment firm's customers may have found other suppliers. Most firms will need additional time to recapture lost business even after the property has been completely restored and may have to offer price concessions to rebuild business.

Another aspect of loss that may continue after the restoration of the physical premises involves loss arising from the cancellation of a license, lease, or contract.

A license to serve as the exclusive distributor of a product may depend on the licensee's selling a certain minimum quantity. Loss of the license because of failure to meet this requirement might reduce a firm's profitability long after its facilities are restored if it cannot obtain a replacement product to sell.

Small Physical Damage Loss, Long Interruption

Business income and extra expense loss exposures would be easier to deal with if physical damage losses and business income losses always occurred in proportionate amounts. Because they do not, risk management and insurance professionals should be alert to situations in which relatively little physical damage could cause a long interruption and therefore a large business income loss. An example of such a situation is a loss involving a "bottleneck."

Bottlenecks in a business operation can cause the business process to slow down or stop. The term "bottleneck" is often applied to situations in which work from several assembly lines or processes must flow through (or depend on continued operation at) a single job site or position. Physical damage confined to the bottleneck position could shut down several undamaged assembly lines. Production bottlenecks are easiest to imagine, but bottlenecks can also exist in purchasing and selling.

Although flowcharts are often effective in identifying bottlenecks, some bottlenecks can be difficult to identify by any method before a loss occurs. For example, suppose that a large plant is prohibited from operating without adequate pollution control devices. A small fire in the pollution control system could shut down the entire plant. This is an important exposure but one that most flowcharts would not identify.

Seasonal Fluctuations

Some organizations earn significantly different amounts of income at different times of the year. For example, retail jewelers and fur dealers may transact as much as half their annual business during their peak three months. Businesses with an even more seasonal pattern (such as ski resorts) might generate their entire annual income in a three-month period.

For such organizations, the business income loss resulting from a shutdown could vary considerably depending on when it occurred.

Foretelling when an interruption will occur is impossible, but the question is important for a company whose earnings vary substantially from month to month. The safest assumption is that the interruption will occur at the worst possible time, that is, during the organization's peak season.

If a seasonal pattern exists, the organization should identify the pattern of fluctuation in earnings by either analyzing the business's past seasonal figures or using figures that show typical seasonal patterns for the same type of business as that being analyzed.

Distinguishing Between Continuing and Noncontinuing Expenses

Not all expenses will continue during a business interruption. Expenses that do not continue reduce the loss that the business would otherwise incur. Estimating which expenses will continue and which will not is a difficult task, but careful analysis can help develop a more accurate estimate of potential loss severity than an estimate based on an assumption that all expenses will continue during a shutdown. See the exhibit "Examples of Expenses That May or May Not Continue."

Measuring Potential Loss Severity

The safest approach to estimating the potential severity of business income losses is to assume a worst-case scenario, that is, a shutdown at the worst possible time of the year, lasting for the maximum amount of time it would take to replace a destroyed building and equipment, restore inventory and personnel to their pre-loss status, and regain lost customers. An organization's potential business income and extra expense loss estimated in this manner is referred to as the estimated maximum loss (EML). However, certain expenses will discontinue even in the worst case.

The objective of calculating EML is to estimate the largest loss that could occur in the future. Past income and expense figures must therefore be analyzed and updated to project them into the future. How far they must be projected depends on the potential duration of a business interruption. Exposure analysis for setting insurance limits is done on a pre-tax basis because business income loss payments will be subject to income tax. When examining retention levels, a risk analyst evaluates losses on an after-tax basis because taxes reduce the effect of the retention.

A useful tool for developing income and expense figures for purposes of setting the EML is a business income worksheet. If completed properly with information derived from the organization's financial statements, the worksheet projects a figure for income and expenses for the twelve months following policy inception. That twelve-month figure, with several important modifications, can serve as the basis for calculating the EML.

Examples of Expenses That May or May Not Continue

Type of Expense	Factors to Consider in Analyzing Whether Expense Will Continue
Payroll expense	• Which employees are needed/not needed while operations are suspended? • Does the company have key employees who would be hard to replace? • Would the local labor market make it difficult to hire back laid-off employees? • Is the company a party to a union contract prohibiting layoffs? • Does the company have severance pay policies that discourage layoffs?
Heat, light, power expenses	• Does the company normally use a large amount of heat, light, or power? • Is the company obligated to pay a minimum charge regardless of usage?
Lease or rental expense	• Do any applicable lease or rental agreements provide for abatement of rent?
Interest expense	• This will continue except that the mortgage interest on a destroyed building will cease until the new loan goes into effect.
Taxes	• Property taxes usually continue. • Sales tax is not an expense; it is a sum the insured collects for the government. • Employer contributions for Social Security and unemployment compensation continue only to the extent that employees are paid during the interruption. • Exposure analysis for setting insurance limits is done on a pre-tax basis because business income loss payments will be subject to income tax.
Advertising expense	• If ads already contracted cannot be canceled, they will be a continuing expense. • Even if ads can be canceled, a company may choose to maintain image-enhancing ads during a long shutdown to reduce residual loss of income after the business reopens. • If the business relocates to a temporary location while its regular location is being repaired, advertising the temporary location may actually increase ad expense.
Franchise and license fees and royalties	• If based on sales or production, such expenses would cease upon suspension of operations. • If a minimum level or flat fee is guaranteed, such expenses could continue.
Postage and telephone expenses	• These expenses could continue in full for a short shutdown. • During a prolonged shutdown, these expenses would probably be reduced or discontinued and then resume shortly before reopening.
Professional fees	• Fees for accounting and legal services normally continue if paid on a retainer basis. • Extra legal and accounting services may be needed as a result of the loss.
Insurance expense	• Coverage on property that is destroyed can be eliminated, and the premium for property insurance on a reporting form basis will be reduced if lower values are reported. • Workers compensation premiums based on payroll and liability premiums based on payroll or sales will be reduced commensurate with any reduction in payroll or sales caused by the interruption.
Depreciation expense	• Although it does not represent a current outflow of cash, depreciation expense does reduce the net income of an ongoing business. • Depreciation ceases on property that is totally destroyed. • Depreciation on property that is not destroyed generally continues unless the charge is linked to usage—for example, a die that can be used only a certain number of times before being discarded or remade.

[DA03575]

ESTIMATING MAXIMUM LOSS OF BUSINESS INCOME

The consequences of improperly estimating the maximum loss of business income that could be incurred by a business may be examined from several points of view: the producer/agent or broker (loss of potential compensation and customer goodwill), the underwriter (management dissatisfaction), the insurer (loss of customers and improper premium collection), or the business owner(s) (potential underinsurance or excessive premium payments).

When estimating an organization's maximum loss of business income for insurance purposes, the goal is to develop a solid foundation that can be used to select an appropriate coinsurance percentage and amount of insurance. In determining an organization's estimated maximum loss (EML) of business income the **coinsurance basis**, which is a projection of income and expenses for the twelve months following policy inception, can be used as a starting point.

However, several factors should also be considered, with corresponding modifications made to the coinsurance basis:

- Business income worksheet
- Noncontinuing expenses
- Time required to restore property
- Peak periods
- Extended business income loss
- Anticipated changes in expenses and profits during restoration period
- Extra expense
- Compensating for possible errors

Business Income Worksheet

The coinsurance basis that is used as a starting point for EML is determined by using a **business income worksheet**. Insurers typically use their own business income worksheets. However, Insurance Services Office (ISO) publishes a Business Income Report/Work Sheet (CP 15 15) that may be used to calculate the amount of insurance necessary to comply with the Coinsurance condition of business income insurance forms and provide underwriters with the information they need to evaluate business income loss exposures and the adequacy of the amount of insurance requested.

For the sake of simplicity, the ISO Business Income Report/Work Sheet is referred to here as the worksheet. It can be used to analyze an organization's business income loss exposure and (if insurance is wanted) determine an appropriate coinsurance percentage and limit of insurance.

Coinsurance basis

The sum of the insured's estimated net income and operating expenses for the twelve months following policy inception, minus only those expenses listed in the business income worksheet.

Business income worksheet

A worksheet for calculating the amount of insurance necessary to comply with the Coinsurance condition of business income insurance forms, for reporting business income values to the insurer, or for providing underwriters with information they need to evaluate an organization's business income loss exposure.

Underwriters often require that the insured submit a completed worksheet to aid them in evaluating the exposure, and loss adjusters follow a procedure similar to the worksheet calculations in determining whether the insured has complied with coinsurance requirements. Even when the insurer has not requested a worksheet, an insured should complete the worksheet as an initial step in determining how much business income insurance to purchase. Thus, a wide range of insurance and risk management professionals need an understanding of how the worksheet is prepared.

In most cases, the worksheet is prepared by the insured's accountant or financial officer, perhaps with some assistance from the insured's insurance agent, broker, or consultant. Generally, neither producers nor underwriters should prepare the worksheet on the insured's behalf.

One of the principal purposes of the worksheet is to determine the amount of insurance needed to comply with the Coinsurance condition in business income forms. The Coinsurance condition requires the insured to carry an amount of insurance equal to the chosen coinsurance percentage times a dollar amount called the coinsurance basis. The coinsurance basis is the sum of the insured's estimated net income and operating expenses for the twelve months following policy inception, minus only those expenses listed in the form as deductions. Although many operating expenses might be reduced or eliminated during a period of business interruption, only those items specifically listed in the worksheet or in optional endorsements are deducted in calculating the coinsurance basis. That is, the coinsurance basis times the applicable coinsurance percentage equals the amount of insurance required to avoid a coinsurance penalty. The worksheet elicits income and expense figures for the insured that, with appropriate calculations, enable the insured to determine the coinsurance basis.

The income and expense figures used in the worksheet are usually found in the insured's income statement. The income statement (sometimes called an earnings statement or a profit and loss statement) reports on the organization's profitability for a stated period of time by comparing the revenues generated in the period with the expenses incurred to produce those revenues. See the exhibit "Sample Condensed Income Statement for Merchandising Business."

The coinsurance basis, referred as the "business income exposure for 12 months" in the worksheet, is not necessarily a reasonable approximation of EML. The maximum interruption period is almost never precisely twelve months. Additionally, some expenses may not continue during a business interruption, thereby reducing the loss of net income actually sustained. These two factors help to explain why the available coinsurance percentages for business income insurance are 50, 60, 70, 80, 90, 100, and 125 percent. (A 50 percent coinsurance percentage, for example, might be chosen if the insured's EML is less than one-half of the insured's coinsurance basis.) Moreover, certain items, such as extra expenses following a loss, are not considered when calculating the coinsurance basis. Thus, several

Sample Condensed Income Statement for Merchandising Business

Net Sales	$10,000,000
Cost of goods sold	− 6,500,000
Gross margin (also called "gross profit")	3,500,000
Operating expenses	− 3,000,000
Operating income	500,000
Other income	+ 50,000
Net income before provision for income tax	550,000
Provision for income tax	− 165,000
Net income after tax	$ 385,000

[DA06065]

adjustments must be made to the worksheet coinsurance basis when it is used to estimate EML.

Nevertheless, the worksheet is a good starting point. As long as the differences between the coinsurance basis and the EML are understood, the worksheet can be a useful tool for analyzing the actual loss exposure and selecting an appropriate amount of insurance.

Noncontinuing Expenses

Only the specific expense items listed in the worksheet can be deducted when completing the worksheet to calculate the coinsurance basis. However, when computing EML, any noncontinuing expenses (not just those listed in the worksheet) can be deducted. For example, Manufacturer, Inc., paid $300,000 rent in the year ending December 31, 20X1. If its lease calls for rent abatement in the event the premises are untenantable, Manufacturer should adjust for that when calculating its business income EML, even though it cannot be deducted from the coinsurance basis.

Time Required to Restore Property

The business income worksheet focuses on the coinsurance requirement, which is based on the consecutive twelve months beginning with the policy inception. Rarely will an organization have a period of restoration that is exactly equal to twelve months. Some organizations will have a shorter period of restoration, and other organizations will require more than a year.

After noncontinuing expenses are deducted, the EML should be adjusted to correspond to the maximum period of restoration anticipated. If, for example, the maximum expected period of restoration for Peg's Toy Store is six months, the EML can be reduced to reflect a six-month period instead of the twelve-month period anticipated by the coinsurance basis. However, care must be exercised in deciding which six-month period to measure.

Peak Periods

Many organizations experience sharp variations in business from month to month. For Peg's Toy Store, September through December account for 72 percent of sales. The remaining 28 percent of sales are divided equally over the other eight months. The estimated maximum restoration period is six months. If a total restoration began on September 1, the store would lose 79 percent of a year's sales rather than 50 percent (72 percent during September through December and 3.5 percent in each of the next two months). Thus, Peg's EML would be 79 percent of the annual estimate, rather than the 50 percent that a six-month restoration period would seem to indicate.

Extended Business Income Loss

Net income does not always return to normal as soon as the damaged property is rebuilt or repaired. Loss of business income that might occur after operations resume needs to be included in the EML. However, only losses that insurance will cover should be included in the EML for insurance purposes.

Business income insurance includes an additional coverage called Extended Business Income (EBI). This coverage insures income loss insured for up to sixty days (thirty days in the pre-2012 editions of ISO commercial property forms) after the damaged property is restored to use. This basic period can be extended up to two years through the Extended Period of Indemnity optional coverage. The EML, for purposes of estimating exposure and arranging business income insurance, should include the EBI exposure only to the extent that it is insured.

Anticipated Changes in Expenses and Profits During the Period of Restoration

The worksheet uses the period of twelve months beginning at the policy inception date. Although it is sometimes recommended that firms review their business income values at least quarterly, few firms examine their business income exposure more than once a year. Technology may enable organizations to increase the frequency of review.

Financial officers now universally use computer-generated spreadsheet projections. If the adjustments necessary to generate a business income worksheet can be incorporated into the spreadsheet, the financial officer could update business income values whenever other business projections are reviewed.

However, to guard against the possibility that this will not happen, insureds must consider how conditions may have changed if the period of restoration commences on the last day of the policy period rather than at inception.

If a firm projects an increase in sales of 15 percent a year and a maximum restoration period of two years, its projected sales volume in the final year of a loss that began on the last day of the policy period would be over 32 percent higher than the sales value projected for the policy period. Even a firm that estimates only a six-month period of restoration must consider the six months beginning on the last day of the policy period. This may yield a significantly different EML if the firm's operations are rapidly changing.

Extra Expense

Many organizations can continue operations at close to normal levels by renting temporary quarters and equipment. The extra expenses incurred for these items are not included in the worksheet when calculating the coinsurance basis. However, anticipated extra expenses should be included in the EML to the extent that they are covered under the subject company's business income insurance.

Compensating for Possible Errors

Errors are inevitable in any estimate. The consequence of underestimating the loss exposure (a partially uninsured loss) is more severe than the consequence of overestimating the loss exposure (the waste of a portion of the premium). It therefore makes sense to increase the EML by a selected percentage (such as 10 percent buffer) to allow for possible underestimates. Such a practice is also justified by insureds' tendency to be overly optimistic about the length of time it would take to restore operations after a severe direct loss.

Coinsurance Percentage

After the coinsurance basis has been calculated in a business income worksheet and the EML has been established, in part by taking the factors discussed previously into consideration, a coinsurance percentage and a limit of insurance can be selected for business income insurance. The appropriate coinsurance percentage can be selected by using the simple calculation and guidelines described in this section. Then, the amount of insurance can be set by following the general rule that the limit of insurance should equal the EML or the amount necessary to satisfy the coinsurance requirement, whichever is higher. See the exhibit "Guidelines for Choosing a Coinsurance Percentage and Limit of Insurance."

For some insureds, EML may constitute only a small fraction of the coinsurance basis. For example, a retail store operating in an area that contains numerous empty stores may be able to relocate and be fully operational within three months if its present location is totally destroyed. Conversely, a

✓ Reality Check

Example of Business Income Loss

An organization can suffer a business income loss because of damage to property at some location other than its own because of acts of civil authorities. In some cases, damage to nearby property creates such a hazardous exposure that the police or fire department will prohibit access to the area. Even though a particular business in the affected area may have sustained no damage within its own premises, the act of civil authority will prevent occupancy, resulting in a loss of business income.

The destruction of the World Trade Center provides a dramatic example of this type of loss. Civil authorities closed most of the area below Canal Street in Manhattan—more than two square miles—to all but essential traffic from September 11 until September 19, 2001. The restricted area was gradually reduced, but more than thirteen square blocks, in addition to the former World Trade Center site, were closed for two months, and small portions of the area remained closed for over eight months.

[DA06066]

Guidelines for Choosing a Coinsurance Percentage and Limit of Insurance

Assume ABR Company has an EML of $3,370,000 and a coinsurance basis of $5,000,000.

The first step is to determine the coinsurance percentage by dividing the company's EML by the coinsurance basis:

$3,370,000 ÷ $5,000,000 = 0.67, which is rounded up to 70 percent coinsurance.

The second step is to determine the limit of insurance to purchase by multiplying the coinsurance percent by the coinsurance basis:

0.70 × $5,000,000 = $3,500,000, then comparing that result with the EML of $3,370,000 and choosing the higher amount, which is $3,500,000.

[DA06068]

manufacturer that depends on sophisticated, special-order machinery might be shut down for eighteen months or more while waiting for replacement equipment if it sustains extensive damage to key equipment. The retail store might need an amount of insurance equal to less than half its coinsurance basis and could thus choose a 50 percent coinsurance clause; the manufacturer might need an amount of insurance much greater than its coinsurance basis. It could select a 125 percent coinsurance clause, which would reduce the rate, because rates are lower when higher coinsurance percentages are selected. However, the premium for a policy with a higher coinsurance percentage will not necessarily be reduced, because the lower rate will be applied to a greater amount of insurance (if the amount of insurance carried is sufficient to comply with the coinsurance requirement).

Given the difficulty of accurately estimating the amount of insurance needed to comply with the coinsurance clause in a business income policy, many experienced risk managers, producers, and consultants advocate elimination or suspension of coinsurance from the business income policy. Smaller businesses often select this option when an insurer makes it available

BUSINESS INCOME (AND EXTRA EXPENSE) COVERAGE FORM

The commercial property program of Insurance Services Office, Inc. (ISO) includes coverage forms for insuring business income and extra expense loss exposures.

The Business Income (and Extra Expense) Coverage Form covers both loss of business income and extra expenses. The form includes an insuring agreement for business income coverage, an insuring agreement for extra expense coverage, additional coverages, a coverage extension, and several conditions.

Business Income Coverage

Two main coverages are provided by the Business Income (and Extra Expense) Coverage Form (CP 00 30): business income coverage and extra expense coverage. An insured can purchase business income coverage without extra expense coverage with the Business Income (Without Extra Expense) Coverage Form, CP 00 32. This form covers extra expenses but only to the extent they reduce business income loss.

Because proving that an extra expense has reduced a business income loss can be difficult, most insureds select the Business Income (and Extra Expense) Coverage Form. That form allows an insured to choose any of three options:

- Business income including rental value
- Business income other than rental value
- Rental value only

The option chosen by the insured should always be clearly indicated on the Declarations page.

Option 1 covers both loss of rental value and loss of other business income. An insurance agency that owns, and operates out of, a multi-tenant office building that it rents in part to other tenants might choose option 1. If the building became physically damaged and untenantable, the insurer would pay for both the insured's loss of rental income from tenants and the insured's loss of business income from (or extra expenses for) its own business.

Option 2 covers business income other than rental value. This option could be chosen by a business that has rental income to lose but does not wish to insure it. A business that has no rental income to lose might choose option 2.

Option 3 is less expensive, but it covers rental value only. The coverage form defines "rental value" to include anticipated net rental income from tenants, as well as all charges that are the legal obligation of the tenants and would otherwise be the insured's obligation (such as real-estate taxes and charges for electrical service).

Rental value also includes the fair rental value of any portion of the described premises occupied by the insured. Option 3 might be purchased by a landlord whose only income is derived from renting property to others.

Regardless of which of the three options the insured selects, it is often said that business income insurance is intended to do for the insured what the insured would have done for itself had no loss occurred. This wording does not appear in business income forms, but it can aid in understanding the basic concept of business income insurance. The exact coverage, of course, depends on the specific wording in the policy.

This passage from the Business Income (and Extra Expense) Coverage Form expresses the key requirements that must be fulfilled for business income coverage to apply:

> We will pay for the actual loss of Business Income you sustain due to the necessary "suspension" of your "operations" during the "period of restoration". The "suspension" must be caused by direct physical loss of or damage to property at premises which are described in the Declarations and for which a Business Income Limit of Insurance is shown in the Declarations. The loss or damage must be caused by or result from a Covered Cause of Loss. With respect to loss of or damage to personal property in the open or personal property in a vehicle, the described premises include the area within 100 feet of such premises.[1]

These are the key requirements in the Business Income (and Extra Expense) Coverage Form:

- Actual loss of business income you sustain
- Due to the necessary suspension of your operations
- During the period of restoration
- Caused by direct physical loss of or damage to property at the described premises
- Loss or damage caused by a covered cause of loss

Actual Loss of Business Income You Sustain

The policy definition of business income is intended to clarify what sums can be included when calculating the amount of loss:

> Business Income means the:
>
> a. Net Income (Net Profit or Loss before income taxes) that would have been earned or incurred; and

b. Continuing normal operating expenses incurred, including payroll.

For manufacturing risks, Net Income includes the net sales value of production.[2]

Calculating the difference between the net income that could have been expected for the period of restoration (had no physical loss occurred) and the actual net income during that period takes into consideration all of the elements of the business income definition.

For example, Pete's Pizza Parlor suffered an $18,000 reduction in net income because of a shutdown following a fire. If Pete had a business income policy, the $18,000 reduction in net income would be covered under that policy. The $18,000 payment from Pete's insurer would cover the $10,000 net profit that Pete would have realized had no loss occurred, and it would cover the $8,000 in continuing expenses during the shutdown.

All of these calculations are performed without consideration of the effect of income taxes, because any loss payment that the insured receives will itself be subject to tax. If the business income loss were calculated on an after-tax basis, the insured would not be fully indemnified.

The form covers only actual loss sustained by the named insured. Thus, the insurer is not obligated to pay anything unless the insured has actually sustained a business income loss, and the extent of the insurer's obligation is limited to the lower of the dollar amount of loss actually sustained, or the limit of insurance.

In contrast with the ISO business income forms, other approaches to covering business income and extra expense loss exposures, such as gross earnings forms and valued business income forms, are available from some insurers. See the exhibit "Non-ISO Business Income Forms."

The actual-loss-sustained approach does not require the insured to have been earning a net profit before the loss occurred in order to receive any benefit. A business already operating at a net loss can sustain a business income loss if a partial or total shutdown increases the net loss beyond what was expected.

"Actual loss sustained" also does not mean that the insured's operations must show a net loss resulting from the interruption of operations. Particularly in the case of a partial shutdown, the insured's operations may continue to be profitable. However, if the profits are less than they would have been had no loss occurred, the insured has sustained a business income loss.

Another problem in determining the actual loss sustained arises when business would have been interrupted by an uninsured event following the covered loss. For example, a restaurant refinished a floor damaged by water from a broken pipe (a covered peril in the insured's policy) during a blizzard that paralyzed local transportation and closed the city for the entire week. Little, if any, actual loss was sustained because no customers would have braved the weather to eat at the restaurant even if it had been open.

Non-ISO Business Income Forms

Description of Other Approaches	Advantage of Using This Form
• Gross earnings form—Covers business interruption as measured by gross earnings less noncontinuing expense, rather than by net income plus continuing expenses.	Because gross earnings minus operating expenses equals net income and all operating expenses are either continuing or noncontinuing following a loss, the amounts payable by an insurer using the gross earnings form will usually equal the amounts payable using the ISO forms. Therefore, there would normally be no advantage or disadvantage to using one of the forms instead of the other in terms of amounts payable. However, the non-ISO forms may contain a clause the ISO form does not have and that the owner of a business prefers.
• Valued business income form—The insurer pays an agreed amount for each day, week, or month that the insured business is shut down (instead of the actual loss sustained).	This form may offer an advantage for a business whose net income or operating expenses may be difficult to determine quickly after a loss. Having an agreed amount can shorten the time required to receive a payment from an insurer, by reducing the calculations and negotiations involved when the amounts payable are determined.

[DA05935]

Business income insurance is also used to cover buildings and other property under construction even though they are not yet producing revenue. If property damage delays the date on which the insured begins to earn rental income or income from operations, business income insurance will pay the owner for the resulting reduction in net income commencing from the date on which the property would have been put to use. It will pay extra expenses (if covered) beginning immediately after the physical loss occurs.

Due to the Necessary Suspension of Your Operations

The business income insuring agreement requires that the loss of business income must be sustained because of a necessary suspension of the named insured's operations. Insurance adjusters have generally interpreted the phrase "suspension of your operations" to encompass business income coverage for either partial or total interruption of operations.

If rental value coverage is included, suspension means that either a part or all of the described premises is rendered untenantable.

Some independently developed business income forms do not contain a definition of suspension. In such cases, the insured or its insurance adviser should request an endorsement or clarification confirming that the broader meaning will apply. The ISO business income forms define "operations" as (1) the named insured's business operations at the described premises and (2) the tenantability of the premises, but only if the policy covers rental value.

During the Period of Restoration

The policy definition of "period of restoration" is the key in determining the extent of business income or extra expense coverage. Business income coverage does not include actual loss sustained before the period of restoration begins or after the period of restoration ends—except for losses covered by the Extended Business Income additional coverage or the Extended Period of Indemnity coverage option.

Period of restoration

The period during which business income loss is covered under the BIC forms; it begins seventy-two hours after the physical loss occurs and ends when the property is (or should have been) restored to use with reasonable speed. (With regard to extra expense coverage, it begins immediately after the physical loss occurs.)

As defined, the **period of restoration** for business income coverage begins seventy-two hours after the physical loss or damage occurs. Consequently, any business income loss sustained during the first seventy-two hours following the physical loss that caused the business income loss is not covered. This seventy-two-hour waiting period is sometimes referred to as an elimination period or a time deductible.

The seventy-two-hour waiting period does not apply to extra expense losses; coverage for such losses begins at the time the loss occurs. This is appropriate because many extra expenses are incurred in the first few days after the damage.

Such expenses could be for the purchase of temporary equipment or moving to and setting up a temporary location. The seventy-two-hour waiting period for business income coverage can be either eliminated entirely or reduced to twenty-four hours through the use of the Business Income Changes—Beginning of the Period of Restoration endorsement (CP 15 56).

For some losses, particularly rental value losses, the period of restoration is determined based on an estimate by the contractor retained by the insurer to estimate the damage. Because it is often only a rough estimate, the loss adjuster will sometimes not deduct the first three days in computing the covered loss. See the exhibit "The Effect of the Seventy-Two-Hour Waiting Period Can Be Severe."

The period of restoration ends on the earlier of these dates: (1) when the property should, with "reasonable speed and similar quality," be repaired or replaced or (2) when business is resumed at a new permanent location.

The period of restoration does not include any increased time required because of the enforcement of any ordinance or law that regulates

---

The Effect of the Seventy-Two-Hour Waiting Period Can Be Severe

This example shows how the seventy-two-hour waiting period can eliminate coverage for a significant business income loss. This type of loss can be covered by omitting the waiting period by endorsement.

Furniture Store holds an annual storewide furniture sale on Labor Day every year. The sale is heavily advertised and widely promoted because Labor Day is an optimal sale day for furniture stores. However, the night before Labor Day, a windstorm struck the store and tore open part of the roof. Temporary repairs enabled the store to reopen on the Wednesday after Labor Day, but the sales that were lost because of the Labor Day closing were never recovered. Because the period of restoration, as defined in Furniture Store's policy, began seventy-two hours after the physical damage occurred, the store could not collect any of its lost income under its business income coverage.

[DA05941]

construction, use, repair, or demolition; or that requires testing for pollutants or cleaning them up.

The reference to "reasonable speed and similar quality" is important. If the insured causes unreasonable delay in obtaining estimates or if extra time is consumed to upgrade the property, the insurer will not pay for loss sustained beyond the reasonably expected repair period.

However, courts have held that time consumed by delays resulting from acts of persons other than the insured, or even by reasonable disputes between the insured and others, is includable in the period of restoration. Moreover, delays resulting from conditions beyond the insured's control are also includable in the period of restoration.

For example, if unusually severe weather or a delay in shipping causes a holdup in rebuilding, the additional time can be included in the period of restoration.

The period of restoration does not cease the instant a damaged or destroyed building is repaired or rebuilt. Time is permitted for the insured to refurnish supplies and to restock merchandise. For a manufacturer, time is allowed to bring the production process to the point it was at before the loss.

Net income often does not return to the normal level as soon as the suspension of operations ends. One of the business income forms' additional coverages, Extended Business Income, covers business income loss for up to thirty days after the period of restoration ends.

In many cases, returning to normal income levels takes more than thirty days. Accordingly, one of the optional coverages included in the business income forms, Extended Period of Indemnity, can be used to increase the number of additional days covered under Extended Business Income.

Caused by Direct Physical Loss of or Damage to Property at the Described Premises

A common misconception about the ISO business income forms is that the physical loss or damage must occur to property covered under the insured's Building and Personal Property Coverage Form (BPP) or another building and contents form. See the exhibit "Elevator Fire Interrupts Engineering Firm's Operations."

Elevator Fire Interrupts Engineering Firm's Operations

C&R Engineering Services was a tenant on the twenty-fifth floor of a multistory office building. A fire commencing at 3 am on March 1 destroyed the building's elevators. Although the fire did not damage C&R's offices, C&R could not use its offices until the elevators were repaired. The building owner completed the repairs, using reasonable speed, on March 27. C&R's resulting business income and extra expense loss was insured under C&R's Business Income (and Extra Expense) Coverage Form. The period of restoration started at 3 am on March 4 (seventy-two hours after the fire occurred) and ended March 27.

[DA05942]

Although some independently filed business income forms do require physical damage to covered property, the ISO business income forms require that the suspension of operations must be caused by loss of or damage to "property at premises which are described in the Declarations."

The property can be real or personal property, owned by the insured or by others. If the insured is a tenant, the period of restoration would include the time necessary to repair or replace the building even though the building is not owned by the insured.

The ISO forms also cover suspension of operations resulting from damage caused by a covered peril to personal property in the open (or in a vehicle) within 100 feet of the described premises.

To illustrate, consider that a hailstorm damages the inventory of new and used autos on an auto dealer's lot and that obtaining replacement inventory will take two to three weeks. Automobiles are not covered property under the BPP.

However, the resulting business income loss would nevertheless be covered under the dealer's business income coverage, if the damaged autos on the lot were at the premises described in the declarations or within 100 feet of the described premises. If the autos had been stored at a remote location not shown in the policy, the business income loss would not be covered.

For an insured that occupies only part of a building, the form states that "premises" means:

a. The portion of the building which you rent, lease or occupy;

b. The area within 100 feet of the building or within 100 feet of the premises described in the Declarations, whichever distance is greater (with respect to loss of or damage to personal property in the open or personal property in a vehicle); and

c. Any area within the building or at the described premises, if that area services, or is used to gain access to, the portion of the building which you rent, lease or occupy.[3]

Not only must there be physical damage to property at the described premises, but also the damage must be the cause of the loss of business income. For example, if a snowstorm damaged the roof of a grocery store and loss of income resulted from the inability of potential customers to reach the store's premises, not from the damage to the roof, the store's loss of income claim would not be payable.

The form contains both an additional coverage (Civil Authority) and a coverage extension (Newly Acquired Locations) that provide some coverage for business income resulting from physical damage occurring away from the described premises. If the insured has an off-premises business income exposure because of dependence on a particular supplier, buyer, manufacturer, or "magnet" property, that exposure can be insured under a separate endorsement.

If the insured's off-premises business income exposure arises from its own property at other locations—for example, property in transit or mobile equipment at job sites—business income coverage can sometimes be obtained as extensions of the inland marine policies covering the property against physical loss.

Caused by a Covered Cause of Loss

The covered causes of loss for business income and/or extra expense coverage are determined by whichever causes of loss form—Basic, Broad, or Special—is designated on the Declarations page as being applicable to business income and/or extra expense. The commercial property causes of loss forms contain some special exclusions that apply only to the ISO business income and extra expense coverage forms. See the exhibit "Special Exclusions Applicable to Business Income and Extra Expense Forms."

Any of the ISO endorsements that are available for adding earthquake or flood or making any other changes to the causes of loss forms can be used for purposes of business income and/or extra expense coverage.

Some causes of loss that may be particularly important as causes of business income loss or extra expenses are generally uninsurable. For example, many businesses are shut down when workers go on strike demanding higher wages

Special Exclusions Applicable to Business Income and Extra Expense Forms

What Is Excluded	Loss Example	Comments
Loss caused by damage to or destruction of finished stock and the time required to reproduce finished stock. (This exclusion does not apply to extra expense coverage.)	If a fire destroys $100,000 worth of finished stock while awaiting shipment from the insured's factory, the insured's business income policy will not cover any part of the resulting loss of sales revenue.	Coverage is limited to what is covered under the insured's BPP. Finished stock can be covered for its selling price by endorsing the BPP with the Manufacturers Selling Price endorsement (CP 99 30) and arranging a limit of insurance that reflects that valuation basis.
Loss resulting from physical damage to radio or TV antennas, including satellite dishes.	If a radio station's transmitting antenna collapsed because of ice buildup, the station's policy would not cover resulting loss of business income or extra expenses to get back on the air.	The exclusion can be deleted by adding the Radio or Television Antennas – Business Income or Extra Expense endorsement (CP 15 50). Inland marine radio and TV policies are also available.
Any increase in loss resulting from delay in rebuilding, repairing, or replacing the property because of interference by strikers or other persons at the location of the rebuilding.	If reconstruction of the building is delayed because of picketing at the building site, the delay would not be covered. But, if the picketing occurred at the general contractor's office, any delay would not be excluded and would be included in the period of restoration.	No ISO endorsement is available to omit or mitigate this exclusion.
Any increase in business income loss resulting from the suspension, lapse, or cancellation of any license, lease, or contract.	Because of poor sales performance over several years, an auto dealer lost its franchise agreement with a major car maker. Notice of the franchise agreement's cancellation arrived while the dealer's operations were suspended because of damage to property at the dealer's premises by a covered cause of loss. Any increase in the dealer's business income loss resulting from losing the franchise is excluded.	If a loss of license, lease, or contract is caused by a suspension of operations because of a covered peril, the insurer will pay such loss that affects the insured's business income during the period of restoration or any extensions of it.
Extra expense resulting from suspension, lapse, or cancellation of any license, lease, or contract beyond the period of restoration.	The insured's operations were suspended because a covered peril damaged the insured's store. As a result, the insured's lease of the store premises was canceled. The insured incurred extra expenses to continue operations at a temporary store location.	Because of the exclusion, the insurer covers these extra expenses only until the period of restoration ends.

or other concessions, and loss of business income caused by strike is not generally insurable. However, if a strike turns into a riot, business interruption resulting from physical damage caused by rioters would be covered by any of the three ISO causes of loss forms.

Extra Expense Coverage

The second of the two main coverages provided by the Business Income (and Extra Expense) Coverage Form is extra expense. The form defines "extra expense" as necessary expenses the insured incurs during the period of restoration that would not have been incurred if there had been no physical loss caused by a covered peril. The coverage provisions describe three categories of covered extra expenses.

The first category includes extra expenses incurred to avoid or minimize the suspension of business and to continue operations, either at the described premises or at temporary or replacement premises. For example, this category would cover the extra expense of renting, moving to, and equipping a temporary location while the original premises are being repaired.

The second category includes extra expenses incurred to minimize the suspension of business if the insured cannot continue operations. For example, a printing company whose plant has been destroyed might have contract obligations to print a certain number of books or magazines by a certain date.

Although the printing company would be unable to do the printing itself, it might hire another printer as a subcontractor to fulfill the contract. The cost of hiring the printing subcontractor would be covered as an extra expense to the extent it exceeded the printing company's normal costs.

The third category includes extra expenses incurred to repair or replace any property, but only to the extent that it reduces the amount of loss that would otherwise have been payable. Examples of this type of extra expenses are: (1) payment of overtime wages to expedite building repairs and (2) payment of above-market prices to obtain replacement merchandise promptly so that sales activities can be resumed more quickly.

The extra expenses described in the first and second categories are covered regardless of whether they reduce the business income loss. Thus, they provide the type of extra expense coverage appropriate for organizations that have a strong need to continue operations or to deliver their services, even if that would cost more than suspending operations.

BUSINESS INCOME ADDITIONAL COVERAGES AND COVERAGE EXTENSION

As with other commercial property coverage forms, additional coverages and coverage extensions are available for business income coverage.

Four additional coverages and a coverage extension apply are available under the Business Income (and Extra Expense) Coverage Form:

- Civil Authority
- Alterations and New Buildings
- Extended Business Income
- Interruption of Computer Operations

Another additional coverage that applies to business income and extra expense coverage is located in each of the causes of loss forms. This additional coverage—Limited Coverage for Fungus, Wet Rot, Dry Rot and Bacteria—provides thirty days of coverage for loss resulting from fungus damage caused by a covered peril. The form also contains a Newly Acquired Locations coverage extension.

Civil Authority

Civil Authority additional coverage

An additional coverage in a business income form, covering loss of business income and/or extra expenses that result when access to the insured's premises is prohibited by a civil authority because of damage by a covered cause of loss to property other than the insured's.

The **Civil Authority additional coverage** extends the Business Income (and Extra Expense) Coverage Form to include actual loss of business income and necessary extra expenses incurred by the insured because access to the insured's premises has been cut off by action of civil authority.

For the Civil Authority additional coverage to apply, four criteria must be met:

- A covered cause of loss must have caused damage to property other than property at the described premises.
- Access to the area immediately surrounding the damaged property must be prohibited by action of civil authority as a result of the damage.
- The described premises must be within the area just described and not more than one mile from the damaged property. (The one-mile limitation is applied as a one-mile radius as opposed to a one-mile road distance.)
- The action of civil authority must have been taken either in response to dangerous physical conditions resulting from the damage or continuation of the covered cause of loss that caused the damage; or to enable a civil authority to have unimpeded access to the damaged property.

For business income losses, the Civil Authority additional coverage begins seventy-two hours after the time of the first action of civil authority that prohibits access to the described premises and continues for up to four consecutive weeks after coverage begins.

For extra expenses resulting from acts of a civil authority, the coverage begins immediately after the time of the first action of civil authority and ends at the later of these times:

- Four consecutive weeks after the date coverage begins
- When civil authority coverage for business income coverage ends

Because coverage of extra expenses ends at the later of these two times, an insured could receive payment for extra expenses for up to four weeks and three days (seventy-two hours) after the first action of civil authority prohibiting access to the insured premises.

Two endorsements are available for modifying the Civil Authority additional coverage:

The Civil Authority Change(s) endorsement (CP 15 32) can be used to increase the four-week limitation to 60, 90, or 180 days and/or the one-mile restriction.

When the Business Income Changes—Beginning of the Period of Restoration endorsement (CP 15 56) is used to eliminate or reduce to twenty-four hours the seventy-two-hour waiting period that applies to business income coverage, the waiting period under the Civil Authority coverage is also changed to the same extent. See the exhibit "Ingress/Egress Coverage."

Ingress/Egress Coverage

A loss exposure not covered by standard business income policies is loss of business income resulting from the inability of customers or employees to reach the insured's premises because of circumstances beyond the scope of the Civil Authority provision. If civil authorities ban access to the insured's premises because of loss by a covered cause at another location, the ISO forms provide some coverage, but if, for example, a windstorm strews debris across roads, making them impassable, the ISO forms do not cover the resulting loss of business income at the insured's premises.

To cover such losses, some insurers are willing to include what is called ingress/egress coverage in their business income policies. ("Ingress" means entrance, and "egress" means exit.) One example of policy wording is shown:

Business income coverage applies to the interruption or interference with the insured's operation and/or ingress to and/or egress from the premises due to damage occurring during the policy period to property in the vicinity of the premises. Coverage applies whether or not the premises have been damaged.

This is very broad wording; other ingress/egress clauses may provide coverage only when access is "prevented," which raises issues related to Civil Authority coverage.

[DA03880]

Alterations and New Buildings

Business income losses do not result only from property damage that disrupts operations currently in progress.

Business income can also be lost if completion of a new building or alterations to an existing building are delayed because the building is damaged during construction. Similarly, if alterations to an existing building are not completed on schedule, operations will not begin when planned and a loss of income may result.

The Alterations and New Buildings additional coverage insures loss of business income sustained because of physical damage to (1) new buildings or structures at the described premises or (2) alterations or additions to existing buildings or structures at the described premises.

The coverage also applies to business income losses resulting from damage to machinery, equipment, supplies, or building materials located on or within 100 feet of the described premises and used in the construction or incidental to the occupancy of new buildings.

If the physical loss or damage delays the start of operations, the "period of restoration" for business income coverage begins on the date operations would have begun if the direct physical loss or damage had not occurred. However, under the Business Income (and Extra Expense) Coverage Form, extra expense payments can be used immediately to try to rush repairs so that the property can be usable by its scheduled date.

The period of restoration for Alterations and New Buildings is not subject to the seventy-two-hour waiting period. And, unlike the Newly Acquired or Constructed Property extension in the BPP and the Newly Acquired Locations extension in business income forms, this coverage is not limited to thirty days.

However, because alterations and new buildings may create a need for increased limits to comply with coinsurance or to cover an increase in estimated maximum loss, insureds may want to review their limits of insurance whenever alterations are made or a new building is constructed on the insured premises.

Extended Business Income

The need for **Extended Business Income (EBI) additional coverage** is best understood by reviewing a basic limitation on recovery for business income loss.

Business income coverage replaces income lost during the period of restoration, which ends on the date when the property at the described premises should be repaired, rebuilt, or replaced with reasonable speed and similar quality. In many cases, the period of restoration ends before the insured's business volume has returned to normal.

A business that has been shut down does not immediately regain all its customers when its doors reopen. The damaged property may be restored, but business activity may still be depressed.

Extended Business Income (EBI) additional coverage

Coverage for business income losses that continue after the period of restoration ends; the coverage begins when the damaged property has been restored and ends when the insured's business returns to normal, subject to a maximum of sixty days.

EBI adds a sixty-day period for which the insured will be reimbursed for loss of business income. EBI begins on the date when the property is actually repaired, rebuilt, or replaced and operations are resumed.

The beginning date of EBI is not necessarily the same as the date on which the period of restoration ends. A gap can occur if the restoration is not completed with reasonable speed.

A gap can also occur if operations do not resume until sometime after the property is restored. Business income coverage ends when the property should have been repaired, rebuilt, or replaced with reasonable speed. EBI does not begin until the property is actually restored and operations are resumed.

EBI is divided into two parts with similar provisions. One part applies to business income other than rental value, and the other part applies to rental value. The provisions in both parts are similar.

In both cases, the coverage ends when the sixty days have expired or on the date the insured, with reasonable speed, could have restored normal conditions, whichever is earlier.

However, what constitutes normal conditions differs between business income other than rental value and rental value. For business income other than rental value, it is the date the insured could restore operations to the level that would generate the business income that would have existed.

For rental value, it is the date the insured could restore tenant occupancy to the level that would generate the rental value that would have existed. Note that in both cases, it is "could restore," not "does restore," that governs.

EBI does not apply to loss of business income or rental value caused by the consequences of the covered cause of loss in the area where the described premises are located.

For example, assume that Gertie's Grocery is damaged by a windstorm on October 2. The store is completely restored by October 10, but business does not return to normal for another thirty days because of impassable roads and bridges in the area that was hit by the storm. Gertie's business income insurance would cover the loss only until October 10.

No coverage would be provided for the loss of business income between October 10 and November 10. "Ingress or egress" provisions are sometimes included in nonstandard business income forms to cover the added business income loss during periods when the premises are inaccessible.

The sixty-day limitation on EBI coverage can be lengthened in thirty-day increments to as long as 730 days (two years) through the **Extended Period of Indemnity** option. This optional coverage, which is printed in the ISO business income forms but requires an additional premium, is activated when the applicable number of days is entered in the appropriate place on the Declarations page. See the exhibit "Bowling Alley Suffers EBI Loss."

Extended Period of Indemnity

An optional coverage that lengthens the duration of the extended business income (EBI) additional coverage for up to two years.

> ## Bowling Alley Suffers EBI Loss
>
> All-American Bowling operates a bowling alley in a suburban town. A major source of its income comes from bowlers who compete weekly in bowling leagues that start in September and end in May. A serious fire occurred on August 15. The insured and the insurer agreed that the period of restoration ended on November 30. However, business did not return to expected normal levels until the following September because some of the leagues shifted to other bowling alleys and did not return to All-American when it reopened. Finding new leagues to replace those that failed to return was not feasible until the start of a new season. All-American was covered for EBI for the first sixty days after the period of restoration. Failure to anticipate the length of time it would take to regain lost business resulted in a large uninsured loss that could have been covered by purchasing the Extended Period of Indemnity option.

[DA03881]

Interruption of Computer Operations

The **Interruption of Computer Operations additional coverage** functions in tandem with another provision of the Business Income (and Extra Expense) Coverage Form. The other provision, titled Additional Limitation—Interruption of Computer Operations, can be summarized this way: neither business income nor extra expense coverage applies when a suspension of operations is caused by destruction or corruption of, or any other loss of or damage to, electronic data except as provided under the Interruption of Computer Operations additional coverage.

Interruption of Computer Operations pays up to $2,500 per policy year (or a higher limit if shown in the declarations) for loss of business income or extra expense due to a suspension of operations resulting from an interruption of computer operations caused by destruction or corruption of electronic data as a result of a covered cause of loss.

As is true with a similar additional coverage in the BPP, the $2,500 is an aggregate limit for all losses sustained in any one policy year. The $2,500 limit is not a meaningful amount of coverage for most insureds covered by commercial package policies; this provision serves more to limit the insurer's exposure than to provide coverage for the insured.

In addition to the low limit, another drawback is that the covered causes of loss for this additional coverage are limited to specified causes of loss, even if the Causes of Loss—Special Form applies to the insured's business income coverage.

If the applicable causes of loss form is endorsed to add a covered cause of loss (for example, flood or earthquake), the added covered cause of loss does not apply to Interruption of Computer Operations.

Interruption of Computer Operations additional coverage

Coverage for loss of business income or extra expense due to a suspension of operations resulting from an interruption of computer operations caused by destruction or corruption of electronic data as a result of a covered cause of loss.

The covered causes of loss for Interruption of Computer Operations include a virus, harmful code, or similar instruction designed to damage or destroy any part of a computer system or to disrupt its normal operation.

Coverage does not apply, however, to loss resulting from the manipulation of a computer system by an employee, including a leased or temporary employee, or by an entity the insured retains to inspect, design, install, maintain, repair, or replace the system.

The Interruption of Computer Operations additional coverage does not apply when loss to electronic data involves only electronic data that are integrated in and operate or control a building's elevator, lighting, heating, ventilation, air conditioning, or security system. This type of loss is specifically excepted from the Additional Limitation—Interruption of Computer Operations and is therefore covered by the business income insuring agreement without any of the restrictions of the additional coverage, such as the $2,500 aggregate limit and the limitation to specified causes of loss.

Limited Coverage for Fungus, Wet Rot, Dry Rot and Bacteria

The Limited Coverage for Fungus, Wet Rot, Dry Rot and Bacteria additional coverage, which is included in the ISO causes of loss forms, includes thirty days of coverage for business income and extra expense due to fungus, wet rot, dry rot, and bacteria damage. The thirty days need not be consecutive, in recognition of the fact that repair of the damage may not be done in one continuous period and that the premises may be usable when cleanup and repair work is not taking place.

When the covered peril that causes fungus, wet rot, dry rot, or bacteria damage results in a suspension of operations, the thirty-day limit applies to the time that the period of restoration is increased by the fungus, wet rot, dry rot, or bacteria damage.

For example, if roof damage caused by windstorm results in mold damage inside the insured building that will take two months to repair, but there is no suspension of operations because of damage other than mold, the insured is covered for thirty days of business income loss. If the windstorm caused other damage that will suspend operations for fourteen days and the mold damage repairs will take two months, the insured will have coverage for a total of forty-four days (forty-one days, if the seventy-two-hour waiting period for the start of the period of restoration has not been reduced or removed).

Newly Acquired Locations

The Newly Acquired Locations coverage extension applies only when 50 percent or greater coinsurance is shown in the declarations. Most policies are written subject to coinsurance, but coinsurance does not apply to the

Maximum Period of Indemnity or the Monthly Limit of Indemnity options. Nor does it apply when the policy is written on a No Coinsurance basis.

Newly Acquired Locations provides up to thirty days' temporary coverage at a new location, which gives the insured time to report the added exposure to the insurer.

Coverage under the extension ceases when the policy expires, when the new location is reported to the insurer, or thirty days after the exposure begins, whichever occurs first. The extension is automatic insurance, not free insurance. The insurer is entitled to charge a premium from the date the exposure begins.

The limit of insurance for the Newly Acquired Locations extension is $100,000 at each location unless a higher limit is shown in the declarations. Unlike the limits for the additional coverages, the limit for Newly Acquired Locations is a separate amount of insurance that applies in addition to the overall limit of insurance for the coverage form.

Coverage for newly acquired locations does not apply to property at fairs and exhibitions. Also, the business income Coinsurance condition does not affect the amount recoverable under the coverage extension.

BI: CONDITIONS

This section examines the conditions that are applicable to the Business Income (and Extra Expense) Coverage Form.

The Business Income (and Extra Expense) Coverage Form contains various conditions, some of which are similar to conditions found in the BPP. Others vary in important ways.

Duties in the Event of Loss

The duties that the insured must perform following a business income and/or extra expense loss are virtually identical to those under the BPP, with one significant exception. The business income forms impose a specific duty with regard to resumption of operations.

If the insured organization intends to continue its operations, it must resume all or part of its operations "as quickly as possible." If the insured does not resume operations as quickly as possible, the insurer will calculate the loss based on the length of time it would have taken to resume operations as quickly as possible.

Loss Determination

The Loss Determination condition contains several parts. The first part lists the various factors that will be taken into account in determining the amount of business income loss:

- The insured's net income before the loss occurred
- The likely net income if no loss had occurred
- Operating expenses, including payroll, necessary to resume operations at the same level of service that existed just before the loss occurred
- Other relevant sources of information, including (but not limited to) the insured's financial records, bills, and invoices

This condition requires the insured to make detailed financial records available for the insurer's use. The insurer uses any of its internal or external resources (such as forensic accountants) required in order to accurately estimate a loss and calculate insurable value.

Determine Extra Expense

The Loss Determination condition in the Business Income (and Extra Expense) Coverage Form also contains an explanation of how the amount of extra expense coverage will be determined. The covered extra expense loss consists of all expenses in excess of normal operating expenses that would have been incurred if the physical loss had not taken place.

The covered loss also includes all necessary expenses that reduce the business income loss that would otherwise have been incurred; there is no requirement that certain types of extra expenses must reduce the otherwise payable loss, provided that such extra expenses are necessary to continue operations or expedite the resumption of operations.

The insurer will deduct from this total the salvage value of any property bought for temporary use during the period of restoration, as well as extra expenses covered by other insurance. To illustrate the provision relating to salvage value, assume that the insured buys a trailer to be placed outside the damaged building for use as a temporary office and a command post for reconstruction efforts.

Although the purchase price is an includable extra expense, the insurer will have the right to deduct the salvage value of the trailer once operations are resumed. Without this provision, the remaining value of property purchased to expedite recovery would be a windfall profit to the insured.

Finally, the insurer reserves the right to reduce its payment for business income loss to the extent that the insured can resume operations in whole or in part using damaged or undamaged property at the described premises or elsewhere. In other words, the insured organization must do what it can to minimize the loss, even if that means setting up temporary operations at another location.

If the insured does not resume operations or does not resume operations as quickly as possible, the insurer will pay only on the basis of what the loss would have been had the insured resumed operations as quickly as possible.

Coinsurance

To encourage insurance to value and to make rates equitable, the Business Income (and Extra Expense) Coverage Form, like the BPP, contains a Coinsurance condition. The Coinsurance condition applies only to business income coverage, not to extra expense.

The business income Coinsurance condition operates in essentially the same manner as the BPP Coinsurance condition, with two important exceptions:

- The business income insured can choose from a wider range of coinsurance percentages.
- The business income coinsurance percentage is not applied against a property value. Instead, it is applied against the total of net income and operating expenses that would have been earned or incurred (had no loss occurred) for the twelve months beginning with the later of policy inception or the last previous anniversary date. (This dollar amount is called the "coinsurance basis.")

The insured may choose business income coinsurance percentages of 50, 60, 70, 80, 90, 100, or 125 percent under *CLM* rules. As in direct damage property insurance, the rates charged for business income insurance decrease as the coinsurance percentage *increases*.

In determining whether the amount of insurance carried under a business income form complies with the Coinsurance condition, the applicable coinsurance percentage is multiplied against net income plus operating expenses that would have developed during the twelve-month period following the inception date of the policy if no loss had occurred.

All operating expenses must be included in the calculation, with only a few exceptions. The items that can be excluded are stated in the Coinsurance condition.

The business income Coinsurance condition is frequently misunderstood. Because the form covers loss of business income, defined as net income plus *continuing* expenses incurred during the interruption, many people assume, erroneously, that the coinsurance percentage is multiplied against the exposure insured: net income plus only those expenses that would continue during a shutdown.

However, the coinsurance percentage is actually multiplied against net income and *all* expenses for the twelve months following policy inception, except the allowable deductions shown in the exhibit.

It might seem more logical if the coinsurance percentage applied to the exposure (net income plus continuing expenses). However, distinguishing continuing expenses from noncontinuing expenses before any loss occurs can be extremely difficult.

Requiring such a distinction might make it hard for policyholders to comply with coinsurance provisions (and even harder for an insurer to prove non-compliance). See the exhibit "Expenses Excluded From the Coinsurance Calculation."

Expenses Excluded From the Coinsurance Calculation

- Prepaid freight—outgoing
- Returns and allowances
- Discounts
- Bad debts
- Collection expenses
- Cost of raw stock and factory supplies consumed (including transportation charges)
- Cost of merchandise sold (including transportation charges)
- Cost of other supplies consumed (including transportation charges)
- Cost of services purchased from outsiders (not employees) to resell that do not continue under contract
- Power, heat, and refrigeration expenses that do not continue under contract (if they have been excluded by endorsement)
- Ordinary payroll expenses excluded by endorsement
- Special deductions for mining properties

Includes copyrighted material of Insurance Services Office, Inc., with its permission. Copyright, ISO Properties, 2007. [DA03587]

BI: OPTIONAL COVERAGES FOR MODIFYING COINSURANCE

Both of the business income forms contain provisions for three optional coverages that can be used to eliminate or suspend the Coinsurance condition.

The Business Income (and Extra Expense) Coverage Form contains provisions for four optional coverages, each of which can be activated by making an appropriate entry on the Declarations page. Three of the optional coverages are designed to eliminate or suspend coinsurance, and an additional option (omitting coinsurance in return for a higher rate) is not printed in the form but is permitted by the *CLM*.

Maximum Period of Indemnity

Maximum Period of Indemnity is a reasonable alternative for organizations that are unlikely to sustain a business interruption of more than four months. The chief advantage of this optional coverage is that it is uncomplicated.

When Maximum Period of Indemnity is in effect, the Coinsurance condition does not apply. Instead, the insurer promises to pay whatever business income loss is sustained for up to 120 days following the physical damage loss or until the limit of insurance is exhausted, whichever comes first.

Premium rates are substantially higher with this option, but lower limits of insurance may be chosen to cover the estimated maximum loss of business income. The result is generally lower premiums for organizations whose only need is for coverage for four months or less and whose estimated maximum loss is much lower than the amount of insurance required by the coinsurance formula. The 120-day limit applies to extra expense as well as business income.

Monthly Limit of Indemnity

Monthly Limit of Indemnity also suspends the Coinsurance condition. With this option, the most the insurer will pay for each period of thirty consecutive days is the actual business income loss sustained, not to exceed the limit of insurance times the fraction shown in the declarations. The fractions ordinarily used are one-third, one-quarter, and one-sixth. In the Monthly Limit of Indemnity option, "month" means a period of thirty consecutive days, not a calendar month.

A simple, rule-of-thumb method can be used to select the fraction and the amount of insurance. In this method, the fraction is selected by using the estimated number of months needed for restoration in a worst-case scenario as the denominator, with 1 as the numerator. Thus, one-third is used for three months, one-fourth for four months, and one-sixth for six months or any period of restoration exceeding six months. The amount of insurance is selected by multiplying the highest possible business income loss in any one month by the denominator.

For example, assume these facts about the RST Company: The period of restoration is estimated as four months. RST conducts a seasonal business with its best month in December. In December, net profits and continuing expenses are expected to be $80,000. Given these facts, the 1/4 monthly limit is selected, and the amount of insurance purchased is four times $80,000, or $320,000.

The rule-of-thumb method is generally used by smaller firms unwilling or unable to estimate the maximum loss for the entire period of a shutdown. It has the advantage of simplicity. Its disadvantages are that it ignores extra expense and EBI exposures and, for insureds with large month-to-month fluctuations in income, that it may overstate the amount of insurance needed.

It may also understate the amount of insurance needed by insureds with long periods of restoration. However, because using the potentially more accurate methods results in low possible savings for smaller insureds, a viable alternative for such firms would be to use the rule-of-thumb method and adjust the result by adding any extra expense that might be necessary in the month with the highest possible loss and adding to the total amount of insurance an amount sufficient to cover EBI.

To illustrate the settlement of losses under the monthly limit of indemnity option, suppose that RST Company is shut down for two weeks and incurs a business income loss of $50,000. The loss will be paid in full because 1/4 of $320,000 yields an $80,000 monthly limit.

The limit is not allocated over the month. In other words, the $80,000 monthly limit is not further prorated into $40,000 for two weeks. The full $80,000 is available for any loss lasting less than one month.

Agreed Value

The Agreed Value option in business income forms is comparable to the Agreed Value option of the BPP. In both cases, the Coinsurance condition is suspended, and the insured and the insurer agree to a set of values reported in a written statement, so it is not necessary to include any increased percentage buffer amount after doing a maximum loss of business income calculation.

If the limit of insurance is no less than the agreed value at the time of the loss, the insured's loss will be covered in full. If not, the payment will be a portion of the loss determined by dividing the amount of insurance by the agreed value and multiplying the result by the loss. In any case, the insurer will not pay more than the policy limit.

The Agreed Value option of the ISO business income forms differs from that of the BPP in some ways. First, the *CLM* requires that the insured complete, sign, and submit to the insurer the business income worksheet. The coinsurance basis calculated in the worksheet (net income plus operating expenses minus the permitted deductions for the next twelve months) is multiplied by the selected coinsurance percentage to determine the amount of insurance necessary to satisfy the Agreed Value requirement.

Second, if the amount of business income insurance is changed without submitting a new worksheet, coinsurance is reactivated. In the BPP, subject to the insurer's approval, the insured may change the amount of insurance without affecting the Agreed Value provision.

Finally, insurers typically charge a 10 percent premium surcharge for the business income Agreed Value option. The surcharge for the BPP Agreed Value option is typically 5 percent.

No Coinsurance

The CLM includes an option to select a No Coinsurance option in lieu of a coinsurance percentage. This option eliminates the Coinsurance condition.

Because of the increased rate for the No Coinsurance option, it is unattractive to insureds and is seldom used. For example, for a mercantile or nonmanufacturing business, the rate for No Coinsurance is more than two-and-a-half times the rate for 50 percent coinsurance. Furthermore, some coverage options, such as agreed value, dependent properties, and premium adjustment, are not available with the No Coinsurance option.

However, under certain circumstances the No Coinsurance option can be useful. Insureds with these characteristics might select the No Coinsurance option:

- Their estimated maximum loss (EML) is a small percentage of the amount needed to satisfy even a 50 percent coinsurance requirement.
- The Maximum Period of Indemnity option does not provide adequate coverage. (For example, insureds with an estimated period of restoration greater than 120 days.)
- The Monthly Limit of Indemnity option requires an amount of insurance much larger than the insured's EML. (This situation could occur when the insured's highest monthly exposure is large compared to its total exposure.)

The No Coinsurance option offers some distinct advantages as compared with other methods of eliminating coinsurance:

- A coinsurance penalty does not apply under any circumstances.
- The insured is not required to file business income worksheets with the insurer (although many underwriters will still want to see a worksheet in order to evaluate the exposure).
- The policy does not impose a 120-day restriction on the length of the period of restoration.
- The policy does not impose a fractional limit of recovery in any one month.

Before using the No Coinsurance option, the insured should decide that its advantages outweigh the costs.

EXTRA EXPENSE COVERAGE FORM

A third time element form is the Extra Expense Coverage Form, which covers extra expense only. It is intended for organizations that must continue their operations "at any cost" and do not want to cover loss of business income.

The Extra Expense Coverage Form insures extra expense only, without any coverage for loss of business income. It is intended for organizations that place a high priority on continuing their operations after sustaining physical loss, even though that alternative may be more costly in the short run than just shutting down and losing income until the property is restored to use.

The Extra Expense Coverage Form is used for certain types of businesses that have unique extra expense loss exposures as opposed to lost income. Additionally, in terms of how the coverage form differs from the BIC, there are differences on the limits on loss payments.

A bank, for example, may want to avoid an interruption of business activities under any circumstances. The flow of money will not stop simply because a bank has been damaged or destroyed. It must remain in operation at all costs. Schools and hospitals and other organizations serving a community may also be unwilling simply to stop operating without providing some continuity of service. Newspapers must continue publishing after a physical loss, particularly so that public notices may appear at appropriate times, advertising contracts can be fulfilled, and readership can be sustained.

To remain in operation despite property damage to buildings or equipment, these organizations will incur substantial extra expenses. Extra expenses are covered as an additional coverage in the Business Income (and Extra Expense) Coverage form, but the primary emphasis of that form is on the replacement of business income.

The Extra Expense Coverage Form, in contrast, is designed for organizations whose business interruption exposure is primarily one of extra expenses rather than lost income and who accordingly wish to purchase only extra expense coverage.

However, even insureds that want to remain in operation at all costs and that therefore do not anticipate having a business income loss may find that certain situations make that impossible. For example, a devastating hurricane may make it impossible to obtain alternative facilities. Insureds should carefully examine their assumptions that extra expense is the only coverage that they will need.

The Business Income (and Extra Expense) Coverage Form provides the same extra expense coverage as the separate Extra Expense Coverage Form in addition to business income coverage. The Maximum Period of Indemnity, Monthly Limit of Indemnity, and No Coinsurance options provide alternative means of avoiding the purchase of the high limits sometimes required to comply with the more usual 50 percent Coinsurance condition. Using the

Business Income (and Extra Expense) Coverage Form instead of the Extra Expense Coverage Form will provide both the needed extra expense coverage and business income coverage, often at little, if any, additional premium.

The Business Income (and Extra Expense) Coverage Form has the added advantage of not limiting the amount of coverage for extra expense to a certain percentage per month of the amount of insurance. The 120-day limitation in the Maximum Period of Indemnity option applies to extra expense as well as business income coverage. The other two options of the Business Income (and Extra Expense) Coverage Form—Monthly Limit of Indemnity and No Coinsurance—provide unrestricted extra expense coverage up to the limit of insurance.

Limits on Loss Payment

The only real difference between the extra expense coverage in the Business Income (and Extra Expense) Coverage Form and the separate Extra Expense Coverage Form is the Limits on Loss Payment condition found only in the Extra Expense Coverage Form.

This condition encourages insurance to value by limiting recovery for certain time periods to stipulated percentages of the overall limit of insurance. The percentages that apply to a particular extra expense policy are listed on the Declarations page, along with the overall limit of insurance.

The omission of this condition is an advantage of the combined Business Income (and Extra Expense) Coverage Form.

The *CLM* shows many combinations of percentages, including 100%-100%-100%. The usual combination of percentages is 40%-80%-100%. With this combination, and a policy with a $100,000 limit of insurance, loss payments would be limited in these ways:

- If the period of restoration is thirty days or less, extra expenses up to $40,000 would be covered.
- If the period of restoration is between thirty and sixty days, extra expenses up to $80,000 would be covered.
- If the period of restoration is longer than sixty days, extra expenses up to $100,000 would be covered.

Using those figures, suppose an interruption lasted thirty days and the insured incurred $50,000 of extra expense. The insured would recover only 40 percent of the overall limit, $40,000. If the insured incurred less than $40,000, the insurer would pay the actual loss sustained.

As another example, suppose an interruption lasted forty-five days and the insured incurred extra expenses of $50,000 the first month and $10,000 the second month. The full $60,000 would be covered. Recovery would not be limited to $40,000 for the first month, because the period of restoration extended into the second month.

Determining the Extra Expense Limit

There is often little relationship between the normal cost of doing business and the extra expenses necessarily incurred to maintain a normal volume of business after loss or damage. This situation makes it difficult to determine how much insurance to purchase.

If a firm anticipates that it will be able to continue operations using emergency measures, it should try to estimate the cost of such measures. There is no principle or rule of thumb on which to base the anticipated extra expense of maintaining a normal volume of business during an interruption. However, the firm should carefully consider how long it would take to rebuild or repair the principal building or equipment or both.

If the extra expense percentage chosen for the first two months is other than 100 percent, the insured must make three estimates:

- The maximum loss in the first thirty days
- The maximum loss in the first sixty days
- The maximum loss for the entire period of restoration

The minimum amount of insurance that should be carried is determined by dividing the estimated extra expense for the first thirty days by the percentage chosen for the first month. The insured would then have to be sure that the amount available in the first sixty days and for the entire period is sufficient. If not, the amount of insurance should be increased.

BUSINESS INCOME COVERAGE OPTIONS

The commercial property program of Insurance Services Office, Inc. (ISO) includes coverage options for insuring business income and extra expense loss exposures.

Various coverage options, in addition to the optional coverages included in the business income forms, are available to modify the business income and extra expense coverage forms to meet particular coverage needs. These coverage options are discussed:

- Blanket business income insurance
- Payroll Limitation or Exclusion endorsement
- Discretionary Payroll Expense endorsement
- Power, Heat, and Refrigeration Deduction endorsement
- Endorsements for dependent property exposures
- Business Income Changes—Educational Institutions endorsement
- Utility Services—Time Element endorsement
- Ordinance or Law—Increased Period of Restoration endorsement
- Food Contamination endorsement

Blanket Business Income Insurance

Many organizations conduct operations at more than one location and face the problem of interdependency among locations. If one of an organization's locations is damaged or destroyed, its other locations may also experience a reduction in output, sales, or other revenue-earning activity.

If its operations are interdependent, an organization may be poorly served by having a separate limit of business income insurance for each building or location. An organization with several interdependent locations can suffer a business income loss far in excess of the limit shown for the one location where the physical damage occurred.

With blanket coverage, one limit of insurance applies to all of the insured's locations, and a blanket rate can be used. (A blanket business income rate can be computed on a weighted average based on floor areas at the various locations.)

According to the *Commercial Lines Manual* (CLM), to be eligible for blanket business income insurance, all premises must be substantially owned, managed, or controlled by the insured. Therefore, a dependent property under separate ownership or management, such as an important supplier, cannot be added to the blanket description.

When operations of the same insured at two or more locations are completely independent (that is, there is no interdependency), either specific or blanket coverage may be appropriate. The application of blanket policy limits provides more flexibility.

Unlike blanket building and contents insurance, which requires at least 90 percent coinsurance, blanket business income coverage may be written with any coinsurance percentage. Insureds do not pay a surcharge for blanket coverage. For insureds with more than one location, blanket coverage is almost always a better choice than specific coverage. ISO forms do not include a margin clause for business income coverage similar to the optional margin clause for building and personal property coverage.

Payroll Limitation or Exclusion Endorsement

Some payroll expenses do not normally continue during a long period of interruption. Payroll expense can be high compared with an insured's other expenses and includes employee benefits, Federal Insurance Contributions Act tax payments, union dues paid by the employer, and workers compensation premiums.

Depending on what the insured selects, remuneration for officers, executives, department managers, and employees under contract may be considered part of payroll. Additional employees may also be removed from or added to the definition of payroll either by name or by job classification.

Payroll expenses can be handled using any one of three approaches.

The first approach is to cover payroll in full, but only to the extent that such expenses are necessary to resume operations. The unmodified business income forms cover all necessary payroll expense, including payroll.

Payroll cost is treated as an operating expense and therefore is included when an organization determines the amount of insurance necessary to meet the coinsurance requirement. However, if a loss occurs, only expenses, including payroll, that are necessary to resume operations with the same level of service that existed before the loss occurred are included in the determination of business income. Therefore, even though payroll is covered in full, the insurer, when settling a claim, might contend that continuing payroll is not a necessary expense and is thus not includable as part of the covered loss.

The second approach is to exclude payroll. This is accomplished by using the **Payroll Limitation or Exclusion endorsement** (CP 15 10).

The third approach is to limit payroll. This approach, which also uses the Payroll Limitation or Exclusion endorsement, covers payroll for a limited period. Payroll coverage can be limited to either 90 or 180 days. If the 90- or 180-day option is selected, the days must fall within the period of restoration.

If payroll is handled using the second or third approach, the Payroll Limitation or Exclusion endorsement is used. The endorsement is written so that the insured can chose which employees' payroll will be included. The choices from which an insured can select include these:

- All employees
- All employees and job classifications except officers, executives, management personnel, and contract employees
- All employees and job classifications except those specifically mentioned
- Only those employees and/or job classifications specifically mentioned

The endorsement also allows the insured to change the selection of which employees' payrolls are included per location. For example, an insured may want to continue the salaries of most of the personnel in a sales office but limit or exclude those of most of the employees at a distribution center.

The purpose of limiting or excluding payroll expense is to allow the insured to satisfy the coinsurance requirement with a smaller amount of insurance. In many cases, the excludable expenses actually do not continue during a business interruption and therefore are not part of the loss. However, unless they are excluded, the insured must include such expenses when calculating the amount of insurance necessary to avoid a coinsurance penalty.

The choice of which approach to use and which employees' payrolls to exclude or limit depends on the possible length of an interruption and the extent to which payroll expenses would continue. Many firms should consider

Payroll Limitation or Exclusion endorsement

Endorsement that limits coverage for payroll expenses to a specified number of days or excludes such expenses altogether, allowing the insured to satisfy the coinsurance requirement with a lower amount of insurance.

reducing the amount of insurance needed to comply with coinsurance (and therefore the policy premium) by limiting or excluding payroll.

Payroll should be limited or excluded entirely only after consideration of the variables that might enter into post-loss handling of payroll, as in these examples:

- Labor might be in short supply in the insured's locale at the time of a loss, and hiring new employees might be difficult. Therefore, retaining existing employees might be necessary to resume operations at the same level of service.
- Training new employees might be more expensive than continuing payroll for existing employees; existing employees are already trained.
- Union or other contracts might require salary continuation.
- The services of certain employees will be needed during a suspension of operations.

When payroll is a large part of a firm's expenses, the firm should carefully examine its options. The *CLM* calls for an increase in rate for all options to limit or exclude payroll, with the exception of the 180-day limitation. The insured must decide whether the savings (if any) because of a lower amount of insurance are of a sufficient amount to make the coverage modification worthwhile.

Discretionary Payroll Expense Endorsement

Another payroll coverage option is to cover payroll on a discretionary basis. An insured that wishes to take this approach—either for humanitarian reasons or to make sure that it will be able to keep key employees on the payroll until operations resume—can do so through use of the **Discretionary Payroll Expense endorsement** (CP 15 04).

Power, Heat, and Refrigeration Deduction Endorsement

Power, heat, and refrigeration expenses are significant for some manufacturing operations. However, if the energy used for power, heat, or refrigeration is consumed in the manufacturing process, most such expenses do not continue when the process is shut down.

When these energy expenses do not continue under contract, they can create a sizable gap between the business income loss exposure and the amount of business income coverage that the insured must purchase to meet coinsurance requirements.

The **Power, Heat, and Refrigeration Deduction endorsement** (CP 15 11), available only for manufacturing and mining firms, provides some relief for those faced with this problem. With the endorsement, the cost of such energy

Discretionary Payroll Expense endorsement
An endorsement that extends business income forms to cover payroll expenses for specified job classifications or employees regardless of whether such expenses are necessary to resume operations.

Power, Heat and Refrigeration Deduction endorsement
Endorsement that eliminates power, heat, and refrigeration expenses from coverage and from the coinsurance calculation, allowing the insured to satisfy the coinsurance requirement with a lower limit of insurance.

used in production operations is not included either in the definition of business income or in coinsurance computations as long as such expenses do not continue under contract.

When energy expenses are excluded, the insured can purchase a lower limit of insurance. However, the CLM calls for an increase in rate when the endorsement is used. Unless energy expense is a significant part of the insured's total operating expenses, no advantage may be gained by using the endorsement.

Endorsements for Dependent Property Exposures

Dependent property loss exposures arise when an organization could suffer a business income loss because of damage occurring at the premises of some other organization that the first organization does not own or control. The other organization might be a main supplier, an important buyer, or a magnet or leader property such as a large department store in a mall that includes several smaller stores.

An unmodified business income policy provides no coverage for dependent property exposures because it covers only business income loss that results from physical loss to property at the insured's premises.

Three basic endorsements are available for insuring dependent property exposures:

- Business Income From Dependent Properties—Broad Form (CP 15 08)— This endorsement is used when the insured wants the same limit that applies to business income loss resulting from damage at its own premises to apply to business income loss resulting from damage to other properties as well.

- Business Income From Dependent Properties—Limited Form (CP 15 09)—This endorsement is used when separate limits are preferred or when the insured wishes to insure only business income from dependent properties.

- Extra Expense From Dependent Properties (CP 15 34)—This endorsement, combined with the Extra Expense Coverage Form, covers extra expenses because of direct loss or damage at other properties. For example, a manufacturer that depends heavily on one supplier may be able to obtain needed materials from other suppliers while the regular supplier's business is interrupted. However, the new suppliers may charge a higher price, which would be an extra expense loss for the manufacturer.

Each endorsement contains definitions, summarized here, for six types of dependent properties:

- Contributing locations—Locations that deliver materials or services to the insured or to others for the account of the insured. These do not include water, power, or communication supply services, which can be covered by another endorsement.

- Secondary contributing locations—Locations that deliver materials or services to the contributing location that, in turn, are used by that contributing location to provide materials or services to the insured. For example, a lumber mill would be a secondary contributing location if it provided lumber to a wholesale lumber yard, which would be a contributing location if it, in turn, provided lumber to a home improvement store that is the insured.

- Recipient locations—Locations that receive products or services from the insured.

- Secondary recipient location—Locations that receive products or services from the recipient location, which, in turn, receives products or services from the insured. For example, a restaurant is a secondary recipient location if it receives shrimp from a fish market, which is a recipient location when it receives shrimp caught by the insured.

- Manufacturing locations—Locations that manufacture products for delivery to the insured's customers under contract of sale.

- Leader locations—Locations that attract customers to the insured's business.

The schedule contained in each endorsement includes space for the insurer to insert the name and address of each dependent property covered by the endorsement. The schedule also includes a space for the insured to indicate that secondary contributing or recipient locations are covered even though they are not named.

Insurance Provisions

The endorsements cover business income losses (or extra expenses) resulting from suspension of the insured's operations because of physical loss or damage resulting from a covered cause of loss to the dependent property described in the endorsement schedule. The dependent property must not be owned, controlled, or operated by the insured. However, the dependent property could be a secondary contributing or recipient location. The maximum amount payable is the business income limit of insurance.

The endorsements do not require that operations at the specified location be shut down. Conversely, a total shutdown at a contributing property might have no effect on the insured's business. For example, the insured could have a large inventory when the loss occurs or might obtain replacement inventory at the same price from another source.

The endorsements limit compensation to the actual loss of business income necessarily sustained by the insured during the period of restoration. The period of restoration is the amount of time required, with reasonable speed and similar materials, to repair or replace the damaged dependent property.

This provision focuses not on the insured's resumption of operations but on conditions at the dependent property location. The endorsements also modify the Resumption of Operations condition in the business income coverage forms to state that the insurer will reduce the insured's recovery to the extent that the insured can resume operations by using other sources of materials or other outlets for its products. The period of restoration for dependent properties coverage begins seventy-two hours after the time of direct physical loss or damage at the premises of the dependent property.

The requirement that the physical loss must occur at a location specified in the endorsement schedule is subject to some exceptions, such as secondary contributing and recipient locations and a Miscellaneous Locations provision, which applies to unscheduled locations other than those operated by the insured. This provision limits coverage to 0.03 percent of the business income limit of insurance for each day's suspension of operations at the miscellaneous location.[4]

Coverage does not apply when the only loss to the dependent property is loss or damage to electronic data (including corruption or destruction). If the dependent property sustains loss to electronic data and other property, coverage is limited to the period of restoration for the other property.

International Coverage

Recognizing the ever-growing global expansion of United States businesses and the use of suppliers located throughout the world, ISO has developed dependent properties forms that provide international coverage: Business Income From Dependent Properties Limited International Coverage (CP 15 01) and Extra Expense From Dependent Properties Limited International Coverage (CP 15 02).

The insured must select a specific limit for contributing locations or manufacturing locations. The endorsements provide no option to cover recipient locations, secondary recipient locations, or leader locations. The selected causes of loss—basic, broad, or special—as well as any endorsements supplementing or restricting the covered causes of loss applying to these coverages must be indicated on the endorsement's schedule (or on the Declarations page). Perils available under the coverage forms can vary based on requested coverage location and underwriter preference.

Amount of Insurance

The amount of insurance for dependent properties should be selected based on analysis of the business income and extra expense losses that could arise from damage to or destruction of the locations on which the insured is dependent.

The choice between the Business Income From Dependent Properties—Broad Form and the Business Income From Dependent Properties—Limited Form depends on whether the amount of insurance needed is equal to the total amount of business income insurance.

If it is, as might be the case when a leader location is key to creating customer traffic by the insured's business or when an insured receives all of its raw materials or supplies from one source, the Broad Form may be the better choice. For most insureds, the dependent property exposure will be less than the regular business income exposure, and the Limited Form may, therefore, be less expensive. Because the rate for the Broad Form is lower than the rate for the Limited Form, it may be necessary to calculate the rate for both forms to determine the better choice.

Educational Institutions

Schools and colleges have a business income loss exposure that differs from that of the typical merchandising or manufacturing organization. If, for example, the building housing Valley Academy, a private college preparatory school, is damaged during the summer recess, the school may be unable to open its doors at the beginning of the fall semester. Even if the school is able to open by early October, it may find that most students have already enrolled elsewhere. Thus, if school property is unusable during a fairly short, but critical, time period, it could cause the school to lose an entire year's tuition.

Business Income Changes—Educational Institutions endorsement
An endorsement that modifies business income coverage forms to make them more appropriate for covering the business income loss exposures of schools.

The **Business Income Changes—Educational Institutions endorsement** (CP 15 25) can be used to modify business income forms to make them more appropriate for covering the business income loss exposures of schools. The endorsement addresses the critical-time-period problem through changes in the definition of period of restoration and changes in the Extended Period of Indemnity provisions.

Period of Restoration

To meet the special needs of educational institutions, the definition of period of restoration is amended to end on the earlier of these times:

- The day before the opening of the next school term following the date when the property should be restored
- The date when the school term is resumed at a permanent new location

In the example of Valley Academy, in which the school's property was not restored until after the start of the fall semester, the endorsement would extend the period of restoration until the day before the start of the spring semester.

Extended Business Income

The endorsement includes an Extended Business Income (EBI) provision that replaces the regular EBI provision of the business income coverage forms.

The modified EBI provision states that if damaged property is actually repaired, rebuilt, or replaced within sixty or fewer days before the scheduled opening of the next school term, the policy will cover the actual loss of business income sustained during that entire school term.

To illustrate the application of this provision, assume that, following a covered loss, Valley Academy had repaired its building in August, fewer than sixty days before the beginning of the fall term, and that Valley Academy's policy included the educational institutions endorsement. In that case, the period of restoration would have ended on the day before the fall term began.

Nevertheless, the EBI provision would have covered any loss of business income occurring during the entire fall term.

Under the circumstances described (repairs completed in August), the EBI provision would not cover any additional loss of business income that Valley Academy might incur during the spring term—a distinct possibility because many students who are unable to enroll in the fall might enroll at another school for the entire school year (or perhaps longer).

An option titled Extension of Recovery Period can be used to cover business income loss sustained for up to twelve months following the end of the period of restoration. The insured can extend coverage over one or more additional school terms by selecting the appropriate number of months. If Valley Academy had selected a twelve-month recovery period extension option, losses in the spring term as well as the fall term would have been covered in the example. The Extension of Recovery Period option replaces EBI; it is not in addition to the endorsement's EBI coverage.

Limited Coverage

The business income coverage forms cover all sources of school income. However, either the insured or the underwriter may wish to restrict the types of income to be covered. This can be done by selecting the limited coverage option in the endorsement.

If this option is chosen, "operations" is defined to include both activities at the insured's premises that generate tuition and related fees from students—including room, board, laboratory, and other similar sources—and the tenantability of the described premises if coverage includes rental value.

Limited coverage does not include income from bookstores, athletic events, activities related to research grants, or any other business activities other than those that generate tuition and related fees from students.

Utility Services—Time Element Endorsement

A business interruption is likely to occur when utilities supplying electricity, water, or communications service to the insured's premises are cut off for a significant period. Even businesses that do not use water in their operations may find it necessary to send employees home if a loss of water service makes restrooms unusable.

Just as the Utility Services—Direct Damage endorsement can be used to cover direct loss resulting from interruption of utility services by damage to utility property resulting from an insured peril, the **Utility Services—Time Element endorsement** (CP 15 45) can be added to either of the ISO business income forms or the Extra Expense Coverage Form to cover the time element aspects of this exposure.

Utility Services—Time Element endorsement

An endorsement that covers loss of business income or extra expense at the insured premises caused by the interruption of utility services to or from the insured premises.

The endorsement modifies the coverage form to include loss of business income and/or extra expense resulting from a suspension of operations at the described premises caused by an interruption in utility service to those premises. The interruption of service must be caused by direct physical loss or damage by a covered cause of loss to a type of supply property that has been checked off in the endorsement's schedule.

These are the categories of supply properties that can be checked off:

- Water supply
- Wastewater removal
- Communication supply (including overhead transmission lines)
- Communication supply (not including overhead transmission lines)
- Power supply (including overhead transmission lines)
- Power supply (not including overhead transmission lines)

It is important for the producer and insured to make sure that each of the categories the insured wants to cover are checked off in the schedule. If a category is not checked off, it is not covered.

The endorsement states that the coverage does not include business income or extra expense related to interruption in utility service that causes loss or damage to electronic data. Only the limit shown applies to the coverage provided by the endorsement, and the limit for the endorsement is part of, not in addition to, the limit of liability applicable to the described premises.

Ordinance or Law—Increased Period of Restoration Endorsement

Ordinance or Law—Increased Period of Restoration endorsement

Endorsement that covers business income loss during the additional time required to comply with building ordinances or laws.

The Ordinance or Law exclusion in the causes of loss forms eliminates coverage for any extra loss resulting from the enforcement of building ordinances or laws—for example, when the undamaged parts of a building must be torn down, following an insured loss, in order for the entire building to be reconstructed in compliance with current building codes. The exclusion also applies to business income and extra expense coverage.

The **Ordinance or Law—Increased Period of Restoration endorsement** (CP 15 31) is available for modifying the business income and/or extra expense forms to cover losses resulting from the enforcement of building laws or ordinances. The enforcement of building laws can increase the length of a business interruption to the extent that additional time is required to demolish the undamaged structure, remove its debris, and rebuild the entire structure to conform to code.

The endorsement extends business income and/or extra expense coverage to encompass the increased period of suspension of operations brought about by the enforcement of building laws. Moreover, the period of restoration is redefined to include the added time necessary to replace damaged property with replacement property that complies with the minimum standards of the law.

Food Contamination Endorsement

The endorsement is designed to address some of the costs an insured such as a restaurant or grocery store is likely to incur if the food it sells is or is suspected to be contaminated. Coverage is triggered if a governmental authority orders the insured to close. The costs that are covered include the expenses to clean equipment, replace contaminated food, have the insured's employees tested for infection, and advertise to restore the insured's reputation. Perhaps the costliest expense the endorsement will cover is the loss of business income incurred until the governmental authority allows the insured to reopen.

DETERMINING WHETHER THE BIC FORM COVERS A LOSS

Knowing how to apply business income coverage to the facts of a case is an important skill. This case study will help you make the transition from knowing policy language to applying policy language to losses to determine whether coverage applies. As you progress through this case study, you can check your understanding of the coverage provided by answering the Knowledge to Action questions.

Case Facts

Given the facts presented by the case, will the business income loss be covered? If so, what amount will the insurer pay for the claim? When answering the questions in this case-based activity, consider only the information provided as part of this case.

Fancy Wear Boutique (FWB), a retail clothing store in Chicago, is insured under a commercial package policy that includes the Business Income (and Extra Expense) Coverage Form, the Causes of Loss—Special Form, the Commercial Property Conditions, and the Common Policy Conditions (as well as other forms that are not relevant to this case).

The Commercial Property Coverage Part Declarations Page describes the insured premises at the address of the store building owned by FWB and shows a $1 million Business Income limit of insurance for the location, subject to option (2), Business Income Other Than "Rental Value." The declarations also show that FWB had purchased the Business Income Agreed Value optional coverage and that the value agreed to by the insurer and FWB was $1 million. None of the other optional coverages of the Business Income (and Extra Expense) Coverage Form are in effect. Moreover, no endorsements apply to FWB's Business Income (and Extra Expense) Coverage Form or Causes of Loss—Special Form. The one-year policy period shown in the declarations began on January 1, 20X1.

On April 1, 20X1, FWB suffered a total direct physical loss to its store building and contents when a tornado touched down on FWB's premises but did not cause widespread damage in the immediate area. Replacement of the building and its contents was accomplished with reasonable speed and required one year. As a result of FWB's direct physical loss, both the revenues and normal operating expenses that FWB expected to experience were reduced as shown in the table. The resulting loss of business income that FWB sustained while operations were suspended at the described premises was $680,000. The business income loss for the first seventy-two hours following the physical loss totaled $4,000. See the exhibit "FWB's Expected and Actual Revenues, Expenses, Net Income."

FWB's Expected and Actual Revenues, Expenses, Net Income

	Expected	Actual
Revenues	$2,000,000	$1,000,000
Expenses	750,000	430,000
Net Income	$1,250,000	$570,000

Business income loss = $1,250,000 − $570,000
= $680,000

[DA07918]

To keep its business operating during the period of restoration, FWB rented and moved into a nearby building one month after the tornado occurred and continued operating the boutique at this location for the duration of the restoration period. During this period, FWB incurred additional costs totaling $34,000 ($20,000 for rent, $3,000 for moving expenses, $5,000 for leased equipment, and $6,000 for additional advertising expenses). FWB would not have incurred any of these expenses had the tornado damage not occurred.

After the period of restoration ended and FWB resumed operations at the insured premises, the boutique continued to sustain loss of business income for sixty days, in these amounts:

- First period of sixty days after reopening: $15,000
- Second period of sixty days after reopening: $10,000

All loss of business income that occurred after FWB reopened its store resulted from changes in customers' shopping behavior during FWB's year-long suspension of normal operations while temporarily relocated. The additional loss of business income did not result from unfavorable business conditions caused by the impact of the tornado in FWB's area. Moreover, there was nothing more that FWB could reasonably have done to restore its normal business income level any sooner than it did.

FWB and the insurer agreed on all loss determinations, and FWB fulfilled all its post-loss duties under the policy.

Necessary Reference Materials

To determine whether FWB's policy provides coverage for business income loss incurred as a result of the tornado, you need copies of the policy forms, and the declarations pages themselves. There are no endorsements that affect Business Income coverage, but if there were, they would need to be reviewed to see how they affect the Business Income (and Extra Expense) Coverage Form.

You will need to have copies of the following forms available for your reference while working on this coverage case:

- Business Income (and Extra Expense) Coverage Form (CP 00 30 10 12)
- Causes of Loss—Special Form (CP 10 30 10 12)
- Commercial Property Conditions (CP 00 90 07 88)

Determination of Coverage

When examining the policy forms to determine whether coverage applies to the losses, you can apply the four steps of the DICE method. This involves analyzing the policy declarations, insuring agreement, conditions, and exclusions and determining whether any information found at each step precludes coverage at the time of the loss. You should also examine other categories of policy provisions such as the insured's duties, general provisions, endorsements (if applicable), and terms defined in the policy in relation to the declarations, insuring agreements, conditions, and exclusions.

DICE Analysis Step 1: Declarations

The first DICE step is to review the declarations pages to determine whether it covers the person or the property at the time of the loss. Action Task:

Review the declarations in FWB's policy. See the exhibit "Excerpt From FWB's Declarations Page."

A basic requirement, expressed in the Policy and Coverage Territory provision in the Commercial Property Conditions, is that the loss or damage must commence during the policy period shown in the declarations and must commence within the coverage territory in order for coverage to apply. The facts of FWB's claim satisfy this requirement because the business income loss commenced on April 1, 20X1, which is within the policy period stated in the declarations; and the loss commenced at the described premises, which is within the coverage territory. Even though the business income and extra expense loss continued for several months after the policy period ended, FWB's claim for the entire business income and extra expense claim would be covered under the policy in effect at the time the loss commenced. This result is supported by this sentence in the policy definition of period of restoration: "The expiration date of this policy will not cut short the 'period of restoration.'"

DICE Analysis Step 2: Insuring Agreement

The second DICE step is to review the insuring agreement to determine whether it is applicable to the described loss. The Business Income (and Extra Expense) Coverage form has two insuring agreements—one for the business income and a second for extra expense. You should determine what part of the loss is covered under the Business Income insuring agreement and what part is covered under the Extra Expense insuring agreement.

To be covered under the Business Income insuring agreement, a loss must be an actual loss of business income as defined and must meet several requirements imposed by the Business Income insuring agreement.

During its suspension of operations at the described premises, FWB sustained a $680,000 loss of business income, as defined in the Business Income insuring agreement. Because the claim is for business income other than rental income, the loss falls within option (2), Business Income Other Than "Rental Value," shown in the declarations. (A claim for loss of rental income, for example, would not be covered under FWB's business income coverage.) Furthermore, the circumstances of the claim meet the other applicable requirements imposed by the insuring agreement:

- The actual loss of FWB's business income was due to the necessary suspension of FWB's operations.
- The suspension was caused by direct physical loss of or damage to property (in this case, building and contents) at the premises described in the declarations and for which a Business Income limit of insurance is shown.
- The loss or damage was caused by a Covered Cause of Loss (in this case, tornado, a type of windstorm that is not excluded by the Causes of Loss—Special Form and is therefore covered).

Excerpt From FWB's Declarations Page

COMMERCIAL PROPERTY
CP DS 00 10 00

COMMERCIAL PROPERTY COVERAGE PART
DECLARATIONS PAGE

POLICY NO. 00123456   **EFFECTIVE DATE** __01__ / __01__ / __20X1__   ☐ **"X" If Supplemental**
                                                                              Declarations Is Attached

NAMED INSURED Fancy Wear Boutique

DESCRIPTION OF PREMISES

Prem. No.	Bldg. No.	Location, Construction And Occupancy
001	001	1234 Main St., Chicago, IL Joisted Masonry Clothing or Wearing Apparel Store

COVERAGES PROVIDED   **Insurance At The Described Premises Applies Only For Coverages For Which A Limit Of Insurance Is Shown**

Prem. No.	Bldg. No.	Coverage	Limit Of Insurance	Covered Causes Of Loss	Coinsurance*	Rates
001	001	Building	600,000	Special	80%	See Sched.
		Your Business Personal Property	700,000	Special		
		Personal Property of Others	50,000	Special		
		Business income/Extra Expense	1,000,000	Special		
		Option (2) Business Income Other Than Rental Value				
		Business Income Agreed Value optional coverage	1,000,000			

CP DS 00 10 00   Copyright, Insurance Services Office, Inc., 1999   Page 1 of 1   ☐

[DA07919]

The Business Income insuring agreement states that the insurer will pay actual loss of Business Income only during the "period of restoration." According to the policy definition of this term, the period of restoration, for purposes of Business Income coverage (as opposed to Extra Expense coverage), begins "seventy-two hours after the time of direct physical loss or damage." Because FWB sustained $4,000 of business income loss during those first seventy-two hours (three days), that sum will be deducted from the covered amount of business income loss.

For expenses to be covered under the Extra Expense insuring agreement, the circumstances of the claim must meet the requirements imposed by that agreement. The requirements of the insuring agreement are satisfied by these case facts:

- FWB incurred $34,000 in additional costs during the period of restoration to continue its operations at a substitute store.
- FWB would not have incurred these costs if there had been no direct physical loss or damage or if the loss or damage had not been caused by or resulted from a Covered Cause of Loss (in this case, tornado).

Knowledge to Action

Do any additional coverages or coverage extensions apply?

Feedback: Yes, but the only additional coverage or coverage extension of the Business Income (and Extra Expense) Coverage Form that applies to FWB's claim is the Extended Business Income (EBI) additional coverage. EBI applies to the claim because FWB continued to sustain loss of Business Income after its property was replaced and operations resumed. Moreover, as explained in the case facts, the additional loss of business income did not result from "unfavorable business conditions caused by the impact of the Covered Cause of Loss in the area where the described premises are located."

Although EBI applies to FWB's claim, it is limited to the sixty consecutive days immediately following the date the property was replaced and operations resumed. FWB could have lengthened this sixty-day period by purchasing the Extended Period of Indemnity optional coverage, but chose not to obtain that optional coverage.

DICE Analysis Step 3: Conditions

The third DICE step is to review the policy conditions to determine whether they preclude coverage at the time of the loss.

Numerous policy conditions are associated with FWB's business income and extra expense coverage. In addition to the conditions contained in the Business Income (and Extra Expense) Coverage Form, the Commercial

Property Conditions and Common Policy Conditions also apply. In investigating the loss, the insurer must ascertain that the insured and the insurer have performed their respective duties imposed by these conditions and that the circumstances of the loss satisfy any other applicable conditions.

As stated in the case facts, the insurer determined that FWB performed all the duties required by the Duties in the Event of Loss condition. Because the insurer and FWB agreed on the determination of the amount of Business Income loss and the amount of Extra Expense incurred, the Appraisal condition was not applicable.

Also, because FWB has a $1 million limit, which satisfies the requirement in the Business Income Agreed Value optional coverage that FWB has purchased, the Coinsurance condition is suspended and therefore there is no possibility of a coinsurance penalty that would reduce the recovery amount. No other conditions had any negative effect on coverage.

Due to FWB complying with all the terms of the coverage part, once the insurer and FWB agree on the amount of loss, the insurer must pay the claim within thirty days after receiving FWB's sworn proof of loss.

Knowledge to Action

Of the following conditions required of the insured, FWB, which are found only as a condition of business income coverage?

a. Timely reporting of claim to the insurer

b. Cooperating with the insurer in investigation of claim

c. Providing a sworn proof of loss statement to the insurer

d. Resuming operations, in whole or in part, as quickly as possible

Feedback: d. Resuming operations is a condition that is unique to business income coverage.

DICE Analysis Step 4: Exclusions

The fourth DICE step is to review the policy exclusions to determine whether they exclude or limit coverage of the loss. The case facts presented provide no indication that any exclusion applies.

Determination of Amounts Payable

Now that you have completed the DICE analysis, you can determine the amounts payable. This involves analyzing the limit(s) of insurance available to pay for the loss and any deductibles that apply. It also involves determining whether more than one policy provides coverage for the same loss. FWB has no other policy that would cover this business income loss and therefore the Other Insurance provisions do not need to be considered.

The full amount of business income loss sustained before FWB's property was restored ($680,000) is covered, minus the amount sustained during the first three days after the physical loss occurred ($4,000), which results in the covered amount of $676,000 of business income loss.

All of FWB's $34,000 in additional costs are covered as extra expense. The period of restoration for Extra Expense coverage begins immediately after the direct physical loss occurs; there is no deductible for loss sustained during the first seventy-two hours, as in the case of business income coverage.

Only the $15,000 of business income loss sustained during the first sixty days following resumption of operations is insured under the EBI coverage extension. The additional $10,000 of business income loss sustained after the initial sixty-day period is not covered. FWB could have covered the additional income loss by purchasing the Extended Period of Indemnity optional coverage. See the exhibit "Amounts Payable to FWB."

Amounts Payable to FWB

Type of Loss	Amount of Loss Covered
Business Income	$676,000
Extra Expense	34,000
EBI	15,000
Total	$725,000

[DA07920]

The limit of insurance for FWB's Business Income (and Extra Expense) Coverage Form is $1 million, which is the maximum amount payable for loss in any one occurrence. Because the covered amount of FWB's losses is $725,000, the limit of insurance does not reduce the amount payable. As discussed in connection with Step 3, the Business Income Agreed Value optional coverage is in effect, suspending the Coinsurance condition and therefore eliminating any possibility of a coinsurance penalty that would reduce the amount payable.

SUMMARY

A business income loss can sometimes be more devastating for an insured than the associated property loss. A business income loss is measured as the reduction in the insured's net income—the difference between expected net income had no loss occurred and actual net income after the loss. The causes of loss are often the same as for direct property losses.

A pre-loss analysis of business income and extra expense exposures serves as the basis for selecting appropriate risk control and risk financing measures. When identifying and analyzing business income loss and extra expense exposures, insurance professionals should consider key factors for all aspects of an organization's business income and extra expense exposure resulting from an accidental property loss.

A business income worksheet can be used to calculate the coinsurance basis, which becomes the starting point for an organization's EML. Other factors are applied to the EML to increase its accuracy. The EML can then be used to select a coinsurance percentage and limit of insurance.

Business income forms cover the actual loss of business income that the named insured sustains because of necessary suspension of operations during the period of restoration. The period of restoration begins seventy-two hours after the time of the damage; it ends when the damaged property should be repaired or when the insured resumes operations at another permanent location. The suspension must have occurred because of physical loss to property at the described premises by a covered cause of loss.

Both business income coverage forms include these additional coverages and extensions:

- Civil Authority additional coverage
- Alterations and New Buildings additional coverage
- Extended Business Income (EBI) additional coverage
- Interruption of Computer Operations additional coverage
- Newly Acquired Locations coverage extension

Noteworthy conditions in both business income forms include Appraisal, Duties in the Event of Loss, Loss Determination, and Coinsurance. The percentages used for the Coinsurance condition range from 50 to 125 percent, reflecting the wide range of restoration periods and estimated maximum losses that different organizations may experience.

Both of the business income forms contain provisions for three optional coverages that can be used to eliminate or suspend the Coinsurance condition: Maximum Period of Indemnity, Monthly Limit of Indemnity, and Agreed Value. A fourth option is simply to omit the Coinsurance condition in return for a significantly higher rate.

A third time element form is the Extra Expense Coverage Form, which covers extra expense only. It is intended for organizations that must continue their operations "at any cost" and do not want to cover loss of business income.

The coverage provided is essentially the same as the extra expense coverage under the Business Income (and Extra Expense) Coverage form. One important difference is that the extra expense form is subject to percentage limitations that correspond to different periods of restoration.

Various coverage options are available for modifying business income and extra expense forms to meet particular needs. These options may be used to provide blanket insurance; modify payroll expense coverage; exclude power, heat, and refrigeration expenses; or cover special exposures such as dependent properties, educational institutions, loss of utility services, or building ordinance and law or food contamination exposures.

You should now be able to apply policy language to business income losses to determine whether the losses are covered and the amount for which they are covered.

ASSIGNMENT NOTES

1. Includes copyrighted material of Insurance Services Office, Inc., with its permission. Copyright, Insurance Services Office, Inc., 2011.

2. Includes copyrighted material of Insurance Services Office, Inc., with its permission. Copyright, Insurance Services Office, Inc., 2011.

3. Includes copyrighted material of Insurance Services Office, Inc., with its permission. Copyright, Insurance Services Office, Inc., 2011

4. In the Business Income From Dependent Properties—Limited Form and the Extra Expense From Dependent Properties endorsement, the limit for miscellaneous locations is 0.03 percent of the sum of all limits shown in the schedule, because these forms may have separate limits that apply to multiple locations.

Direct Your Learning ▶▶

Inland Marine and Ocean Cargo

Educational Objectives

After learning the content of this assignment, you should be able to:

▹ Identify loss exposures that are generally eligible for inland marine insurance.

▹ Describe the general characteristics of inland marine insurance.

▹ Explain the following factors affecting transportation loss exposures:

- Parties involved in transportation
- Ownership of goods
- Carrier responsibility for loss

▹ Describe the specific purpose and typical provisions of common inland marine and ocean marine policies.

▹ Recommend appropriate inland marine or ocean cargo coverages for a described organization.

Inland Marine and Ocean Cargo | 8

OVERVIEW OF INLAND MARINE INSURANCE

Marine insurance, as it is understood internationally, is insurance on vessels and their cargoes. In the United States, marine insurance has a broader definition and consists of two distinct lines: ocean marine and inland marine. Ocean marine insurance corresponds to the international meaning of marine insurance. Inland marine insurance covers a wide range of usually land-based risks that have some link to transportation or communication.

The present scope of inland marine insurance is based not only on logical distinctions but also on historical events. Understanding how inland marine insurance developed contributes to understanding the current scope of inland marine insurance, including these topics:

- Development of Inland Marine
- Nationwide Inland Marine Definition
- Status of Inland Marine

Development of Inland Marine

Certain policies were first identified as "inland marine" in the early 1900s. At that time, the insurance business in the U.S. was compartmentalized by state regulation. In most states, an insurer could be licensed to transact only (1) fire and marine insurance (or in some cases, only one or the other), (2) casualty insurance and surety, or (3) life insurance. This rigid regulatory scheme made it impossible for a fire or casualty insurer to meet all the coverage needs of a customer.

For example, fire insurers could not insure crime perils in their policies, because crime perils were a subject of casualty insurance, and casualty insurers could not include fire insurance in their policies. An individual or a business that wanted to insure its property against both fire and theft had to purchase two policies from two insurers.

Marine insurers, in contrast, could provide "all-risks" insurance on marine exposures. When the trucking industry took off in the 1920s, shippers wanted to obtain broad coverage on goods in transit. Marine insurers, who had "all-risks" policies and experience in underwriting goods in transit, were well equipped for providing the new coverage, which was a logical extension of marine insurance. Pursuing premium growth, marine insurers extended the marine concept even further and provided "all-risks" insurance on various other land-based risks, including even property at fixed locations. The jewelers block policy, providing "all-risks" coverage on the contents of jewelry stores, was one of the policies developed by marine insurers in this era.

Nationwide Marine Definition

By the late 1920s, fire insurers were losing premiums to marine insurers writing inland marine policies on properties that had formerly been covered by fire insurance. Fire insurance forms and rates were more strictly regulated than inland marine forms and rates and therefore could not compete as effectively. Fire insurers felt threatened by inland marine insurance and viewed it as encroaching on the fire insurance business.

To resolve the resulting disputes between fire underwriters and marine underwriters, insurance regulators in 1933 introduced the **Nationwide Marine Definition**, which most states adopted as a regulation. The Nationwide Marine Definition restricted marine insurers to covering the loss exposures included in the definition. All other loss exposures (except for the few that could be considered casualty lines) could be covered only by approved fire insurance forms and rates.

In the 1950s, strict adherence to the separation of underwriting powers began to disappear from the regulations and from company practices. Some insurers began to write multiple-line policies, a practice that started with automobile insurance, continued with the development of homeowners policies, and finally extended into commercial coverages. The Nationwide Marine Definition was no longer used as a definition of what types of loss exposures an insurer could underwrite.

However, the Definition, with some modernization, continued to be used for classification purposes. A regulatory definition of marine insurance was still needed because insurance regulatory laws exempted most classes of marine insurance from form and rate-filing requirements. That is, insurers were not required to obtain regulatory approval of the forms and rates used in ocean marine and many inland marine policies. Thus, the Definition remained useful in determining which types of insurance were exempt from the filing requirements. (The Definition, last revised in 1976, is summarized in the exhibit.) See the exhibit "Summary of Nationwide Marine Definition."

Status of Inland Marine

Today, many classes of inland marine insurance remain exempt from filing requirements.

Such types of inland marine insurance are referred to as **nonfiled classes (uncontrolled classes)**. A justification for this exemption from filing requirements is that the types of exposures being insured can vary greatly among insureds. For those exposures, using standard forms and class rates is

Nationwide Marine Definition
Statement of the types of property that may be insured on inland marine and ocean marine insurance forms.

Nonfiled classes (uncontrolled classes)
The classes of inland marine business for which neither policy forms nor rates must be filed with the state insurance department.

Summary of Nationwide Marine Definition

A. Imports.

B. Exports.

C. Domestic shipments.

D. Instrumentalities of transportation and communication, such as bridges, tunnels, piers, wharves, docks, pipelines, power and telephone lines, radio and television towers and communication equipment, and outdoor cranes and loading equipment.

E. Various types of property owned or used by individuals, such as jewelry, furs, musical instruments, silverware, coin collections, and stamp collections.

F. Various types of property pertaining to a business, profession, or occupation. Examples of such property include mobile equipment, builders' risks, property in the custody of bailees, live animals, property at exhibitions, electronic data processing equipment, and the filed classes shown in the next exhibit.

[DA03602]

impractical. The filing exemption allows insurers the flexibility needed to determine appropriate policy provisions and rates for individual risks.

Filed classes (controlled classes) of inland marine insurance are those for which forms or rates or both must be filed with the insurance regulatory officials of a particular state in order for an insurer to issue policies for that class of business in that state. Generally, a filed class of business is one that has a large number of insureds with similar loss exposures.

Insurance Services Office, Inc. (ISO) and the American Association of Insurance Services (AAIS) file forms and rates for these classes of business on behalf of their member companies. See the exhibit for examples. See the exhibit "Classes of Commercial Inland Marine Insurance Filed by ISO and AAIS."

Many states, however, specify additional classes for which forms and rates must be filed. To comply with regulations, insurers must ascertain which classes of inland marine are filed in each state in which they operate.

When insuring the filed classes, the underwriter has less flexibility in modifying rates and forms. However, the inland marine manual rules filed by ISO and AAIS allow insurers to substitute various valuation clauses and other policy provisions for those contained in the standard filed forms. Moreover, most states permit insurers to charge higher rates for riskier exposures as long as the insured's written consent is filed with the appropriate insurance department. The regulations that allow this practice are called consent-to-rate rules.

Although the Nationwide Marine Definition makes no distinction between inland and ocean marine, they are treated as separate lines in the Annual

Filed classes
(controlled classes)

The classes of inland marine business for which policy forms and/or rates must be filed with the state insurance department.

Classes of Commercial Inland Marine Insurance Filed by ISO and AAIS

- Accounts receivable
- Camera and musical instrument dealers
- Film
- Floor plan merchandise
- Equipment dealers (implement dealers)
- Jewelers block (jewelry dealers)
- Mail (ISO only)
- Musical instruments
- Photographic equipment
- Physicians, surgeons, and dentists equipment
- Signs
- Theatrical property
- Valuable papers and records

[DA03603]

Statement that insurers use to report their financial data to state regulators. In practice, many insurers offer only inland marine insurance and not ocean marine. Insurers that offer both types of insurance often underwrite them in separate departments.

Insurers customarily subdivide inland marine insurance into several classes of business that correspond closely to the risks and policies named in the Nationwide Marine Definition. The largest classes of commercial inland marine business, measured by premiums written, are contractors' equipment, builders' risk, motor truck cargo, electronic data processing equipment, property in domestic transit, and "difference in conditions."

A difference in conditions (DIC) policy is typically an "all-risks" policy that supplements a basic named perils commercial property policy. DIC policies, although they are named in the Nationwide Marine Definition, are not always identified with the inland marine line.

GENERAL CHARACTERISTICS OF INLAND MARINE POLICIES

Many provisions of inland marine policies are similar or identical to those contained in commercial property forms. Moreover, the AAIS and ISO inland marine forms and many nonfiled forms are designed to be included in a commercial package policy or to be issued as monoline policies.

Other general characteristics of inland marine insurance involve these topics:

- Coverage for property in transit
- Loss exposures covered
- Broad coverage of perils
- Valuation provisions

Coverage for Property in Transit

Inland marine policies almost always provide an element of coverage for property in transit or at locations other than the insured's premises. Covering property in the course of transit or at other locations is the main purpose of several inland marine forms, such as annual transit, trip transit, and contractors' equipment policies.

In other inland marine forms, the transit coverage is incidental. For example, an inland marine art dealer's policy may cover the dealer's merchandise while located at the dealer's gallery or while in transit to or from or located at other places. Commercial property forms such as the Building and Personal Property Coverage Form provide little coverage for property while away from the described location.

Inland marine policies that cover property of a mobile or "floating" nature are often called **floaters**. Examples of floaters are the contractors equipment floater, the commercial articles floater, and the fine arts floater.

Floater

A policy designed to cover property that floats, or moves, from location to location.

Loss Exposures Covered

Although many inland marine policies are limited to covering physical loss, some policies cover loss of business income and extra expense as well. For example, electronic data processing equipment policies are sometimes extended to cover time element losses resulting from damage to or destruction of the insured computer system or its data. And inland marine builders' risk policies are frequently extended to cover time element losses resulting from damage to or destruction of the insured building during the course of construction.

Some inland marine policies cover the insured against legal liability for damage to property of others. These are examples of inland marine liability insurance:

- Motor truck cargo liability insurance, which covers a trucking company's liability for damage to property of others being transported by the trucking company
- Warehouse legal liability insurance, which covers a warehouse operator's legal liability for damage to property of others being stored in the warehouse

Broad Coverage of Perils

One of the reasons inland marine insurance developed in the United States is that it met a demand for "all-risks" coverage (now more commonly referred to as open perils coverage). Although open perils coverage is now available in standard commercial property forms, the open perils coverage provided in inland marine policies is often subject to fewer exclusions.

For example, many inland marine policies do not exclude (and therefore cover) flood and earthquake. With the nonfiled classes of inland marine insurance, the underwriter has the flexibility to delete other exclusions when doing so is appropriate. For instance, mechanical breakdown and utility services failure are standard exclusions in commercial property forms. However, coverage for mechanical breakdown utility services failure is readily provided in most inland marine electronic data processing equipment policies (subject to an additional premium charge).

Although open perils coverage is common in inland marine, it is not universal. Some inland marine policies apply on a named perils basis. And in some cases, an open perils inland marine form may contain stricter exclusions than those of the Causes of Loss—Special Form used in commercial property policies.

Valuation Provisions

Inland marine policies use the same approaches to valuation of covered property as other property policies do, including actual cash value, replacement cost, and selling price. Additionally, many inland marine policies contain special valuation provisions to address the unique valuation problems inherent in these classes of business. Two such valuation provisions are valuation at invoice and agreed value, or valued policy.

Invoice value

A valuation basis that values covered property at its invoice value, including freight.

Invoice value is frequently used in policies covering property in transit between buyers and sellers. An advantage of valuation at invoice is that the amount of loss can be determined quickly and without dispute.

Another advantage of valuation at invoice is that it covers whatever profit the seller has in that price. Many policies providing for valuation at invoice also state that freight and other charges that have been either prepaid or guaranteed to the carrier will also be paid if the insured property is lost or destroyed.

Another valuation method used in some inland marine policies is **agreed value method**. With this method, the insured and insurer agree to the value of the property at policy inception, and that amount is paid in the event of a total loss. (This valuation method should not be confused with the agreed value optional coverage of the Building and Personal Property Coverage Form, which values property only for purposes of suspending the coinsurance provision, not for determining the amount of a covered loss.) In inland marine policies, the agreed value approach is typically used for property that is hard to value objectively, such as works of art and irreplaceable documents.

> **Agreed value method**
>
> A method of valuing property in which the insurer and the insured agree, at the time the policy is written, on the maximum amount that will be paid in the event of a total loss.

TRANSPORTATION LOSS EXPOSURES

Most inland marine policies include some coverage for property in transit. Some inland marine policies cover nothing but property in transit. Thus, being able to analyze transportation loss exposures is an essential skill for anyone working with inland marine insurance.

Almost all organizations have transportation loss exposures. In this context, the term "transportation exposures" is limited to the possibility of loss to property being transported and not to the conveyances on which it is carried. Manufacturers typically receive raw materials from suppliers and ship finished goods to others. Merchandisers receive goods from manufacturers or distributors and, after selling the goods, may ship or transport them to customers.

Even a service organization that sells no goods, such as an accounting firm or an insurance agency, may be exposed to loss of property in transit during a move from an old location to a new location. These are the issues one should consider when analyzing transportation loss exposures:

- Parties involved in transportation
- Ownership of goods
- Carrier responsibility for loss

Parties Involved in Transportation

Loss exposures involving property in transit can be uncomplicated or highly complex, depending to a large degree on how many parties are involved in the transportation. A shipment from a manufacturer's factory to its own retail outlet store on its own truck is an example of an uncomplicated exposure. The manufacturer will bear any loss that occurs to the goods being shipped during the course of transit.

Transit exposures become more complicated as additional parties become involved. Many shipments of goods are between a seller (often called the **shipper**) and a buyer (often called the **consignee**). In addition, many shipments of goods are transported not by the buyer or seller of the goods but

> **Shipper**
>
> The person or organization shipping goods, often the seller of the goods.
>
> **Consignee**
>
> The person or organization that receives property being transported by a carrier.

by a third party called a carrier—an individual or organization in the business of transporting property of others.

Complicating things even further, a single shipment of goods may be transported by two or more carriers using two or more modes of transportation. Modes of transportation that can be used to transport property include trucks, aircraft, railcars, river barges, oceangoing cargo vessels, and even oil and natural gas pipelines.

An auto parts wholesaler in the United States might purchase a container-load of auto parts from an overseas manufacturer. The transportation of the container might involve these trip segments:

- A carrier transports the container by truck from the manufacturer's factory to a seaport in the seller's country.
- The container is left in the custody of an ocean carrier, which loads the container aboard one of its vessels and transports the container across the Pacific Ocean to Seattle.
- In Seattle, a stevedoring company unloads the container from the vessel and places it aboard a railcar operated by an interstate railroad. The railroad transports the container to a rail terminal more than 1,000 miles inland.
- From the rail terminal, a local trucking firm transports the container by truck to the buyer's warehouse.

If the goods are lost in transit between the seller's factory and the seaport, who suffers the loss? The seller? The buyer? The carrier? Would the answer differ if the goods were lost while aboard the vessel? Or aboard the train or truck in the U.S.? The answers to these questions are necessary for applying the risk management process to property in transit.

Ownership of Goods

When goods are shipped between a seller and a buyer, either party may be exposed to loss while the goods are in transit. Generally, the party that owns the goods at the time they are damaged bears the loss. If a shipment is damaged in transit after title (ownership) has passed to the buyer, the buyer will suffer the loss. The question of who owns the goods during the course of transit is answered by the terms of sale, which are usually stated in the purchase order or contract of sale. An understanding of common terms of sale in international commerce helps identify who owns the goods.

If the shipment of auto parts had been sold under FOB Vessel terms, title would have passed to the buyer as soon as the goods were loaded aboard the overseas vessel. Thus, if the goods had been damaged before they reached the vessel, the seller would have borne the direct loss. If the goods had been damaged at any point in transit after they were loaded onto the vessel, the buyer would have borne the direct loss. See the exhibit "Some Terms of Sale Used in International Commerce."

Some Terms of Sale Used in International Commerce

Ex Point of Origin

The buyer takes delivery of the goods at the point of origin specified in the terms, such as "Ex Warehouse, Philadelphia." The buyer is responsible for any loss that occurs after taking delivery of the goods.

FOB (Free on Board) Vessel

The buyer assumes responsibility for loss as soon as the goods are placed aboard the vessel at the port named in the terms, such as "FOB Vessel, Port of San Diego."

FAS (Free Along Side) Vessel

The buyer assumes responsibility for loss as soon as the goods are placed alongside the vessel at the port named in the terms, such as "FAS Vessel, Port of Los Angeles."

CIF (Cost, Insurance, Freight)

The seller quotes a price that includes the cost of insurance and all transportation charges (freight) incurred to the named destination. The buyer assumes responsibility for loss or damage as soon as the goods are placed into the custody of the ocean carrier or delivered on board the vessel.

[DA03607]

In domestic shipments—that is, shipments between two points in the U.S.—the selling terms of FOB Point of Origin and FOB Destination are often used.

With FOB Point of Origin terms, the title (and the risk of loss) passes from seller to buyer when the goods are accepted by the carrier for transit. With FOB Destination, title passes when the goods are delivered to the buyer's premises. A store that receives all of its shipments of merchandise on FOB Destination terms is not directly at risk for those shipments. In contrast, a manufacturer that ships its finished goods under FOB Destination terms is exposed to direct loss of all such shipments until they reach their destinations. In any event, ownership exposures can be identified only after the terms of sale are known.

Carrier Responsibility for Loss

When a carrier transports goods, the carrier may be held responsible for any damage or loss that occurs to the goods, thus providing a source of recovery for the owner. Carrier responsibility for loss does not eliminate the owner's loss exposure; it merely provides a possible source of recovery. If the carrier is insolvent and unable to pay a cargo claim for which it is liable, the loss still falls on the owner.

The extent of a carrier's responsibility for loss depends in part on whether the carrier is a common carrier or a contract carrier. A **common carrier** offers its transportation services to the general public; in contrast, a **contract carrier** carries the goods of certain customers only, often to meet special needs that common carriers cannot meet. In practice, the distinction between common carriers and contract carriers is sometimes unclear. However, their liabilities for cargo loss can differ substantially. Carriers' cargo liabilities also differ among the various modes of transportation, such as land transit and water and air transit.

Common Carriers of Goods by Land

A common carrier ordinarily has a higher degree of responsibility for customers' property than a contract carrier. Common carriers, regardless of whether they have acted negligently, are usually liable to the shipper for any cargo losses except those that occur in narrowly defined circumstances. These are the exceptions to common-carrier liability:

- Acts of God—An " **act of God**" is an occurrence of nature, such as a tornado, a storm, an earthquake, or a flood.

- Acts of a public enemy—The public enemy referred to is a nation or government at war with the nation in which the carrier is domiciled. It does not refer to common thieves, rioters, or other criminals.

- Exercise of public authority—Confiscation of cargo is an example of an act by public authorities for which a common carrier would not be held liable.

- Shipper's fault or neglect—The common carrier is not held liable if property is damaged as a result of the shipper's negligent packing or shipping of property that is unfit for transportation.

- **Inherent vice**—A destructive condition within property. For example, perishables such as eggs and lettuce will spoil quickly if they are shipped without refrigeration.

Outside of these exceptions, a common carrier cannot escape liability for cargo loss. However, a carrier can limit the amount of its cargo liability. Such limitations are usually expressed in the **bill of lading**, which is the contract of carriage between the carrier and the shipper. In a so-called released bill of lading, the carrier charges a lower freight rate (a "released rate") if, in return, the shipper agrees to accept a limitation on how much the shipper can recover from the carrier if the carrier becomes liable for cargo loss. The limitation is expressed as a dollar amount per pound, package, or other shipping unit.

Contract Carriers of Goods by Land

A contract carrier's liability depends on the contract terms agreed to by the carrier and the shipper. To evaluate the exposure properly, one must examine the specific contract of carriage. Typically, a contract carrier's liability for

---

Common carriers

Airlines, railroads, or trucking companies that furnish transportation to any member of the public seeking their offered services.

Contract carriers

Carriers that furnish transportation services to shippers with whom they have contracts.

Act of God

A natural and unavoidable catastrophe that interrupts the expected course of events.

Inherent vice

A quality of or condition within a particular type of property that tends to make the property destroy itself.

Bill of lading

A document acknowledging receipt of goods from the shipper, given by the carrier, which includes the terms of the contract of carriage for the goods.

cargo loss is not as strict as a common carrier's. A common approach is for the contract carrier to be liable for cargo loss that results from the carrier's negligence. If, for example, property being transported by a contract carrier is stolen despite the carrier's use of prudent antitheft measures, the carrier will probably not be held liable for the loss. In contrast, a common carrier can be held liable for theft losses even though it did not act negligently.

Waterborne Carriers

Carriers of goods shipped by water (either inland waterways or the sea) can also be classified as common carriers or contract carriers.

A common carrier's liability for goods shipped in foreign trade to or from the U.S. by sea is specified under the U.S. Carriage of Goods by Sea Act (COGSA). Domestic shipments over either inland waterways or the coastwise sea lanes by common carrier are subject to another U.S. law, the Harter Act, unless the carrier and shipper agree to be subject to COGSA. COGSA is far less strict than the rules that apply to common carriers of goods in surface transit. It contains a much longer list of exceptions that relieve the carrier of liability. In addition to the exceptions applicable to truckers, COGSA excuses the carrier from liability for loss caused by any "act, neglect, or default" of the master or crew in navigation or management of the vessel; perils of the seas; and several other occurrences.

COGSA also provides that the carrier will not be held liable for cargo loss arising from unseaworthiness of the vessel unless the loss is caused by "want of due diligence on the part of the carrier" to make the vessel seaworthy. The Harter Act imposes a similar, but slightly more stringent, standard on the carrier. Thus, both laws relieve the carrier of liability in many instances. Even if the carrier is liable, COGSA provides for a package limitation, which limits the carrier's liability to $500 for loss to a single package or customary freight unit (such as each metric ton of grain). The Harter Act does not include a package limitation.

Contract carriage by water is called chartering. Chartering is typically used by shippers of bulk commodities such as grain or oil. The shipper obtains a **charter** on the entire vessel (or sometimes part of the cargo space on the vessel) for either a specified voyage or a specified period of time. The vessel is operated by the shipowner, although the shipper (charterer) may have responsibility for loading and unloading. The shipowner's liability for damage to the charterer's property is determined by the contract of carriage, which is called the charter party. In many cases, the shipowner and charterer agree to abide by the rules of COGSA.

Charter

A travel contract in which transportation is temporarily hired for a specific trip.

Air Carriers

The liability of air carriers engaged in international service is governed by the rules of the international Warsaw Convention. Under these rules, an air carrier is not liable for loss to property (for example, baggage, or cargo) if it can prove that it took all of the necessary steps to avoid the loss or that the loss was caused by pilot error. The bills of lading used for international flights limit the shipper's recovery for cargo loss to $9.07 per pound of cargo when no value is declared to the carrier. If the shipper declares a higher amount, the carrier will charge a higher air freight rate and will be liable up to the declared amount.

Domestic air carriers have considerable latitude in choosing the liability rules under which they operate. They may be subject to a negligence standard or to rules like those that apply to common carriers on land. They may also limit their liability to a certain amount per pound unless the shipper declares a higher value and pays a higher freight rate. See the exhibit "Risk Control for Transportation Loss Exposures."

Risk Control for Transportation Loss Exposures

Loss Exposure	Property Type	Risk Controls
Collision	All types	• Adequate packaging • Selection of carriers, modes of transportations, and routes
Theft	All types (especially valuable property, limited-supply property, and controlled substances)	• Adequate packaging with trademarks and descriptions of valuables not shown • Warehouse security measures • In transit security measures • Work rules (refusing hitchhikers or parking where load is visible) • Selection of carriers, modes of transportation, routes, terminals, and warehouses
Fire	All types (especially flammable liquids, gases, or solids)	• Adequate packaging • Work procedures for proper handling and storage
Weather damage or delay	All types (especially perishable)	• Adequate packaging • Covering shipment with shrink-wrap • Arrangements and relations with parties
Shipper's negligence	All types	• Adequate packaging • Selection of shipper • Stacking and binding of smaller parcels on a single pallet • Covering shipment with shrink-wrap and enclosing desiccants and packaging with vapor-proof liners • Bills of lading • Warsaw Convention

Loss Exposure	Property Type	Risk Controls
Unseaworthy vessel	All types	• Adequate packaging • FOB Vessel Terms • Carriage of Goods by Sea Act (COGSA) • Harter Act
Miscounts, erroneous or illegible shipping labels, other human errors or weaknesses	Most types	• Accounting and supervisory systems for shipments in and out • Clear markings to show final destinations, number in package, special handling instructions, and universal pictorial symbols
Spurious or hypercritical rejections of shipments by consignees	All types	• Arrangements and relations with parties at other end (sending or receiving) • Released bill of lading • Contract of Sale
General	All types	• FOB Point of Origin • Released bill of lading • Contract of Sale • Arrangements for handling damaged or incomplete shipments, billing, and payment procedures

[DA06035]

TYPES OF INLAND MARINE AND OCEAN CARGO INSURANCE POLICIES

Inland and ocean marine policies provide coverage for transportation loss exposures. In addition, inland marine policies can insure a variety of mobile articles, construction projects, machinery, and equipment.

Various types of inland and ocean marine policies are available for covering transportation exposures, such as an **annual transit policy** and an **open cargo policy**. The Nationwide Marine Definition is used to determine whether a particular coverage is classified as marine insurance (inland or ocean) and helps to frame and regulate the many categories of inland marine "floaters" that cover various types of property.

Annual transit policy

Policy that covers all shipments made or received by the insured throughout a one-year policy period.

Open cargo policy

Policy that covers all goods shipped or received by the insured during the policy's term; comparable to an inland marine annual trip transit policy, but without a set policy expiration date.

Transportation Insurance

These are the common types of inland and ocean marine policies used for covering transportation loss exposures:

- Annual transit insurance
- Open cargo insurance
- Trip transit insurance
- Mail insurance
- Motor truck cargo insurance

With the exception of one type, mail insurance, all of these are nonfiled classes of business in most states; that is, those classes of inland marine business for which neither policy forms nor rates must be filed with a state's insurance department for use in that state. The provisions used in a nonfiled policy are those agreed on by the insurer and the insured. See the exhibit "Common Types of Inland/Ocean Marine Insurance."

Annual Transit Insurance

Annual transit insurance is designed for organizations that frequently ship or receive property in transit. Thus, an annual transit policy covers all shipments made by or received by the insured throughout the policy period, which is ordinarily one year.

The primary purpose of annual transit insurance is to cover property while being transported by carriers. However, not all types of transportation are automatically covered. When arranging transit insurance, the insured should make sure that all possible modes of transportation that the insured might use are clearly indicated on the Declarations page as being covered.

In addition to covering property transported by carriers, many transit policies also cover property shipped by any land vehicle owned or operated by the insured. For some insureds, this exposure is incidental to carrier-borne shipments; for other insureds, the "owner's goods on owner's trucks" exposure is substantial. For example, a plumbing supply wholesaler's incoming shipments may be transported by common carriers, whereas its outgoing shipments to its customers may be transported on the insured's own trucks. When the "owner's goods on owner's trucks" exposure is significant, it is sometimes insured under the owner's form of a motor truck cargo policy.

Any annual transit policy excludes certain types of property. Contraband, for example, is not insurable as a matter of public policy, and most insurance forms make this clear by excluding contraband. Other types of property are commercially insurable, but they are especially attractive to thieves and therefore expensive to insure. Examples are precious metals, furs, jewelry, money, and securities. These items are typically excluded. If the insured is willing to pay an additional premium to cover such items, the insurer will usually delete or modify the exclusions to provide coverage.

Common Types of Inland/Ocean Marine Insurance

- Annual transit insurance—Also known simply as transportation insurance, this inland marine coverage is purchased by frequent shippers to cover all shipments made or received during the annual policy period.

- Open cargo insurance—This is the ocean marine counterpart of annual transit insurance. It covers all waterborne shipments (and, often, international air shipments) in which the insured has an insurable interest.

- Trip transit insurance—Purchased by infrequent shippers, trip transit insurance covers the particular shipment of goods specified in the policy.

- Mail insurance—Various forms are available for insuring property being transported by the United States Postal Service or another country's postal service.

- Motor truck cargo insurance—This class contains two basic variations. The "carrier's form" covers the insured's legal liability as a motor carrier for loss to customers' property. The "owner's form" provides transit coverage for organizations that use their own trucks to transport their own goods.

[DA06056]

An annual transit policy typically contains any of several exclusions of property in particular situations. For example, some exclusions are intended to prevent annual transit insurance (an inland marine coverage) from covering ocean marine cargo exposures. Therefore, a policy may exclude overseas shipments made by the insured (1) after being placed on the overseas vessel or (2) after ocean marine insurance attaches to the shipment (whichever occurs first). Similarly, import shipments are usually excluded as long as ocean marine insurance applies to the shipment. In many cases, ocean marine insurance applies on a "warehouse to warehouse" basis, automatically covering shipments until they reach their final inland destinations.

Annual transit policies contain various coverage extensions, such as providing coverage for the insured's property while in the course of transit back to the insured if the shipment was rejected by the buyer.

Most annual transit policies cover on an open perils basis. The approach used is similar to that of the commercial property Causes of Loss—Special Form. However, an annual transit policy does not contain as many exclusions as the Special Form and thus covers a broader scope of perils. For example, flood and earthquake are usually covered.

Many annual transit policies cover only within the continental United States and Canada, including airborne shipments between these places. The "continental United States" does not include Hawaii, Puerto Rico, or any overseas possessions. This language precludes the insurer from having to cover air or water shipments to or from overseas locations. Insurers generally prefer to insure such shipments under ocean cargo policies. Land shipments to Mexico or other nations south of the U.S. are not within the typical coverage territory, but some underwriters will modify the policy territory accordingly for an additional premium.

Property covered under an annual transit policy is usually valued at the amount of invoice (including shipping charges) if the property is being transported between buyer and seller. When no invoice applies (such as when a company is shipping property between its own locations), the property may be valued at actual cash value.

Open Cargo Insurance

The open cargo policy is an ocean marine insurance contract that covers overseas shipments by vessel or aircraft. The open cargo policy, like the annual transit policy, is designed for frequent shippers because it automatically covers all shipments for which the insured is at risk.

In an ocean marine policy, the party named as insured is usually referred to as the **assured**. In addition to a clause that names the parties insured, open cargo policies contain a loss payable clause stating that losses will be paid to the assured "or order." The phrase "or order" means that the assured can direct payment to the consignee, a bank, or some other party that has an insurable interest in the shipment.

Open cargo policies contain a clause, often titled Goods Insured, stating that the policy will cover "all shipments of lawful goods and merchandise of every kind and description consisting principally of…." A general description of the product or products shipped by the assured is inserted in the space provided. Coverage is not limited to the type of commodity named in the clause. However, the policy may state that goods of a type not named will be subject to restricted terms of coverage.

In addition to covering the assured's interest in property being shipped, open cargo policies cover the assured's responsibility for general average and sue and labor charges. In maritime law, "average" refers to a partial loss to a vessel or its cargo. **General average** is either an expenditure or a sacrifice of part of the vessel or cargo, made in a time of danger to save the voyage.

Open cargo policies contain a **sue and labor clause** obligating the assured to preserve the covered property at a time of loss. In return, the insurer agrees to pay, in addition to the policy limit, the cost of such measures the assured takes.

The attachment clause states that the insurance will "attach and cover all shipments made on and after" the date and time shown in the policy. A shipment made before the date of attachment is not covered even if it is still in transit after the date of attachment. Open cargo policies are so named because they do not specify an expiration date. The policy remains in force continuously until canceled by either the assured or the insurer.

Assured
In ocean marine policies, the party named as the insured.

General average
Partial loss that must, according to maritime law, be shared by all parties to a voyage (cargo owners and vessel owner).

Sue and labor clause
Clause that covers the cost of reasonable measures that the insured is required to take to protect property from damage at the time of loss.

The cancellation provision indicates that usually either the assured or the insurer can cancel the policy by giving thirty days' notice. Once the cancellation date is reached, coverage terminates only for shipments that commence after that date. Property in transit before cancellation occurs remains covered until delivery.

Many open cargo policies contain the broadest possible description of where ocean shipments are covered, stated in a geographical limits provision (for example: "to and from ports or places in the world"). Every open cargo policy contains a clause that describes the types of conveyances by which covered shipments can be made—for example, by aircraft and connecting conveyances.

Ocean cargo insurance is said to provide **warehouse-to-warehouse coverage**. This phrase means that shipments are covered from the point of origin to the point of destination, even if the connecting transportation on either end of the ocean voyage (or international flight) is by land conveyances. Ocean cargo insurance is thus not limited to covering cargo while afloat (or aloft). However, unless the policy has been modified accordingly, ocean cargo insurance does not cover land-only shipments, such as a shipment from New York City to Chicago by truck or train.

> **Warehouse-to-warehouse coverage**
>
> Clause in open cargo policies that covers the insured cargo during the ordinary course of transit (including land transit) from the time the cargo leaves the point of shipment until it is delivered to its final destination.

The warehouse-to-warehouse clause and the marine extension clauses included in virtually every open cargo policy specify the precise scope of warehouse-to-warehouse coverage. Together, these clauses provide an extremely broad scope of coverage for deviations, delays, forced discharges, and transshipments (cargo moved from one ship or other conveyance to another) beyond the assured's control. Although the exact terms are not described here, assureds should be cautioned that these clauses do not cover every possible interruption of transit that might occur. Accordingly, when the assured becomes aware that an interruption has occurred, the best course of action for the assured is to bring the situation to the underwriter's attention. If needed, an additional coverage extension can then be arranged.

Open cargo policies may insure on an "all-risks" basis or for named perils. Most open cargo policies apply on an "all-risks" basis. (Unlike most other property insurance policies, ocean marine cargo policies still commonly use the "all risks except as excluded" language.) The principal exclusions of a cargo policy are called warranties, but they are equivalent to exclusions in a nonmarine policy. These are the principal warranties (or exclusions):

- **Free of capture and seizure (FC&S) warranty**—Eliminates coverage for losses caused by any taking of the vessel by another party or cause. This includes governmental taking, such as capture, arrest, seizure, and restraint, as well as taking by piracy or military actions, such as war. (This warranty does not eliminate coverage under an "all-risks" policy for ordinary theft or pilferage.)

- **Strikes, riots, and civil commotion (SR&CC) warranty**—Eliminates coverage for any type of loss that results from labor disputes or riots,

> **Free of capture and seizure (FC&S) warranty**
>
> A warranty that excludes loss caused by war, piracy, virtually any lawful or unlawful taking of the vessel, a nuclear weapon, a mine, or a torpedo.

> **Strikes, riots, and civil commotion (SR&CC) warranty**
>
> A warranty that excludes loss caused by strikes, labor disturbances, riots, vandalism, sabotage, or malicious acts.

including related property damage from vandalism, sabotage, and similar causes.

- **Delay clause**—Eliminates coverage for financial or property loss that occurs when a shipment is delayed, such as spoilage of produce and interruptions to business processes that are dependent on the shipment.

Delay clause
A clause that excludes coverage for loss caused by delay, such as loss of market, spoilage, and business interruption.

Traditionally, ocean cargo policies covered on a named perils basis, and some open cargo policies still do. More commonly, however, an open cargo policy applies "all-risks" coverage to all covered property except that which is shipped subject to an "on deck" bill of lading. Cargo shipped on deck (with the exception of cargo in watertight intermodal containers) has a much greater exposure to loss than cargo in the vessel's hold. Insurers usually prefer to insure on-deck shipments against a more limited scope of named perils.

Accordingly, many "all-risks" open cargo policies contain one or more clauses for naming the covered perils that are applicable to on-deck shipments. The first such clause found in these types of open cargo policies is called the Perils Clause. See the exhibit " Common Perils Found in Ocean Cargo Perils Clause."

Inchmaree clause
A clause that adds coverage to an ocean marine cargo policy for loss resulting from bursting of boilers, breakage of shafts, latent defects in the vessel, or faults or errors in the navigation or management of the vessel.

In a named perils policy, additional perils can be insured by adding clauses to the policy. The most common of these additional clauses is the **Inchmaree clause**, named after a vessel that was the subject of an English court case in which the traditional perils clause was held not to cover a particular type of loss. To provide coverage for similar losses (such as bursting of boilers or errors in navigation), the Inchmaree clause was developed. It covers loss resulting from bursting of boilers, breakage of shafts, latent defects in components of the vessel, and faults or errors in navigation or vessel management.

FPA/AC (free of particular average/American conditions) warranty
An exceptive warranty that excludes particular average unless the loss is actually caused by the stranding, sinking, or burning of the vessel or its collision with another vessel.

Some open cargo policies contain **FPA/AC (free of particular average/American conditions) warranties**, which restrict the scope of covered perils with regard to "particular average." In marine insurance and maritime law, the term **particular average** is used to describe a partial loss other than a general average. An example is water damage to part of the contents of a container that occurs under circumstances other than general average. An FPA English Conditions alternative is also used at times. Insurers use FPA warranties less frequently today than in the past.

Particular average
Partial loss that is borne by only one party to a voyage (such as a cargo owner).

Ocean cargo policies are among the longest and most complicated of all insurance policies and contain many provisions. However, the provisions relating to maximum limits and the provisions relating to type of loss valuation are the more essential general provisions found in open cargo policies.

Virtually every open cargo policy places a maximum limit on the amount the insurer will pay for cargo on any one vessel or connecting conveyance or in any one place at any one time. It is extremely important for the assured to understand that cargo policy limits apply on a per-conveyance basis and not on a per-shipment basis. Because several shipments could be stowed on the same vessel, the assured must exercise care to select adequate limits. The

---

Common Perils Found in Ocean Cargo Perils Clause

- Perils of the seas—Perils of the sea are fortuitous causes of loss peculiar to the sea and other bodies of water such as rivers, lakes, and seaports. Abnormally high winds or waves are examples of perils of the seas, as are accidents in navigation, such as collisions, strandings, and groundings, even though they may have resulted from negligence of the vessel's master or crew.

- Fire—The peril of fire includes damage resulting from the direct action of fire as well as loss resulting from measures taken to fight the fire, such as water damage.

- Jettison—Jettison is the voluntary throwing overboard of cargo (or other property) in an emergency, usually to lighten the vessel's load or to eliminate a hazard. In most cases, jettison of cargo is considered a general average loss to be shared by all parties to the venture.

- Assailing thieves—The assailing thieves peril refers to the theft of cargo by force and does not include clandestine theft, pilferage, or theft by the passengers or crew.

- Barratry of the masters and mariners—Barratry includes any wrongful act willfully committed by the master or crew with criminal intent, to the detriment of the shipowner or charterer. Mutiny and malicious destruction of cargo are examples of barratry.

- All other like perils—The phrase "all other like perils" includes only perils similar to those described above. It does not provide "all-risks" coverage.

[DA06058]

accumulation clause contained in most open cargo policies provides some relief to the assured in this matter. See the exhibit "Essential General Open Cargo Provisions."

For shipments between buyers and sellers, most open cargo policies state that the value of covered property will include certain elements, as described in the exhibit.

When a shipment involves no sale, the shipment can be valued at declared value or market value plus freight and other charges. A market value approach may also be used for commodities whose values can fluctuate widely within a relatively short period of time.

Open cargo policies typically require the insured to report the full value of all shipments to the insurer. Premiums are calculated by applying the applicable insurance rate to that value, even if it exceeds the policy limit. This provision encourages insureds to carry a limit of insurance that is no less than the highest possible shipment value.

Trip Transit Insurance

A **trip transit policy** covers cargo on a specified trip. Depending on where the shipment is going, the policy may be inland marine or ocean marine. A trip

Accumulation clause

A clause in open cargo policies that doubles the policy limit when, for reasons beyond the control of the assured, shipments accumulate at some point in transit.

Trip transit policy

Policy that covers a particular shipment of goods specified in the policy.

Essential General Open Cargo Provisions

Provision	Description
Provision on Maximum Limits	• Cargo on any one vessel or connecting conveyance or in any one place at any one time
	• Cargo while on deck of any one vessel subject to on-deck bills of lading
	• Cargo shipped by any one aircraft or connecting conveyance
	• Cargo in any one package transported by mail or parcel post
	• Cargo in any one approved metal barge (other than as a connecting conveyance)
Provision on Value of Covered Property	• The amount of the invoice, including all charges in the invoice
	• Any prepaid, advance, or guaranteed freight charges
	• An "advance" equal to 10 percent of the invoice and freight, or a higher percentage if so agreed upon

[DA06059]

transit policy is commonly used to cover property such as a valuable piece of machinery being moved from its place of manufacture to its place of use.

For example, several turbines built in Europe may be shipped to a utility company in Illinois. Such equipment might be worth millions of dollars and might exceed any limited liability assumed by the carrier. Loss exposures (and insurance rates) are affected by the value and the chances of loss under the method of shipment chosen, as well as other factors.

Mail Insurance

Property in the custody of the United States Postal Service (USPS) can be insured through the purchase of insurance from the USPS. The limits of insurance offered by the USPS, as well as the rates for such insurance, depend on the type of mail service used. However, mail insurance is also available through commercial insurers. Many organizations find it useful because the cost is frequently lower than that of government insurance, the amount of insurance available from the USPS is limited, and commercial insurance may provide faster claim settlements.

Mail Coverage Form
Form that covers a financial institution against loss of securities and other negotiable instruments while in transit through specified types of mail.

Additional coverage is available as provided under ISO's **Mail Coverage Form** (CM 00 60). *Commercial Lines Manual* rules permit the Mail Coverage Form to be used by corporations acting as security transfer agents or registrars for their own security issues. Examples of the types of property covered include bonds, stock certificates, certificates of deposit, money orders, checks, bills of lading, and other commercial papers. If sent by registered mail, bullion, currency, unsold traveler's checks, precious and semiprecious stones, and similar valuables are covered as well.

A **parcel post policy** provides coverage against loss due to nondelivery (failure of the package to arrive at its destination). However, the policy may exclude coverage for loss caused by improperly or insecurely wrapped packages or for packages bearing labels that describe the nature of the contents. Coverage applies while the property is in the custody of the USPS. A comparable policy can also be written to cover shipments by commercial parcel carriers.

Parcel post policy
Inland marine policy that provides broad coverage on parcel post shipments.

Motor Truck Cargo Insurance

Annual transit insurance applies to the property of shippers, protecting the owners of such property from loss in transit. The carrier transporting the property from one place to another may be held legally liable for loss of or damage to the property in its custody. Motor truck carriers can insure this liability loss exposure by purchasing a **motor truck cargo liability policy**. Similar insurance could be written for airlines and railroads, although airlines and railroads often retain their cargo liability exposures. Waterborne carriers can insure their cargo liability exposure by purchasing protection and indemnity insurance.

Motor truck cargo liability policy
Policy that covers a trucker's liability for damage to cargo of others being transported by the trucker.

Another type of motor truck cargo insurance, sometimes called the **owners' goods on owners' trucks policy**, is purchased by firms that transport their own property with their own vehicles. In essence, the owner's form of motor truck cargo insurance resembles an annual transit policy, and annual transit policies are often extended to cover owners' goods on owners' trucks. The discussion that follows describes only the motor truck cargo liability insurance purchased by carriers.

Owners' goods on owners' trucks policy
A type of motor truck cargo policy that covers any type of organization (not just a trucking company) for damage to its own cargo while being transported on its own trucks.

Motor truck cargo liability applies only to cargo damage for which the motor carrier is legally liable. It is not direct property insurance for the benefit of the cargo owner. For example, a cargo loss may have resulted from an "act of God" (such as a hurricane) without any negligence on the part of the motor carrier. The motor carrier would not be liable under such circumstances, and the insurance would not cover the loss.

In addition to limiting coverage to losses for which the insured is legally liable, some policies also limit coverage to losses caused by specified perils. Other forms cover any loss for which the insured is liable as long as the loss is not subject to any of the exclusions stated in the form.

The description of covered property usually encompasses most property accepted by the insured for transportation. However, as in transit policies, certain types of valuable property likely to be targeted by thieves are commonly excluded, such as precious metals, jewelry, and fine arts. Some policies exclude liquor and cigarettes, two other commodities that attract hijackers. A motor carrier that transports such commodities can usually have the exclusions deleted in return for an additional premium.

The property is covered only while in or on a land vehicle operated by the insured (including connecting carriers) or while located at the insured's terminal. Terminal coverage is usually limited to a certain time period, such as seventy-two hours; however, the insurer will usually extend the duration of terminal coverage for an additional premium.

Regulations of the U.S. Department of Transportation (USDOT) require insurers to include a special endorsement when providing motor truck cargo policies to interstate carriers. Public utilities commissions and other regulatory bodies within individual states require similar endorsements to be attached to motor truck cargo policies of intrastate carriers.

BMC 32—Endorsement for Motor Common Carrier Policies of Insurance for Cargo Liability

An endorsement that insurers must attach to motor truck cargo liability policies of interstate carriers stating that the insurer will pay cargo claims for which the insured is liable, up to the limits required by the U.S. Department of Transportation, even if such claims are not covered under the policy.

The endorsement is designated **BMC 32—Endorsement for Motor Common Carrier Policies of Insurance for Cargo Liability**. The endorsement states that the insurer will pay cargo claims for which the insured is liable, up to the limits required by USDOT, even if such claims are not otherwise covered under the policy. However, the policy contains a provision that obligates the insured to reimburse the insurer for any losses that are covered under the policy only because of the endorsement. Thus, the endorsement is a means of ensuring that shippers can receive some compensation for their losses, even if the loss is not ultimately covered by the carrier's motor truck cargo policy.

Instrumentalities of Transportation and Communication

In the early 1900s, marine insurers were the only insurers willing to insure bridges. The practice was so firmly established by the time the first Nationwide Marine Definition was written that it was considered proper for a marine policy to cover a bridge or tunnel. In time, the practice was expanded to include coverage on other types of property with similar exposure and coverage problems.

Eventually, a designation for this category of coverages became necessary, and "instrumentalities of transportation and communication" was chosen. The Nationwide Marine Definition lists these instrumentalities of transportation and communication:

- Bridges, tunnels, and other similar instrumentalities.
- Piers, wharves, docks, slips, dry docks, and marine railways. (Marine railways are the structures on which vessels can be launched into the water or hauled out of the water.)
- Pipelines, including on-line propulsion, regulating, and other equipment.
- Power transmission and telephone and telegraph lines.

- Radio and television communication equipment.
- Outdoor cranes, loading bridges, and similar equipment used to load, unload, and transport.

Huge values can be at risk from a variety of perils when a major bridge, tunnel, or other "instrumentality" is being constructed. Specialized builders risk policies are available from inland marine underwriters to cover such construction projects. Once the structure is completed, it can be insured under an inland marine form designed for completed structures of that type. Business income and extra expense coverages can usually be obtained in connection with both the builders risk policy and the policy for the completed structure.

The designation "instrumentalities of transportation and communication" is not limited to the classes of property listed in the Definition. For example, communication satellites, satellite receiving dishes, cellular phones, traffic signaling equipment, and automated toll collection systems can also be insured as inland marine.

Equipment Floaters

Several types of inland marine policies can be classified as **equipment floaters**. In many cases, the main exposure covered by such policies is equipment normally used away from the insured's premises, such as a building contractor's tools and mechanized equipment. In contrast, other equipment floaters cover property, such as computers or medical equipment that normally remains at a fixed location but may be taken off premises.

Two of the most important types of equipment floaters cover these types of property:

- Contractors equipment
- Electronic data processing equipment

The Nationwide Marine Definition does not limit inland marine insurance to these particular classes. Virtually any type of mobile articles, machinery, and equipment (other than motor vehicles designed for highway use) can be insured under an inland marine equipment floater.

Contractors Equipment

Contractors equipment is the largest class of commercial inland marine insurance. The equipment used by contractors when constructing buildings, highways, dams, tunnels, bridges, and other structures ranges from small hand tools to large machines worth hundreds of thousands or even millions of dollars. Such equipment may include cranes, earthmovers, tractors, stone crushers, bulldozers, mobile asphalt plants, portable offices, and scaffolding. A **contractors equipment floater** can be used to insure this type of equipment.

Equipment floaters
A category of inland marine policies covering various types of equipment, wherever it may be located in the policy period.

Contractors equipment floater
A policy that covers mobile equipment or tools while located anywhere in the coverage territory.

The property that can be insured under a contractors equipment floater is not limited to tools and equipment used by contractors. For example, mobile equipment used in mining and lumbering operations, as well as snow-removal and road-repair equipment owned by municipalities, is commonly insured under contractors equipment floaters.

A contractors equipment floater normally contains a schedule that lists each piece of equipment and its corresponding limit of insurance. A policy may also provide blanket coverage on unscheduled hand tools and miscellaneous equipment. Maintaining an up-to-date schedule of all items can be difficult or impossible for a large contractor that uses perhaps hundreds of pieces of equipment. Therefore, a large contractor may obtain blanket coverage applying to all equipment it uses, whether owned, rented, or borrowed.

Coverage may be on an open perils basis or for named perils. When coverage is for named perils, the following perils are commonly covered: fire, lightning, explosion, windstorm, hail, vandalism, theft, earthquake, flood, collision, overturn, and collapse of bridges and culverts.

Policies designed for equipment used in specialized operations may include some unusual perils. For example, a policy covering underground mining equipment may cover, in addition to the perils just listed, "roof fall," "cave-in," and "squeeze." Squeeze is the pressure of surrounding rock or coal on augers or drill bits, which can break the augers or bits. Policies covering exploratory oil or natural-gas well-drilling rigs usually add the perils of "blow-out" and "cratering." Blowout is the uncontrolled flow from inside the well of drilling fluid, oil, gas, or water. Cratering is the formation of a basin-like opening around the rig by the erosive action of air, oil, gas, or water.

Contractors equipment floaters frequently include rental reimbursement coverage, which pays the cost of renting substitute equipment when covered property has been put out of service by a covered cause of loss. Rental reimbursement coverage is comparable to the extra expense coverage provided by the Business Income (and Extra Expense) Coverage Form.

Computer Equipment

Computer equipment (also called electronic data processing [EDP] equipment) may be insured under inland marine insurance. Although computer equipment is also covered as unscheduled business personal property in commercial property forms such as the Building and Personal Property Coverage Form, an inland marine EDP equipment floater can provide added benefits. Many EDP floaters cover special perils such as mechanical or electrical breakdown, which otherwise can be covered only in an equipment breakdown policy. They also typically insure covered property while in transit. Moreover, because EDP is a nonfiled class of inland marine, an EDP floater provides the opportunity to tailor policies to meet individual coverage needs. EDP equipment floaters can go by various names, such as "computer equipment coverage" or "computer coverage form."

An EDP policy typically covers equipment, data, and media owned by the insured, as well as similar property of others in the insured's care, custody, or control. Extra expense coverage is also usually included. Business income coverage can often be added when requested.

In an EDP policy, "equipment" is defined broadly. A typical policy definition is "your electronic data processing equipment, word processing equipment, and telecommunications equipment, including their component parts."

Equipment can be valued at its actual cash value, replacement cost, or **upgraded value**. For data and media, valuation can be on either an "actual reproduction cost" basis or a valued basis. With the valued approach, a stated value is placed on each item.

Data is information that has been converted to a form usable in computer equipment. Data includes both computer programs, which direct the processing of data, and data files, which store data that has been processed (such as a customer mailing list or an inventory of merchandise). Media are the material on which data are stored, such as discs and tapes. Media containing data can be valuable for the information they contain.

For purposes of data and media coverage, most EDP policies exclude accounts, bills, evidences of debt, valuable papers, abstracts, records, deeds, manuscripts, and other documents. However, if any of these are converted to data, many EDP policies will cover them in that converted form. Some EDP policies include optional valuable papers and records insurance and accounts receivable insurance.

If their EDP systems become damaged, many organizations can stay in operation or decrease the shutdown period by incurring extra expenses. Extra expenses can be incurred in several ways, including these:

- Through using a "hot site" disaster recovery facility, which for a fee performs the insured's data processing operations
- Through using manual procedures until computer service has been restored, which can involve additional labor costs
- Through expediting repair services by paying employees or contractors overtime

The regular commercial property Business Income and Extra Expense Coverage Form does not exclude losses resulting from damage to EDP equipment or media. However, that form covers only the perils insured against by the commercial property causes of loss forms.

Some EDP policies offer business income coverage for those insureds whose incomes depend on the functioning of their computer systems. A major advantage of purchasing business income insurance in an EDP policy is the broader scope of perils covered by an EDP policy.

One of the main reasons for buying an EDP policy is that it covers a broader range of perils than commercial property policies. Coverage is on an open

Upgraded value
The cost to replace covered equipment with the latest comparable state-of-the-art equipment available; can be used as a valuation basis in an EDP floater.

perils basis, but usually with fewer of the exclusions found in the Causes of Loss—Special Form.

Breakdown coverage

Coverage, in an EDP equipment floater, for perils such as mechanical failure, electrical disturbance, and damage to electronic data when covered equipment breaks down.

Most important, the insured often has the option of purchasing **breakdown coverage**. Subject to a separate deductible, breakdown coverage insures loss to equipment resulting from such perils as mechanical failure or faulty design of the covered property, or changes in temperature resulting from breakdown of air conditioning equipment.

EDP policies typically cover computer virus losses if they can be attributed to a covered cause of loss. If, for example, the virus was planted in the system by an outsider with malicious intent, the loss will be covered if the policy covers vandalism (and does not exclude computer virus losses). However, if the virus was maliciously introduced by a disgruntled employee of the insured and the policy excludes employee dishonesty, the loss will not be covered.

Builders Risks and Installation Risks

Although the ISO commercial property program includes a Builders Risk Coverage Form, one of the categories of insurance listed in the Nationwide Marine Definition is "builders' risks and/or installation risks." The Definition includes builders risks and installation risks in the same category because they are similar coverages. These are the fundamental differences between a builders risk policy and an installation floater:

- A *builders risk policy* covers an entire building or other structure during the course of construction, including the building supplies and material that will become part of the covered structure. The entity insured is usually the owner, the builder, or perhaps both.

- An *installation floater* usually covers property installed at a work site by a particular contractor or subcontractor. The coverage normally applies while the property is in transit or in temporary storage and during the installation and testing process. The entity insured is usually the contractor or subcontractor installing the property.

Builders Risk Policies

Although an ISO Builders Risk Coverage Form can be issued as a component of a commercial property coverage part, buildings or other structures in the course of construction can also be insured under an inland marine builders risk policy, which is a policy that covers a building in the course of construction, including building materials and supplies while on or away from the building site. Inland marine builders risk policies usually provide broader coverage than the commercial property version of builders risk coverage and allow for rating flexibility.

Inland marine builders risk policies typically cover the structure under construction, temporary structures at the building site, and building materials that have not yet become part of the building. Building materials are covered while on the insured location, in transit, or in storage at another location. Business income coverage may be provided as part of the policy.

Inland marine builders risk policies usually cover on a special perils basis, and many insurers provide coverage for losses usually excluded under standard commercial property forms:

- Flood
- Earthquake
- Theft of building materials that have not been installed
- Boiler explosion

Coverage is provided for collapse during the course of construction resulting from use of defective materials or methods. (The commercial property builders risk form does not cover such collapse unless the coverage is added by endorsement.)

Most insurers that write inland marine builders risk policies offer an endorsement providing "soft costs" coverage. Soft costs coverage endorsements differ among insurers. Examples of items these endorsements cover are additional architects' and engineers' fees and additional legal and accounting fees.

Installation Floaters

Contractors and subcontractors commonly purchase **installation floaters** to cover the property they are installing at job sites. These persons might also purchase an installation floater:

- A property owner to cover property being installed at the owner's premises
- A seller of property who is responsible for loss to the property until it is installed in the buyer's premises

Installation floaters are generally associated with plumbing, heating, cooling, and electrical systems but can be used to insure any property being installed. Carpeting, tile, windows, elevators, and machinery are examples of property that can be covered.

A typical installation floater covers the property during the course of transit and while being installed and tested at the work site. The point at which coverage ends is usually the earliest of these times:

- When the insured's financial interest ceases
- When the purchaser accepts the property as complete
- When the policy expires or is canceled

Installation floater
Policy that covers a contractor's interest in building supplies or fixtures that the contractor has been hired to install.

Bailee/Bailor Policies

Bailee
The party temporarily possessing the personal property in a bailment.

Bailor
The owner of the personal property in a bailment.

A commercial **bailee** is a party that holds the property of another (the **bailor**) for some purpose beneficial to both of them. Examples of commercial bailments are the laundering of clothes, the storing of furs, and the repairing of jewelry.

Generally, a commercial bailee is legally responsible for loss of or damage to a customer's property that results from the bailee's negligence (failure to exercise reasonable care to safeguard the property). Even if a bailee cannot be held legally liable for loss of or damage to a customer's property, the customer (bailor) is likely to expect the bailee to pay for the loss. Thus, many bailees want to buy insurance that will pay for damage to customers' property regardless of whether the bailee is legally liable. Additionally, bailor policies protect an insured's property while it is in the custody of a bailee.

Warehouse operators legal liability policy
Policy that covers warehouse operators against liability for damage to the property of others being stored in operators' warehouses.

One type of bailee policy is a bailee liability policy, which covers loss by an insured peril to property in the bailee's care, custody, or control *only if the bailee is legally liable* for the loss. A common type of bailee liability insurance is the **warehouse operators legal liability policy**. The policy covers the liability of the insured as a warehouse operator for direct physical loss of or damage to property of others while contained in the specified premises. The coverage is subject to various exclusions, many of which resemble those contained in special-form property insurance policies.

The bailee liability policy responds only if the insured is legally obligated to pay for loss to customers' property. If the insured is not held liable, the policy will not respond. Consequently, bailees require a higher level of coverage knowing they face a significant "loss of goodwill" exposure in addition to their legal liability exposure for customers' property.

For example, if a dry cleaning plant were destroyed by a fire originating in a neighboring building, the bailee would usually have no legal liability to the customers for loss of their clothing. Thus, it might appear that the bailee would incur no loss. However, the public image created by a dry cleaner who failed to reimburse its customers for their losses might be so bad that the cleaner would lose many customers and perhaps even go out of business. For most types of bailees, it has become customary to cover both the legal liability exposure and the goodwill exposure through a single policy called a **bailees' customers policy**.

Bailees' customers policy
A policy that covers damage to customers' goods while in the possession of the insured, regardless of whether the insured is legally liable for the damage.

Bailor policies are designed specifically to cover the insured's property while it is in the custody of a bailee. Two common examples of such policies are pattern and die floaters and processing floaters.

In some manufacturing operations, parts of the work are subcontracted to other manufacturers or processors. This arrangement may require that the manufacturer send various patterns, dies, or other tools for cutting, forming, or shaping materials to the subcontractor's premises. In many cases, these items remain indefinitely at the subcontractor's premises in anticipation of future use there. A **pattern and die floater** covers the insured's tools while off-premises for such purposes. Similar coverage can be provided on other types of property, such as a publisher's manuscripts, artwork, positives, and negatives, while on the premises of the publisher's printing contractors.

Whereas a pattern and die floater covers the tools a subcontractor uses to perform manufacturing operations for another firm, a **processing floater** covers the property that the subcontractor is actually working on. For example, a furniture manufacturer may send some of its stock in process to a mill for sanding operations. Alternatively, a machine parts manufacturer may send certain items to a contractor for chrome plating. A processing floater can be obtained to cover such property from the time it leaves the insured's premises until it is returned there.

Dealers Policies

The inventories and other business personal property of various types of dealers can be insured under inland marine **dealers policies**. (The term "dealer" is usually applied to retailers but can also include wholesalers.) The Nationwide Marine Definition lists several specific types of dealers, but it does not limit the category to the types listed.

As long as the property sold by the dealer could be insured by the ultimate purchaser under an inland marine policy, it can be insured under an inland marine policy while held by the dealer. A computer dealer or a bicycle dealer, for example, could insure its inventory under an inland marine dealer policy. In practice, many dealers are insured under businessowners policies rather than under inland marine forms.

The Nationwide Marine Definition also states that such policies may cover money in locked safes or vaults on the insured's premises, furniture, fixtures, tools, machinery, patterns, molds, dies, and a tenant insured's interest in improvements and betterments. Thus, an inland marine dealers policy can cover both the dealer's inventory and most other business personal property of the dealer. See the exhibit "Types of Dealers Eligible for Inland Marine Dealer Policies."

Dealers policies, particularly those written for jewelers and furriers, are also called **block policies**. The name is derived from the French *en bloc*, meaning "all together" or "complete." When the phrase was coined in the early 1900s, jewelers and furriers were the principal types of dealers insured.

Filed inland marine forms are available from both ISO and AAIS for jewelers, dealers in mobile and agricultural and construction equipment, camera dealers, and musical instrument dealers.

The property covered by a dealers form typically includes the insured's "stock in trade" (inventory) and similar property of others in the insured's care, custody, or control. This property is covered while it is (1) on the insured's premises, (2) away from the insured's premises in transit or in the custody of

Pattern and die floater

A policy that covers the insured's patterns and dies while located at the premises of others and also while in transit to and from those premises.

Processing floater

A policy that covers the insured's goods while being worked on at a subcontractor's or processor's premises and while in transit to and from those premises.

Dealers policy

A policy that covers the inventory and other property of any of the types of dealers that qualify for inland marine coverage (such as jewelers, equipment dealers, fine arts dealers, and furriers).

Block policy

A dealers policy, particularly one written for a jeweler or furrier.

Types of Dealers Eligible for Inland Marine Dealer Policies

- Jewelers
- Equipment (farm or construction) dealers
- Fine arts dealers
- Furriers
- Camera dealers
- Musical instrument dealers
- Stamp and coin dealers
- Dealers of any other property that, when sold to the ultimate purchaser, may be covered, by the owner, under an inland marine policy

[DA03616]

the insured's employees, or (3) located elsewhere. Separate limits may apply to loss of property in each of these categories. In addition to covering the insured's stock in trade, the form can be extended for an additional premium to cover these items:

- Furniture, fixtures, and office supplies
- Machinery, tools, and fittings
- Patterns, dies, molds, and models
- Tenants' improvements and betterments

Accounts, bills, currency, deeds, evidences of debt, money, notes, and securities are excluded.

Dealers forms cover on an open perils basis, subject to many of the same exclusions as in the commercial property Causes of Loss—Special Form. However, the flood and earthquake exclusions are often omitted from dealer policies.

Theft is a frequent and sometimes severe cause of loss for many dealers, especially jewelers. Thus, most dealers forms contain several theft-related exclusions to encourage loss prevention and avoid coverage for exposures that would be very expensive to insure. Common examples of such theft exclusions include theft of property from an unlocked vehicle (unless in the custody of a carrier for hire), employee dishonesty, and unexplained disappearance. The Jewelers Block Coverage Form contains a theft exclusion relating to theft from show windows (unless specifically covered).

Miscellaneous Inland Marine Coverages

In addition to the broader classes of inland marine insurance, various inland marine coverages are available to meet special exposures that are not fully covered under basic commercial property forms. Three such coverages are sign coverage, accounts receivable coverage, and valuable papers and records coverage.

Sign Coverage

The **Signs Coverage Form** (CM 00 28), filed by ISO, must be scheduled with a limit of insurance shown for each item. The signs form is used by many businesses because commercial property forms exclude or severely limit coverage for signs. A coinsurance requirement (typically 100 percent) applies to all covered property at all locations. The coinsurance requirement does not apply to property in transit.

Coverage is on an open perils basis, subject to various exclusions. Two exclusions specific to the signs form eliminate coverage for these events:

- Breakage during transportation, installation, repair, or dismantling of covered property.
- Loss caused by short circuit or other electrical disturbance within a covered sign caused by artificially generated current. (Loss caused by resulting fire is not excluded.)

Signs Coverage Form
Form that covers neon, fluorescent, automatic, or mechanical signs.

Accounts Receivable Coverage

Accounts receivable insurance does not cover credit losses that result simply because a customer defaults or becomes bankrupt. Accounts receivable coverage is triggered only if a covered cause of loss damages or destroys the insured's records of accounts receivable, interrupting the insured's billing procedures.

In addition to paying the sums that the insured is unable to collect from its customers, accounts receivable insurance covers these expenses:

- Interest charges on any loan required to offset the uncollectible amounts
- Collection expenses in excess of normal collection expenses that were made necessary by the damage to the records of accounts receivable
- Other reasonable expenses the insured incurs to reconstruct the damaged records

Accounts receivable insurance
Insurance that covers the sums the insured is unable to collect when records of accounts receivable are destroyed by a covered cause of loss.

Many businesses that extend credit to their customers operate without accounts receivable coverage. Some firms are simply unaware of the exposure and the relatively low cost of insuring it. Other firms rely wholly on duplicate records to replace the original records if they are destroyed. Even if an organization keeps duplicate records in a fire-resistant safe or vault or at another location, such risk control measures are not foolproof and should not entirely discount the need for coverage. Errors or omissions can be made in copying records, and duplicate records in storage may themselves become damaged or lost. Accounts receivable coverage on an inland marine form can be used to supplement coverage limits an insured is able to obtain in a package policy.

Additionally, the Building and Personal Property Coverage Form (BPP) provides only nominal coverage for loss of records of accounts receivable. When such records are in electronic form (as is usually the case), the BPP's additional coverage for electronic data limits recovery to only $2,500 per policy year for the cost to restore lost data. Moreover, the BPP does not cover any sums that the insured is unable to collect from customers because of the loss of the records. Finally, the covered causes of loss are limited to named perils even if the insured has purchased the special form, so accounts receivable coverage could be an option for insureds who require coverage beyond what the BPP insures.

Valuable Papers and Records Coverage

Records of accounts receivable are not the only "valuable papers and records" in organizations. Other examples of valuable papers and records include specifications, plans, and drawings; mailing lists; formulas; legal documents; medical records; and a variety of accounting, financial, and personnel records. Duplicating such records and storing the duplicates at a separate location are effective risk control measures for records that can be readily reproduced.

**Valuable papers and
records insurance**

Insurance that covers direct physical loss to valuable papers and records, such as architect's blueprints and plans.

Valuable papers and records insurance can be obtained to cover loss of either replaceable or irreplaceable documents. For irreplaceable items, coverage is for an agreed value on each specified item. Items that can be reconstructed are covered for actual cash value and on a blanket basis. The policy will pay nothing for property that cannot be replaced unless such property has been scheduled and valued.

CASE STUDY OF INLAND MARINE AND OCEAN CARGO INSURANCE

Commercial property coverage forms either provide limited coverage for property in transit or at locations other than the insured's premises or provide no coverage for transportation-related loss exposures. Ocean marine and inland marine insurance forms are designed to meet the shipping and transportation-related needs of most commercial customers.

A general understanding of transportation and inland marine loss exposures and of the provisions of various transportation and inland marine insurance forms can enable an agent to recommend suitable insurance coverages for a commercial customer that best meet its transportation-related needs.

Case Facts

Logan and Wayne established a business partnership and purchased an after-market auto parts distribution business, renamed as Auto Parts—Central Distributor (AP-CD). The AP-CD business office and primary warehouse are located along the Mississippi River in St. Louis. AP-CD purchases auto parts from manufacturers in Minneapolis and transports them by cargo vessel, trains, and their own fleet of trucks to smaller distributors in St. Louis, Kansas City, Indianapolis, Toledo, and Memphis. Because these distribution routes were already established and relatively successful, Logan and Wayne decided to maintain these routes as they took over the business.

To complement its shipping business and better serve its customer's needs, AP-CD has one warehouse in St. Louis to which smaller auto part components, available from local manufacturers, are shipped by common carrier trucks. AP-CD acts as an intermediary for these local manufacturers to supply parts to its customers. These non-owned parts are temporarily stored in the AP-CD warehouse to be packaged with the larger parts and shipped to the buyers/owners at their respective warehouses along AP-CD's normal delivery routes.

Sales are handled by cash and through customer charge accounts.

Recognizing the need for transportation insurance in addition to the commercial package policy they have that covers their premises locations and business operations, Logan and Wayne contacted their insurance agent to develop an insurance program that would cover all their shipping and transportation exposures. With the help of their agent, Logan and Wayne determine that their loss exposures include these:

* Consignee for cargo vessel shipments FOB Point of Origin from the manufacturers in Minneapolis
* Shipper for cargo vessel shipments FOB Point of Destination to warehouse owners in Memphis
* Shipper for shipments by truck or rail to the purchasers at warehouses in Kansas City, Indianapolis, and Toledo
* Shipper of own property to warehouses in St. Louis
* Receiver of customer property (smaller auto parts) held for shipment with AP-CD parts in one warehouse
* Owner of accounts receivable

Case Analysis Tools and Information

Knowledge of transportation insurance (including terminology and responsibilities) and various other types of inland marine coverages is required to resolve this case.

Logan and Wayne's agent will help them answer these questions: What transportation-related inland marine insurance coverages will best cover AP-CD's transportation-related loss exposures? What other inland marine or ocean cargo coverages are best suited to AP-CD's additional inland marine exposures? To answer these questions, the agent must first complete three case analysis steps.

These free on board (FOB) contract terms are crucial to correctly answering these questions:

- FOB Point of Origin contract terms—Title (and the risk of loss) passes from seller to buyer when the goods are accepted by the carrier for transit.
- FOB Destination contract terms—Title (and the risk of losses) passes when the goods are delivered to the buyer's premises.

The agent will make a recommendation from among these inland marine/ocean cargo insurance options the coverages that are most appropriate for AP-CD:

- Annual transit insurance
- Open cargo insurance
- Trip transit insurance
- Motor truck cargo insurance
- Mail insurance
- Instrumentalities of transportation and communication
- Equipment floaters
- Builders risks and installation risks
- Bailee/bailor policies
- Dealers Policies
- Sign Coverage
- Accounts receivable coverage
- Valuable papers and records coverage

Case Analysis Steps

To recommend appropriate inland marine and ocean cargo coverages for AP-CD, these steps should be followed:

1. Identify all loss exposures.
2. Describe the responsibility, if any, that AP-CD bears for its customers' property and new merchandise in transit.
3. Recommend appropriate coverages for these loss exposures.

Identify All Loss Exposures

In the first step, all loss exposures that could affect AP-CD's transport operations should be identified.

What transportation exposures affect AP-CD's operations? What inland marine or ocean cargo loss exposures affect AP-CD's operations?

With the help of their agent, Logan and Wayne determine that their loss exposures include these:

- Consignee for cargo vessel shipments FOB Point of Origin from the manufacturers in Minneapolis—The seller transports a container of car parts from the factory to the river, where it is left in the custody of a river carrier. The carrier loads the container aboard a vessel for transport to St. Louis. At the port, AP-CD loads the container on its own truck for transport to its warehouse near the river, where it removes the parts from the container and stores some parts, while distributing other parts to buyers.

- Shipper for cargo vessel shipments FOB Destination to warehouse owners in Memphis—AP-CD loads auto parts into a container and leaves it in the custody of a river carrier, who loads it on a vessel and transports it to Memphis. At that port, the container is loaded on the truck of the buyer and the sales transaction is complete.

- Shipper for shipments by truck or rail to the purchasers at warehouses in Kansas City, Indianapolis, and Toledo—AP-CD loads auto parts into containers and transports them by common carrier or train car to warehouses in Kansas City, Indianapolis, and Toledo. Upon delivery, these sales transactions are complete.

- Shipper of own property to warehouses in St. Louis—Some auto parts are loaded into AP-CD's own cargo trucks for transport to various warehouses around the city.

- Receiver of customer property held for shipment with AP-CD property in one warehouse—Supply companies in St. Louis load smaller auto component parts into trucks for delivery to an AP-CD warehouse, where they are received and unloaded by AP-CD. These smaller parts are stored and later packed with larger AP-CD parts for delivery to various customers throughout their delivery area.

Throughout the transport and deliveries, the shipments are susceptible to pirating and other theft, flood, fire, windstorm, collision, employee theft, employee errors, shipper's negligence, unseaworthy vessel, and spurious or hypercritical rejections by consignees. Some of these perils are insurable; however, the latter three must be controlled through loss control measures.

Describe Responsibility for Customers' Property and New Merchandise in Transit

To determine who has responsibility for the shipments in each transaction, the insurance agent must examine the contracts of sale. Each contract must be analyzed for indications of ownership or responsibility in the terms of sale. These responsibilities may be determined from the previously examined exposures:

- Consignee for cargo vessel shipments FOB Point of Origin from the manufacturers in Minneapolis—Under FOB Point of Origin, the seller bears responsibility for the goods until the goods are transferred to the carrier, in this case, the shipping company. At that point, AP-CD bears responsibility for the goods. The shipper, however, may also bear some liability for goods lost or damaged while in its possession. At the port in St. Louis, AP-CD assumes full responsibility for the shipment when it loads the container on its own truck for transport to its warehouse near the river.

- Shipper for cargo vessel shipments FOB Destination to warehouse owners in Memphis—When shipping FOB Destination, AP-CD retains responsibility for the goods shipped to the warehouse owners in Memphis until the product is delivered to the buyer's premises. Again, the river carrier would also assume some responsibility for the cargo while in its possession, during loading and unloading, and shipping. Once it is loaded on the buyer's truck, title passes to the buyer for the goods.

- Shipper for shipments by truck or rail to the purchasers at warehouses in Kansas City, Indianapolis, and Toledo—Because AP-CD uses common carriers for distributing its goods by truck or train to warehouses in Kansas City, Indianapolis, and Toledo, the carrier may be held liable for any damage or loss that occurs to the goods, even if the carrier has not acted negligently, with few exceptions. A bill of lading would indicate any limitations specified for the common carrier's liability for cargo loss.

- Shipper of own property to warehouses in St. Louis—For shipments of its property using its own trucks, AP-CD retains responsibility for its goods.

- Receiver of customer property held for storage and later shipment with AP-CD property in one warehouse—Because AP-CD receives property from another organization, it becomes a bailee and the non-owned property is in its care, custody, or control. Therefore, AP-CD is liable for any loss to those goods, until the goods are delivered to the buyer.

Recommend an Appropriate Coverage for These Loss Exposures

For each loss exposure identified previously, the agent could suggest a type of policy to insure AP-CD's exposure to loss. In some cases, other forms of loss control besides risk financing may be required to entirely cover the loss exposures. These products would cover AP-CD's responsibility for loss:

- Consignee for cargo vessel shipments FOB Point of Origin from the manufacturers in Minneapolis—AP-CD could insure this exposure under an Open Cargo Policy in which it is the assured. Any loss payee could be included in the policy, as "or order," (to direct a loss payment to the consignee, a bank, or some other party that has an insurable interest in the shipment). Ideally, the shipper will have its own Open Cargo policy to cover its liability for the shipment, as well.

- Shipper for cargo vessel shipments FOB Destination to warehouse owners in Memphis—An Open Cargo policy with warehouse-to-warehouse coverage would provide the needed coverage for AP-CD's liability for shipments until it reaches the buyer's premises. Again, the river carrier could also insure its liability for loss through an open cargo policy.

- Shipper for shipments by truck or rail to the purchasers at warehouses in Kansas City, Indianapolis, and Toledo—An annual transit policy with open perils coverage would meet AP-CD's common carrier transportation needs. This would insure its shipments by common carrier truck and train. Because AP-CD uses common carriers for distributing its goods by truck or train to warehouses in Kansas City, Indianapolis, and Toledo, the carrier may be held responsible for any damage or loss that occurs to the goods, even if the carrier has not acted negligently, with few exceptions. A bill of lading would indicate any limitations specified for the common carrier's liability for cargo loss.

- Shipper of own property to warehouses in St. Louis—An owners' goods on owners' truck motor truck cargo policy would cover AP-CD's interests in its own property for this transportation, as well as for any use of its own trucks in conjunction with common carriers.

- Receiver of customer property held for storage and later shipment with AP-CD property in one of its warehouses—A warehouse operator's legal liability bailee policy would cover AP-CD's liability for the care, custody, or control of such property while stored in its warehouse. Once the non-owned property is packaged for delivery, other policies would insure the property.

Failure to adequately insure its property and its liability for other's property in transit or in AP-CD's care, custody, or control could prove devastating to the organization's financial resources and longevity. Purchase of some or all of the coverages mentioned would reduce or limit AP-CD's risk of loss. Other loss control techniques could help avoid losses, such as favorable contract of sale terms, adequate packaging, warehouse and transit security measures, accounting and supervisory systems, and enforcement of work procedures for proper handling and storage of goods. See the exhibit "Correct Answer."

Correct Answer

Insurance Proposal for AP-CD:

- Open Cargo Policy with warehouse-to-warehouse coverage for all river vessel shipments to and from AP-CD's warehouse

- Annual transit policy with open perils coverage for its shipments via common carrier truck and rail

- Owners' goods on owners' truck motor truck cargo policy to protect interests in its own property transported using its own trucks

- Warehouse operators legal liability bailee policy for its liability for the care, custody, or control of property of others while stored in its warehouse

*This solution might not be the only viable solution. Other solutions could be exercised if justified by the analysis. In addition, specific circumstances and organizational needs or goals may enter into the evaluation, making an alternative action a better option.

[DA06061]

SUMMARY

Inland marine insurance evolved from marine insurance in the early 1900s to meet the public's need for broad insurance coverages.

The general characteristics of inland marine policies involve coverage of property in transit, loss exposures covered, broad coverage of perils, and valuation provisions.

Transportation loss exposure analysis involves a review of the parties involved in transportation; ownership of goods; carrier responsibility for loss; waterborne carriers; and air carriers.

Various types of inland and ocean cargo insurance policies exist for covering transportation and transportation-related exposures. Coverages protect the insured and others who have an insurable interest in the covered property.

Inland marine and ocean marine insurance coverages and endorsements can provide solutions for customers with specific transportation and transportation-related needs that are not adequately covered by other commercial property and liability coverage forms.

9

Commercial Crime Insurance

Educational Objectives

After learning the content of this assignment, you should be able to:

▷ Describe the basic characteristics of the ISO commercial crime program and financial institution bonds.

▷ Summarize the seven insuring agreements of the Commercial Crime Coverage Form in terms of these elements:

- Covered causes of loss

- Covered property

- Where coverage applies

▷ Apply the Commercial Crime Coverage Form's Limit of Insurance and Deductible provisions to a claim.

▷ Identify losses that the Commercial Crime Coverage Form excludes.

▷ Explain how the Commercial Crime Coverage Form's conditions address each of these issues:

- Interests insured

- Where coverage applies

- When coverage applies

- Claim-related duties and procedures

- Conditions applicable to Employee Theft only

▷ Explain how each of these endorsements modifies the Commercial Crime Coverage Form:

- Clients' Property

- Extortion

- Inside the Premises—Theft of Other Property

9

- Inside the Premises—Robbery of a Watchperson or Burglary of Other Property
- Employee Theft—Name or Position Schedule
- Lessees of Safe Deposit Boxes
- Securities Deposited With Others
- Guests' Property
- Destruction of Electronic Data or Computer Programs
- Unauthorized Reproduction of Computer Software by Employees

▶ Explain how the ISO government crime forms differ from the ISO commercial crime forms.

▶ Given a case, determine whether, and for how much, a described loss would be covered by the Commercial Crime Coverage Form.

Commercial Crime Insurance

9

OVERVIEW OF COMMERCIAL CRIME INSURANCE

Organizations use various techniques to manage their loss exposures resulting from criminal acts such as robbery, burglary, and other forms of theft. Among these techniques are avoidance (for example, paying employees by check or direct deposit instead of in cash), risk control (for example, installing burglar alarms), and insurance.

Many types of insurance provide coverage against some property losses that result from criminal acts. Because crime loss exposures can vary significantly among policyholders and require special underwriting skills, insurers prefer to insure certain types of crime-related property loss under separate commercial crime insurance forms. These forms allow organizations to cover crime losses that are not insured under other insurance policies.

Briefly described, commercial crime insurance covers money, securities, and other property against a variety of criminal acts, such as employee theft, robbery, forgery, extortion, and computer fraud. Many insurers use Insurance Services Office, Inc. (ISO) commercial crime forms. Financial institution bonds are used to meet the crime insurance needs of banks, insurance companies, and other types of financial institutions.

ISO Commercial Crime Program

The ISO commercial crime program includes crime coverage forms that can be added to a commercial package policy, as well as crime policy forms that can be written as monoline crime policies. The principal difference between the coverage forms and the policy forms is that the policy forms include the conditions contained in the ISO Common Policy Conditions form, thus eliminating the need to attach them to a monoline crime policy. Each coverage form and policy form comes in two versions: a discovery form and a loss sustained form. See the exhibit "Crime Forms: Discovery Form Versus Loss Sustained Form."

The ISO commercial crime coverage forms and policy forms are designed for insuring any type of nongovernment commercial or not-for-profit entity other than a financial institution. A separate set of ISO government crime coverage forms and policy forms is used to insure government entities, such as states, counties, and public utilities. See the exhibit "ISO Crime Forms and Policies."

Crime Forms: Discovery Form Versus Loss Sustained Form

Discovery Form	Loss Sustained Form
Form that covers losses discovered during the policy period even though they may have occurred before the policy period.	Form that covers losses actually sustained during the policy period and discovered no later than one year after policy expiration.

[DA07817]

Financial Institution Bonds

Few industries have crime loss exposures equal to those faced by banks and other financial institutions. A financial institution bond is an insurance policy that covers the crime loss exposures of financial institutions. Financial institution bonds were developed by the Surety & Fidelity Association of America (SFAA) and are called "bonds" because one of the key coverages that they provide is employee dishonesty insurance, which was traditionally called a "fidelity bond."

Although banks are the most common type of financial institution, other entities—such as savings and loan associations, credit unions, stockbrokers, finance companies, and insurance companies—are also eligible to be insured under financial institution bonds. Entities eligible for financial institution bonds are not eligible for the ISO commercial crime program.

The most widely used financial institution bond is Standard Form No. 24, used to insure banks and savings and loan associations. For many years, this form was called the "bankers blanket bond," a term still often used informally to refer to this coverage. The forms used for other types of financial institutions are similar to Form 24. ISO also publishes financial institution forms similar to the SFAA forms, and many of the insurers that specialize in financial institution coverage have developed their own forms.

ISO Crime Forms and Policies

Form	Form #	Type of Form	Description
Commercial Crime Coverage Form	CR 00 20	Discovery*	Designed for attachment to another policy to provide crime coverage (eight insuring agreements) for organizations other than financial institutions** and government entities.
Commercial Crime Coverage Form	CR 00 21	Loss sustained***	Designed for attachment to another policy to provide crime coverage (eight insuring agreements) for organizations other than financial institutions and government entities.
Commercial Crime Policy	CR 00 22	Discovery	Designed as a stand-alone policy to provide crime coverage (eight insuring agreements) for organizations other than financial institutions and government entities.
Commercial Crime Policy	CR 00 23	Loss sustained	Designed as a stand-alone policy to provide crime coverage (eight insuring agreements) for organizations other than financial institutions and government entities.
Government Crime Coverage Form	CR 00 24	Discovery	Designed for attachment to another policy to provide crime coverage (nine insuring agreements) for government entities.
Government Crime Coverage Form	CR 00 25	Loss sustained	Designed for attachment to another policy to provide crime coverage (nine insuring agreements) for government entities.
Government Crime Policy	CR 00 26	Discovery	Designed as a stand-alone policy to provide crime coverage (nine insuring agreements) for government entities.
Government Crime Policy	CR 00 27	Loss sustained	Designed as a stand-alone policy to provide crime coverage (nine insuring agreements) for government entities.
Employee Theft and Forgery Policy	CR 00 28	Discovery	Designed to provide only employee theft and forgery or alteration coverage in a monoline policy.
Employee Theft and Forgery Policy	CR 00 29	Loss Sustained	Designed to provide only employee theft and forgery or alteration coverage in a monoline policy.

* Loss is discovered during the policy period and sustained during the policy period, before it, or both.

**Financial institutions include banks, savings and loan associations, credit unions, insurers, and similar institutions. These organizations obtain their crime insurance under financial institution bonds (a specialized policy).

***Loss is sustained during the policy period and discovered no longer than one year after the policy period.

[DA05994]

COMMERCIAL CRIME INSURING AGREEMENTS

The Insurance Services Office, Inc. (ISO) Commercial Crime Coverage Form offers optional insuring agreements that enable organizations to customize crime coverage to meet their business needs.

The ISO Commercial Crime Coverage Form includes these insuring agreements, numbered in the form as shown:

1. Employee Theft
2. Forgery or Alteration
3. Inside the Premises—Theft of Money and Securities
4. Inside the Premises—Robbery or Safe Burglary of Other Property
5. Outside the Premises
6. Computer and Funds Transfer Fraud
7. Money Orders and Counterfeit Money

Insureds may select one or more of these insuring agreements and can add other crime coverages by endorsement.

Employee Theft

Insuring Agreement 1 covers an employer against theft of its property by its own employees. The scope of the coverage is determined by policy definitions of various terms. See the exhibit "Summary of Employee Theft Coverage."

Summary of Employee Theft Coverage

Cause of Loss	"Theft" committed by any "employee."
Property Covered	"Money," "securities," and "other property."
Where Coverage Applies	Covered territory is the United States (including its territories and possessions), Puerto Rico, and Canada. Coverage also applies to loss caused by an employee who is temporarily outside the covered territory for not more than ninety consecutive days.

[DA02511]

The policy defines "theft" as the unlawful taking of "money," "securities," or "other property" to the deprivation of the insured. No police report or criminal conviction is required for coverage to apply.

The Employee Theft insuring agreement also states that the term "theft" includes forgery—thereby clarifying that forgery committed by an employee is covered under this insuring agreement, not under the Forgery or Alteration insuring agreement.

The policy definition of "employee" is a natural person (not a corporation) who is currently employed by the insured or who was employed by the insured within the past thirty days; who is compensated by the insured by salary, wages, or commissions; and who is subject to the control and direction of the insured. The definition includes further details that are not discussed here.

The policy defines these types of covered property:

- "Money" means currency, coins, and bank notes in current use with a face value, and travelers' checks, register checks, and money orders held for sale to the public. Under insuring agreements 1, 2, and 6, money also includes deposits in the named insured's account at any financial institution as defined in the form.

- "Securities" means negotiable and nonnegotiable instruments or contracts representing money or other property, such as stocks, bonds, tokens, tickets, stamps, and evidences of debt issued in connection with credit cards other than cards issued by the insured.

- "Other property" means all other tangible property that has intrinsic value. Computer programs, electronic data, and other specified property are excluded. "Tangible" means "possible to touch." Copyrights, patents, intellectual property, and other intangible items are not covered property under the crime coverage form.

The Employee Theft insuring agreement extends the coverage territory to include loss caused by any employee while temporarily outside the regular policy territory (the United States, including its territories and possessions, Puerto Rico, and Canada) for up to ninety consecutive days.

Forgery or Alteration

Insuring Agreement 2 covers loss sustained for these reasons:

> "forgery" or alteration of checks, drafts, promissory notes, or similar written promises, orders or directions to pay a sum certain in "money" that are:
>
> (1) Made or drawn by or drawn upon you; or
>
> (2) Made or drawn by one acting as your agent;
>
> or that are purported to have been so made or drawn.[1]

The coverage pays losses of the insured or its representatives resulting from forgery or alteration of checks and similar instruments; it does not pay losses resulting from the insured's knowing acceptance of instruments that have been forged or altered by others. See the exhibit "Summary of Forgery or Alteration Coverage."

Forgery or alteration coverage does not apply to loss resulting from dishonest acts of the insured or of its partners, members, directors, trustees, representatives, or employees. Forgery committed against the insured by the insured's employees is covered under the Employee Theft insuring agreement, not under the Forgery or Alteration insuring agreement.

Summary of Forgery or Alteration Coverage

Causes of Loss	"Forgery" and alteration
Property Covered	Checks, drafts, promissory notes, or similar instruments made or drawn by the insured or the insured's agent
Where Coverage Applies	Worldwide

[DA07838]

Inside the Premises—Theft of Money and Securities

Insuring Agreement 3 covers money and securities inside the "premises" or "financial institution premises" against theft, disappearance, or destruction.

Under this insuring agreement, "premises" means the interior of any commercial building the named insured occupies. The form defines financial institution premises as the interior of that portion of any building occupied by a financial institution.

For purposes of Insuring Agreement 3, the form defines "financial institution" as "(1) A bank, savings bank, savings and loan association, trust company, credit union or similar depository institution; or (2) An insurance company."[2]

The insuring agreement extends coverage to apply to loss or damage to the premises if the insured is the owner or is liable for the damage, and to containers that hold covered property if damage is caused by safe burglary or attempted safe burglary.

The policy definition of theft includes any type of "unlawful taking" of covered property "to the deprivation of the insured." Hence, an insured loss (subject to exclusions) can be caused by burglary, robbery, observed or unobserved theft, or any other unlawful taking of money or securities.

However, for this coverage to apply, the thief must be present inside the premises or the banking premises; thus, theft committed through a remote computer is not covered.

Disappearance or destruction includes losses regardless of whether they are caused by unlawful acts. For example, coverage is provided for money and securities destroyed by fire, and disappearance of property is covered regardless of whether theft appears to be the cause. See the exhibit "Summary of Inside the Premises—Theft of Money and Securities Coverage."

Summary of Inside the Premises—Theft of Money and Securities Coverage

	Basic Coverage	Extension for Damage to Premises	Extension for Containers
Covered Causes of Loss	"Theft," disappearance, destruction	Actual or attempted "theft" of "money" or "securities"	Actual or attempted "theft" or unlawful entry
Covered Property	"Money," "securities"	The "premises" or their exterior	Locked safe, vault, cash register, cash box, or cash drawer
Where Coverage Applies	Inside the "premises" or "financial institution premises" (The thief must be present inside the premises.)	At the "premises"	Inside the "premises"

[DA02514]

Inside the Premises—Robbery or Safe Burglary of Other Property

Insuring Agreement 4 covers "other property" from actual or attempted "robbery" of a "custodian" and actual or attempted "safe burglary."

According to the policy definition, the unlawful taking of property is considered "robbery" if the person taking the property has caused or threatened to cause bodily harm to the person having care or custody of the property or if the custodian witnesses an obviously unlawful act (for example, seeing someone run out of the store with property for which he or she has not paid). See the exhibit "Summary of Inside the Premises—Robbery or Safe Burglary of Other Property Coverage."

For robbery coverage to apply, the property must be inside the premises when taken from the named insured, the named insured's partners, or any employee who is a custodian as defined in the policy. A custodian may be a salesperson or cashier working inside the insured's store but cannot be a watchperson (hired exclusively to have care and custody of property inside the premises with no other duties) or janitor (a doorkeeper or person who cleans or maintains the premises).

The other covered peril, "safe burglary," is the unlawful taking of a safe or vault from inside the premises or of property from within a locked safe or vault by a person unlawfully entering the safe or vault as evidenced by marks

Summary of Inside the Premises—Robbery or Safe Burglary of Other Property Coverage

	Basic Coverage	Extension for Damage to Premises	Extension for Containers
Covered Causes of Loss	Actual or attempted "robbery" of a "custodian" or "safe burglary"	Actual or attempted "robbery" or "safe burglary" of "other property"	Actual or attempted "robbery" or "safe burglary"
Covered Property	"Other property"	The "premises" or their exterior	Locked safe or vault
Where Coverage Applies	Inside the "premises"	At the "premises"	Inside the "premises"

[DA02521]

of forcible entry. Coverage is only provided if a burglar leaves marks of forcible entry into the safe or vault.

In an actual or attempted robbery or safe burglary, coverage extends for resulting damage to the premises and for loss of or damage to a locked safe or vault located inside the premises.

Outside the Premises

Insuring Agreement 5 covers money, securities, and other property while outside the premises and in the care and custody of either a "messenger" or an armored vehicle company. The policy defines "messenger" as the named insured, a relative of the named insured, any partner or member of the named insured, "or any 'employee' while having care and custody of property outside the 'premises.'" For example, an employee who takes cash and checks to the bank for deposit in the insured's account is a messenger.

The perils insured against vary by the type of property involved in the loss. Money and securities are covered against theft, disappearance, or destruction. Other property is covered against actual or attempted robbery.[3] See the exhibit "Summary of Outside the Premises Coverage."

Computer and Funds Transfer Fraud

Insuring Agreement 6 covers two types of loss that were, before the introduction of the 2012 editions of the ISO commercial crime forms, covered by separate Computer Fraud and Funds Transfer Fraud insuring agreements.

Summary of Outside the Premises Coverage

	Coverage for "Money" and "Securities"	Coverage for "Other Property"
Covered Causes of Loss	"Theft," disappearance, destruction	Actual or attempted "robbery"
Where Coverage Applies	Outside the "premises" while in care or custody of a "messenger" or an armored car company and inside the United States (including its territories and possessions), Puerto Rico, and Canada	Outside the "premises" while in care or custody of a "messenger" or an armored car company and inside the U.S. (including its territories and possessions), Puerto Rico, and Canada

[DA02522]

The first part of the Computer and Funds Transfer Fraud insuring agreement covers loss resulting directly from fraudulent entry of electronic data or computer program into, or change of electronic data or computer program within, a computer system owned, leased, or operated by the named insured. The fraudulent entry or change must cause either of these results:

- Money, securities, or other property to be transferred, paid, or delivered
- The named insured's account at a financial institution to be debited or deleted

The second part of the insuring agreement covers loss resulting directly from a fraudulent instruction directing a financial institution to debit the named insured's transfer account and transfer, pay, or deliver money or securities from that account. See the exhibit "Summary of Computer and Funds Transfer Fraud Coverage."

Money Orders and Counterfeit Money

Insuring Agreement 7 covers loss from money orders that are not paid when presented and "counterfeit money" that the insured has accepted in good faith in exchange for merchandise, money, or services. See the exhibit "Summary of Money Orders and Counterfeit Money Coverage."

Summary of Computer and Funds Transfer Fraud Coverage

	Coverage for Computer Fraud	Coverage for Funds Transfer Fraud
Covered Cause of Loss	Use of a computer to fraudulently cause a transfer of covered property or cause the named insured's account at a financial institution to be debited or deleted.	Fraudulent instruction directing a financial institution to debit the named insured's transfer account and transfer covered property from that account.
Covered Property	"Money," "securities," and "other property."	"Money" or "securities."
Where Coverage Applies	Coverage applies to loss resulting directly from an occurrence taking place anywhere in the world.	

[DA11294]

Summary of Money Orders and Counterfeit Money Coverage

Covered Cause of Loss	Good-faith acceptance of: (1) Money orders that are not paid upon presentation or (2) "Counterfeit money"
Covered Property	Money orders issued by any post office, express company, or financial institution; and "counterfeit money" acquired during the regular course of business
Where Coverage Applies	United States (including its territories and possessions), Puerto Rico, and Canada

[DA02525]

COMMERCIAL CRIME LIMITS AND DEDUCTIBLE

Applying an insurance policy's limit of insurance and deductible to a claim covered under the policy is crucial to determining the amount payable. The Insurance Services Office, Inc. (ISO) Commercial Crime Coverage Form contains provisions that specify the manner in which the policy's limits and deductible(s) should be applied.

The Commercial Crime Coverage Form's Limit of Insurance provision states that the most the insurer will pay for all loss resulting directly from an "occurrence" (as defined in the policy) is the applicable limit shown in the declarations. Therefore, whether an act meets the policy's definition of occurrence and the limit that applies to the claim that stems from that act are components of the determination of the amount payable. The Deductible provision, which indicates how the deductible shown in the policy's declarations affects the insurer's payment, must also be applied to the claim.

Limit of Insurance

Under the Commercial Crime Coverage Form, a separate limit of insurance can be shown in the declarations for each insuring agreement that the insured selects. If a loss is covered under more than one insuring agreement, the insurer will pay no more than the highest limit of the insuring agreements that apply.

Definition of Occurrence

The definition of "occurrence" is key in determining how much the insurer is obligated to pay for a covered crime loss. Slightly different definitions of occurrence apply to employee theft coverage, forgery or alteration coverage, and all other coverages. Each of these definitions states that "occurrence" includes an individual act, the combined total of all separate acts (whether or not related), or a series of acts (whether or not related).

As defined for employee theft, the definition of occurrence requires that the act or acts must be committed by an employee (as defined in the form) acting alone or in collusion with others. Thus, if the employee theft limit is $100,000, the most the insurer would be required to pay for one instance of embezzlement—regardless of how many employees might have been involved in the crime—is $100,000. In addition, because of the definition of occurrence, the applicable limit is the most the insurer will pay for an individual act or a series of acts involving the same employee.

The definition of occurrence that applies to forgery or alteration requires that the act or acts must be committed by a person acting alone or in collusion with others and must involve one or more instruments. Therefore, if one person or a ring of perpetrators forged multiple documents, the resulting loss would be considered as having been caused by a single occurrence, and the insurer would pay no more for the combined loss than the forgery or alteration limit.

The definition of occurrence that applies to all coverages other than employee dishonesty and forgery or alteration includes not only acts but also events. The word "event" is included because some of the perils covered by these other coverages are events rather than acts committed by persons. For example, money and securities can be covered for theft, disappearance, or destruction. Although theft is an act committed by persons, disappearance and destruction can be caused by events such as windstorm or earthquake.

Each definition of occurrence comes in two different versions: one for the loss sustained forms and another for the discovery forms. The difference is found at the end of each definition:

- The loss sustained forms state that the act must be committed (or the event must occur) "during the Policy Period shown in the Declarations, except as provided" in the conditions pertaining to loss sustained under prior insurance
- The discovery forms state that the act must be committed (or the event must occur) "during the Policy Period shown in the Declarations, before such Policy Period or both."[4]

Special Limits of Insurance

In addition to the limits of insurance shown in the policy declarations for each insuring agreement, three of the insuring agreements are subject to special limits that apply only to specified types of covered property.

Inside the Premises—Robbery or Safe Burglary of Other Property is subject to a special limit of $5,000 per occurrence for these types of property:

(1) Precious metals, precious or semiprecious stones, pearls, furs, or completed or partially completed articles made of or containing such materials that constitute the principal value of such articles; or

(2) Manuscripts, drawings, or records of any kind or the cost of reconstructing them or reproducing any information contained in them.[5]

Outside the Premises coverage is subject to a special limit of $5,000 per occurrence for the types of property listed in items (1) and (2). Computer and Funds Transfer Fraud coverage is subject to a special limit of $5,000 per occurrence for loss of or damage to the types of property listed in item (2).

Deductible

No loss in any one occurrence is payable by the insurer unless the amount of loss exceeds the deductible shown in the declarations. If the amount of loss exceeds the deductible, the insurer will pay the amount of the loss in excess of the deductible, up to the limit of insurance.

To illustrate application of the deductible with a hypothetical case, assume that Tri-State Supply Company has employee theft coverage with a $100,000 limit and a $1,000 deductible. If one employee stole $5,000 of covered property, the insurer would pay the amount of loss in excess of the $1,000 deductible, or $4,000. If the amount of loss exceeded the limit of insurance by the deductible amount or more, the insured would be able to recover the full amount of insurance. For example, on a loss of $101,000 or more, the insurer would pay the full $100,000 limit in excess of the $1,000 deductible. In other words, the deductible is taken off the amount of the loss, not off the limit.

Apply Your Knowledge

An independent audit of the accounting records of a business insured under a Commercial Crime Coverage Form reveals that several employees in the organization's accounting department colluded over five years (and five policy periods) to embezzle $200,000 annually. The policy's limit of insurance is $500,000, with a per-occurrence deductible of $1,000. The insured submits a claim to its insurer for $1,000,000, the total that was stolen. Will the Commercial Crime Coverage Form apply to this claim and, if so, what amount will the insurer pay for this loss?

Feedback: Yes, the Commercial Crime Coverage Form will apply to this claim. The definition of "occurrence" applicable to employee theft coverage requires that the act or acts be committed by an employee, whether acting alone or in collusion with others, and that the act must be committed "during the Policy Period shown in the Declarations, before such Policy Period, or both." The facts of the claim meet this condition, as the theft occurred over a number of years prior to the discovery during the audit. Additionally, the definition of occurrence states the limit of insurance is the most the insurer will be liable for as a result of an individual act or a series of acts involving the same employee. In this circumstance, the most the insurer will pay for the act of employee theft, regardless of how many employees were involved and—equally importantly—regardless of the number of acts of employee theft, is $500,000. Finally, the amount of loss the insurer is obligated to pay under the Commercial Crime Coverage Form is the amount in excess of the deductible. The amount of the loss, $1,000,000, exceeds the limit of $500,000, so the insurer will pay the full limit in excess of the $1,000 deductible. The deductible is subtracted from the amount of the loss, not the limit of insurance.

COMMERCIAL CRIME EXCLUSIONS

As with most insurance coverage forms, the Commercial Crime Coverage Form excludes losses that are best covered under other insurance, are not insurable, or are not anticipated in the policy premium.

In the Insurance Services Office, Inc. (ISO) Commercial Crime Coverage Form, the basic crime insuring agreements are subject to several exclusions. The exclusions are divided into different groups, depending on whether they apply to all or only some insuring agreements.

Exclusions are presented in the coverage form and described in this section based on these groupings:

- General exclusions
- Exclusions applicable only to employee theft

- Exclusions applicable to inside the premises and outside the premises
- Exclusions applicable only to computer and funds transfer fraud

General Exclusions

Eleven general exclusions are applicable to any of the crime insuring agreements:

- Acts Committed by You, Your Partners or Your Members—The exclusion eliminates coverage for loss resulting from theft or any other dishonest act committed by the named insured, the named insured's partners, or (if the named insured is a limited liability company) the named insured's members, whether acting alone or in collusion with other persons.

- Acts Committed by Your Employees Learned of by You Prior to the Policy Period—The exclusion eliminates coverage for loss resulting from theft or any other dishonest act committed by an employee if the named insured, the named insured's partners, or the named insured's members, or any managers, officers, directors, or trustees, not in collusion with the employee, knew that the employee had committed theft or a dishonest act before the policy's effective date. This exclusion prevents the insurer from having to cover employee theft committed by employees who are known, prior to the policy period, to have committed any type of dishonest act.

- Acts Committed by Your Employees, Managers, Directors, Trustees or Representatives—The commercial crime form excludes theft or other dishonest acts committed by the named insured's employees, managers, directors, trustees, or authorized representatives. The exclusion applies regardless of whether such persons acted alone or in collusion with others and while such persons performed services for the named insured or otherwise. The exclusion states that it does not apply to loss covered under the Employee Theft insuring agreement.

- Confidential or Personal Information—The form excludes losses resulting from the use of another person's or organization's confidential or personal information, including, but not limited to, patents, trade secrets, processing methods, customer lists, credit card information, or health information.

- Data Security Breach—The form excludes fees, costs, fines, penalties, and other expenses the insured incurs related to the access to or disclosure of another person's or organization's confidential or personal information, which includes, but is not limited to, patents, trade secrets, processing methods, customer lists, financial information, credit card information, health information, or any other type of nonpublic information.

- Governmental Action—Like virtually any policy covering property loss, the commercial crime form excludes loss resulting from seizure or destruction of property by order of government authority.

- Indirect Loss—The form lists three examples of indirect loss that are not covered: (1) business income losses; (2) payment of damages for which the insured is legally liable (other than compensatory damages arising directly from a loss covered by the policy); and (3) expenses incurred in establishing either the existence or the amount of loss under the policy. The exclusion is not limited to just those three types of indirect loss; any indirect loss is excluded.

- Legal Fees, Costs and Expenses—The form excludes fees, costs, and expenses related to any legal action except when covered under the Forgery and Alteration insuring agreement.

- Nuclear Hazard—The exclusion eliminates coverage for loss or damage caused by any nuclear reaction, radiation, or radioactive contamination.

- Pollution—This exclusion eliminates coverage for any loss or damage that in any way results from pollution, which the exclusion defines as "the discharge, dispersal, seepage, migration, release or escape of any solid, liquid, gaseous, or thermal irritant or contaminant." Pollution includes residuals of pollutants, such as smoke, vapor, fumes, and so forth, along with materials to be recycled, reconditioned, or reclaimed.

- War and Military Action—This exclusion eliminates coverage for loss or damage resulting from war or civil war, whether declared or undeclared; warlike actions by a military force; or acts of rebellion or revolution, including governmental action to defend against such acts.

Exclusions Applicable Only to Employee Theft

This group of exclusions applies only to the Employee Theft insuring agreement:

- Inventory Shortages—The insurer will not pay for any loss that depends on inventory or profit-and-loss calculations to prove either the existence or the amount of the loss. An inventory shortage is the difference between a physical inventory and the inventory shown in the insured's books and records. An inventory shortage may occur for reasons other than employee theft. For example, there may have been bookkeeping or arithmetic errors, obsolete inventory may have been discarded, or samples may have been sent to customers but not deleted from the inventory records. Therefore, insurers will not accept an inventory calculation as proof that the insured has sustained an employee theft loss. However, if an insured establishes without inventory computations that it has sustained a loss, the form allows the insured to offer inventory records and actual physical count of inventory in support of the amount of loss claimed.

- Trading—An employer may sustain a large financial loss resulting from an employee's unauthorized trading in stocks, bonds, futures, commodities, or other similar items. Because employee theft coverage rates do not contemplate such losses, the form excludes loss resulting from trading, whether the trading occurs in the named insured's name or in a "genuine or fictitious account."

- Warehouse Receipts—The Warehouse Receipts exclusion eliminates coverage for "loss resulting from fraudulent or dishonest signing, issuing, canceling or failing to cancel, a warehouse receipt or any papers connected with it." Such a loss may occur, for example, when an employee releases merchandise without canceling the receipt or issues a receipt without having received the merchandise. The customer could then make a claim for missing goods based on the erroneous receipts. Such claims would not be covered because of this exclusion.

Exclusions Applicable Only to Inside the Premises and Outside the Premises

These eight exclusions apply specifically to the Inside the Premises—Theft of Money and Securities; Inside the Premises—Robbery or Safe Burglary of Other Property; and Outside the Premises insuring agreements:

- Accounting or Arithmetical Errors or Omissions—The form excludes losses resulting from accounting or arithmetical errors or omissions. Although many losses of this type are within the policy deductible, some losses could be sizable. The exposure falls within the general category of business risks that should be addressed by loss control measures, with any losses retained by the business.

- Exchanges or Purchases—Loss resulting from giving or surrendering property in an exchange or purchase is excluded. Thus, a fraudulent transaction that involves the loss of money, securities, or other property is not covered. For example, the loss sustained when a purchaser pays with a forged cashier's check is excluded from coverage.

- Fire—The three insuring agreements do not cover loss or damage resulting from fire, regardless of its cause. However, the exclusion does not apply to fire damage to a safe or vault. The exclusion also does not apply (under Inside the Premises—Theft of Money and Securities) to money or securities damaged or destroyed by fire. Nearly all organizations have commercial property insurance to cover the fire losses that the crime form excludes; money, however, is not covered under commercial property coverage forms.

- Money Operated Devices—Loss of property from money-operated devices (such as vending machines, amusement devices, or change machines) is not covered unless a continuous recording instrument inside the machine keeps track of the amount of money deposited. In the absence of a recording device, establishing the amount of the loss would be difficult or impossible.

- Motor Vehicles or Equipment and Accessories—The form excludes loss of or damage to motor vehicles, trailers, or semi-trailers, or for equipment and accessories attached to them. Theft of automobiles and related equipment can be insured under automobile physical damage coverage, and theft of mobile equipment can be insured under inland marine forms.

- Transfer or Surrender of Property—Loss of or damage to property after it has been transferred or surrendered to a person or place outside the premises or financial institution premises is excluded under several specified circumstances. For example, loss of property that the insured has voluntarily sent to an imposter on the basis of unauthorized instructions is excluded.

- Vandalism—Coverage extensions stated in the two inside the premises insuring agreements cover damage to the premises and their exterior and loss of or damage to various types of receptacles containing covered property if directly caused by a covered peril. The Vandalism exclusion eliminates coverage for damage to those types of property by vandalism or malicious mischief. Commercial property forms normally include coverage for damage to such property by vandalism or malicious mischief, including building damage caused by the breaking in or exiting of burglars.

- Voluntary Parting With Title to or Possession of Property—The voluntary parting exclusion eliminates coverage when the insured or an agent of the insured is tricked into voluntarily surrendering property to a thief. For example, a business owner tells the firm's cashier that a bank messenger is to pick up money at a given time each day. If a wrongdoer impersonates the messenger and succeeds in getting the cashier to part with the money voluntarily, the loss would not be covered by Inside the Premises—Theft of Money and Securities.

Exclusions Applicable Only to Computer and Funds Transfer Fraud

These five exclusions apply only to the Computer and Funds Transfer Fraud insuring agreement:

- Authorized Access—Loss resulting from fraudulent entry of or a fraudulent change to electronic data or a computer program in any computer system that is owned, leased, or operated by the insured that is executed by a person or organization with authorized access to the insured's computer system is excluded. The exclusion does not apply if the fraudulent entry or change is made by an employee acting on a fraudulent instruction from a computer software contractor who has a written agreement with the insured. It also does not apply to losses that may be covered under the Employee Theft Insuring Agreement.

- Credit Card Transactions—Loss resulting from the use or purported use of credit, debit, charge, access, convenience, identification, stored-value, or other cards or the information contained on such cards is excluded.

- Exchanges or Purchases—Loss resulting from the giving or surrendering of property in any exchange or purchase is excluded. For example, this exclusion may apply to an Internet-based transaction in which an insured knowingly exchanges a product for compensation whose value is less than the value the insured intended to receive in exchange for that product.

- Fraudulent Instructions—Loss resulting from an employee or financial institution acting upon a fraudulent instruction to transfer, pay, or deliver money, securities, or other property or from an employee or financial institution acting upon a fraudulent instruction to debit or delete the insured's account is excluded. However, the exclusion does not apply if the loss results directly from a fraudulent instruction that directs a financial institution to debit the insured's transfer account and pay, transfer, or deliver money or securities from that account. It also does not apply if the fraudulent entry or change is made by an employee acting on a fraudulent instruction from a computer software contractor who has a written agreement with the insured.

- Inventory Shortages—A separate Inventory Shortages exclusion applies to computer fraud coverage. Unlike the general exclusion, this exclusion does not include the wording permitting the insured to use inventory records in support of the amount of loss claimed.

Apply Your Knowledge

Identify any exclusions of the Commercial Crime Coverage Form that would apply to these losses. In each case, the insured has purchased all of the insuring agreements under this coverage form:

Tom, an employee of the insured, commits an act that meets all of the requirements under the Employee Theft insuring agreement. The insurer's claims investigation reveals that Tom had been arrested for shoplifting before the policy period began. However, Tom's employer had no knowledge of Tom's prior dishonesty until it was revealed by the investigation. Would the Acts of Employees Learned of by You Prior to the Policy Period exclusion eliminate coverage for this loss?

Feedback: No. The exclusion applies only if the insured learns of the prior dishonest act before the beginning of the policy period. In this case, Tom's employer did not know about Tom's prior dishonest act before the policy period, so the exclusion does not apply.

Vandals set the insured's building on fire. In addition to damaging the building and its contents, the fire destroys $5,000 of money that was in the insured's building. The loss of money meets all the requirements under the Inside the Premises—Theft of Money and Securities insuring agreement, which covers money and securities against theft, disappearance, or destruction. Would the Fire exclusion eliminate coverage for this loss?

Feedback: No. The Fire exclusion does not apply to loss of or damage to money or securities.

A thief breaks into and steals money from vending machines located in a convenience store. The vending machines do not contain recording instruments to track the money that was deposited. The loss of money meets all the requirements under the Inside the Premises—Theft of Money and Securities insuring agreement. Would the Money Operated Devices exclusion eliminate coverage for this loss?

Feedback: Yes. The Money Operated Devices exclusion eliminates coverage from such devices that do not have a continuous recording instrument inside them to keep track of the amount of money deposited.

COMMERCIAL CRIME CONDITIONS

The Insurance Services Office, Inc. (ISO) Commercial Crime Coverage Form includes numerous policy conditions that affect the application or extent of coverage provided.

As with all insurance policies, conditions are included in the ISO Commercial Crime Coverage Form that extend or eliminate coverage under various circumstances. Some conditions apply only to certain insuring agreements. Other conditions apply to all of the insuring agreements. The latter group, although listed alphabetically in the form, are presented here in logical order followed by two conditions that apply only to the Employee Theft insuring agreement.

Interests Insured

Several conditions help to clarify issues concerning the interests insured under a crime policy.

The Ownership of Property; Interests Covered condition states that the insurance applies only to property owned, leased, or held by the named insured, or for which the insured is legally liable, provided that the insured was liable for the property before the loss occurred. However, the insurance is for the insured's benefit only; any claim must be made by the insured. If the insured does not want to present a claim, the owner of the property cannot make a direct claim on the insurance. Coverage for theft by the insured's employee of client's property may be added by endorsement.

The Joint Insured condition appoints the first named insured as agent for all other insureds with regard to all transactions under the policy. It also provides that an employee of any insured is considered to be an employee of every insured and that knowledge possessed by any insured or any partner, officer, or limited liability company (LLC) member of any insured is considered to be known to all insureds.

If, during the policy period, the insured adds additional premises or employees other than by consolidation, merger, or acquisition, the Additional

Premises or Employees condition states that policy coverage will be extended automatically.

No notice is required, and no additional premium is charged for the remainder of the policy period. On renewal, the insured must give the insurer full information, and the renewal premium will reflect the revised exposure.

If the insured acquires additional employees or premises by consolidation, merger, or acquisition, the Consolidation—Merger or Acquisition condition states that coverage will be extended automatically for ninety days to the new employees or premises. If the insured wishes to extend coverage beyond ninety days, the insured must notify the insurer of the consolidation, merger, or acquisition promptly and pay the appropriate additional premium.

Where Coverage Applies

Many of the crime insuring agreements limit coverage to occurrences inside the premises described in the policy. When coverage is not restricted to the premises, the Territory condition defines the geographical scope of coverage. This condition limits coverage for all insuring agreements to acts committed or events occurring within the United States (including its territories and possessions), Puerto Rico, and Canada. The territorial provision for employee theft coverage is extended to include coverage for loss caused by employees temporarily outside the coverage territory for not more than ninety days. The territorial provisions for forgery or alteration coverage and computer and funds transfer fraud coverage are extended to cover loss resulting from occurrences taking place anywhere in the world.

When Coverage Applies

Three conditions are principally concerned with determining when a loss must occur in order to be covered under the loss sustained version of the Commercial Crime Coverage Form:

- Extended Period to Discover Loss
- Loss Sustained During Prior Insurance Issued by Us or Any Affiliate
- Loss Sustained During Prior Insurance Not Issued by Us or Any Affiliate

Extended Period to Discover Loss

Under the loss sustained form, the insurer will pay for loss that the named insured sustains through acts committed or events occurring during the policy period. Moreover, coverage applies only to acts discovered during the policy period or within one year after the policy is canceled. However, the discovery period terminates immediately as of the effective date of any other insurance that the insured obtains (from any insurer) that replaces coverage in whole or in part. See the exhibit "Discovery Form."

Discovery Form

All of the ISO crime forms are available in loss sustained and discovery versions. The discovery form covers losses regardless of when they occurred if they are first discovered during the policy period or during the sixty-day discovery period that applies to most claims under the discovery form.

To limit the broad coverage for prior occurrences that discovery forms provide, the insurer may attach a retroactive date endorsement. This endorsement states that coverage is limited to losses the insured sustains through acts committed or events occurring after the retroactive date shown in the policy schedule. For coverage to apply, the loss must still be discovered during the policy period or the extended loss discovery period.

[DA07834]

Loss Sustained During Prior Insurance Issued by Us or Any Affiliate

Some losses occurring before the current policy period of a loss sustained crime policy may be covered by the policy currently in effect. Under the Loss Sustained During Prior Insurance Issued by Us or Any Affiliate condition, the insurer agrees to pay a loss that meets these criteria:

- The loss is discovered during the policy period shown in the declarations.
- The loss occurred while prior insurance, issued by the same insurer or an affiliated insurer, was in effect.
- The current insurance became effective when the prior insurance was canceled.
- The loss would have been covered by the present insurance if the insurance had been in force at the time of loss.

If these requirements are met, the current policy applies, but the most the insurer will pay is the amount recoverable under the prior insurance, if it had remained in effect.

The same condition also contains provisions for settling covered losses that occurred over more than one policy period. Such losses typically are associated with employee theft, in which an employee may have embezzled funds for years before the employer discovers the loss.

Coverage must be continuous; that is, the renewal policy must have commenced when the prior policy expired, but no limit of insurance accumulates from year to year. A policy in force for ten years with a $50,000 limit will pay a maximum of $50,000 for any one covered loss, not ten times $50,000. This is important to consider when selecting the amount of insurance for employee theft coverage. A dishonest employee often steals smaller amounts on numerous occasions over many years that can accumulate in significant losses.

This condition is found in the loss sustained form only; it is not needed in the discovery form because the discovery form covers loss, regardless of when it occurred, that is discovered during the current policy period.

Loss Sustained During Prior Insurance Not Issued by Us or Any Affiliate

If the prior insurance was not provided by the current insurer or an affiliate, the Loss Sustained During Prior Insurance Not Issued by Us or Any Affiliate condition applies. Under this condition, which is found in the loss sustained form but not in the discovery form, the insurer agrees to pay a loss that meets all of these criteria:

- The loss is discovered during the policy period shown in the declarations.
- The loss occurred while prior insurance, issued by another unaffiliated insurer, was in effect.
- The current insurance became effective when the prior insurance was canceled or terminated.
- The loss would have been covered by the present insurance if the insurance had been in force at the time of loss.

If these requirements are met, the insurer will pay the *lesser* of the amount recoverable under the present insurance or the prior insurance (if it had remained in effect).

The essential difference between these two provisions concerns the available limits. If the loss is covered by both the current insurance and prior insurance issued by the same or an affiliated company, the highest limit in force under any of the policies covering the loss will be available to the insured. If the loss occurred under prior insurance issued by another insurer, recovery is limited to, at most, the applicable limit in the policy in effect at the time of the loss.

Claim-Related Duties and Procedures

Several conditions establish the duties and procedures to follow after a loss involving covered property.

The insured's duties stated in the Duties in the Event of Loss condition in a crime policy are essentially the same as such duties under other property policies. After discovering a loss or a situation that may result in a loss, the insured has these duties:

- Notify the insurer as soon as possible and, except for employee theft and forgery and alteration losses, notify the police if the insured believes that the loss involves a violation of law
- Submit a detailed, sworn proof of loss within 120 days
- Cooperate with the insurer in its investigation of the loss
- Produce all pertinent records for the insurer to examine

✓ Reality Check

Loss Sustained During Prior Insurance Not Issued by Us

This hypothetical example illustrates why an insurer would be willing to cover a loss that occurred during the prior policy period of another insurer.

Joanie, the proprietor of an electronics store, was alarmed when her commercial crime insurer raised the premium on her loss sustained crime policy by 20 percent. She consulted Mark, her insurance agent, because she wanted to change insurers. However, she was concerned that she would not be covered for any crime loss that occurred when that policy was in effect but was not discovered until after the policy was canceled.

Mark explained that another insurer offers loss sustained coverage using ISO's Commercial Crime Coverage Form. He told Joanie that the form has a condition that would cover a loss sustained during prior insurance not issued by the new insurer if the loss met specified criteria.

After Mark explained the criteria and quoted Joanie a lower premium on the new crime policy, Joanie was surprised that the new insurer would be willing to cover such a loss. Mark explained that without the offer of such coverage, it would be nearly impossible to persuade an insured to switch to a new insurer. In effect, providing this coverage for a prior period is one of an insurer's costs of acquiring new policyholders.

[DA07835]

- Submit to examination under oath if requested by the insurer
- Secure all rights of recovery that the insured has against others responsible for the loss and do nothing to impair those rights.

The Records condition in a crime policy requires the insured to keep sufficient records to enable the insurer to verify the amount of loss.

Under the Valuation—Settlement condition of a crime policy, the value of a covered loss is determined differently for each of the three categories of covered property:

- Money is valued at its face value. If foreign money is lost, the insured has the option of receiving payment for the loss at the face value of the money or at its equivalent U.S. value on the date of the loss.
- Securities are valued as of the close of business on the day the loss is discovered. In many cases, duplicate securities can be issued if the insured posts a bond. The insurer will pay the cost of the bond as part of the loss. The insurer has the option of paying the market value of lost securities or replacing them in kind. If securities are replaced, the insured must assign to the insurer all rights, title, and interest in the lost securities.
- If property other than money and securities is lost or damaged, the insurer has the option of paying the replacement cost of the property, repairing

the property, or replacing it. If the property is not promptly repaired or replaced as soon after the loss or damage as possible, the insurer will pay the loss on an actual cash value basis.

The Recoveries condition of a crime policy specifies how any subrogation or salvage recoveries will be divided between the insurer and the insured. First the insured is reimbursed for its covered loss that exceeded the limit of insurance.

The remaining amount of the recovery is paid to the insurer until it has recovered all that it paid. Any remaining value is paid to the insured to reimburse it for the deductible amount and for any loss not covered by the insurance.

As with most insurance policies, the crime general provisions include a subrogation provision. Under the Transfer of Your Rights Against Others to Us condition, for any loss the insurer pays to the insured, the insured must transfer its rights of recovery against others to the insurer. Moreover, the insured must do nothing after loss to impair those rights. (The insured is permitted to waive its rights of action against other parties if the waiver is made before loss occurs.)

The Other Insurance condition is split into two parts: primary and excess.

If the insurance is written as primary, a loss will be shared on a pro rata by limits basis with other insurance subject to the same terms and conditions. If the other insurance is not subject to the same terms and conditions, the insurance will apply as excess coverage over any other insurance available to the insured to cover a loss. Often, the other policy will have a similar clause. When two or more policies cover a loss and all policies purport to be excess over other insurance, courts usually require the insurers to contribute on a pro rata basis if the insurers are unable to agree on a mutually acceptable method.

If the insurance is written on an excess basis, the insurer will only pay the amount of loss that exceeds the limit and deductible of the other insurance.

Conditions Applicable to Employee Theft Only

The Termination as to Any Employee condition and the Employee Benefit Plans condition apply only to the Employee Theft insuring agreement.

The first part of the Termination as to Any Employee condition automatically terminates employee theft coverage with respect to any employee who has committed a dishonest act as soon as the act is known to the insured or any partner, officer, or director not in collusion with the employee. Coverage on the employee is terminated regardless of whether the act was committed against the insured or others (before or after the employee was hired by the insured) and regardless of whether the employer learns of it before or after policy inception.

If the insured first learns of an employee's dishonest act after the employee has committed an employee theft, the loss will be covered (assuming no other exclusions apply), but coverage with respect to that employee for any further claims will be terminated.

If, in another situation, a claim investigation of an employee theft loss reveals that the insured knew about a prior dishonest act by the same employee, the current claim will not be covered, because coverage for that employee was automatically terminated when the insured learned of the prior dishonest act.

The second part of the Termination as to Any Employee condition gives the insurer the right to cancel coverage with respect to any employee by providing thirty days' advance notice to the insured.

The Employee Benefit Plans condition explains how employee theft coverage applies when the policy includes one or more employee benefit plans as insureds for the Employee Theft insuring agreement. This condition eliminates the need to attach the Employee Retirement Income Security Act of 1974 (ERISA) compliance endorsement to the policy to satisfy the ERISA fidelity bonding requirement. Employee theft coverage was traditionally called a fidelity bond, and the term "fidelity" is still used to refer to employee theft coverage.

Apply Your Knowledge

On August 5, Millright Foods canceled its crime insurance policy, which it had purchased from Insurer A. Millright then purchased a new crime policy from Insurer A's affiliate, Insurer B, which took effect on the cancellation date of Insurer A's policy. Insurer B's policy uses the ISO Commercial Crime Coverage Form. Four months after Insurer B's policy became effective and during its policy period, Millright discovered that one of its former managers, who left Millright's employment on July 15 of that year, had been embezzling funds over the previous three months. Insurer A denied coverage for the loss because the loss was not discovered until after Insurer A's policy was canceled.

How would the Loss Sustained During Prior Insurance Issued by Us or Any Affiliate condition in Insurer B's policy affect coverage for this loss?

Feedback: This condition specifies that the loss will be covered under Insurer B's policy if these requirements are met: the loss is discovered during the policy period shown in the declarations, the loss occurred while the affiliate's insurance was in effect, the current insurance became effective when the prior insurance was canceled, and the loss would have been covered by the present insurance if the insurance had been in force at the time of loss.

COMMERCIAL CRIME ENDORSEMENTS

The Insurance Services Office, Inc. (ISO) Commercial Crime Coverage Form can be modified for various purposes through the addition of coverage endorsements.

Endorsements that may be added to the ISO Commercial Crime Coverage Form include these:

- Clients' Property
- Extortion
- Inside the Premises—Theft of Other Property
- Inside the Premises—Robbery of a Watchperson or Burglary of Other Property
- Employee Theft—Name or Position Schedule
- Lessees of Safe Deposit Boxes
- Securities Deposited With Others
- Guests' Property
- Destruction of Electronic Data or Computer Programs
- Unauthorized Reproduction of Computer Software by Employees

Clients' Property

The Commercial Crime Coverage Form contains an Ownership of Property; Interests Covered condition, which limits coverage to property that the insured owns, leases, or holds, or for which the insured is liable (provided that the insured's liability precedes the loss). Moreover, the policy definition of "theft" is the unlawful taking of property to the deprivation of the insured.

Consequently, the Employee Theft insuring agreement does not cover theft by the insured's employees of property owned or leased by a client of the insured (unless the insured is leasing or holding the client's property at the time of theft), nor does the Employee Theft insuring agreement cover theft of property being held by a client of the insured.

The Clients' Property endorsement (CR 04 01) modifies these and other commercial crime provisions to cover theft of money, securities, or other property belonging to any client of the insured by an identified employee of the insured. "Client" means any entity for whom the insured performs services under a written contract.

The insurer covers such losses only if they are presented to the insurer by the insured. This coverage can be important to firms whose employees work on clients' premises, such as equipment-servicing contractors and cleaning contractors.

Extortion

Two endorsements—one for commercial entities (CR 04 03) and one for government entities (CR 04 04)—are available for insuring loss resulting from extortion. Both endorsements cover the surrender of money, securities, or other property as a result of a threat communicated to the insured to cause bodily harm to certain classes of persons (such as employees, directors, or partners of the insured or any of their relatives) who have been captured (or allegedly captured) or to cause damage to the insured's premises or the property therein.

In other words, the endorsements cover ransom but do not provide any other coverages commonly contained in kidnap, ransom, and extortion policies. For an extortion threat to be covered under the endorsements, the first communication of the threat must occur during the policy period, and the surrender of the ransom must occur away from the insured premises. See the exhibit "Kidnap, Ransom, and Extortion Coverage."

Kidnap, Ransom, and Extortion Coverage

In addition to the Extortion endorsements, the ISO commercial crime program includes a Kidnap/Ransom and Extortion Coverage Form (CR 00 40) and a stand-alone policy form (CR 00 41), together with several coverage options.

Although the Extortion endorsements cover ransom payments, organizations that believe they have a substantial kidnap, ransom, and extortion (KR&E) exposure may want to consider purchasing KR&E policies. An organization may consider doing so because KR&E insurers typically have international security expertise and provide risk control and response services to their insureds. Additionally, the coverage territory of a KR&E policy is usually worldwide, although it may be subject to some exceptions. Another advantage of KR&E policies is that they pay for a variety of expenses beyond the ransom, including expenses associated with a kidnapped person's release, the cost of repatriating kidnap victims, death or dismemberment benefits of a kidnapped person, and other costs associated with these acts.

KR&E policies typically contain a confidentiality condition requiring every insured not to divulge the existence of the insurance. This condition is justified because when potential kidnappers or extortionists know that insurance is available, the likelihood of a kidnapping or an extortion threat increases.

[DA11295]

Inside the Premises—Theft of Other Property

The Inside the Premises—Theft of Other Property (CR 04 05) endorsement, instead of being limited to covering robbery and safe burglary, covers theft. The policy definition of "theft" is broad enough to include robbery, safe burglary, regular burglary, or any other instance of theft while the premises are open or closed, regardless of whether there are signs of forcible entry or exit. This is about the same level of premises theft coverage as provided by the Causes of Loss—Special Form.

Inside the Premises—Robbery of a Watchperson or Burglary of Other Property

The Inside the Premises—Robbery of a Watchperson or Burglary of Other Property (CR 04 06) endorsement, instead of covering robbery of a custodian, covers robbery of a watchperson ("any person you retain specifically to have care and custody of property inside the 'premises' and who has no other duties"). The endorsement also covers burglary, defined as "the unlawful taking of property from inside the 'premises' by a person unlawfully entering or leaving the 'premises' as evidenced by marks of forcible entry or exit."

Employee Theft—Name or Position Schedule

The Employee Theft insuring agreement covers employee theft committed by anyone who meets the policy definition of "employee."

Insurers or insureds sometimes prefer to limit coverage to theft committed by an employee whose name (such as "Jane Rogers") or position (such as "Bookkeeper") is listed in the policy. The Employee Theft—Name or Position Schedule endorsement (CR 04 08) permits an insurer to use this approach, which is usually limited to firms that have only one or two employees for whom coverage is wanted.

The endorsement replaces the regular policy definition of employee with one that applies on either a name-schedule basis or a position-schedule basis. When written on a name-schedule basis, employee theft coverage is restricted to covering theft committed by employees whose names are scheduled.

When written on a position-schedule basis, employee theft coverage is restricted to covering theft committed by employees whose position titles are scheduled. If more than the stated number of employees in a particular position are employed at the time of loss, coverage is prorated based on the number stated in the policy divided by the number of employees actually employed in that classification.

Lessees of Safe Deposit Boxes

Banks and other organizations maintain safe deposit boxes for their customers' use. As a lessor, the bank or other depository is liable only for losses of customers' property resulting from its negligence.

The Lessees of Safe Deposit Boxes endorsement (CR 04 09) enables a customer to insure property that the customer keeps in a safe deposit box on the premises of a bank or other depository. The endorsement provides that securities can be covered against theft, disappearance, or destruction and that property other than money and securities can be insured against burglary, robbery, and vandalism.

The coverage enables the lessee (customer) to recover from its insurer for losses to covered property without having to prove that the lessor (bank or depository) was liable for the loss. If the insurer pays a loss, it is subrogated to any recovery rights the lessee may have against the lessor.

Thus, the lessor needs to have its own insurance on the property in its custody. Banks and other financial institutions can obtain this insurance under a financial institution form called the Combination Safe Depository Policy. Depository companies that are ineligible for the Combination Safe Depository Policy Form can obtain similar coverage under a Safe Depository endorsement that can be attached to commercial crime forms.

Securities Deposited With Others

In some cases, the owner of securities will place the securities in the temporary custody of another organization. For example, the custodian might be a creditor that is holding stock certificates as collateral or security for repayment of a loan by the owner of the stock.

The Securities Deposited With Others endorsement (CR 04 10) enables the owner of the securities to insure them while they are in the custodian's possession or on deposit by the custodian for safekeeping in a depository. The covered causes of loss are theft, disappearance, and destruction.

Guests' Property

The Guests' Property endorsement (CR 04 11) is designed for lodging facilities—such as hotels, motels, and bed-and-breakfasts—to protect themselves against liability for property loss sustained by their guests. Under the common law, lodging facilities (traditionally referred to as "innkeepers") are liable for all losses to a guest's property.

The common-law rule has been modified by state statutes that limit innkeeper liability for property of guests. Because the limitation of liability usually applies separately to each guest, an innkeeper can incur a large liability loss if many guests' belongings are destroyed in one occurrence—even if the innkeeper was not negligent.

The Guests' Property endorsement covers loss to guests' property for which the insured is legally liable, subject to applicable exclusions.

If the insured is sued for refusing to pay for loss of guests' property and the insurer has given the insured its written consent to defend, the insurer will also pay reasonable legal expenses incurred and paid by the insured. Covered legal expenses are payable in addition to the limit of insurance.

Destruction of Electronic Data or Computer Programs

Most commercial property policies provide inadequate coverage for the cost to restore damaged electronic data. To partially close this coverage gap, insureds can obtain the Destruction of Electronic Data or Computer Programs endorsement (CR 04 13).

This endorsement covers the costs to restore or replace electronic data or computer programs stored in the insured's computer system if such property is damaged or destroyed by a computer virus or by vandalism committed by a person who has gained unauthorized access to the insured's computer system.

The usual crime policy exclusion of acts of employees, managers, directors, trustees, or representatives does not apply to this coverage. Because damage by employees is believed to be the most frequent source of such losses, the omission of this exclusion is a valuable expansion of coverage.

Unauthorized Reproduction of Computer Software by Employees

Software piracy—the unauthorized reproduction of computer software—is a serious problem for the software industry. Industry groups, and some of the largest software manufacturers, vigorously pursue users of unlicensed software.

The Unauthorized Reproduction of Computer Software by Employees endorsement (CR 04 14) can protect insureds against the cost of fines and penalties for the unauthorized reproduction of computer software by an employee in violation of a licensing agreement with a third-party vendor. However, the violation must be without the knowledge of the insured, any of the insured's partners, limited liability company members, officers or directors, and any other person responsible for compliance with the terms of the software licensing agreement.

GOVERNMENT CRIME FORMS

The ISO crime insurance program includes two government crime coverage forms (discovery and loss sustained) and two government crime policies (discovery and loss sustained) for insuring governmental entities. These forms contain most of the provisions found in the ISO commercial crime forms. However, the government crime forms differ from the commercial crime forms in these elements of the forms:

- Employee theft insuring agreements
- Territory condition
- Termination as to Any Employee condition

- Employee theft exclusions
- Indemnification condition

Employee Theft Insuring Agreements

Each government crime form contains two Employee Theft insuring agreements instead of a single Employee Theft insuring agreement in the commercial crime forms. One of these insuring agreements provides "per loss coverage," and the other provides "per employee coverage." With per loss coverage (as in the commercial crime forms), the limit of insurance is the most that the insurer will pay for a single loss. With per employee coverage, the limit of insurance is the most that the insurer will pay for all loss caused by a single employee.

Per employee coverage is available for government entities because the statutes in some jurisdictions require that coverage apply per employee. For example, assume that five employees colluded to steal funds from the insured employer, and it could be proven that each had stolen $1 million for a total of $5 million.Per loss coverage with a $1 million limit would pay only $1 million for the entire loss. Per employee coverage with a $1 million limit would pay $5 million for the loss.

This analysis is based on the assumption that the amount stolen by each employee could be proven. If only the involvement of one or more employees and the amount of the loss, $1 million, could be proven, but not the separate amount stolen by each employee, neither form would pay more than $1 million. Because (1) it is rare that multiple employees are involved in a loss and (2) establishing the amount stolen by each employee is usually difficult, per loss coverage with an adequate limit is generally preferable to per employee coverage.

Territory Condition

The Territory condition in the government crime forms does not include Canada, and the forms' coverage territory is therefore limited to the United States, its territories or possessions, and Puerto Rico. However, the Forgery or Alteration and Computer and Funds Transfer Fraud insuring agreements in the government crime forms are subject to worldwide coverage, as in the commercial crime forms.

In addition, under the Employee Dishonesty insuring agreements, the insurer agrees to pay for loss caused by an employee while temporarily outside the United States, its territories or possessions, or Puerto Rico for a period not to exceed ninety consecutive days.

Termination as to Any Employee Condition

In the government crime forms, the Termination as to Any Employee condition applies to any employee whose theft or other dishonest act is discovered by the named insured or any official or employee authorized to manage, govern, or control the insured's employees. The government crime forms therefore encompass a broader group of employees whose knowledge is imputed to the insured. For example, knowledge by a supervisor who is not an officer would not trigger automatic termination under the commercial crime forms but would do so under the government forms.

Employee Theft Exclusions

The government crime forms contain two additional exclusions that are not contained in the commercial crime forms. These exclusions eliminate coverage for loss caused by (1) any employee required by law to be individually bonded or (2) any treasurer or tax collector.

Some insurers will eliminate the treasurer or tax collector exclusion by adding endorsement CR 25 12 (Include Treasurers or Tax Collectors as Employees).

Indemnification Condition

The government crime forms contain an Indemnification condition, not included in the commercial crime forms. The condition states that the insurer will indemnify any of the insured's officials who are required by law to provide faithful performance bonds against loss resulting from theft committed by employees who serve under these officials.

When such bonding requirements exist, the official may be held responsible to the insured public entity for loss resulting from theft committed by the official's subordinates. The Indemnification condition confirms that the insurer will indemnify the official for such losses, enabling the official to indemnify the insured as required by law. This condition prevents the insured from having to proceed against its own officials to recover for employee theft committed by the officials' subordinates. The amount that the insurer will pay to indemnify an official of the insured is limited to the amount of insurance provided.

Faithful performance of duty coverage can be added to government crime policies by endorsement CR 25 19 (Add Faithful Performance of Duty Coverage for Government Employees). The endorsement broadens employee theft coverage to include loss "resulting directly from the failure of any 'employee' to faithfully perform his or her duties as prescribed by law." This language provides coverage for various breaches of faithful performance that might not meet the criteria for employee theft.

DETERMINING WHETHER THE COMMERCIAL CRIME COVERAGE FORM COVERS A LOSS

Knowing how to apply commercial crime coverage to the facts of a case is an important skill. This case study will help you make the transition from knowing policy language to applying policy language to losses to determine whether coverage applies. As you progress through this case study, you can check your understanding of the coverage provided by answering the Knowledge to Action questions.

Case Facts

Office Myria, Inc. (OM) is an office supply store. Each day, the shift manager on duty at the end of the day prepares the deposit from all of the daily receipts and takes the deposit to the night depository of a nearby bank. Each night, $2,000 in cash is stored in a safe for use in the cash drawers the next day.

Brad, the principal owner and president of OM, purchased a commercial package policy that includes the Insurance Services Office (ISO) Commercial Crime Coverage Form (Loss Sustained Form). The Crime and Fidelity Coverage Part Declarations page shows the coverages, limits, and deductibles that Brad selected. See the exhibit "Excerpt From Office Myria's Crime Coverage Declarations Page."

Excerpt From Office Myria's Crime Coverage Declarations Page

Insuring Agreements	Limit Of Insurance Per Occurrence	Deductible Amount Per Occurrence
1. Employee Theft	$100,000	$1,000
2. Forgery Or Alteration	$100,000	$1,000
3. Inside The Premises – Theft Of Money And Securities	$25,000	$1,000
4. Inside The Premises – Robbery Or Safe Burglary Of Other Property	$25,000	$1,000
5. Outside The Premises	$25,000	$1,000
6. Computer And Funds Transfer Fraud	$100,000	$1,000
7. Money Orders And Counterfeit Money	Not Covered	

If "Not Covered" is inserted above opposite any specified Insuring Agreement, such Insuring Agreement and any other reference thereto in this policy are deleted.

In 20X1, OM sustained several losses. On July 3, 20X1, a thief entered OM through an unlocked window while the store was closed and broke into the safe, causing $1,200 damage to the safe. The thief found only $2,000 in cash in the safe, so he also stole $1,500 worth of electronic devices from the selling floor on his way out. OM repaired the safe and replaced the stolen property promptly after the loss.

Two employees, Daryl (OM's bookkeeper) and Jared (a shipping clerk), in collusion, stole money and merchandise from OM during 20X1. The thefts occurred as shown in the exhibit, "Office Myria Employee Thefts From 20X1." When Daryl and Jared were hired, neither Brad nor anyone else at OM was aware of any criminal history of either of these men.

Because Brad had a high degree of trust in Daryl and did not check the store's accounting records frequently, he did not discover any of the thefts until late December, 20X1, after all the thefts had been committed. During a police investigation, Daryl and Jared blamed one another for the thefts, but later they both confessed to all the thefts. Brad immediately fired both Daryl and Jared. See the exhibit "Office Myria Employee Thefts From 20X1."

Office Myria Employee Thefts From 20X1

Date of Theft	Item(s) Stolen	Value of Stolen Item(s)
April 30, 20X1	Money	$10,000
September 12, 20X1	Merchandise	$15,000
August 20, 20X1	Merchandise	$30,000
November 24, 20X1	Merchandise	$20,000
December 18, 20X1	Money	$35,000
TOTAL		$110,000

[DA07924]

Given the facts presented in the case and assuming that no endorsements to OM's policy affect the coverage in these losses, determine whether the commercial crime form will cover the losses, and if so, what amount the insurer will pay for each loss. When answering the questions in this case-based activity, assume that the insured reported each loss to its crime insurer promptly after discovering it, cooperated with the insurer, and maintained records of all property covered under the policy. Otherwise, consider only the information provided as part of this case.

Necessary Reference Materials

To determine whether OM's crime form provides coverage for any losses of money, securities, or other property incurred as a result of criminal acts such as robbery, burglary, and other forms of theft, you need a copy of the crime form and the declarations page.

Overview of Steps

When examining the declarations page and crime form to determine whether coverage applies to each loss, you can apply the four steps of the DICE method. Doing this involves analyzing the policy declarations, insuring agreement, conditions, and exclusions and determining whether any information found at each step precludes coverage at the time of each loss. You should also examine other policy provisions such as the limit of insurance, deductible, endorsements (not applicable in this case), and terms defined in the policy.

Next, you determine the amounts payable for each loss under the applicable policy. Doing this involves analyzing the limit(s) of insurance and any deductibles that apply. Assume OM has no other policy that provides coverage for the same losses.

Determination of Coverage

To determine coverage, you must apply the four DICE steps to the case facts for each of OM's losses.

DICE Analysis Step 1: Declarations

The first DICE step is to review the declarations page to ascertain basic facts about the coverage.

Action Task: Review OM's Common Policy Declarations included with its commercial package policy. See the exhibit "Excerpt From Office Myria's Common Policy Declarations Page."

Knowledge to Action

To complete Step 1, answer these questions about the Common Policy Declarations:

- Is OM listed as an insured under the policy?
- Were the losses sustained during the policy period?

Feedback: The declarations page shows OM as the named insured. A review of the insuring agreements is needed to confirm whether coverages apply to each of the losses. The case facts indicate that each of the losses was sustained (and discovered) during the policy period.

Excerpt From Office Myria's Common Policy Declarations Page

POLICY NUMBER:

IL DS 00 09 08

COMMON POLICY DECLARATIONS

COMPANY NAME AREA	PRODUCER NAME AREA

NAMED INSURED: **Office Myria, Inc.**

MAILING ADDRESS: **1225 East Nevada Avenue**

Anytown, US 12345

POLICY PERIOD: FROM **03/12/20X1**   TO **03/12/20X2**   AT 12:01 A.M. STANDARD

TIME AT YOUR MAILING ADDRESS SHOWN ABOVE

BUSINESS DESCRIPTION	Office supply store with loading dock

Includes copyrighted material of Insurance Services Office, Inc. with its permission. Copyright, ISO Properties, Inc., 2007. [DA07925]

DICE Analysis Step 2: Insuring Agreement

The second DICE step is to review the insuring agreements to determine whether those for which coverage is provided apply to the described losses.

Action Task: Refer to the insuring agreements in the excerpt from the crime coverage declarations page, and then examine the applicable insuring agreements from the Commercial Crime Coverage Form.

The $2,000 theft of money from the safe and $1,200 damage to the safe are covered under the Inside the Premises—Theft of Money and Securities insuring agreement.

We will pay for:

a. Loss of "money" and "securities" inside the "premises" or "financial institution premises":

(1) Resulting directly from "theft" committed by a person present inside such "premises" or "financial institution premises"; or

(2) Resulting directly from disappearance or destruction.

b. Loss from damage to the "premises" or its exterior resulting directly from an actual or attempted "theft" of "money" and "securities", if you are the owner of the "premises" or are liable for damage to it.

c. Loss of or damage to a locked safe, vault, cash register, cash box or cash drawer located inside the "premises" resulting directly from an actual or attempted "theft" of, or unlawful entry into, those containers.[6]

The $1,500 theft of electronic devices is not covered under the Inside the Premises—Theft of Money and Securities insuring agreement, because the stolen property does not qualify as money or securities. This theft is also not covered under the Inside the Premises—Robbery and Safe Burglary of Other Property, because the cause of the loss does not meet the policy definition of "robbery" or "safe burglary."

> 20. "Robbery" means the unlawful taking of property from the care and custody of a person by one who has:
>
> a. Caused or threatened to cause that person bodily harm; or
>
> b. Committed an obviously unlawful act witnessed by that person.[7]

In this case, the cause of loss was not robbery, because the thief did not harm or threaten a person having custody of the property, nor was there any custodian present to witness the thief's obviously unlawful act. Moreover, the cause of loss was not safe burglary because the devices were stolen from the selling floor, not from a locked safe or vault, as is required by the policy definition of safe burglary.

The Employee Theft insuring agreement applies to the employee theft losses committed by Daryl and Jared. Daryl and Jared both meet the policy definition of employee, they committed theft as defined, and their acts of theft resulted in the loss of money and other property as defined.

> We will pay for loss of or damage to "money", "securities" and "other property" resulting directly from "theft" committed by an "employee", whether identified or not, acting alone or in collusion with other persons.[8]

DICE Analysis Step 3: Conditions

The third DICE step is to review the policy conditions to determine whether they preclude coverage at the time of the loss.

Action Task: Refer to the applicable Commercial Crime Coverage Form policy conditions.

OM has complied with the standard policy conditions contained in the Commercial Crime Coverage Form, such as Cooperation, Duties in the Event of Loss, and Records. The only other condition that would apply is the Valuation—Settlement condition. This condition, which explains how money and property are valued, will be helpful to you when you determine the amounts payable for the insured's claims.

If OM had not immediately fired Daryl and Jared, then the Termination As to Any Employee condition (provision E.2.a.) that applies to the Employee Theft insuring agreement would have automatically terminated OM's employee theft coverage with regard to any further acts committed by Daryl or Jared.

DICE Analysis Step 4: Exclusions

The fourth DICE step is to review the policy exclusions to determine whether they exclude or limit coverage of the loss.

Action Task: Refer to the exclusions in the Commercial Crime Coverage Form, (section D).

Based on these loss scenarios, no exclusions apply. However, under different circumstances, two exclusions might have been applicable to the employee theft loss.

If Brad had been aware of any past criminal acts of either Daryl or Jared prior to the policy period, the Acts of Employees Learned of by You Prior to the Policy Period exclusion (D.1.b.) would apply.

If the only evidence of the employee theft loss was the inventory shortage that Brad noticed in January, then the Inventory Shortages exclusion that applies to the Employee Theft insuring agreement (A.1) would apply. However, in this case, Daryl and Jared confessed their crime to the police.

> Insuring Agreement A.1. does not cover:
>
> a. Inventory Shortages
>
> Loss, or that part of any loss, the proof of which as to its existence or amount is dependent upon:
>
> (1) An inventory computation; or
>
> (2) A profit and loss computation.
>
> However, where you establish wholly apart from such computations that you have sustained a loss, then you may offer your inventory records and actual physical count of inventory in support of the amount of loss claimed.[9]

Knowledge to Action

Based on the Inventory Shortages exclusion in the commercial crime form, would OM's inventory records from January of 20X2 serve any useful purpose in OM's claim for merchandise losses from employee theft? Explain your answer.

Feedback: Yes, OM could use the inventory records from January 20X2 to support the amount of loss it claims from the employee theft because Brad was able to "establish wholly apart from such computations" that OM sustained a loss.

Determination of Amounts Payable

Now that you have completed the DICE analysis, you can determine the amounts payable. Doing this involves applying the limits of insurance available to pay each of the losses and any deductibles that apply. Typically, it also involves determining whether more than one policy provides coverage for the same loss; however, in this case no other policy applies. See the exhibit "Office Myria's Claims and Applicable Limits."

Office Myria's Claims and Applicable Limits

Claim	Applicable Insuring Agreement(s)	Coverage Limit(s)	Claim Amount(s)
July 3, 20X1 Theft:			
• Theft of money from safe ($2,000)	Inside the Premises—Theft of Money and Securities	$25,000	$3,200
• Damage to safe ($1,200)			
• Theft of small electronics (not covered)			
20X1 Employee Theft:			
• Theft of money ($45,000)	Employee Theft	$100,000	$110,000
• Theft of merchandise ($65,000)			

[DA07926]

The Limit of Insurance provision (B) in the Commercial Crime Coverage Form restricts the amount that the insurer will pay for losses.

The most we will pay for all loss resulting directly from an "occurrence" is the applicable Limit Of Insurance shown in the Declarations.

If any loss is covered under more than one Insuring Agreement or coverage, the most we will pay for such loss shall not exceed the largest Limit of Insurance available under any one of those Insuring Agreements or coverages.[10]

The Commercial Crime Coverage Form's definition of "occurrence" is crucial in applying the Limit of Insurance provision correctly. Part a. of the definition (F.17.a.) applies specifically to the Employee Theft insuring agreement.

"Occurrence" means:

a. Under Insuring Agreement A.1.:

(1) An individual act;

(2) The combined total of all separate acts whether or not related; or

(3) A series of acts whether or not related; committed by an "employee" acting alone or in collusion with other persons, during the Policy Period shown in the Declarations, except as provided under Condition E.1.k. or E.1.l.[11]

Consequently, all the separate acts of employee theft that Daryl and Jared committed (for both money and merchandise) qualify as only one occurrence when applying the limit of insurance applicable to employee theft loss. Therefore, the most the crime insurer will pay for OM's employee theft losses is $100,000.

The July 3, 20X1, theft of money from the safe and safe damage claim is within the policy limit for the applicable coverage and will be paid fully, minus the deductible.

The Deductible provision of the crime form explains how the deductible should be applied to a loss.

> We will not pay for loss resulting directly from an "occurrence" unless the amount of loss exceeds the Deductible Amount shown in the Declarations. We will then pay the amount of loss in excess of the Deductible Amount, up to the Limit of Insurance.[12]

The July 3 money theft amounts to $3,200, which is less than the applicable limit of insurance. The insurer will pay OM the amount of loss in excess of the $1,000 deductible: $2,200.

The employee theft losses (one occurrence) amount to $110,000, which exceeds the $100,000 limit of insurance for employee theft. The insurer will pay the amount of the loss in excess of the deductible ($110,000 − $1,000 = $109,000), up to the limit of insurance. Therefore the insurer's loss payment is $100,000. (The deductible comes off the amount of the loss, not the limit.)

SUMMARY

The ISO commercial crime program includes crime coverage forms that can be added to a commercial package policy and crime policy forms that can be written as monoline crime policies. ISO offers two versions of crime forms, the discovery form and the loss sustained form. Financial institution bonds provide employee dishonesty insurance and other crime coverages designed for banks, insurance companies, and other types of financial institutions.

Insureds can select from among the seven insuring agreements of the ISO Commercial Crime Coverage Form to tailor coverage for their businesses. These insuring agreements cover money, securities, and other property against a variety of covered perils, such as employee theft, forgery or alteration, robbery, safe burglary, theft, disappearance, destruction, computer and funds transfer fraud, and good-faith acceptance of counterfeit money.

The ISO Commercial Crime Coverage Form contains provisions that specify the policy's limits and the manner in which a deductible should be applied.

In the commercial crime form, the exclusions are divided into different groups, depending on whether they apply to all or only some insuring agreements.

The ISO Commercial Crime Coverage Form includes numerous policy conditions that extend or eliminate coverage under various circumstances. While some conditions apply only to particular insuring agreements, such as two that apply to Employee Theft, other conditions apply to all insuring agreements.

The Insurance Services Office, Inc. (ISO) Commercial Crime Coverage Form can be modified for various purposes through the addition of coverage endorsements.

The ISO crime insurance program includes two government crime coverage forms (discovery and loss sustained) and two government crime policies (discovery and loss sustained) for insuring governmental entities. These forms and policies differ from the ISO commercial crime forms and policies in several significant ways.

You should now be able to apply policy language to commercial crime losses to determine whether the losses are covered and the amount for which they are covered.

ASSIGNMENT NOTES

1. Includes copyrighted material of Insurance Services Office, Inc. Copyright, Insurance Services Office, Inc., 2012.
2. Includes copyrighted material of Insurance Services Office, Inc. Copyright, Insurance Services Office, Inc., 2012.
3. Includes copyrighted material of Insurance Services Office, Inc. Copyright, Insurance Services Office, Inc., 2012.
4. Includes copyrighted material of Insurance Services Office, Inc., with its permission. Copyright, Insurance Services Office, Inc., 2012.
5. Includes copyrighted material of Insurance Services Office, Inc., with its permission. Copyright, Insurance Services Office, Inc., 2012.
6. Copyright, Insurance Services Office, Inc., 2012.
7. Copyright, Insurance Services Office, Inc., 2012.
8. Copyright, Insurance Services Office, Inc., 2012.
9. Copyright, Insurance Services Office, Inc., 2012.
10. Copyright, Insurance Services Office, Inc., 2012.
11. Copyright, Insurance Services Office, Inc., 2012.
12. Copyright, Insurance Services Office, Inc., 2012.

Direct Your Learning ▶▶

Equipment Breakdown Insurance

Educational Objectives

After learning the content of this assignment, you should be able to:

▷ Identify the types of equipment and causes of loss that can be covered by equipment breakdown insurance.

▷ Summarize the insuring agreements included in the Equipment Breakdown Protection Coverage Form.

▷ Summarize the policy provisions contained in each of the following sections of the Equipment Breakdown Protection Coverage Form:

- Exclusions
- Limits of Insurance
- Deductibles
- Conditions

▷ Given a case describing a claim, determine whether the Equipment Breakdown Protection Coverage Form would cover the claim.

Equipment Breakdown Insurance

EQUIPMENT BREAKDOWN LOSS EXPOSURES AND COVERED EQUIPMENT

Equipment breakdown insurance, also known as boiler and machinery insurance, covers loss resulting from the accidental breakdown of covered equipment. The covered equipment can be almost any type of equipment that operates under pressure or that controls, transmits, transforms, or uses mechanical or electrical power.

Organizations of all types and sizes can have significant equipment breakdown loss exposures. The apparent causes of equipment breakdown losses can include heat, pressure, electrical energy, centrifugal force, or reciprocating motion. These categories of equipment can be covered under equipment breakdown policies:[1]

- Boilers and pressure vessels
- Electrical equipment
- Mechanical equipment
- Air conditioning and refrigeration equipment
- Office equipment and systems

Equipment Breakdown Loss Exposures

If one looks below the surface of these apparent causes of loss (such as a boiler explosion resulting from excessive pressure), the initiating causes are often operator error, faulty maintenance, or faulty design or installation of the equipment. Consequently, efforts to prevent equipment breakdown losses focus on operator training, regular maintenance of the equipment, and inspections to help detect and correct hazards before accidents occur. See the exhibit "Example of Operator Error."

Example of Operator Error

A diesel generator used by a hospital was severely damaged when the operator inadvertently added glycol to the engine's oil systems in the mistaken belief that he was adding lubricating oil. The repairs cost $180,000, and the hospital was forced to spend another $25,000 to purchase additional power from the local utility.

[DA03670]

Insurance is available to cover equipment breakdown. The insurance has several distinct characteristics. See the exhibit "Characteristics of Equipment Breakdown Insurance."

Characteristics of Equipment Breakdown Insurance

Characteristic	Description
Small, specialized field	Most insurers have chosen not to acquire the specialized underwriting, risk control, and claim personnel required to insure these loss exposures, on the basis that they would have insufficient volume; therefore the few insurers that have the expertise dominate the field.
Role of reinsurance	Many insurers include equipment breakdown coverage in their commercial package policies and then reinsure the equipment breakdown coverage with an insurer that specializes in that line. The specialized insurer assumes the financial consequences of the loss exposure and provides underwriting, risk control, and claim services. The specialized insurer may also purchase reinsurance for the financial consequences of the loss exposures.
Importance of risk control	Most states have laws requiring periodic inspection of boilers and pressure vessels by licensed inspectors, who could be the risk control representatives of equipment breakdown insurers. A key goal of the inspections is to spot dangerous conditions before trouble occurs. An inspector may take any of these actions: • Comment on suitability of equipment for the job • Request the testing of controls and safety devices • Check equipment maintenance • Review operators' logs • Review the insured's training programs • Provide underwriters with information they need to keep rates and coverages in line with the exposures

[DA05977]

Boilers and Pressure Vessels

Boilers are the most common type of **fired pressure vessel**. Many buildings are heated by boilers. The exhibit shows a common type of boiler and describes its operation. See the exhibit "Firetube Scotch Marine Boiler."

Examples of fired pressure vessels other than boilers are economizers, which preheat water being fed into or returned to a boiler; and separately fired

Boiler

A fired pressure vessel constructed of cast iron or steel in which water is heated to produce steam or hot water.

Fired pressure vessel

A closed container that is heated by the direct fire of burning fuel and can withstand internal pressure.

Firetube Scotch Marine Boiler

The firetube Scotch marine boiler is one of the oldest boiler designs in current use. This design is widely used in hospitals, laundries, and apartment buildings, as well as in commercial/light industrial processes, for both steam and hot water production. It is called a firetube boiler because the combustion process and the resulting gases are contained inside the tubes; water (and steam) are outside the tubes.

The boiler shown is a four-pass, natural-gas-fired unit (two- and three-pass designs are also popular). The burner, located in the front of the boiler (on the left-hand side of the sketch), mixes air and fuel in the correct proportions to burn the fuel safely and completely. Flame extends from the burner into the center of the furnace tube, where the combustion process is completed. Products of combustion (flue gas) continue through the furnace tube toward the rear of the boiler (right-hand side of the sketch). These hot gases then turn around at the rear of the boiler and pass through firetubes three times (in this particular design) before exiting from the top of the boiler to the stack.

The furnace (first pass) and three firetube passes transfer heat to the pressurized water surrounding them. Steam bubbles rise to the surface of the water above the topmost firetubes. From there the steam is piped to apparatus that use the energy (such as radiators for comfort heating, steam-jacketed kettles for cooking, or other process use). As the steam gives off its energy and loses heat, it condenses back into water, which returns to the boiler to repeat the cycle.

Courtesy of Cleaver-Brooks [DA03671]

superheaters, which raise the temperature of steam after it leaves the boiler. These are the common types of breakdown losses to fired pressure vessels:

- Explosion caused by excessive internal pressure of steam.
- Overheating (referred to as "dry-firing") caused by continued firing when there is insufficient water in the vessel, usually because of the failure of

the low-water cutoff. The low-water cutoff is designed to shut down the furnace when the water falls below a safe level.

- Cracking of cast iron sections because of expansion and contraction stresses, rust growth between sections, porous castings, and tie rods that are too tight.
- Bulging or "bagging" (swelling), usually caused by improper heat transfer because of buildup of scale or sediment.

When a steam boiler malfunctions in a way that results in the buildup of pressure that exceeds the boiler's ability to contain the pressure, it explodes. As illustrated in the exhibit, such an explosion can destroy the boiler and extensively damage the building and personal property around the boiler. See the exhibit "Building Damage Caused by Boiler Explosion."

Building Damage Caused by Boiler Explosion

Courtesy of The Hartford Steam Boiler Inspection and Insurance Company, Hartford, Conn. [DA03672]

Commercial property policies exclude loss (other than resulting fire) caused by the explosion of steam boilers, steam pipes, steam engines, and steam turbines that are owned or leased by the insured or operated under the insured's control. Overheating losses are more frequent than explosion but generally less severe.

In some **unfired pressure vessels**, heat is generated by chemical action within the vessel or by the application of a heating medium such as electric heat or steam. Other unfired pressure vessels are not heated, and still others are refrigerated.

Unfired pressure vessel

A closed vessel that can withstand internal pressure or vacuum but is not heated by the direct fire of burning fuel.

Examples of unfired pressure vessels include compressed air tanks, liquefied gas tanks (which are sometimes refrigerated to maintain the gas in a liquefied state), and steam-jacketed vessels. Steam-jacketed vessels are used in food and chemical processing operations to heat liquid mixtures. Unfired pressure vessels are subject to the perils of explosion, bulging, cracking, and implosion (collapse). The exhibit shows a storage tank that collapsed because of internal vacuum. See the exhibit "Collapsed Storage Tank."

Collapsed Storage Tank

Courtesy of The Hartford Steam Boiler Inspection and Insurance Company, Hartford, Conn. [DA03673]

The steam boiler explosion exclusion in commercial property policies does not extend to explosion of unfired pressure vessels, which is therefore covered under commercial property forms and usually excluded under equipment breakdown policies.

Commercial property policies specifically cover a type of explosion involving boilers, called combustion explosion or furnace explosion. Combustion explosion occurs when unburned fuel or gases that have accumulated in a steam boiler or another type of fired vessel are ignited. Because commercial property policies cover combustion explosion, equipment breakdown policies exclude combustion explosion unless it is added by endorsement. See the exhibit "Common Perils Affecting Equipment—Which Policy Covers?."

Electrical Equipment

Common types of electrical equipment include power transformers, switchboards, distribution panels, circuit breakers, cables, motors, and generators.

Common Perils Affecting Equipment—Which Policy Covers?

Peril	Covered by Commercial Property Policy?	Covered by Equipment Breakdown Policy?
Boiler explosion	No	Yes
Electrical breakdown	No	Yes
Mechanical breakdown	No	Yes
Rupture or bursting from centrifugal force	No	Yes
Explosion of unfired pressure vessels	Yes	No
Furnace explosion	Yes	No
Fire	Yes	No

[DA03674]

Frequent types of losses include electrical shorting of windings; insulator, connector, or control failure; bearing failure in rotating equipment; casing, rotor, or shaft damage; and distortion or mechanical breakage of parts.

Common causes of these accidents include supply line surges, excessive moisture, insulation deterioration, overload conditions, lubrication failure, and improper repairs. Here are some examples of electrical equipment breakdown:

- The aluminum bus (an electrical conductor) in an apartment building short circuited, causing extensive damage to the building's electrical cables and wiring. Residents were temporarily relocated. The total loss was $192,000, consisting of physical damage of $120,000 and extra expenses of $72,000.

- A rectifier transformer winding at the premises of a manufacturer short-circuited because of loose lead connections. The relatively small physical damage loss of $10,000 resulted in a business income loss of nearly $80,000.

Commercial property policies exclude damage caused by artificially generated electric current to electrical devices, appliances, or wires. Consequently, they do not cover the electrical breakdown of motors, generators, circuit breakers, electrical distribution boards, cables, or transformers caused by short circuits or line surge unless as the result of lightning.

Commercial property policies do cover damage resulting from lightning, including damage to electrical components that are covered property. Commercial property policies also cover fire damage that results from any electrical breakdown.

Mechanical Equipment

Mechanical equipment—such as compressors, pumps, blowers, fans, engines, turbines, and gear sets—is subject to various types of breakdown. Examples of such breakdown losses include breaking or chipping of rotating elements; scoring of cylinder walls; breaking of gears or couplings; failure of bearings or shafts; and seizing of moving parts. See the exhibit "Examples of Mechanical Equipment Breakdown."

Examples of Mechanical Equipment Breakdown

At a milk processing plant, a spring broke on a check valve in a milk processing machine, causing raw milk to mix with processed milk. The resulting spoiled milk amounted to a $256,000 loss.

The operator of a milling and boring machine failed to ensure that the cutting head was fully withdrawn before changing from vertical to horizontal drilling. The ensuing collision caused extensive damage to the cutting head spindle and the ceramic shaft bearings. Despite all efforts to expedite replacement, it took almost two months to obtain the replacement parts from the foreign-based manufacturer. The combined property damage and business income loss totaled $111,000.

[DA03675]

These breakdowns can result from metal fatigue, weld failure, insufficient lubrication, overspeed, mechanical stress, shock loads, and many other causes. Commercial property policies exclude loss resulting from mechanical breakdown, including rupture or bursting caused by centrifugal force.

Air Conditioning and Refrigeration Equipment

Air conditioning and refrigeration systems include components such as motors, compressors, fans, switchboards, coils, pipes, and vessels. A wide range of causes—such as control failure, vibration, lack of lubrication, improper control settings, and electrical disturbance—can result in many different types of breakdown losses. Examples of such losses include cracks or breaks in refrigerant piping, rupture or collapse of condenser or evaporator vessels, freezing and bursting of chiller or cooling coils, motor winding short-out, compressor valve failure, seizing of moving parts, and scoring of cylinder sleeves. See the exhibit "Examples of Air Conditioning and Refrigeration Equipment Breakdown."

Ammonia refrigeration systems present an additional hazard. Ammonia can cause severe contamination losses, especially to foodstuffs. The mechanical and electrical breakdown exclusions in commercial property policies exclude most breakdown losses to air conditioning and refrigeration equipment.

> **Examples of Air Conditioning and Refrigeration Equipment Breakdown**
>
> - A hotel's compressor motor short-circuited, causing a partial loss of air conditioning during a July convention, resulting in a 50 percent loss of occupancy in the hotel. The physical damage loss was $30,000, and the business income loss was $44,000.
> - A portion of a compressor became detached and fell into the evaporator, puncturing several tubes. The cooling water from the tubes contaminated the refrigerant and caused severe damage to the driving motor windings. The loss amounted to $45,000.

[DA03676]

Office Equipment and Systems

Traditionally, boiler and machinery insurance did not provide coverage for accidents to regular office equipment. However, the widespread use of complex office equipment such as computer systems, automated telephone systems, copiers, and fax machines created an opportunity for breakdown insurers to offer coverage on such items.

Examples of losses in this category include circuit board failures; electrical arcing; distortion or breakage of parts; insulator, connector, or control failure; bearing failure; and gear or coupling breakage. These losses can result from electrical line surges, deterioration of insulation, electrical overload, excessive moisture, poor contacts or connections, operator error or abuse, misalignment, improper adjustment or clearance of parts, and the presence of foreign objects in the system. See the exhibit "Example of Office Equipment Breakdown Loss."

> **Example of Office Equipment Breakdown Loss**
>
> A voltage fluctuation caused two terminal boards in an office building's phone computer to short-circuit, resulting in a $52,000 physical damage loss.

[DA05301]

Insureds sometimes assume that breakdown coverage on office equipment duplicates manufacturers' warranties or maintenance contracts that they already have on the equipment. In reality, breakdown coverage on such equipment covers many losses and expenses that are not covered by a warranty or maintenance contract.

Equipment Breakdown Exposures by Market Segment

A common misconception is that only large industrial accounts have equipment breakdown loss exposures. Actually, many types of organizations have such exposures, and the number of policies provided to smaller customers far exceeds the number provided to large industrial accounts. Equipment breakdown coverage can meet the somewhat different loss exposures of market segments ranging from small business, or what are sometimes called "Main Street" insureds; midsize commercial insureds; and large industrial insureds.

The Main Street segment includes relatively small insureds; they are often thinly financed and therefore vulnerable to business income or extra expense losses. They also often have uncomplicated breakdown exposures, such as retail stores, apartment and office buildings, theaters, churches, restaurants, and dry cleaners. Heating and air conditioning equipment are their principal exposures, but other ones can also be significant. For example, refrigerating equipment can be a significant exposure for grocery stores, and retail stores of all types are highly dependent on integrated scanning/checkout/inventory control systems.

Examples of insureds in the midsize commercial segment include food processors, printers, publishers, and manufacturers. In this group, the equipment breakdown exposures can become more complex, including production machinery and processing equipment in addition to heating and air conditioning equipment. Covered equipment tends to be larger and receives a more detailed inspection by the insurer.

Large industrial insureds are an important market segment for equipment breakdown insurers. Examples of these insureds include utilities, chemical companies, oil and natural gas companies, heavy manufacturers, and mining companies. In this category, property values exposed to loss can be very high.

EQUIPMENT BREAKDOWN INSURING AGREEMENTS

Insurance Services Office, Inc. (ISO) and the American Association of Insurance Services (AAIS) both file equipment breakdown coverage forms.

Although equipment breakdown coverage is usually provided as part of a commercial package policy (CPP), the Equipment Breakdown Protection Coverage Form (EB 00 20) of ISO can be used in either a monoline equipment breakdown policy or a CPP. Other approaches to providing equipment breakdown coverage are to include it as an endorsement to a commercial property form or as an optional coverage in a businessowners policy. An advantage of including equipment breakdown coverage and commercial property coverage in the same policy is avoiding claim disputes that can arise when the two coverages are written by separate insurers.

The ISO Equipment Breakdown Protection Coverage Form contains ten insuring agreements. The insuring agreements that apply in a particular policy are indicated by the appropriate entries (such as a limit of insurance or the number of days covered) on the Declarations page. A policy might not include all ten insuring agreements, either because the insured does not want to purchase all of them or because the insurer is unwilling to provide all of them. See the exhibit "Insuring Agreements in the Equipment Breakdown Protection Coverage Form."

Insuring Agreements in the Equipment Breakdown Protection Coverage Form

- Property Damage
- Expediting Expense
- Business Income and Extra Expense—Or Extra Expense Only
- Spoilage Damage
- Utility Interruption
- Newly Acquired Premises
- Ordinance or Law Coverage
- Errors and Omissions
- Brands and Labels
- Contingent Business Income and Extra Expense—Or Extra Expense Only

Includes copyrighted material of Insurance Services Office, Inc., with its permission. Copyright, ISO Properties, Inc., 2006. [DA03721]

The covered cause of loss for all of the insuring agreements is "breakdown" to "covered equipment." The policy definition of breakdown includes failure of pressure or vacuum equipment, mechanical failure, and electrical failure, subject to exclusions. See the exhibit "Policy Definition of "Breakdown"."

The policy definition of covered equipment includes a wide range of equipment, also subject to exclusions. See the exhibit ""Covered Equipment"."

A common misconception is that equipment breakdown insurance covers only loss to the covered equipment itself. In reality, breakdown to covered equipment during the policy period is the event that triggers coverage. Once equipment breakdown coverage is triggered, it covers any of the types of loss described in any of the insuring agreements that apply to the policy.

Policy Definition of "Breakdown"

"Breakdown":

a. Means the following direct physical loss, that causes damage to "Covered Equipment" and necessitates its repair or replacement:

    (1) Failure of pressure or vacuum equipment;

    (2) Mechanical failure including rupture or bursting caused by centrifugal force; or

    (3) Electrical failure including arcing;

unless such loss or damage is otherwise excluded within this Coverage Form.

b. Does not mean or include:

    (1) Malfunction including but not limited to adjustment, alignment, calibration, cleaning or modification;

    (2) Defects, erasures, errors, limitations or viruses in computer equipment and programs including the inability to recognize and process any date or time or provide instructions to "Covered Equipment";

    (3) Leakage at any valve, fitting, shaft seal, gland packing, joint or connection;

    (4) Damage to any vacuum tube, gas tube, or brush;

    (5) Damage to any structure or foundation supporting the "Covered Equipment" or any of its parts;

    (6) The functioning of any safety or protective device; or

    (7) The cracking of any part on an internal combustion gas turbine exposed to the products of combustion.

Includes copyrighted material of Insurance Services Office, Inc., with its permission. Copyright, ISO Properties, Inc., 2006. [DA03722]

Property Damage

Under the Property Damage insuring agreement, the insurer agrees to pay for direct damage to covered property. The policy definition of "covered property" is distinct from, and much broader than, the policy definition of "covered equipment." Covered property can be one or both of these types:

• Property that the named insured owns

• Property that is in the named insured's care, custody, or control and for which the named insured is legally liable. In either case, the property must be situated at a location described in the declarations

For example, a steam boiler explosion (one example of breakdown to covered equipment) can destroy the steam boiler and also damage other covered property, such as the insured's building, business personal property, and a customer's property in the insured's care, custody, or control. An equip-

"Covered Equipment"

a. Means and includes any:

(1) Equipment built to operate under internal pressure or vacuum other than weight of contents;

(2) Electrical or mechanical equipment that is used in the generation, transmission or utilization of energy;

(3) Communication equipment, and "Computer Equipment"; and

(4) Equipment in Paragraphs (1), (2) and (3) that is owned by a public or private utility and used solely to supply utility services to your premises.

However, if Coverage A.2.e. Utility Interruption is provided, then Paragraph 6.a.(4) does not apply.

Except for Paragraph 6.a.(4), Utility Interruption and Contingent Business Income And Extra Expense—Extra Expense Only Coverages, the "Covered Equipment" must be located at a premises described in the Declarations and be owned, leased, or operated under your control.

b. Does not mean or include any:

(1) "Media";

(2) Part of pressure or vacuum equipment that is not under internal pressure of its contents or internal vacuum;

(3) Insulating or refractory material, but not excluding the glass lining of any "Covered Equipment";

(4) Non-metallic pressure or vacuum equipment, unless it is constructed and used in accordance with the American Society of Mechanical Engineers (A.S.M.E.) code or another appropriate and approved code;

(5) Catalyst;

(6) Vessels, piping and other equipment that is buried below ground and requires the excavation of materials to inspect, remove, repair or replace;

(7) Structure, foundation, cabinet or compartment supporting or containing the "Covered Equipment" or part of the "Covered Equipment" including penstock, draft tube or well casing;

(8) Vehicle, aircraft, self-propelled equipment or floating vessel including any "Covered Equipment" that is mounted upon or used solely with any one or more vehicle(s), aircraft, self-propelled equipment or floating vessel;

(9) Dragline, excavation, or construction equipment including any "Covered Equipment" that is mounted upon or used solely with any one or more dragline(s), excavation, or construction equipment;

(10) Felt, wire, screen, die, extrusion plate, swing hammer, grinding disc, cutting blade, non-electrical cable, chain, belt, rope, clutch plate, brake pad, non-metal part or any part or tool subject to periodic replacement;

(11) Machine or apparatus used solely for research, diagnosis, medication, surgical, therapeutic, dental or pathological purposes including any "Covered Equipment" that is mounted upon or used solely with any one or more machine(s) or apparatus unless Diagnostic Equipment is shown as INCLUDED in the Declarations; or

(12) Equipment or any part of such equipment manufactured by you for sale.

ment breakdown policy can cover all these types of property. A commercial property policy would not cover any of this loss because it was caused by an excluded peril.

In connection with its coverage for property in the insured's care, custody, or control for which the insured is legally liable, the coverage form contains a loss condition, titled Defense. This condition gives the insurer the right, but not the duty, to defend the insured against suits arising from claims of property owners (such as the owner of property in the insured's care, custody, or control). If the insurer chooses to defend against a claim or suit, it will pay the resulting expenses. In contrast, some other equipment breakdown policies obligate the insurer to provide defense and describe the covered defense expenses in more detail.

Expediting Expenses

Under the Expediting Expenses insuring agreement, the insurer agrees to pay such expenses that the insured necessarily incurs. Examples of **expediting expenses** are the payment of overtime wages to make repairs, or the use of overnight shipping to obtain needed parts.

Coverage for expediting expenses overlaps extra expense coverage to some degree, but expediting expenses coverage is not as broad as extra expense coverage. For example, the cost of renting substitute facilities to continue operations could be covered as extra expense but not as expediting expenses.

Expediting expenses
Expenses incurred to speed up the repair or replacement of covered property.

Explosion of Steam Boiler—What Is Covered?

The explosion of a steam boiler in Acme Manufacturing Company's factory caused these losses:

1. Destruction of the boiler
2. Damage to Acme's building
3. Damage to Acme's business personal property
4. Damage to a customer's patterns in Acme's possession
5. Damage to the building of a neighboring firm
6. Bodily injury to some of Acme's employees

Because the explosion was "breakdown" to "covered equipment," Acme's equipment breakdown insurance would cover items 1, 2, 3, and 4. Acme's equipment breakdown insurance would not cover damage to the neighboring firm's building (item 5), because equipment breakdown insurance does not cover property of others unless it is in the insured's care, custody, or control at a described location. Acme's liability for damage to its neighbor's building would be covered by Acme's commercial general liability (CGL) insurance. Acme's equipment breakdown insurance also would not cover item 6, because such insurance does not cover bodily injury of any kind. Instead, Acme's responsibility for injury to its own employees would be covered under Acme's workers compensation insurance.

Spoilage Damage

The Spoilage Damage insuring agreement covers spoilage damage to raw materials, property in process, or finished products while in storage or in the course of being manufactured. The spoilage damage must result from the lack or excess of power, light, heat, steam, or refrigeration, and the insured must own or be legally liable for the property.

If, for example, the insured is a cold storage warehouse and its refrigeration system fails because of breakdown to covered equipment, spoilage damage coverage would pay for loss resulting from the spoilage of food in the warehouse. The insurer also agrees to pay expenses the insured incurs to reduce the amount of spoilage loss, not to exceed the amount that would otherwise have been payable.

Insuring Agreements for Time Element Coverages

Most organizations have a need for time element coverages in connection with equipment breakdown perils. The breakdown of equipment or the resulting damage to covered property can interrupt operations and cause the insured to lose business income and incur extra expenses. Such time element losses are not covered under regular business income and extra expense forms, because the cause of loss is not covered. Accordingly, the ISO equipment breakdown form contains these insuring agreements:

- Business Income and Extra Expense—Or Extra Expense Only
- Utility Interruption
- Contingent Business Income and Extra Expense—Or Extra Expense Only

Insureds can select any or all of these coverages, subject to the underwriter's approval.

Business Income

The first insuring agreement can provide business income and extra expense coverage or only extra expense coverage. Entries in the declarations indicate which coverages apply.If business income coverage applies, the insurer agrees to pay the insured's actual loss of business income during the period of restoration resulting from breakdown to covered equipment. (The policy defines "business income" to include net income that would have been earned, plus continuing normal operating expenses incurred, including employee payroll.) Extra expense coverage applies to extra expense the insured necessarily incurs to operate the business during the period of restoration.

The "period of restoration," as defined in the ISO form, continues for five consecutive days after the damaged property is repaired or replaced with reasonable speed. The period of restoration can be extended for the number of additional days shown in the declarations.

Utility Interruption

The second insuring agreement is comparable to the Utility Services—Time Element endorsement used with commercial property business income coverage. It extends any business income, extra expense, or spoilage damage coverage provided by the policy to include loss resulting from breakdown of covered equipment owned, operated, or controlled by the local private or public utility or distributor from whom the insured receives electrical power, communication services, air conditioning, heating, gas, sewer, water, or steam. If, for example, a utility's electrical transformer is destroyed by a breakdown, shutting off all electrical power to the insured's premises for several days, utility interruption coverage will cover the resulting loss of business income following the waiting period shown in the declarations.

Contingent Business Income

Like dependent properties coverage in commercial property business income insurance, the third insuring agreement covers business income and extra expense (or only extra expense) arising from breakdown to covered equipment at the location, shown in the declarations, that is not owned or operated by the insured. The breakdown must either (1) wholly or partially prevent the delivery of services or materials to the insured or from the insured to others for the insured's account or (2) result in the loss of sales at the named insured's premises shown in the declarations.

Newly Acquired Premises

This insuring agreement extends the other coverages provided by the policy to apply at newly acquired premises the insured buys or leases. The coverage begins when the insured acquires the property and continues for the number of days shown in the declarations for Newly Acquired Premises. The insured must inform the insurer in writing of the newly acquired premises as soon as practicable and agree to pay additional premium determined by the insurer.

Ordinance or Law Coverage

Ordinances or laws that regulate the repair or construction of buildings can cause the insured to sustain losses (such as the cost of demolishing undamaged parts of a building or the increased cost of construction) in addition to the direct loss resulting when breakdown to covered equipment damages covered property subject to such ordinances or laws. The Ordinance or Law Coverage insuring agreement provides a way to cover such losses.

Errors and Omissions

Errors and Omissions coverage commits the insurer to pay for loss or damage not otherwise covered under this form solely because of any of these reasons:

- Any error or unintentional omission in the description or location of insured property
- Any failure through error to include any premises owned or occupied by the insured on the policy's inception date
- Any error or unintentional omission by the insured that results in cancellation of any premises insured under the policy

The error or unintentional omission must be reported and corrected when discovered, and the policy premium will be adjusted to reflect the date the premises should have been added to the policy if no error or omission had occurred. No coverage is provided as a result of any error or unintentional omission in the reporting of values or the coverage that the insured requested.

Many equipment breakdown forms do not contain an Errors or Omissions provision. This is a broadening of coverage that risk managers and knowledgeable insureds and producers often ask insurers to add to their property insurance policies.

Brands and Labels

The Brands and Labels insuring agreement is similar to the Brands and Labels endorsement available for commercial property policies. The insurer agrees to pay reasonable costs the insured incurs in stamping merchandise with the word "Salvage" or removing brands and labels, but the total the insurer will pay for such costs and the value of the damaged property cannot exceed the applicable limit of insurance on such property.

Insuring Computers and Electronic Data

How best to insure computers and electronic data can be a difficult issue. In some cases, equipment breakdown coverage can be a good solution. Generally, computers and electronic data can be insured by using one of three approaches:

- Insure these items as business personal property in a commercial property policy. The weakness of this approach is that even Special Form coverage excludes many perils. For example, the Special Form excludes damage caused by artificially generated electrical current, and electronic equipment is easily damaged by current surges and spikes. Also, commercial property coverage for electronic data is very limited, as to both the amount of coverage and the covered perils. Nevertheless, this alternative is a viable risk management technique for many firms because computers have become so inexpensive, and regular backup of data, with off-premises storage, reduces the risk of losing data.

- Use an inland marine electronic data processing (EDP) equipment floater. This approach can provide broader coverage for EDP equipment and data than commercial property policies, but the premium can be higher than that for covering the equipment under a commercial property policy.

- Use a combination of equipment breakdown coverage and commercial property coverage. This approach closes some of the coverage gaps that exist when only commercial property coverage is purchased. Equipment breakdown coverage effectively complements commercial property coverage for electronic equipment, but the combination may not provide adequate limits for loss of data from perils other than breakdown of covered equipment. Some equipment breakdown policies include an insuring agreement that covers the cost to research, replace, or restore data that are lost because of covered equipment breakdown. If the policy also covers business income and extra expense, those coverages may be extended to cover loss of business income or the incurring of extra expense because of data losses.

POLICY PROVISIONS IN EQUIPMENT BREAKDOWN COVERAGE

As with other commercial property coverages, an insurance professional should be knowledgeable of the policy provisions in equipment breakdown forms to properly advise insureds of how to use the coverage.

Equipment breakdown forms contain exclusions that eliminate coverage for certain perils covered under commercial property policies and various other exclusions. An equipment breakdown policy has a limit of insurance that applies to all loss resulting from any one breakdown. Loss covered by each insuring agreement may also be subject to a smaller limit that is part of the overall limit per breakdown. Various sublimits also apply to certain types of loss such as ammonia contamination and restoration of data and media.

Four types of deductibles can be used with equipment breakdown insurance: dollar, time, multiple of daily value, and percentage of loss. Many of the conditions in equipment breakdown policies are comparable to those in commercial property policies. Other conditions that are unique to equipment breakdown coverage include the Suspension condition, the Joint or Disputed Loss Agreement, and (in some policies, but not the Insurance Services Office [ISO] form) a condition addressing jurisdictional inspections.

Exclusions

The policy definitions of breakdown and covered equipment each contain several exclusions that eliminate coverage for certain causes of loss and types of equipment. In addition to the exclusions within the policy definitions, equipment breakdown policies contain additional exclusions:

- Exclusions similar to exclusions contained in commercial property policies
- Exclusions that eliminate coverage for perils usually insured in other policies
- Other exclusions

All these exclusions are subject to anti-concurrent causation language similar to that found in ISO commercial property forms.

Exclusions Similar to Commercial Property Exclusions

Several exclusions in the ISO form are comparable to the commercial property exclusions regarding ordinance or law; earth movement; water; nuclear hazard; war or military action; wear and tear or gradual deterioration (unless a breakdown occurs); neglect to use all reasonable means to save covered property from further damage at and after the time of a loss; and fungus, wet rot, and dry rot.

Exclusions for Perils Usually Insured in Other Policies

Most equipment breakdown policies exclude loss caused by certain perils that are commonly covered by other policies. Some of the exclusions apply only if the insured has other insurance, and some apply regardless of other insurance. Equipment breakdown policies vary as to which perils are excluded in this category.

The ISO form excludes these causes of loss:

- Fire or combustion explosion that results in a breakdown, that occurs at the same time as a breakdown, or that ensues from a breakdown
- Water or other means of extinguishing a fire
- Breakdown caused by any of the following perils if coverage for that peril is provided by another policy of the insured's, whether collectible or not: aircraft or vehicles; freezing caused by cold weather; lightning; sinkhole collapse; smoke; riot, civil commotion, or vandalism; or weight of snow, ice, or sleet
- Breakdown caused by windstorm or hail

This category also includes exclusions that duplicate exclusions or conditions applicable to time element coverages in other policies. The ISO form, for example, excludes these exposures with respect to the business income, extra expense, and utility interruption coverages:

- Business that would not or could not have been conducted if the breakdown had not occurred
- The insured's failure to use due diligence and dispatch in operating the business
- The suspension, lapse, or cancellation of a contract

Other Exclusions

Various other exclusions can be found in equipment breakdown policies. For example, equipment breakdown policies usually exclude certain types of testing that place above-normal stresses on equipment. The ISO form excludes "damage to 'Covered Equipment' undergoing a pressure or electrical test." When such testing occurs in a newly constructed building, it is often covered by endorsement to the builders risk policy covering the entire construction project. Builders risk equipment breakdown forms are also available, and these forms typically omit the testing exclusion.

Limits of Insurance

An equipment breakdown policy can have several limits of insurance. Ordinarily, every policy has one overall limit, which is the most that the insurer will pay for loss or damage resulting from any one breakdown. The ISO form refers to this limit as the "limit per breakdown" and defines "one breakdown" to include all additional breakdowns that result from an initial breakdown at the same premises. In addition to the limit per breakdown, separate limits may be shown for some of the insuring agreements. See the exhibit "Equipment Breakdown—Setting Limits of Insurance."

Equipment Breakdown—Setting Limits of Insurance

Setting limits for equipment breakdown coverages other than business income differs from the procedure used in commercial property policies because there is little catastrophic exposure from an equipment breakdown loss and because coinsurance seldom applies to equipment breakdown coverages other than business income. When a policy covers a single location, the equipment breakdown limit should be set equal to the covered property's value. When the policy covers more than one location, there is virtually no possibility of a catastrophic loss affecting separate locations. The limit for such a policy is usually set higher than the estimate of maximum possible loss at the highest valued location, but less than the total insurable value at all locations.

The limit for equipment breakdown business income coverage should be set equal to the amount needed to comply with the Coinsurance condition or equal the estimated maximum loss of business income, whichever is greater.

[DA06026]

"Included" in Declarations

If the word "Included" is shown beside a coverage in the declarations, any limit shown for that coverage is part of, not in addition to, the limit per breakdown. The insurer will not pay more under each coverage than the limit of insurance applicable to that coverage. Any payments for those losses reduce the Property Damage limit or the limit per breakdown.

Unless a higher limit or "Included" is shown in the declarations, the most the insurer will pay for each of these exposures is $25,000:

- Spoilage damage to covered property resulting from ammonia contamination. (Ammonia is used in some cooling equipment and can escape as the result of a breakdown to such equipment.)
- The reduction in value of undamaged parts of a product that becomes unmarketable because of physical loss or damage to another part of the product.
- The cost to research, replace, or restore damaged computer data or media, including the cost to reprogram instructions used in any computer equipment.
- Additional expenses the insured incurs to clean up, repair, replace, or dispose of covered property that is damaged or contaminated by a hazardous substance. The form defines "hazardous substance" as any substance other than ammonia that a government agency has declared to be hazardous to health.
- Damage to covered property by water. However, no coverage applies to water damage resulting from leakage of a sprinkler system or domestic water piping.

Fungus, Wet Rot, and Dry Rot

The Limits of Insurance section also contains a lengthy provision titled Limited Coverage for "Fungus", Wet Rot and Dry Rot. This limited coverage is subject to a $15,000 aggregate limit unless the declarations show a higher limit for this coverage or indicate that the limit applies separately to each covered location. The coverage applies to the cost of removing fungus, wet rot, or dry rot that result directly from a breakdown to covered equipment.

Deductibles

The ISO form addresses both the application of deductibles and the determination of deductibles.

Application of Deductibles

Regarding application of deductibles, the insurer will not pay for loss resulting from any one breakdown until the amount of loss exceeds the applicable deductible. After subtracting the deductible, the insurer will pay the remaining amount of loss up to the limit of insurance. That is, the deductible does not reduce the applicable limit of insurance.

Another aspect of applying deductibles concerns situations in which an equipment breakdown policy has insuring agreements with separate deductibles. The form says that deductibles apply separately for each applicable coverage. For example, if a breakdown loss involved both property damage and loss of business income, one deductible might apply to the property damage part of the loss and another deductible might apply to the business income part of the loss.

However, if the declarations show "Combined" deductibles for two or more coverages, the insurer will subtract the combined deductible only once from the aggregate amount of loss under the coverages to which the combined deductible applies. Similarly, if more than one item of covered property is involved in "one breakdown" (as defined in the form), only the highest applicable deductible will apply for each of the coverages.

Determination of Deductibles

The equipment breakdown form also addresses how deductible amounts will be determined for four possible types of deductibles:

- Dollar deductible
- Time deductible
- Multiple of daily value deductible
- Percentage of loss deductible

A dollar deductible is simply the dollar amount shown as such in the declarations.

Time deductibles are often used for time element coverages such as business income and extra expense. When a time deductible applies, the insurer is not liable for any loss occurring during the specified number of hours or days immediately following the breakdown.

The multiple of daily value is an alternative deductible for time element coverages. It is shown in the declarations as a number (such as 3) times the insured's daily value, calculated as the amount of business income that the insured would have earned during the period of restoration if no breakdown had occurred, and divided by the number of working days in that period. See the exhibit "Example of Multiple of Daily Value Deductible."

Example of Multiple of Daily Value Deductible

The insured's business was interrupted for six days because of a breakdown to covered equipment. If the breakdown had not occurred, the business income for those six days would have been $30,000. If the business income and extra expense deductible is three times the daily value, the amount of the deductible would be calculated in these two steps:

1. $30,000 ÷ 6 = $5,000.
2. 3 × $5,000 = $15,000.

[DA03678]

An equipment breakdown deductible can also be expressed as a specified percentage of loss. This type of deductible is most frequently used with spoilage damage coverage. The dollar amount of the deductible for a particular claim is calculated by multiplying the specified percentage by the gross amount of the loss (before application of any deductible or coinsurance penalty).

The multiple of daily value and percentage of loss deductibles can be subject to minimum and/or maximum deductibles at the underwriter's discretion:

- If a minimum deductible is specified in the declarations, it will apply to a loss if the dollar amount calculated for the multiple of daily value deductible or the percentage of loss deductible is less than the minimum deductible.

- If a maximum deductible is specified in the declarations, it will apply to a loss if the dollar amount calculated for the multiple of daily value deductible or the percentage of loss deductible is more than the maximum deductible.

Conditions

Most of the conditions contained in equipment breakdown policies are comparable to those contained in other property insurance policies. Several conditions of the ISO equipment breakdown form distinguish this type of policy from commercial property policies.

Valuation

The Valuation condition, which differs from the valuation provisions of commercial property policies, addresses a number of topics related to how much the insurer will pay for a covered loss.

Coverage applies on a replacement cost basis. The insurer will determine the value of covered property that has been lost or damaged based on the cost to repair, rebuild, or replace the damaged property with property of like kind, capacity, size, or quality on the same site or another site, whichever is less costly. However, the insurer will not pay for property that is obsolete and useless to the insured.

If the insured does not repair or replace the damaged property within twenty-four months after the time of loss, the insurer will pay no more than (1) what it would have cost to repair the property at the time of loss or (2) the property's actual cash value at the time of loss, whichever amount is less.

By endorsement, the underwriter can amend the valuation for certain items, typically outdated equipment, to an actual cash value basis.

If manufactured by the insured, property held for sale by the insured is valued at its selling price, less any discounts and expenses the insured otherwise would have had. Computer data and media that are mass produced and commercially available are valued at replacement cost, and all other computer data and media are valued at the cost of blank materials.

Insureds often upgrade their equipment after a loss. To cover the added expense, the policy provides that the insurer will pay the additional cost to replace covered equipment with equipment that is better for the environment, safer, or more efficient than the equipment being replaced. The most that the insurer will pay under this extension is an additional 25 percent of the property damage amount otherwise collectible. This type of coverage extension is seldom offered in other types of property insurance because of morale and moral hazards. The complex nature of most covered equipment and the extensive risk control services provided by insurers combine to make this coverage commercially viable for equipment breakdown.

For purposes of spoilage damage coverage, separate valuation methods apply to raw materials, property in process, and finished products. Raw materials are valued at replacement cost. Property in process is valued at the sum of the replacement cost of the raw materials, the labor expended, and the proper proportion of overhead charges. Finished products are valued at their selling price, less any discounts the insured offered and expenses the insured otherwise would have had.

Coinsurance

Some equipment breakdown policies include coinsurance, and others do not. In practice, coinsurance generally applies only to time element coverages. The ISO equipment breakdown form contains a Coinsurance condition that applies only to business income loss, and then only if the insurer does not receive the insured's annual report of business income values within three months of the Business Income Report Date shown in the declarations.

Any insured that has business income and extra expense coverage must complete an annual report of values, and the report must reach the insurer within three months of the Business Income Report Date shown in the declarations. The report shows actual values for the preceding policy period and estimated values for the next policy period. After receiving the report, the insurer determines the amount of premium it earned during the preceding policy period. If the earned premium is greater than the premium charged, the insurer will bill the insured for the difference. If the earned premium is less than the premium charged, the insurer will refund the difference to the insured, but the refund will not exceed 75 percent of the original premium.

If the Coinsurance condition applies (because the report was not received on time), the insurer will not pay the full amount of any loss if the estimated annual business income value (shown in the insured's latest report of values) is less than the actual annual business income value for the current period (as might be determined in the insurer's investigation of the claim). Instead, the amount of recovery is reduced by the proportion that the estimated value bears to the actual value.

Because the Coinsurance condition does not refer to a coinsurance percentage, the condition operates as a 100 percent coinsurance clause. However, the ISO advisory declarations form contains a blank space for showing a business income coinsurance percentage. If a coinsurance percentage lower than 100 is shown, the percentage would presumably be multiplied by the actual business income value, and the resulting number would be divided into the estimated business income value.

Policy Period, Coverage Territory

The insurer covers loss or damage commencing during the policy period shown in the declarations. The loss or damage must also occur within the coverage territory, which is defined as the United States (including its territories and possessions), Puerto Rico, and Canada.

Premium and Adjustments

An insured that has business income and extra expense coverage must file an annual statement of business income values with the insurer. The Premium and Adjustments condition requires the insured to also report to the insurer annually the total insurable property values at each insured location as of the policy's anniversary date. The insurer uses the reported property values and the rates in effect at the policy renewal date to calculate the premium for the ensuing policy period. The insured must keep the records available to the insurer during the ensuing policy year and for an additional year after that policy period ends.

Suspension

Suspension condition

Condition that allows the insurer to immediately suspend equipment breakdown insurance on an item of equipment that the insurer determines to be in a dangerous condition.

If the insurer or its representative finds that covered equipment is in, or exposed to, a dangerous condition, the **Suspension condition** allows the insurer or any of its representatives to immediately suspend the insurance against loss to that equipment. The insurer can suspend coverage by delivering or mailing a written notice of suspension to the named insured. Once coverage has been suspended, it can be reinstated only by endorsing the policy.

The Suspension condition may seem harsh, but it is reasonable when one considers the dangers posed by poorly maintained or operated equipment. This condition allows a boiler inspector or another representative of the insurer to take action when danger of an accident is imminent. The goal of an inspection is to help detect adverse conditions so that corrective actions—such as replacing a defective pressure relief valve on a steam boiler—can be taken before an accident occurs. See the exhibit "Success Story—A Timely Boiler Inspection Prevents a Loss."

Success Story—A Timely Boiler Inspection Prevents a Loss

During a routine boiler inspection at a middle school, a Hartford Steam Boiler (HSB) inspector found cracks in four cast iron sections. The boiler was less than a year old, one of an identical pair that had been installed to provide hot water for heating. A closer look showed that both boilers had been set up without support rails. The heavy sections were "suspended in air," with nothing supporting their weight, the inspector reported. Similar cracks would almost certainly have developed in the second unit.

The school district was lucky. The inspector discovered the cracks before serious damage and a boiler breakdown had occurred. The sections were repaired and support rails installed properly to prevent further cracks in the two boilers. Since the school had equipment breakdown insurance, the coverage paid for the damage. But the service did not stop there. The HSB inspector provided advice on making repairs and arranged for another inspection to make sure the problems were fixed correctly.

Courtesy of The Hartford Steam Boiler Inspection and Insurance Company, Hartford, Conn. [DA06127]

Joint or Disputed Loss Agreement

When different insurers provide an organization's equipment breakdown insurance and its commercial property insurance, coverage disputes may occur. For example, the insurers may disagree as to whether an explosion was a steam boiler explosion (covered by the equipment breakdown policy) or a combustion explosion (covered by the commercial property policy).

Disputes can also occur when fire breaks out following breakdown to covered equipment. The insurers may disagree about how much of the damage was caused by the accident and how much by the fire. See the exhibit "Fire Resulting From Equipment Breakdown."

If these or other coverage disputes arise, the insured may receive no payment until the insurers settle their differences. The **Joint or Disputed Loss Agreement condition** provides a way for the insured to receive prompt payment. The agreement applies only if the commercial property policy contains a similar provision with substantially the same conditions. Moreover, several other requirements must be met for the insurers to be obligated to adhere to the agreement.

When all the requirements of the condition are met, each insurer will pay the entire amount of loss that each agrees is covered under its own policy plus one-half of the amount in dispute. In this way, the insured is fully paid without having to wait for the insurers to reach agreement on their respective liabilities. After the insured has been compensated, the agreement requires the insurers to settle their differences through arbitration.

Jurisdictional Inspections

Although the ISO form does not contain this condition, many equipment breakdown policies do. A **jurisdictional inspections condition** typically states that if any covered equipment requires inspection to comply with state,

Joint or Disputed Loss Agreement

Condition that addresses claim situations in which the insured's equipment breakdown insurer and the insured's commercial property insurer disagree on which insurer covers a loss; each insurer pays half the loss to quickly indemnify the insured; insurers then resolve their differences.

Jurisdictional inspections condition

A condition in equipment breakdown policies that provides that the insurer will perform required inspections of boilers and other equipment on the insured's behalf.

Fire Resulting From Equipment Breakdown

This transformer fire was caused by the breakdown of a turbine inside the building. The turbine breakdown propelled a turbine blade through the turbine casing and the building wall, ultimately causing the transformer fire. This loss illustrates how a single incident can involve both equipment breakdown insurance and commercial property insurance.

Photo courtesy of The Hartford Steam Boiler Inspection and Insurance Company, Hartford, Conn. [DA03682]

county, or municipal boiler and pressure vessel regulations, the insurer will perform jurisdictional inspections on the insured's behalf. For many insureds, obtaining inspection service is one of their major reasons for purchasing equipment breakdown insurance.

EQUIPMENT BREAKDOWN PROTECTION CASE STUDY

It is important to understand the types of loss exposures related to equipment breakdown and how equipment breakdown insurance, also called boiler and machinery insurance, can assist organizations with these exposures.

It will be necessary to refer to the Equipment Breakdown Protection Coverage Form during the analysis of this case study.

Most organizations have equipment breakdown loss exposures that are commonly excluded under commercial property forms. Equipment breakdown insurance, such as that provided under the Insurance Services Office, Inc.

(ISO) Equipment Breakdown Protection Coverage form, provides a way to insure these exposures.

An analysis of a hypothetical loss scenario provides an opportunity to understand the types of loss exposures organizations face from equipment breakdown and how equipment breakdown insurance can address those exposures. This type of analysis also develops an understanding of how to determine coverage after equipment breaks down.

Case Facts

Garden Goodness is a food-processing company that produces a variety of canned fruits, vegetables, and pasta sauces. The company is insured under a commercial package policy (CPP) that includes the ISO Equipment Breakdown Protection Coverage form (EB 00 02). An explosion of one of the main steam boilers in Garden Goodness's processing plant damages the building and its contents. Two trucks owned and operated by Cross-Country Shipping are also damaged. Cross-Countrys drivers arrived an hour before the shipment they were going to load for transport was ready, and the drivers decided to park the trucks on the road outside the plant and walk to a nearby diner for lunch.

The plant has to shut down immediately after the accident and because it is the height of the summer, the fresh produce on hand spoils quickly, before the insured can arrange to move it to an alternative, refrigerated storage location. In addition, during the period required to repair the damage and return to full operations, the company loses income and incurs additional costs by having to rent temporary office and warehouse space in a neighboring building.

Immediately after the accident, the general manager reports the loss to the company's insurer. The insurer assigns the loss to Gerald, an experienced equipment breakdown loss adjuster. See the exhibit "Garden Goodness Equipment Breakdown Losses."

How would Gerald determine coverage for this hypothetical loss?

Garden Goodness Equipment Breakdown Losses

Loss	Amount
Steam boiler damage	$25,000
Damage to building	$750,000
Damage to building contents (conveyor, labeler, canned goods, office, and office equipment)	$530,000
Produce lost	$20,000
Warehouse and office rent	
Loss of business income	$60,000
$160,000	
Cross-Country's truck damage	$35,000

[DA05989]

Case Analysis Steps

In reviewing the form, Gerald will follow these steps:

- Review the policy declarations to confirm that the loss occurred at an insured location and determine which coverages or insuring agreements have been purchased
- Review the policy's insuring agreements and any related definitions to ascertain whether coverage may apply
- Review the policy exclusions to determine whether any exclusion applies to the company's loss
- Review other applicable policy terms and conditions to ascertain whether any other provisions may limit or preclude coverage

Review the Declarations

By checking the policy declarations, Gerald can ascertain whether the location at which the loss occurred is an insured location under the policy. In this case, the boiler explosion did occur at an insured location listed on the policy declarations. The declarations indicate which of the available coverages Garden Goodness purchased as well as the limits of insurance. The declarations for Garden Goodness list these coverages:

- Property Damage $10,000,000
- Extra Expense Only $1,000,000
- Spoilage Damage $500,000

The combined deductible is $250,000.

Review the Insuring Agreements

The basic insuring agreement indicates that the policy covers losses resulting from "breakdown" of "covered equipment." Because both terms are in quotation marks, Gerald knows that he will need to refer to the policy definitions to determine specifically what each term means. The definition of "breakdown" includes the wording "failure of pressure or vacuum equipment." The definition of "covered equipment" includes the wording "equipment built to operate under internal pressure or vacuum other than weight of contents." Gerald determines that the breakdown of the steam boiler meets the policy definitions.

Gerald next reviews the descriptions of the three coverages purchased by Garden Goodness.

In relation to the Property Damage coverage, the policy states that "covered property" includes any property that "you own" or that "is in your care, custody, or control and for which you are legally liable." The agreement regarding property damage states that the insurer "will pay for direct damage to 'Covered Property' located at the premises described in the Declarations." The damage to Garden Goodness's building and contents is covered based on this insuring agreement and the definitions.

However, the damage to Cross-Country Shipping's trucks would not be covered under this policy because the trucks are not in the care, custody, or control of Garden Goodness. The trucks are in the control of Cross-Country's drivers; at the time of the explosion, they were not located on Garden Goodness's premises and instead were parked on the road outside the premises. (Garden Goodness's CGL policy, however, may provide coverage.)

Regarding the Extra Expense coverage, because Garden Goodness has purchased only the Extra Expense coverage without the Business Income coverage, the company's loss of income during the period required to repair the building and restore its contents would not be covered. However, the additional expense the insured incurs by renting temporary warehouse and office space in the neighboring building would be covered under the Extra Expense coverage.

The fresh produce that spoiled immediately following the accident would be covered under Spoilage Damage. The produce constituted raw material intended for use in the company's products; Garden Goodness owned the produce at the time of the loss, and the loss occurred due to a lack of refrigeration. Although Garden Goodness attempted to find alternative storage for the fruit and vegetables, it was unable to do so quickly enough. Had the company been able to relocate some of the produce quickly, the policy would have covered related expenses to the extent that those expenses reduced the insured's spoilage loss.

Review Policy Exclusions

To make an accurate coverage determination, Gerald knows he must examine the policy exclusions as well as the insuring agreements and their coverage descriptions. A review of the Exclusions section of the policy identifies one that might apply—an exclusion for losses caused directly or indirectly by explosion. However, an exception to the exclusion allows for coverage if the explosion involves specific types of equipment, one of which is a steam boiler. Therefore, this exclusion does not apply to Garden Goodness's loss.

Review Other Policy Terms and Conditions

Gerald finally reviews several other policy terms and conditions to determine whether any would affect the coverage for Garden Goodness's claim. One of the provisions he examines is entitled "Duties in the Event of Loss or Damage." Gerald knows that, even in the case of a covered loss, if an insured fails to fulfill these duties, the insurer is under no obligation to pay the insured's claim.

Garden Goodness did provide prompt notice of the loss, and representatives of the company cooperated with Gerald during the investigation.

The Coinsurance condition does not apply because Garden Goodness submitted its Annual Report of Values Form by the due date.

This solution might not be the only viable solution. Other solutions could be exercised if justified by the analysis. In addition, specific circumstances and organizational needs or goals may enter into the evaluation, making an alternative action a better option. See the exhibit "Coverage Determination for Garden Goodness's Steam Boiler Explosion."

Coverage Determination for Garden Goodness's Steam Boiler Explosion

Loss	Is Loss Covered?	Amount Payable
Damage to building	Yes	$750,000
Damage to steam boiler	Yes	$25,000
Damage to building contents	Yes	$530,000
Total for Covered Property		$1,305,000
Damage to produce	Yes	$20,000
Total for Spoilage Damage		$20,000
Expenses of moving the office and warehouse	Yes, (during the restoration period)	$60,000
Total for Extra Expense		$60,000
Loss of business income	No	$0
Damage to Cross-Country's trucks	No	$0

The damages for covered property, spoilage, and extra expense are under the limits for each of these coverages.

$1,305,000 Covered Property + $20,000 Spoilage + $60,000 Extra Expense = $1,385,000

$1,385,000 Covered Loss − $250,000 deductible = $1,135,000 payable

[DA05990]

SUMMARY

Equipment breakdown insurance, also known as boiler and machinery insurance, covers loss resulting from the accidental breakdown of covered equipment. Covered equipment includes boilers and other pressure vessels; electrical equipment; mechanical equipment; air conditioning and refrigerating equipment; and office equipment such as copiers, fax machines, and computers. All sizes and types of businesses can have equipment breakdown exposures.

The ISO form contains ten insuring agreements. The insuring agreements that apply in a particular policy are indicated by the appropriate entries (such as a limit of insurance or the number of days covered) on the Declarations page.

Policy provisions contained in the Equipment Breakdown Protection Coverage Form include exclusions, limits of insurance, deductibles, and conditions.

Equipment breakdown insurance, also known as boiler and machinery insurance, provides coverage for loss exposures resulting from the accidental breakdown of equipment that is often excluded in other commercial property policy forms.

ASSIGNMENT NOTE

1. The equipment categories and the examples of losses and causes of loss given for each are adapted, with permission, from *Whistle Stop*, a publication of The Hartford Steam Boiler Inspection and Insurance Company, Hartford, Conn.

Direct Your Learning ▶▶

Businessowners Policies

Educational Objectives

After learning the content of this assignment, you should be able to:

▷ Describe the typical businessowners policy (BOP) in terms of these elements:

- The categories of loss exposures that can be covered by a BOP
- The advantages of the BOP to insurers, producers, and insureds
- Why BOP eligibility rules are necessary
- How the BOP is rated

▷ Summarize the property coverage provisions of the ISO businessowners policy and how they differ from comparable provisions in the ISO commercial package policy program.

▷ Summarize the liability coverage provisions of the ISO BOP and how they differ from comparable provisions in the commercial package policy program.

▷ Given a case describing a businessowners claim, explain whether the Businessowners Coverage Form would cover the claim.

▶▶

Businessowners Policies

OVERVIEW OF THE BUSINESSOWNERS POLICY

The businessowners policy (BOP) is widely used to insure eligible small to mid-size businesses against most of their property and liability loss exposures.

Both Insurance Services Office, Inc. (ISO) and the American Association of Insurance Services (AAIS) have developed businessowners programs for use by their member insurers. In addition, many insurers use their own independently developed BOP forms. This discussion examines these characteristics shared by most BOPs:

- Loss exposures covered by the BOP
- Advantages of the BOP
- The need for BOP eligibility rules
- Rating the BOP

Loss Exposures Covered by the BOP

BOPs usually cover most of the property and liability loss exposures that can be insured under the various ISO commercial package policy coverage parts. Most BOPs cover these common exposures:

- Buildings
- Business personal property
- Personal property of others
- Business income and extra expense
- Premises and operations liability
- Products and completed operations liability
- Contractual liability
- Personal and advertising injury liability
- Employee dishonesty
- Theft of money and securities
- Forgery and alteration
- Equipment breakdown

The BOP does not provide commercial auto coverage for owned autos. However, hired and nonowned auto coverage, as well as a variety of other coverages, can be added to the BOP by endorsement.

Advantages of the BOP

The manner in which the BOP packages basic coverages and uses simplified rating procedures is similar to that of a homeowners policy and offers advantages to the insurer, the producer, and the insured. Packaging several coverages reduces **adverse selection** and, combined with simplified rating, lowers handling costs for insurers.

Adverse selection

In general, the tendency for people with the greatest probability of loss to be the ones most likely to purchase insurance.

Underwriting and processing policies through an automated system rather than through individual underwriting also reduces costs for insurers. The resulting lower premiums and broader coverage enable an insurer and its producers to compete effectively with other insurers and producers. Producers also benefit from the simplified rating procedures when quoting coverage. Insureds gain the convenience and economy of having one policy that meets most of their property and liability insurance needs.

The Need for BOP Eligibility Rules

Every insurer that writes BOPs has eligibility rules limiting its program to applicants for which the BOP approach is designed. These rules are needed because the rating structure of all BOPs contemplates a relatively homogeneous group of small to mid-size insureds. Writing BOP coverage for insureds that do not fall within this group can create a mismatch of premium and exposure.

BOP eligibility rules are based on criteria that relate to business size and complexity of loss exposures. Examples of these criteria are total floor area, building height in stories, annual gross sales, occupancy or business type, and characteristics of the applicant's operations.

Since the first BOP was written in the 1960s, insurers have continually expanded their eligibility rules to remain competitive and to increase or maintain market share. For example, BOP eligibility rules once excluded restaurants and contractors. Most insurers now write BOPs for both, subject to certain size and hazard restrictions required to maintain rating integrity.

Under ISO *Commercial Lines Manual* rules for the BOP, eligible risks, generally, may not exceed 35,000 square feet in total floor area or $6 million in annual gross sales at each location. Furthermore, certain types of businesses are not eligible for the ISO Businessowners Program. Examples of ineligible businesses are automobile-related businesses, bars, financial institutions, general contractors, and buildings occupied in whole or in part for manufacturing.

Insurers that have developed their own businessowners programs may have eligibility rules that are either broader or stricter than ISO's. Because of the variation in businessowners eligibility rules and their ongoing expansion, such rules are not discussed in further detail here.

Rating the BOP

Rating a BOP is much less complicated than rating comparable coverages in a commercial package policy. BOP property coverage is rated based on the amounts of coverage provided for building and personal property. BOP property rates include loadings (built-in charges) for business income and any additional coverages that are automatically included. As a result, the rates do not have to be computed separately for each of those coverages.

The ISO BOP requires separate liability rating for all classes of business. However, in calculating the BOP liability premiums for most classifications, the liability rate is applied to the property insurance amount rather than to a rating basis such as that used to rate commercial general liability (CGL) coverage. For example, under the ISO BOP, the liability premium for an apartment building is based on the amount of building insurance; under the CGL coverage form, the number of apartment units determines the rate. The AAIS BOP program and most independent insurers use separate liability rating only for certain classes of business.

Most insurers that write BOPs for eligible contractors rate the liability coverage apart from the property coverages by applying a separate liability rate to the insured's payroll, receipts, or number of full- and part-time employees.

Typically, the BOP rater or processor enters some basic data into a computer application, which automatically calculates the premium. BOP rating incorporates these variables:

- Territory. (For example, tornadoes are more frequent in the Midwestern United States; theft losses are higher in metropolitan areas; and so forth.)
- Type of construction. (For example, frame, joisted masonry, or fire resistive.)
- Public fire protection.
- Occupancy of the building.
- Presence of sprinklers.
- Deductible. (The standard deductible for most insurers is $250 or $500 per loss. The deductible can be increased or decreased, with a corresponding premium adjustment.)

If the insured wants increased limits for liability insurance, the rates are increased by appropriate factors. If the insured has purchased optional coverages, the policy premium is increased either by adding a premium charge for each optional coverage requested or by applying an increased rate factor to the insured values.

ISO BUSINESSOWNERS PROGRAM: PROPERTY COVERAGE

In most respects, businessowners property coverages are similar or identical to those found in the commercial package policy program. However, to properly advise insureds, an insurance professional should be aware of several differences between them.

Insurance Services Office, Inc. (ISO) introduced its standardized Businessowners Program in 1976 and has revised it several times. An ISO businessowners policy (BOP) consists of the Businessowners Policy Declarations (BP DS 01), the Businessowners Coverage Form (BP 00 03), and applicable endorsements. The Businessowners Coverage Form contains three major sections of policy provisions: Section I—Property, Section II—Liability, and Section III—Common Policy Conditions.

How the ISO BOP differs from comparable forms used in the ISO commercial package policy (CPP) program is discussed in connection with covered property, property not covered, covered causes of loss, additional coverages, coverage extensions, limits of insurance, deductibles, loss conditions, optional coverages, and endorsements.

Covered Property

The description of covered property in the BOP differs from that in the Building and Personal Property Coverage Form (BPP) in two ways:

- The BOP description of building property includes the named insured's personal property in apartments or rooms furnished by the named insured as landlord. Such property is not included under building coverage in the BPP. Therefore, for example, an apartment building owner with no personal property to insure other than apartment furnishings can cover both the building and the apartment furnishings under the BOP for a single amount of building insurance. Under the BPP, a landlord that wants to insure his or her personal property in furnished apartments must purchase a limit of coverage for Your Business Personal Property. The BOP description of building property also includes the landlord's property in common areas. The BPP does not refer to such furnishings, but they may be considered covered as property used to maintain or service the building under the BPP's building definition.
- The BOP covers personal property of others in the insured's care, custody, or control under the same limit that applies to personal property owned by the named insured. In contrast, the BPP divides coverage for personal property into two sections: (1) Your Business Personal Property and (2) Personal Property of Others.

If a BOP written for a tenant shows no limit of insurance for building property, the business personal property definition includes exterior building glass owned by the tenant or in the tenant's care, custody, or control. This definition closes a gap under the BPP when a tenant that has not purchased building coverage is responsible for damage to building glass under the terms of its lease.

Property Not Covered

The BOP's Property Not Covered section is shorter than the corresponding section in the BPP. As a result, in a given situation an insured could have significant additional coverage under the BOP.

For example, excavations, foundations, and underground pipes and flues, which are susceptible to damage by many insured perils, are covered by the BOP but excluded by the BPP unless it has been endorsed to cover those items. However, the value of this property, because it is not excluded, should be included in the determination of whether the insured has met the insurance-to-value provision of the ISO BOP. (See Businessowners Coverage Form Section I—Property, E. Property Loss Conditions, 5. Loss Payment.)

Covered Causes of Loss

The BOP uses the same approach as the Causes of Loss—Special Form. Named perils coverage can be substituted by endorsement. The named perils are equivalent to those covered by the Causes of Loss—Basic Form, plus additional perils applicable to covered property in transit.

Important differences between the BOP and the Causes of Loss—Special Form concern coverage for computers. Smaller firms may not have sufficient exposure to warrant purchasing a separate electronic data processing (EDP) equipment policy. The BOP provides broader coverage than the BPP and the Causes of Loss—Special Form for computers and electronic data and media. The BOP provides this coverage through exceptions to policy exclusions:

- The Power Failure exclusion does not apply to loss or damage to computers and electronic data.
- The Electrical Apparatus exclusion states that the insurer will pay for loss or damage to computers resulting from artificially generated electrical current if the loss or damage is caused by or results from (1) an occurrence taking place within 100 feet of the described premises or (2) interruption of electricity, power surge, blackout, or brownout if the cause of the occurrence takes place within 100 feet of the premises.
- The exclusion of mechanical breakdown does not apply to the breakdown of computers.

However, the BOP contains several additional exclusions applicable to computers and electronic data, which eliminate coverage for these losses:

- Errors or omissions in programming, processing, or storing data or processing or copying valuable papers and records
- Errors or deficiencies in design, installation, testing, or repair of computer systems
- Electrical or magnetic injury, disturbance, or erasure of electronic data, except as provided for under the additional coverages

In addition, the BOP does not contain these exclusions or limitations found in the Causes of Loss—Special Form:

- The exclusion of theft of building materials and supplies not attached as part of the building or structure
- The exclusion of business income or extra expense losses arising from loss or damage to antennas or satellite dishes
- The limitation of coverage for loss of animals to specified perils and only if the animals are killed or their destruction is necessary

Additional Coverages

The exhibit lists all the BOP's additional coverages and compares them with the comparable coverages in ISO commercial property forms such as the BPP, the Causes of Loss—Special Form, and the Business Income (and Extra Expense) Coverage Form. This section also discusses several of the BOP's additional coverages and, where relevant, how they differ with comparable coverages. See the exhibit "Additional Coverages in the ISO Businessowners Coverage Form."

Additional Coverages in the ISO Businessowners Coverage Form

Additional Coverage in BOP	Description
Debris Removal	Same as in BPP
Preservation of Property	Same as in BPP
Fire Department Service Charge	$2,500 limit in BOP and $1,000 limin in BPP
Collapse	Similar to collapse coverage in Causes of Loss—Special Form
Water Damage, Other Liquids, Powder, or Molten Materials Damage	Same as in Causes of Loss—Special Form
Limited Coverage for Fungi, Wet Rot, Dry Rot and Bacteria	Same as in Causes of Loss—Special Form
Business Income (Including Extended Business Income)	Similar to ISO business income forms except that a one-year limit applies instead of a specific dollar limit
Extra Expense	Similar to extra expense coverage in Business Income (and Extra Expense) Coverage Form
Pollutant Clean Up and Removal	Same as in BPP
Civil Authority	Same as in ISO business income forms
Business Income From Dependent Properties	Similar to endorsements to ISO business income forms
Money Orders and Counterfeit Money	Similar to coverage in ISO commercial crime program
Forgery or Alteration	Similar to coverage in ISO commercial crime program
Increased Cost of Construction	Same as in BPP
Glass Expenses	Unique to BOP
Fire Extinguisher Recharge Expense	Unique to BOP
Electronic Data	Similar to additional coverage in BPP except broader perils and higher limit apply to BOP version
Interruption of Computer Operations	Similar to additional coverage in Causes of Loss—Special Form
Limited Coverage for "Fungi", Wet Rot or Dry Rot	Similar to additional coverage in Causes of Loss—Special Form

Business Income and Extra Expense: Key Differences

The Business Income and Extra Expense additional coverages in the BOP differ from the separate ISO business income and extra expense forms in three ways that can be significant for many insureds:

- The BOP coverages are subject to a *one-year limit* instead of the dollar limits in other forms. The Business Income additional coverage insures actual loss of business income sustained during the period of restoration, and the Extra Expense additional coverage insures necessary extra expense incurred during the period of restoration. However, under both coverages, the insurer will pay only for losses or expenses that occur within the twelve consecutive months after the date of direct physical loss or damage. Most small businesses can restore damaged property in less than a year; a one-year limitation seldom poses a problem for the insured. Because of the possibility of having to pay a large business income loss under a BOP that generates little premium, some insurers impose a specific dollar limit on business income and extra expense coverage in their BOPs.

- The BOP coverages are not subject to coinsurance; therefore, coverage is simplified and any possibility of a coinsurance penalty is eliminated. Coinsurance can be omitted from the regular ISO business income and extra expense forms, but the techniques for omitting coinsurance complicate the coverage and impose restrictions not found in the BOP.

- The BOP coverages limit ordinary payroll coverage to sixty days following the date of the physical loss unless a greater number of days is shown in the declarations. The regular ISO business income forms impose no restriction on coverage of payroll expense unless an endorsement eliminating ordinary payroll or limiting it to 90 or 180 days is added to the policy.

Business Income and Extra Expense: Waiting Period

As in the ISO business income forms, the period of restoration in the BOP begins seventy-two hours after the physical damage occurs. This waiting period may be eliminated from a BOP by endorsement. The ISO *Commercial Lines Manual* (CLM) calls for a 1 percent increase in the building and personal property coverage premiums to make this change. Most small businesses would probably prefer to have the waiting period eliminated. Even a short interruption can be critical to a small business.

The BOP's additional coverage for business income also includes Extended Business Income (EBI), which covers business income loss for sixty additional days after the damaged property is restored and operations are resumed. It is the same as the EBI additional coverage in ISO's business income forms except that the sixty-day time limit can be increased by an entry in the

BOP declarations, eliminating the need for a separate Extended Period of Indemnity option.

Other Additional Coverages

The BOP contains other additional coverages that differ from comparable coverages, including these:

- Business Income From Dependent Properties—This additional coverage insures the actual loss of business income resulting from damage at the premises of a dependent property caused by any covered cause of loss up to $5,000, or a higher limit shown in the declarations. The types of dependent properties and the applicable conditions are similar to those of the dependent properties endorsements available in the commercial package policy (CPP) program.

- Money Orders and Counterfeit Money—This additional coverage is comparable to the Money Orders and Counterfeit Money insuring agreement in the ISO commercial crime program. However, the additional coverage is subject to a $1,000 limit that cannot be increased under CLM rules.

- Forgery or Alteration—This additional coverage is similar to the Forgery or Alteration insuring agreement in the ISO commercial crime program. The additional coverage is subject to a $2,500 limit that may be increased for an additional premium.

- Glass Expenses—This additional coverage pays the cost to install temporary plates or to board up openings if repair or replacement is delayed. Although the BPP does not specifically provide such coverage, the same expenses would, in most cases, be payable in accordance with policy provisions requiring the insured to protect covered property from further loss.

- Fire Extinguisher Systems Recharge Expense—This additional coverage pays up to $5,000 per occurrence to cover the cost of recharging or replacing (whichever is less) the insured's fire extinguishers and fire extinguisher systems if they are discharged on or within 100 feet of the insured premises. The coverage includes hydrostatic testing, if necessary.

- Electronic Data—This additional coverage is similar to one in the BPP but differs in two significant ways. First, the businessowners version covers a broader range of perils because it is not restricted to specified causes of loss. Second, it has an aggregate limit of $10,000 (or a higher limit shown in the declarations), rather than $2,500 as in the BPP.

- Interruption of Computer Operations—This additional coverage is similar to one in the ISO business income forms, except that the businessowners version has an aggregate limit of $10,000 (or a higher limit shown in the declarations), rather than $2,500 in the business income forms.

Coverage Extensions

The BOP contains seven coverage extensions. The BOP does not include the BPP extension for non-owned detached trailers. See the exhibit "Coverage Extensions in the ISO Businessowners Coverage Form."

Coverage Extensions in the ISO Businessowners Coverage Form

Coverage Extension in BOP	Description
Newly Acquired or Constructed Property	Essentially the same as in BPP
Personal Property Off Premises	Similar to Property Off-Premises extension in BPP
Outdoor Property	Same as Outdoor Property extension in BPP except that BOP provides higher limits
Personal Effects	Same as Personal Effects part of the Personal Effects and Property of Others extension in BPP
Valuable Papers and Records	Provides broader perils and higher limits than the Valuable Papers and Records extension in BPP
Accounts Receivable	No equivalent extension in BPP
Business Personal Property Temporarily in Portable Storage Units	Same as in BPP

Includes copyrighted material of Insurance Services Office, Inc., used with its permission. Copyright, Insurance Services Office, Inc., 2012. [DA03691]

A comparison of the BOP coverage extensions and those of the BPP reveals similarities and differences:

- Newly Acquired or Constructed Property—Like the BPP, the BOP covers, for up to thirty days, newly constructed or acquired buildings (up to $250,000) and newly acquired business personal property or business personal property in a newly constructed or acquired building (up to $100,000).

- Personal Property Off Premises—The Personal Property Off Premises extension in the BOP has the same $10,000 limit as the comparable extension in the BPP. The BOP extension is broader than the BPP version in that it includes coverage for property while it is in the course of transit.

- Outdoor Property—The BOP Outdoor Property extension is the same as its counterpart in the BPP except that the limit for outdoor property in the businessowners policy is $2,500, subject to a sublimit of $500 for any one tree, shrub, or plant. The comparable limits in the BPP are $1,000 and $250.

- Personal Effects—The limit for personal effects is $2,500 in both forms, but in the BPP, personal effects and property of others are combined in a single extension, and the $2,500 limit applies to the combination of both types of loss in a single occurrence. The businessowners policy has no extension for property of others because it includes personal property of others under its definition of covered business personal property.

- Valuable Papers and Records—The BOP Valuable Papers and Records extension provides broader coverage than the comparable extension in the BPP, in two basic ways. First, the BPP extension is limited to "specified causes of loss," while the BOP extension broadens the scope of Special Form coverage by specifying that only seven of the property exclusions apply to valuable papers and records. Second, the BOP extension has limits of $10,000 on premises and $5,000 off premises, whereas the BPP has a $2,500 limit.

- Accounts Receivable—The Accounts Receivable extension in the BOP is similar to the coverage provided by the ISO Accounts Receivable Coverage Form. Under the BOP, accounts receivable coverage for loss or damage at the described premises is limited to $10,000 unless a higher amount is shown in the declarations, and off-premises coverage is limited to $5,000.

Limits of Insurance

The Limits of Insurance provisions that apply to the BOP's property section differ from those of the BPP in two ways:

- The BOP automatically includes a provision titled Building Limit—Automatic Increase. The BPP contains a comparable Inflation Guard provision, but it is optional.

- The BOP includes a provision titled Business Personal Property Limit—Seasonal Increase, which has no counterpart in the BPP.

The Building Limit—Automatic Increase provision increases the stated limit for buildings by an annual percentage shown in the declarations. The annual percentage is applied on a pro rata basis throughout the policy year.

The **seasonal increase provision** automatically increases the business personal property limit to cover increases in inventory values. The limit for business personal property is automatically increased by 25 percent (or another percentage if shown in the declarations), but only if the limit for personal property is 100 percent or more of the insured's average monthly personal property value for the twelve months preceding the date of loss.

Although this provision can be helpful in covering moderate seasonal increases, an insured that carries an amount of insurance equal to the average

Seasonal increase provision

A provision commonly included in businessowners policies that addresses fluctuating personal property values by automatically increasing the amount of insurance.

value for the preceding twelve months still may not have adequate coverage for peak periods.

For example, the value of personal property in Grandma's Gift Shop for January through October was $100,000 each month, rising to $150,000 in November and to $200,000 in December as more inventory was added for the busy holiday season. The average monthly value for the year was $112,500. If Grandma's Gift Shop carried a business personal property limit of $112,500, a loss up to 25 percent greater than the policy limit (or, in this case, $140,625) would be paid in full, but that would not be sufficient to cover a total loss in November or December. Alternatively, Grandma's Gift Shop could have its personal property limit increased by endorsement in November and December and reduced in January.

Deductibles

Under CLM rules, a basic deductible of $500 applies to all BOP property coverages other than Business Income, Extra Expense, Civil Authority, Fire Extinguisher Systems Recharge Expense, and Fire Department Service Charge. Optional deductibles are available. No deductible applies to the five additional coverages just listed.

Windstorm or hail percentage deductibles equal to 1 percent, 2 percent, or 5 percent of the amount of insurance are also available. These deductible options are most likely to be used in areas subject to frequent or severe windstorm or hail losses.

Property Loss Conditions

The property loss conditions of the BOP are comparable in most respects to the loss conditions of the BPP. The major differences concern the Loss Payment condition, which provides for replacement cost valuation if the insured carries insurance equal to at least 80 percent of the insured property's replacement value.

The BOP covers buildings and personal property on a replacement cost basis. As in the BPP replacement cost option, certain types of property are covered only on an actual cash value (ACV) basis. In the BOP, these types of property are used or secondhand merchandise and most types of household contents.

If, because of a written contract, the insured is liable for loss or damage to an item of personal property of others, the valuation will be based on the amount for which the insured is liable under the contract, not to exceed the lesser of the property's replacement cost or the applicable limit of insurance.

Underwriters sometimes require ACV to make a given property eligible for a BOP. Insureds have no incentive to choose ACV, because they would collect at least ACV even if they did not meet the insurance-to-value requirement.

The BOP does not have a Coinsurance condition like the BPP but instead has an insurance-to-value requirement that resembles that found in many homeowners policies. Although less stringent than coinsurance, it encourages insureds to insure to at least 80 percent of the covered property's value. No agreed value option is available with the BOP, but the insurance-to-value requirement can be eliminated by endorsement.

The insurance-to-value requirement differs from the BPP Coinsurance condition in several ways, including these examples:

- It applies only to replacement cost, not also to ACV coverage.
- It does not apply if the insured elects an ACV settlement.

For full replacement cost coverage to apply under the BOP, the amount of insurance at the time of the loss must equal at least 80 percent of the full replacement cost of the covered property immediately before the loss. If the amount of insurance is less than 80 percent of the full replacement cost, the insurer will pay the greater of two amounts, not to exceed the limit of insurance:

- The ACV of the lost or damaged property.
- A proportion of the cost to repair or replace, after applying the deductible but without a deduction for depreciation.[1] The proportion is the applicable limit of insurance divided by 80 percent of the property's replacement cost.

Optional Coverages

The BOP includes provisions for four optional coverages: Outdoor Signs, Money and Securities, Employee Dishonesty, and Mechanical Breakdown. These coverages are put into effect by appropriate entries in the declarations.

The BOP covers outdoor signs, but with important limitations. Outdoor signs attached to buildings are insured against all covered causes of loss under the policy but only up to $1,000 per sign in any one occurrence. Outdoor signs that are not attached to buildings, although they are listed as Property Not Covered, are covered for up to $2,500 per occurrence under the Outdoor Property extension but are covered only against fire, lightning, explosion, riot, civil commotion, or aircraft.

The Outdoor Signs optional coverage allows an insured to purchase a higher amount of insurance on outdoor signs located at the described premises and owned by or in the care, custody, or control of the insured. The insurance applies on a Special Form basis.

The Money and Securities optional coverage insures money and securities used in the named insured's business against theft, disappearance, or destruction. The money and securities are covered while at the described premises, at a bank or savings institution, within the living quarters of the named insured or any partner or of any employee having care and custody of the property, or in transit between any of these places. This optional coverage applies only to money and securities because the BOP covers theft of property other than money and securities.

Under the Employee Dishonesty optional coverage, the insured is covered for direct loss of or damage to business personal property, including money and securities, that results from dishonest acts of any of the insured's employees, whether acting alone or in collusion with others (except the named insured or the named insured's partners). Under CLM rules, various limits are available.

The Mechanical Breakdown optional coverage insures direct damage to covered property (building and business personal property) caused by a mechanical breakdown or electrical failure to pressure, mechanical, or electrical machinery or equipment, including computers used to operate production machinery. Because the optional breakdown coverage omits the BOP exclusions relating to electrical apparatus, mechanical breakdown, and steam apparatus, these perils are covered causes of loss that also trigger the BOP's additional coverages for business income and extra expense.

Businessowners Property Endorsements

The original businessowners policies offered few optional endorsements. Requests from insureds, as well as competitive pressures from insurers that use independently developed businessowners programs have led ISO to broaden program eligibility and coverages. Broadened eligibility has generated the need for additional endorsements to tailor the policy to newly eligible businesses; also, demand for an increased number of coverages has required more endorsements. See the exhibit "Selected Businessowners Property Coverage Endorsements."

Insurers that use independently developed businessowners programs have been credited for causing ISO to broaden its BOP program's eligibility and coverages. However, some independently developed businessowners programs have both broader and more restrictive coverages than ISO's BOP. See the exhibit "Examples of Broader and More Restrictive Coverage in Independently Developed Businessowners Programs."

Selected Businessowners Property Coverage Endorsements

- Spoilage Coverage (BP 04 15)
- Food Contamination (BP 04 31)
- Water Back-up and Sump Overflow (BP 04 53)
- Utility Services—Direct Damage (BP 04 56)
- Utility Services—Time Element (BP 04 57)
- Computer Fraud and Funds Transfer Fraud (BP 05 47)
- Electronic Commerce (E-Commerce) (BP 05 94)
- Contractors' Installation, Tools and Equipment Coverage (BP 07 01)
- Earthquake (BP 10 03)
- Condominium Association Coverage (BP 17 01)
- Condominium Commercial Unit-Owners Coverage (BP 17 02)

[DA03692]

Examples of Broader and More Restrictive Coverage in Independently Developed Businessowners Programs

Broader Coverage	More Restrictive Coverage
• No coinsurance or insurance-to-value provision	• Limits business income coverage to specific dollar limit
• Automatically includes coverage for employee dishonesty and money and securities	• Provides no coverage if building is vacant for over 60 days
• Covers flood losses, including property in transit	• Limits extra expense coverage to the amount business income loss is reduced
• Covers cost of preparing a proof of loss	• Does not provide for seasonal increase

[DA06069]

ISO BUSINESSOWNERS PROGRAM: LIABILITY COVERAGE

Section II—Liability of the Businessowners Coverage Form (BCF), commonly referred to as the ISO BOP, is similar in most ways to the occurrence version of the ISO Commercial General Liability (CGL) Coverage Form. This section of the policy contains two insuring agreements:

- Business Liability, which provides the equivalent of Coverage A—Bodily Injury and Property Damage Liability and Coverage B—Personal and Advertising Injury Liability of the CGL coverage form
- Medical Expenses, which provides the equivalent of Coverage C—Medical Payments of the CGL coverage form.

Businessowners liability coverage and CGL coverage differ in several ways, mostly minor.

Limits of Insurance

The businessowners policy (BOP), like the CGL, has two aggregate limits, which apply in the same manner as the General Aggregate Limit and Products—Completed Operations Aggregate Limit of the CGL. The Products-Completed Operations Aggregate Limit in the BOP may be increased to three times the Liability and Medical Expenses Limit by endorsement. In contrast, the CGL's aggregate limits can be set at various multiples of the each occurrence limit.

The BOP's Liability and Medical Expense Limit is the most the insurer will pay for the sum of all damages because of all bodily injury, property damage, and medical expenses arising out of any one occurrence; and all personal or advertising injury sustained by any one person or organization. The Liability and Medical Expense Limit is thus equivalent to both the Each Occurrence Limit and the Personal and Advertising Injury Limit of the CGL.

The BOP's liability section, like the CGL, is also subject to a Damage to Premises Rented to You Limit and a per person Medical Expenses Limit.

Professional Services Exclusion

Businessowners liability coverage is subject to an exclusion eliminating coverage for bodily injury, property damage, or personal and advertising injury resulting from the rendering of, or failure to render, any professional service. The CGL form does not contain a similar exclusion, but when a CGL policy is issued to a provider of professional services, the *Commercial Lines Manual (CLM)* requires that a professional services exclusion be added to the policy.

Several optional professional liability coverage endorsements are available for use with businessowners liability coverage. Examples of such endorsements are those for barbers, beauticians, veterinarians, funeral directors, optical and hearing aid establishments, and printers. These endorsements do not have ISO CGL counterparts. A number of insurers offer similar coverage as part of independently developed CGL forms or as standalone professional liability or errors and omissions liability policies.

Hired and Nonowned Auto Liability Coverage

Almost every business, at some time or another, has an exposure to liability for hired or nonowned autos. Just having an employee drop off the mail at the post office on the way home may impose vicarious liability on the employer if the employee is involved in an accident while running the errand.

A businessowners insured that does not have separate commercial auto coverage can obtain hired and nonowned auto liability coverage by endorsement to its BOP. This is a major advantage for small businesses. If they do not own any autos, they often overlook the need for, or cannot obtain, a separate policy covering hired and nonowned auto liability.

The Hired Auto and NonOwned Auto Liability endorsement (BP 04 04) provides coverage like that provided by symbols 8 and 9 of the Business Auto Coverage Form. In addition to covering the named insured for hired or nonowned autos, the endorsement includes the named insured's employees, partners, or executive officers as insureds for the use of hired or nonowned autos in the named insured's business.

Other Liability Options

To meet the needs of certain business classifications now eligible for a BOP, the ISO program offers various liability coverage options by endorsement. Examples of such options are coverage of self-storage facilities' liability for customers' goods, coverage of motels' liability for guests' property, and liquor liability coverage. The ISO program also includes endorsements for liability coverages that almost any type of business might want to buy, such as pollution liability, employment-related practices liability, and employee benefits liability.

BUSINESSOWNERS COVERAGE FORM CASE STUDY

The Businessowners Coverage Form (BCF) is designed to meet the insurance needs of small and mid-sized businesses. It provides broad coverage in a package format at a reasonable price.

This case will help you learn how to apply the Businessowners Coverage Form (BCF) to a claim.

Case Facts

Given the facts of this case, will the loss be covered under the BCF? If so, will all the items claimed be covered? What amounts will be paid? Are there any coverage limitations that apply?

Diane is the owner of Sweet Peggie's Home Décor, a retail store specializing in home decorating items. The store sells lamps, small tables, vases, picture frames, and other similar household items. It also sells a small amount of second-hand items, mostly unique watering cans and gardening items that Diane finds at flea markets. She leases 1,500 square feet in a one-story shopping center containing a total of six retail stores and a restaurant. The store space is primarily used for the display of merchandise and contains a small office and stock room in the rear.

On October 4, an electrical fire started overnight in an adjoining store. The fire spread to Diane's store, causing considerable damage. She had just completed a display of new fall items, including a line of popular collectibles. In addition, several shipments of holiday items were in storage in the stock room awaiting display. The sign attached to the building over the front door was also damaged because of the fire.

Diane's agent assisted her in promptly notifying the insurer of the loss and in determining what property was damaged and the values for the damaged property. See the exhibit "Damage Estimate."

Sweet Peggie's Home Décor is covered under a Businessowners Coverage Form. Diane's agent had recommended this approach and determined that, based on the square footage and annual sales amounts, the business was eligible for this program. This package policy provides all the coverages that Diane requires at a reasonable premium compared with a commercial package policy. See the exhibit "Coverage Facts."

Case Analysis Tools

In this case, a claim representative named Fred will determine if this fire loss is covered under the BCF. Fred will need to review the information on the declarations page, which identifies who is covered, which locations are covered, the policy period, coverage limits, any coverage options that apply, and any applicable limits for additional coverage.

Fred will also need a copy of the BCF and any applicable endorsements. Section I of the BCF describes the types of property that are and are not covered, the covered causes of loss, any coverage extensions or limitations that may apply, and how losses will be valued.

Damage Estimate

Item	Description	Amount
Personal property	Damage to new merchandise on display and in storage	$112,000
Computer equipment in office	Fire and water damage to computer and printer in office area	$3,500
Second-hand items of personal property	Damage to secondhand items held for sale	$2,800
Outdoor sign	Smoke and water damage to wooden sign attached to the building over front door	$850
Loss of business income	The store was closed for 50 days while repairs were completed. Includes $2,800 in ordinary payroll.	$17,000
Exterior glass	The large front window (4' by 8') was shattered and required temporary boarding up immediately after the fire as well as replacement.	$500
Total		$136,650

[DA06053]

Coverage Facts

Policy form	Businessowners Coverage Form
Policy period	07-01-20x0 to 07-01-20x1
Insured	Diane Smith d/b/a Sweet Peggie's Home Décor
Business Personal Property Limit	$100,000. Replacement cost
Deductible	$500
Endorsements	None
Occupancy	Retail sales of home accessories including office and stock room
	1,500 square feet of leased space within a 12,500 square-foot strip shopping center with seven attached retail occupancies

[DA06054]

Determination of Coverage

To determine if the BCF covers this fire loss, Fred will first examine the declarations page. This declarations page shows Diane as the insured and lists the location of the shopping center as the insured location. The date of loss falls within the policy period. Diane has complied with all the terms and conditions stated in the BCF.

Fred must then determine if fire is a covered cause of loss under the BCF. Because the BCF covers on a special form basis and there are no exclusions for fire, this is a covered cause of loss.

The next step is to examine the list of damages and the "Covered Property" and "Property Not Covered" paragraphs of the BCF. Based on this review, it is determined that the new merchandise in the store, any fixtures or displays installed by Diane that are part of the building, the second-hand merchandise, and the front exterior show window are covered under the policy as Business Personal Property.

> BCF, SECTION I - Property
>
> b. Business Personal Property located in or on the buildings or structures at the described premises or in the open (or in a vehicle) within 100 feet of the buildings or structures or within 100 feet of the premises described in the Declarations, whichever distance is greater, including:
>
> (1) Property you own that is used in your business;
>
> (2) Property of others that is in your care, custody or control, except as otherwise provided in Loss Payment Property Loss Condition Paragraph E.5.d.(3)(b);
>
> (3) Tenant's improvements and betterments. Improvements and betterments are fixtures, alterations, installations or additions:
>
> (a) Made a part of the building or structure you occupy but do not own; and
>
> (b) You acquired or made at your expense but cannot legally remove;
>
> (4) Leased personal property which you have a contractual responsibility to insure, unless otherwise provided for under Paragraph 1.b.(2); and
>
> (5) Exterior building glass, if you are a tenant and no Limit Of Insurance is shown in the Declarations for Building property. The glass must be owned by you or in your care, custody or control. [2]

The computer and printer would also be covered as Business Personal Property that is owned by Diane and used in her business. She has not submitted a claim for any lost electronic data, as she frequently backs up the data and keeps discs of all stored data in a safe deposit box at a local bank.

The sign would also be covered under the BCF based on the Property Not Covered provision, Item e. This item excludes most outdoor property, but indicates that "signs attached to the building" are considered an exception to the Property Not Covered provision and are, therefore, covered.

BCF, SECTION I - Property

e. Outdoor fences, radio or television antennas (including satellite dishes) and their lead-in wiring, masts or towers, signs (other than signs attached to buildings), trees, shrubs or plants (other than trees, shrubs or plants which are part of a vegetated roof), all except as provided in the:

(1) Outdoor Property Coverage Extension; or

(2) Outdoor Signs Optional Coverage;[3]

Business income is covered under A. Coverage, Section 5 Additional Coverages, Item f—Business Income in the BCF. Business Income coverage also includes ordinary payroll expenses for up to sixty days. Diane is seeking ordinary payroll coverage for one full-time employee who assists her in operating the store. Fred determines that this employee's salary qualified as ordinary payroll and is therefore includable in the covered business income loss along with other continuing operating expenses.

Determination of Amounts Payable

Having completed the policy analysis for coverage, Fred now determines the amounts payable under the policy. This will require a review of Section 1, C.—Limits of Insurance in the BCF, which indicates that the most the insurer will pay is the applicable limits of insurance under the policy. Fred has established that Diane has met the insurance-to-value provisions of the BCF and the loss will be paid on a replacement cost basis for the new merchandise. The second-hand items will be paid on an actual cash value (ACV) basis (see BCF, Section E, Item 5.d.3.a) with a 50 percent depreciation percentage.

Diane is listing total damages of $112, 000 for merchandise on display and in storage, which exceeds the policy limit of $100,000. A further review of the policy identifies Business Personal Property Limit—Seasonal Increase.

BCF, SECTION I - Property

5. Business Personal Property Limit – Seasonal Increase

a. Subject to Paragraph 5.b., the Limit of Insurance for Business Personal Property is automatically increased by:

(1) The Business Personal Property — Seasonal Increase percentage shown in the Declarations; or

(2) 25% if no Business Personal Property — Seasonal Increase percentage is shown in the Declarations;

to provide for seasonal variances.

b. The increase described in Paragraph 5.a. will apply only if the Limit Of Insurance shown for Business Personal Property in the Declarations is at least 100% of your average monthly values during the lesser of:

(1) The 12 months immediately preceding the date the loss or damage occurs; or

2. The period of time you have been in business as of the date the loss or damage occurs.[4]

This coverage provision automatically increases the business personal property limit to cover increases in inventory values as long as the conditions noted in the policy are met. Diane's values are higher in October because of the seasonal items she is currently stocking for sale. Based on the policy provision, Fred requests that Diane provide records of values for the past twelve months. A review of these records indicates that the average inventory values were $98,600. Because this amount does not exceed the limit of insurance and no seasonal increase percentage is indicated on the declarations page, the $100,000 Personal Property limit will be increased by 25 percent, to $125,000. Diane will receive full payment for the $112,000 as well as the $3,500 for the damaged computer and printer in the office. After applying a depreciation factor of 50 percent, the amount paid for the secondhand items is $1,700. All of these items are included under the category of business personal property coverage.

The outdoor sign attached to the building is covered for the full amount of $850. The BCF indicates that a limit of $1,000 applies per outdoor sign in any one occurrence (see BCF, Section 1.C.2).

The Business Income loss will be paid for the full amount of $17,000. The period of restoration will begin after a seventy-two hour waiting period following the time of direct physical damage. The fifty-day period required to repair the building and resume operations falls within the one-year limitation in the BCF. Because the suspension of operations was less than sixty days, none of the ordinary payroll expense that necessarily continued during the period of restoration will be deducted from the covered loss of business income, which includes all continuing normal operating expenses, including payroll. Moreover, the $17,000 of covered business income loss is not subject to the limit of insurance applicable to business personal property.

BCF, Business Income

f. Business Income

(1) Business Income

(a) We will pay for the actual loss of Business Income you sustain due to the necessary suspension of your "operations" during the "period of restoration". The suspension must be caused by direct physical loss of or damage to property at the described premises. The loss or damage must be caused by or result from a Covered Cause of Loss. With respect to loss of or damage to personal property in the open or personal property in a vehicle, the described premises include the area within 100 feet of such premises....

(b) We will only pay for loss of Business Income that you sustain during the "period of restoration" and that occurs within 12 consecutive months after the date of direct physical loss or damage. We will only pay for ordinary payroll expenses for 60 days following the date of direct physical loss or damage, unless a greater number of days is shown in the Declarations.

(c) Business Income means the:

(i) Net Income (Net Profit or Loss before income taxes) that would have been earned or incurred if no physical loss or damage had occurred, but not including any Net Income that would likely have been earned as a result of an increase in the volume of business due to favorable business conditions caused by the impact of the Covered Cause of Loss on customers or on other businesses; and

(ii) Continuing normal operating expenses incurred, including payroll.

(4) This Additional Coverage is not subject to the Limits of Insurance of Section I — Property.[5]

The $500 to replace the glass will be covered at replacement cost (see BCF, Section E, Item 5.d.4). In addition, the cost of boarding up the window is covered under the Glass Expenses additional coverage (see BCF, Section A, Item 5.n.1).

As result of the analysis of amounts payable under the BCF, the total amount paid for this loss is $134,750. See the exhibit "Correct Answer."

Correct Answer

Item	Amount Paid
New inventory	$112,000
Computer equipment	$3,500
Secondhand inventory	$1,400
Outdoor sign	$850
Loss of business income (Business personal property limit does not apply)	$17,000
Exterior glass	$500
Minus deductible	$500
Total	134,750

[DA11284]

SUMMARY

The businessowners policy (BOP) is designed to insure eligible small to mid-size businesses. Common exposures generally included in the BOP are buildings, business personal property, personal property of others, business income and extra expense, premises and operations liability, and several others. With its package approach and simplified rating procedures, the BOP can meet the needs of insurers, producers, and policyholders.

Section I of ISO's BOP covers buildings and business personal property and, through additional coverages and coverage extensions, several other loss exposures. Section I also includes optional coverages for outdoor signs, money and securities, employee dishonesty, and mechanical breakdown.

Businessowners liability coverage is comparable in most ways to the Commercial General Liability (CGL) Coverage Form. However, several liability coverage endorsements that are not available for use with the CGL form are included in the ISO businessowners program.

As this case illustrates, the Businessowners Coverage Form (BCF) can fully cover (less the deductible) a property loss that exceeds the business personal property limit, thanks to the Business Personal Property Limit—Seasonal Increase provision and the fact that the Business Income additional coverage is not subject to the business personal property limit of insurance.

ASSIGNMENT NOTES

1. The ISO businessowners policy calls for the amount of the loss to be reduced by the deductible before it is multiplied by the percentage of insurance to value. The Coinsurance condition in the ISO Building and Personal Property Coverage Form calls for deducting it after coinsurance has been applied. The procedure in the businessowners policy is more favorable to the insured: it increases the amount that an insured can collect if the amount of insurance is not equal to 80 percent of the replacement cost.

2. Includes copyrighted material of Insurance Services Office, Inc., with its permission, Copyright Insurance Services Office, Inc., 2012.

3. Includes copyrighted material of Insurance Services Office, Inc., with its permission, Copyright Insurance Services Office, Inc., 2012.

4. Includes copyrighted material of Insurance Services Office, Inc., with its permission, Copyright Insurance Services Office, Inc., 2012.

5. Includes copyrighted material of Insurance Services Office, Inc., with its permission, Copyright Insurance Services Office, Inc., 2012.

12

Industry-Specific Policies

Educational Objectives

After learning the content of this assignment, you should be able to:

▷ Describe the ISO farm program in terms of each of the following:

- Main forms and endorsements
- Insuring agreements
- Causes of loss form

▷ Describe what is covered by each of the following:

- Crop hail insurance
- Multiple Peril Crop Insurance
- Animal mortality insurance
- Feedlot insurance
- Federal livestock insurance

▷ Summarize the provisions applicable to each of the following elements of Financial Institution Bond, Standard Form 24:

- Insuring agreements A through G
- Exclusions
- Coverage trigger
- Notice of loss
- Limits of liability
- Deductible

▷ Describe what is covered by each of the following:

- SFAA Computer Crime Policy
- SFAA Combination Safe Depository Policy
- Mortgage impairment insurance

12

- Mortgage guarantee insurance
- Title insurance

▶ Explain how the ISO Market Segments Program broadens standard coverage forms for insureds in particular industries.

Industry-Specific Policies

ISO FARM PROGRAM

Special modularized insurance forms for farms address the loss exposures presented by the wide variety of farm sizes, farm ownership arrangements, and agricultural outputs.

Traditional farms are owned by families who live and work on their own land. Such a farm is both a residence and a business. Accordingly, the package policies used for covering traditional farms—called "farmowners policies" or simply "farm policies"—are designed to cover both residential loss exposures and farming business loss exposures. A significant number of farms are owned by agribusiness corporations and are worked by employees who may or may not live on the property. To accommodate both, insurers offer farm insurance policies that use a modular format:

- When the insured is a traditional farm family that lives on its own farm, a form covering residential property exposures is included in the policy along with other forms that cover the farm business exposures.
- When the insured is an agribusiness corporation, the form covering residential property exposures can be omitted.
- When a farm engages in additional business activities, the farm coverage forms can be combined with other commercial property and liability forms in a commercial package policy.

Insurance Services Office (ISO) and the American Association of Insurance Services (AAIS) both file forms, rules, and loss costs for farm insurance. Some of the leading writers of this line of business have developed their own coverage forms. (Throughout this section "farm" and "farmer" are used to include the terms "ranch" and "rancher.")

Insuring Agreements (A Through G) of ISO Farm Property Coverage Forms

The ISO farm program includes various forms and endorsements that can be combined into either a separate farm policy or a coverage part in a commercial package policy. The insured can select any combination of three property coverage forms:

- Farm Dwellings, Appurtenant Structures and Household Personal Property Coverage Form (FP 00 12)—This form contains four insuring agreements for covering residential structures and personal property on a farm.

- Farm Personal Property Coverage Form (FP 00 13)—This form contains two insuring agreements for covering farm personal property, on either a scheduled or an unscheduled basis.
- Barns, Outbuildings and Other Farm Structures Coverage Form (FP 00 14)—This form contains a single insuring agreement for covering non-residential buildings and structures used in farming.

The Causes of Loss Form—Farm Property (FP 10 60) contains provisions for basic, broad, and special causes of loss. The Other Farm Provisions Form (FP 00 90) contains provisions for various additional coverages, conditions, and definitions that are common to more than one of the other farm forms.

The three ISO farm property coverage forms include insuring agreements for covering these types of property:

- Dwellings
- Appurtenant structures (other than farm structures)
- Household personal property
- Loss of use of the preceding types of property
- Scheduled farm personal property
- Unscheduled farm personal property
- Barns and other farm buildings

Farm Dwellings, Appurtenant Structures and Household Personal Property Coverage Form

The Farm Dwellings, Appurtenant Structures and Household Personal Property Coverage Form covers residential building and personal property exposures, as well as additional living expenses and loss of fair rental value resulting from damage to such property.

The form contains these four coverages, which are comparable in most respects to Coverages A through D of homeowners policies:

- Coverage A—Dwellings
- Coverage B—Other Private Structures Appurtenant to Dwellings
- Coverage C—Household Personal Property
- Coverage D—Loss of Use

Coverage B excludes structures, other than private garages, that the named insured uses principally for farming purposes. Thus, Coverage B does not cover farm structures such as barns and silos, which can be covered under the Barns, Outbuildings and Other Farm Structures Coverage Form.

Similarly, Coverage C insures only household personal property and excludes "farm personal property" other than office fixtures, furniture, and office equipment. "Farm personal property" is defined as "equipment, supplies and products of farming or ranching operations, including but not limited to feed, seed, fertilizer, 'livestock', other animals, 'poultry', grain, bees, fish, worms, produce and agricultural machinery, vehicles and equipment."

"Farm personal property" can be insured under the Farm Personal Property Coverage Form. Although the ISO farm forms distinguish between "household personal property" and "farm personal property" and insure them under separate forms, some independently filed farm policies do not make this distinction. They simply insure all of the insured's personal property under a single coverage agreement.

Farm Personal Property Coverage Form

The Farm Personal Property Coverage Form contains two coverages: Coverage E—Scheduled Farm Personal Property and Coverage F— Unscheduled Farm Personal Property. The insured can choose either or both of these coverages.

Coverage E applies to only those classes of farm personal property for which a specific limit of insurance is shown in the declarations. There is no coinsurance requirement. Property that can be insured under Coverage E includes (but is not limited to) these types:

- Farm machinery (individually described)
- Rented or borrowed farm machinery, vehicles, and equipment
- Livestock (limited to cattle, sheep, swine, goats, horses, mules, and donkeys)
- Poultry
- Bees, worms, and fish
- Grain and feed
- Hay, straw, and fodder
- Farm products, materials, and supplies
- Computers

In addition, Coverage E can be used to cover individually scheduled items of farm personal property, such as a particular tractor, combine, or irrigation equipment owned by the insured. Coverage restrictions and sublimits apply to some of the eligible classes. For example, a $2,000 limit applies to loss of any one head of livestock, and a $10,000 limit applies to any one stack of hay, straw, or fodder.

The scheduled classes or items of property are insured up to their specified limits while situated at the location described in the policy. An extension insures most classes of scheduled property while away from the insured premises and within the coverage territory (the United States, Puerto Rico, and Canada) for up to 10 percent of their specified limits. However, livestock and individually described farm machinery, vehicles, and equipment while off premises are covered for their full, specified limits.

Coverage F insures unscheduled farm personal property under a single limit subject to an 80 percent Coinsurance condition. For property at the insured location, all items of "farm personal property" (as defined in the form) are covered unless excluded. Property that can be excluded under Coverage F includes (but is not limited to) these types:

- Household personal property used for the dwelling
- Animals other than "livestock"
- "Poultry," bees, fish, or worms
- Contents of chicken fryer or broiler/duck/turkey houses, laying houses, "poultry" brooder or duck or turkey houses
- Racehorses and show horses
- Crops in the open
- Trees, plants, shrubs, or lawns
- Tobacco, cotton, vegetables, root crops, potatoes, bulbs, fruit, or nursery stock
- Motor vehicles primarily designed and licensed for road use, watercraft, or aircraft
- Fences, windmills, or windchargers
- Outdoor radio or television equipment
- Bulk milk tanks, bulk feed tanks or bins attached to buildings, barn cleaners, pasteurizers, or boilers
- Portable buildings or structures
- Irrigation equipment
- Cotton pickers and harvester-thresher combines

Coverage for property away from the insured location is limited to livestock, farm machinery, equipment, implements, tools and supplies, and grain, ground feed, fertilizer, fodder, hay, herbicides, pesticides, and similar items.

Off-premises coverage (under both Coverage E and F) is subject to some restrictions. For example, none of the three listed classes is covered while in the custody of a common or contract carrier. However, the form provides an extension covering property in the custody of a common or contract carrier, subject to a $1,000 limit that can be increased by an entry on the declarations page.

Coverage F is written with a single limit. This approach is often preferred because it is less complicated to arrange and is less likely to leave the insured with an inadequate amount of insurance for a particular class of property. Of course, the 80 percent coinsurance requirement must be met.

Despite the advantages of Coverage F, some types of farm personal property are excluded and can therefore be insured only under Coverage E. These types of property include poultry, bees, fish, and worms; other animals that are not within the definition of "livestock"; and portable buildings and portable structures.

Barns, Outbuildings and Other Farm Structures Coverage Form

An insured might choose to schedule certain items of farm personal property under Coverage E and to insure the remaining farm personal property for a blanket limit under Coverage F. The division of property between Coverages E and F may also depend on the underwriter's preferences.

The Barns, Outbuildings and Other Farm Structures Coverage Form contains the provisions for Coverage G, which is designed to insure all types of farm buildings and structures (other than dwellings and private garages) on either a scheduled or a blanket basis. The form lists these types of covered property:

- Farm buildings and structures other than dwellings
- Silos individually described in the declarations
- Portable buildings and portable structures
- Fences (other than field and pasture fences), corrals, pens, chutes, and feed racks
- Outdoor radio and television equipment, antennas, masts, and towers
- Improvements and betterments
- Building materials and supplies

When farm structures are insured on a blanket basis, the insurer ordinarily requires the insured to submit to the insurer annually (and whenever a material change in the property occurs) a statement of values listing the covered buildings or structures and their values. Except for improvements and betterments, Coverage G can be arranged on either a replacement cost basis or an actual cash value basis, as indicated in the declarations. Functional replacement cost provisions are available by endorsement.

The Barns, Outbuildings and Other Farm Structures Coverage Form and the Farm Personal Property Coverage Form both include extra expense coverage if the declarations show a limit for that coverage. An ISO farm policy can also be endorsed to cover loss of farm income resulting from damage to farm buildings or farm personal property by a covered cause of loss through the Disruption of Farm Operations (FP 15 01) endorsement.

Although farm machinery and equipment and livestock can be insured under the Farm Personal Property Coverage Form, an insured who wishes to insure either or both of these two classes of property, and no others, can obtain the insurance under inland marine forms:

- Mobile Agricultural Machinery and Equipment Coverage Form (FP 00 30)
- Livestock Coverage Form (FP 00 40)

Causes of Loss Form—Farm Property

The ISO Causes of Loss Form—Farm Property (FP 10 60) contains provisions for basic, broad, and special causes of loss. These three levels of coverage correspond, in most ways, to the basic, broad, and special causes of loss in commercial property policies. The farm causes of loss also include several, such as flood or electrocution, that can kill covered livestock. The basic and broad perils covered are shown in the exhibit. The insurer marks the declarations page accordingly to indicate which level of coverage applies.

Basic Causes of Loss

With the exception of theft and the last three causes of loss listed in the exhibit, the basic covered causes of loss for the farm policy are the same as the causes of loss covered by the commercial property Causes of Loss—Basic Form.

The collision peril has three aspects: (1) collision damage to covered farm machinery, (2) death of covered livestock resulting from collision or overturn of vehicles, and (3) collision damage to other farm personal property. Earthquake and flood are covered perils only when they cause loss to covered livestock.

Broad Causes of Loss

The broad covered causes of loss in the ISO farm program include all of the farm basic causes of loss plus twelve additional causes of loss. The first five additional perils listed apply to covered livestock only.

Various restrictions apply to these perils. For example, the peril of attacks on covered livestock by dogs or wild animals is subject to an exclusion of loss or damage (1) to sheep or (2) caused by dogs or wild animals owned by the named insured, the named insured's employees, or other persons residing on the insured location. See the exhibit "Perils Covered by Causes of Loss Form—Farm Property."

Similarly, the accidental shooting peril does not include loss or damage caused by the named insured, any other insured, employees of the named insured, or other residents of the insured location. The remaining seven perils of the broad causes of loss are comparable to covered perils in either the homeowners broad form or the commercial property Causes of Loss—Broad Form.

Perils Covered by Causes of Loss Form—Farm Property

Basic and Broad Causes of Loss Include

- Fire or lightning
- Windstorm or hail
- Explosion
- Riot or civil commotion
- Aircraft
- Vehicles
- Smoke
- Vandalism
- Theft
- Sinkhole collapse
- Volcanic action
- Collision—Coverages E and F only*
- Earthquake loss to covered livestock*
- Flood loss to covered livestock*

Broad Causes of Loss Also Include

- Electrocution of covered livestock*
- Attacks on covered livestock by dogs or wild animals*
- Accidental shooting of covered livestock*
- Drowning of covered livestock*
- Loading/unloading accidents (livestock only)*
- Breakage of glass or safety glazing materials
- Falling objects
- Weight of ice, snow, or sleet
- Sudden and accidental tearing apart, cracking, burning, or bulging of a steam or hot water heating system, an air conditioning or automatic fire protective system, or an appliance for heating water
- Accidental discharge or leakage of water or steam from within a plumbing, heating, air conditioning, or other system or appliance
- Freezing of a plumbing, heating, air conditioning, or automatic fire protective system or a household appliance
- Sudden and accidental damage from artificially generated electrical current (Coverages A through D only)

*These covered causes of loss are not included in the commercial property causes of loss forms or in homeowners forms.

Includes copyrighted material of Insurance Services Office, Inc., with its permission. Copyright, ISO Properties, 2002.
[DA03694]

Special Causes of Loss

The farm special causes of loss correspond to those of the homeowners special form and the commercial property Causes of Loss—Special Form. Livestock, poultry, bees, fish, worms, and other animals are not eligible for the special causes of loss and can only be covered for the basic or broad causes of loss.

Grain in the open and hay, straw, and fodder are covered only against limited named perils.

If the insured wants to cover eligible farm personal property on an unscheduled basis under Coverage F with the special causes of loss and also wants to insure under Coverage F the types of property that are not eligible for the special causes of loss, an entry can be made on the declarations indicating that the ineligible types of property are covered for the broad (or basic) perils and all other personal property is covered for the special causes of loss. Another approach is separate scheduling of the livestock, poultry, or other restricted classes of property under Coverage E for the broad (or basic) perils.

Farm Liability Coverage Forms

The Farm Liability Coverage Form (FL 00 20) covers both personal and farm business liability exposures. The form combines elements of homeowners liability coverage and commercial general liability coverage and contains special provisions that address liability loss exposures unique to farms.

The Farm Umbrella Liability Policy (FB 00 01) or Farm Excess Liability Policy (FE 00 01) can be used to provide limits of liability in excess of underlying policies for farm liability, auto liability, farm employers liability, recreational motor vehicle liability, and watercraft liability. The basic difference between the two policies is that the umbrella policy, in some instances, provides broader coverage than the underlying policies, while the excess policy does not provide broader coverage than the underlying policies.

SPECIALTY FARM COVERAGES

The coverage that standard farm policies provide for crops and livestock is inadequate for many insureds. Various types of specialty crop insurance and livestock insurance are available from both private insurers and the United States government.

These forms can provide specialty coverage needed by agricultural and related operations:

- Crop hail insurance
- Multiple Peril Crop Insurance
- Animal mortality insurance
- Feedlot insurance
- Federal livestock insurance

Crop Coverages

The Insurance Services Office (ISO) Farm Personal Property Coverage Form provides only minimal coverage on unharvested crops. Under Coverage E—

Scheduled Farm Personal Property, unharvested crops are not an eligible class for coverage. Coverage F—Unscheduled Farm Personal Property excludes crops in the open, but by means of an extension, provides up to 10 percent of the Coverage F limit to cover unharvested barley, corn, oats, rye, wheat and other grains, flax, soybeans, and sunflowers against loss caused by fire or lightning only. Farmers can obtain broader coverage for crops through either a crop hail insurance policy or a crop insurance plan offered by an agency of the U.S. government.

In addition to covering hail damage to growing crops, **crop hail insurance** policies are often extended to cover additional perils such as fire, windstorm accompanying hail, damage caused by livestock, and vehicles. Such policies may also cover harvested crops against named perils while being transported to the first place of storage.

> **Crop hail insurance**
> Insurance offered by private insurers that covers crops against loss caused by hail and often other perils.

The Federal Crop Insurance Corporation (FCIC) offers several crop insurance programs that are administered by the U.S. Department of Agriculture's Risk Management Agency (RMA). These programs are marketed and serviced by participating private insurers and agents but are reinsured by the FCIC.

One of FCIC's crop insurance plans provides **Multiple Peril Crop Insurance (MPCI)**, which insures farmers against unexpected production losses (as measured against the insured farmer's actual production history), however, these policies do not cover losses resulting from neglect, poor farming practices, or theft.

> **Multiple Peril Crop Insurance (MPCI)**
> Insurance offered by the federal government that covers unexpected crop production losses due to natural causes such as drought, excessive moisture, hail, windstorm, and flood.

Livestock Coverages

The livestock coverage provided by standard farm policies may be inadequate for several reasons. Farm policies are subject to per-head limits that are inadequate for many farmers. Also, farm policies are subject to eligibility requirements that exclude certain types of livestock. Finally, farm policies cover livestock against the basic or broad form causes of loss only. Owners of high-valued animals often want to insure against loss of their animals by any fortuitous cause, including illness or disease.

Two livestock coverages that can be obtained from private insurers to supplement a regular farm policy are animal mortality insurance and feedlot insurance. Additionally, livestock insurance is also available in some states from the FCIC.

Animal mortality insurance is essentially term life insurance on animals. This type of insurance might be purchased to cover farm animals such as valuable horses, registered cattle, or calves being grown and exhibited under sponsorship of a club (such as 4-H). Animal mortality insurance is also bought by owners of race horses, show dogs, circus animals, and even laboratory animals.

> **Animal mortality insurance**
> Insurance that covers loss of valuable animals by (1) death resulting from accident, injury, sickness, or disease or (2) theft, subject to exclusions.

Because animal mortality insurance covers death resulting from injury, sickness, or disease, it provides much broader protection than conventional livestock coverage under a farm policy. Moreover, an animal mortality policy can be written for whatever limit of insurance is agreeable to the insurer and the owner of the insured animal. A prize bull, for example, might be insured for $250,000, in contrast with the $2,000 per-head livestock limit in a standard farm policy.

The insurance does not cover reduction in the animal's value because of its becoming incapable of fulfilling the functions or duties for which it is kept. However, some insurers will endorse the policy to cover loss resulting from the infertility of a breeding animal.

These are other causes of loss that animal mortality policies often exclude:

- Neglect in providing the animal with proper care or treatment
- Elective surgery unless the insurer has given its prior approval
- Unauthorized instructions to transfer the animal to any person or place
- Seizure or destruction by a governmental authority
- War and nuclear risks

Acts committed by the insured or at the insured's direction with intent to cause a loss are also excluded. However, most animal mortality policies cover the intentional destruction of an insured animal that is suffering from an irreversible or incurable condition, as long as the condition results from a cause that is not excluded and the intentional destruction is necessary for humane reasons. In addition, before destroying the animal, the insured must have either the insurer's consent or a veterinarian's certification that destruction was immediately required (as in the case of some bone fractures).

 **Reality Check**

Animal Mortality Coverage

Race horses are commonly covered under animal mortality policies. The value of these specially bred and trained animals can range from several hundred thousand dollars to millions of dollars. Such policies cover the owners in event of the death or theft of a race horse and often include extensions for surgical and medical costs, loss of use, and other coverages.

Less commonly covered under animal mortality policies are show dogs. These animals may also be valuable, but the need for mortality coverage is often overlooked. A case that spotlights the need occurred last year, after the Westminster show in New York, when a whippet named Vivi escaped from her crate at the Newark Airport. Although the dog's value was approximately $20,000, Delta airlines paid only $2,800—the cost of a lost piece of luggage of that size and weight.

If it were subsequently determined that the show dog had been killed or stolen, an animal mortality policy would cover the dog's value to its owners.

Caroline McDonald, "Show Dog Owners' Coverage Is Bare Bones, Expert Says," National Underwriter Property & Casualty, February 2008, www.property-casualty.com/News/2008/2/Pages/Show-Dog-Owners--Coverage-Is-Bare-Bones--Expert-Says.aspx (accessed April 22, 2010) [DA05914]

The market for animal mortality insurance is highly specialized and consists of only a few insurers. Because of the possibility of moral hazard, insurers are extremely careful in their underwriting and may require certification by a licensed veterinarian that the insured animal is in good health at the time insurance takes effect.

A second type of livestock coverage is **feedlot insurance**. A feedlot is a commercial facility that fattens (or "custom feeds") a farmer's animals and then markets them for slaughter at the best possible time. The feedlot operator usually does not take ownership of the animals but is paid on a commission basis.

Feedlot operators have a bailee liability exposure for animals in their custody. They may also assume liability by contract for loss resulting from causes that would not otherwise be a bailee's responsibility. To cover animals in their custody, feedlot operators can purchase feedlot insurance. Few insurers have the underwriting and claims expertise to handle this class of business. Animals at feedlots are generally not eligible for livestock coverage under farm policies.

Coverage under feedlot policies is usually limited to named perils, such as fire, explosion, windstorm, electrocution, drowning, and attack by dogs or wild animals. Loss caused by smothering (which commonly occurs during blizzards) may or may not be covered. Loss resulting simply from exposure to the elements is often not covered.

Livestock policies are also available from the FCIC for covering cattle, swine, and lamb in eligible states.[1] Coverage may be obtained in either Livestock Gross Margin (LGM) policies or Livestock Risk Protection (LRP) policies.

> **Feedlot insurance**
> A specialized type of livestock coverage that covers animals while in the custody of a commercial feedlot operator.

FINANCIAL INSTITUTION BONDS

Financial institution bonds are similar in many ways to commercial crime coverage forms. The differences are in large part accounted for by the nature of the loss exposures faced by financial institutions and the regulations requiring financial institutions to carry crime coverage.

The Surety & Fidelity Association of America (SFAA) maintains several different policy forms to cover the exposures faced by financial institutions. The SFAA financial institution policies are called **financial institution bonds** because their principal coverage was traditionally referred to as a fidelity bond, a type of surety bond that covered employee dishonesty.

> **Financial institution bond**
> A policy that covers the crime loss exposures of financial institutions such as banks, savings and loan institutions, and insurance companies.

Insurance Services Office, Inc. (ISO) also maintains financial institution coverage forms and endorsements. Financial institution bonds that differ from the SFAA or ISO forms also are available in both the United States and foreign markets. A significant number of financial institutions, particularly large ones, have at least part of their insurance placed in the London or Bermuda markets.

Insurance requirements may be imposed on financial institutions by either governmental or industry bodies—for example, the Federal Deposit Insurance

Corporation with regard to banks, stock exchanges with regard to their members, and state insurance departments with regard to insurers.

Financial Institution Bond Form 24

Form 24, used to insure commercial banks and savings and loan associations, is one of the most widely used SFAA financial institution bonds. For many years, this form was called the Bankers Blanket Bond, and that term is still used as a generic description of this type of insurance. Familiarity with Form 24 can serve as the basis for analyzing other financial institution forms. Form 24 contains these insuring agreements:

- A—Fidelity
- B—On Premises
- C—In Transit
- D—Forgery or Alteration
- E—Securities
- F—Counterfeit Money
- G—Fraudulent Mortgages

Agreements A, B, C, and F are required components of the policy. Agreements D, E, and G, although printed in the policy form, are optional. Appropriate entries on the Declarations page indicate which optional insuring agreements, if any, have been purchased.

In addition to agreements D, E, and G, many other optional coverages can be added by attaching riders. (The word "rider" has the same meaning as "endorsement": an amendment to an insurance policy.)

Insuring Agreement A—Fidelity

The Fidelity insuring agreement covers losses resulting directly from dishonest or fraudulent acts committed by an employee acting alone or in collusion with others. Because employee dishonesty accounts for the vast majority of financial institution losses, fidelity, the historical name for employee dishonesty coverage, is the most important element of the bond.

Since being revised in 2004, the Fidelity insuring agreement no longer uses the "manifest intent" wording common to most employee dishonesty forms. Instead, the insuring agreement requires the employee's acts to have been committed with "the active and conscious purpose to cause the Insured to sustain such loss." This change in language is intended to clarify the meaning of the coverage requirement and avoid arguments that have complicated interpretation of manifest intent wording.

A provision of the Fidelity insuring agreement precludes coverage for "any employee benefits, including: salaries, commissions, fees, bonuses, promotions, awards, profit sharing or pensions, *intentionally paid by the insured*" (emphasis added). The emphasized phrase would seem to allow coverage for situations when employees dishonestly increase the amount of their salaries or other employee benefits without such increases being intended by their employers.

The Fidelity insuring agreement does not require the employee to have acted with intent to derive a financial benefit—unless some or all of the insured's loss results from trading, in which case the loss is not covered unless the employee receives "an improper financial benefit." The insuring agreement clarifies that "an improper financial benefit does not include any employee benefits received in the course of employment, including salaries, commissions, fees, bonuses, promotions, awards, profit sharing or pensions."

There is also a special provision regarding losses resulting directly or indirectly from loans. Such losses are not covered unless the employee colluded with one or more parties to the loan transaction(s) and received an improper financial benefit other than any employee benefit.

The applicable definition of "employee" is broader than that used in commercial crime forms in that it includes (1) attorneys and their employees retained by the insured while performing legal services for the insured and (2) corporations or partnerships and their employees performing data processing of checks or other records for the insured.

Insuring Agreement B—On Premises

The On Premises insuring agreement provides broader coverage than most commercial crime forms. It covers "Property" located at any office or premises anywhere in the world against a broad range of named perils. The applicable definition of "Property" is extremely broad, encompassing money, securities, gems, jewelry, precious metals, and all other tangible personal property.

> Property means Money, Certificated Securities, Negotiable Instruments, Certificates of Deposit, Documents of Title, Evidences of Debt, Security Agreements, Withdrawal Orders, Certificates of Origin or Title, Letters of Credit, insurance policies, abstracts of title, deeds and mortgages on real estate, revenue and other stamps, tokens, unsold state lottery tickets, books of account and other records stored on tangible media, gems, jewelry, precious metals in bars or ingots, (which are collectively the enumerated items of Property), and tangible items of personal property which are not hereinbefore enumerated. [2]

The On Premises insuring agreement covers the "enumerated items of Property," as specified in the definition of Property, against loss by robbery, burglary, misplacement, and mysterious unexplained disappearance, as well as damage to or destruction of the property, while the property is "lodged or deposited within offices or premises located anywhere." To be covered against those perils, the property need not be at the insured's premises.

The property could be at other banking premises in a foreign country, for example, and still be covered. Loss caused by riot or civil commotion outside the U.S. and Canada is excluded.

Additional covered perils, if committed by a person present at the insured's premises, are theft, false pretenses, and common-law or statutory larceny. The inclusion of loss caused by false pretenses is noteworthy because most commercial property and crime forms exclude it.

The On Premises insuring agreement also applies to loss of or damage to furnishings, fixtures, supplies, or equipment within a covered office of the insured if caused by actual or attempted larceny, theft, burglary, or robbery; or by vandalism or malicious mischief. However, to be covered for the losses described in this paragraph, the insured either must be the owner of, or must be legally liable for, the furnishings, fixtures, supplies, equipment, or office.

Moreover, loss to furniture, fixtures, supplies, or equipment must not be caused by fire. If, for example, burglars set the insured's premises on fire, the resulting loss by fire to those types of property would not be covered. The insured's commercial property insurance generally covers such items against fire loss. However, loss by fire to money or any other "enumerated items of Property" would be covered because these items are covered against damage or destruction.

Insuring Agreement C—In Transit

The In Transit insuring agreement insures "property" (as defined) while in transit anywhere in the custody of certain types of individuals or organizations. The covered perils are "robbery, common-law or statutory larceny, theft, misplacement, mysterious unexplainable disappearance, and damage thereto or destruction thereof."

The property in transit must be (1) in the custody of a "messenger" (an employee in possession of the insured's property away from the insured's premises or any other person acting as custodian of the property during an emergency arising out of the incapacity of the employee messenger) or (2) in the custody of a transportation company and being transported in an armored vehicle.

Insuring Agreement D—Forgery or Alteration

The Forgery or Alteration insuring agreement covers loss resulting from forgery of a signature or alteration involving most types of negotiable instruments and certain other listed instruments. Losses resulting from written instructions directed towards the insured that have been altered or that bear a forged signature are also covered.

Form 24 defines "forgery" to mean only the signing of the name of another with the intent to deceive. It does not include the genuine but unauthorized signature of the signer. A genuine but unauthorized signature could be, for example, a corporate officer's signature on a check that exceeds the officer's authority. Another example is a machine-produced signature placed on an instrument without required approval. Although these examples might be dishonest acts covered under other policy agreements, they would not be covered under the Forgery or Alteration agreement. Some independently developed forms offer riders to cover loss resulting from unauthorized signatures.

Insuring Agreement E—Securities

The Securities insuring agreement covers loss sustained by the insured because of the insured's reliance on certain listed instruments that bear a forged signature, that are altered, or that are counterfeit or stolen. Often, these instruments are securities that the bank holds as collateral for a loan. The bank may discover that the securities are counterfeit when it attempts to sell them after the borrower has defaulted on the loan. The Securities insuring agreement would cover the insured against the resulting loss.

Insuring Agreement F—Counterfeit Money

The Counterfeit Money insuring agreement covers loss when the bank, acting in good faith, receives any counterfeit or altered paper securities, money, or coins of the U.S., Canada, or another country in which the insured maintains a branch office.

Insuring Agreement G—Fraudulent Mortgages

The Fraudulent Mortgages insuring agreement covers loss resulting from the insured's good-faith acceptance of a mortgage or deed of trust that proves to be defective because the signature on the mortgage or deed was obtained through fraud or false pretenses.

A loss covered under this insuring agreement could occur, for example, in this way: A customer of the insured defaults on a mortgage loan, and the insured seeks (in accordance with the loan agreement) to foreclose the loan and sell the property to recoup its credit loss. However, the mortgage on the property proves to be defective because of a signature on the mortgage that was obtained fraudulently. As a result of the defective mortgage, the bank cannot sell the property and recoup its loss. The Fraudulent Mortgages insuring agreement covers the loss resulting directly from the insured's acceptance of the faulty mortgage as collateral for the loan.

Exclusions

Form 24 contains several exclusions. Some of the more significant ones are described here.

Loan exclusion—If the insured advances funds to a borrower with the expectation of repayment in the normal course of business, but such repayment is not made, the bond excludes coverage for the resulting loss. As with many of the exclusions in the bond, an exception to the loan exclusion provides coverage if employee dishonesty is involved.

Exclusion of property contained in customers' safe deposit boxes—Form 24 does not cover loss resulting from a burglary or robbery of customers' property from a safe deposit box unless the loss is caused by dishonesty on the part of a bank employee. The separate Combination Safe Depository Policy for financial institutions is available to cover this exposure.

Trading exclusion—Losses related to unauthorized securities trading, often referred to as "rogue trading," are excluded. The form can be extended by endorsement to cover trading losses, but even when this coverage is added, trading losses will often not be covered because of the Fidelity insuring agreement's requirement that the employee must have acted "with the active and conscious purpose to cause the Insured to sustain such loss." In many of these cases, the loss results from the employee's unauthorized efforts to make profits for the firm.

Uncollected funds exclusion—This exclusion eliminates coverage for loss involving items of deposit that "are not finally paid for any reason." For example, Form 24 does not cover losses sustained because the bank honored a bad check or another item of deposit. The simplest way of managing this exposure is not to pay the item until it is collected through the clearing process.

Extortion exclusion—Although Form 24 excludes loss by extortion, SFAA riders can be added to the bond to cover, for an additional premium, threats against persons or property.

Coverage Trigger

Financial institution bonds apply on a discovery basis, covering loss sustained by the insured at any time but discovered during the bond period. If a bond is replaced by another bond that applies on a discovery basis, the new bond will cover all losses discovered during the new bond period, regardless of when they occurred.

Notice of Loss

Like most other insurance policies, financial institution bonds require that the insured give prompt notice of loss to the insurer. Unlike most other policies, the financial institution bond adds the requirement that the report be made within a period not to exceed thirty days after the discovery of loss. This can create problems for insureds. Insureds are often reluctant to report employee dishonesty losses, perhaps because they believe that such losses reflect on the firm's management supervision. Failure to report a discovered loss promptly can jeopardize coverage.

Limits of Liability

An aggregate limit of liability applies to the entire bond. This limit is the most that the insurer will pay under all coverages during the bond period. Additionally, a single-loss limit applies to each of the basic insuring agreements. Optional insuring agreements may have a single-loss limit in an amount less than that of the basic insuring agreements.

ISO's financial institutions program includes both aggregate and nonaggregate forms. Under a nonaggregate form, the amount collectible is subject to the single-loss limit, but no limit applies to the total paid under the policy for multiple claims. Nonaggregate forms are primarily used to cover smaller community banks.

Determining appropriate fidelity limits for banks is difficult because the possibility of a catastrophic loss is real. In one case, a senior bank officer stole $29 million over three years from his employer. Bank officials were unable to explain the loss until divorce proceedings between the officer and his wife revealed that he was maintaining a separate lavish residence with a female companion. [3]

One method of covering severe employee dishonesty exposures of banks is by means of the Excess Bank Employee Dishonesty Bond, Standard Form No. 28. This bond applies only to the Fidelity coverage agreement and is usually written for amounts of $1 million or more, applying in excess of other applicable bonds and insurance. Under SFAA manual rules, this form is available only to commercial banks. Other types of financial institutions desiring higher fidelity limits or higher limits for other coverages can increase the limit in their financial institution bond or purchase a nonstandard excess bond.

Deductibles

The SFAA manual requires a minimum $1,000 deductible. In practice, most financial institution bonds are issued with deductibles much larger than $1,000. Deductibles for the largest financial institutions can run into the millions and are coordinated with sophisticated loss funding plans.

SFAA AND OTHER POLICIES BEYOND COMMERCIAL PROPERTY AND INLAND MARINE

Financial institutions may need coverages in addition to what is normally covered under commercial property and inland marine forms.

The Surety and Fidelity Association of America (SFAA) provides two policies—Computer Crime and Combination Safe Depository—that insure exposures outside of the scope of commercial property and inland marine coverages. Three other policies, designed to protect mortgageholders, also insure against exposures outside of the scope of commercial property.

Computer Crime Policy

Loss or damage to computer systems and data can cause enormous loss to a financial institution. Although the computer systems of financial institutions are generally highly secure, no system is completely invulnerable.

Commercial property and inland marine coverages can be used to insure most of the physical damage exposures to which computer systems are exposed. However, some losses resulting from criminal activity involving computers are outside the scope of such coverage. To insure these exposures, the SFAA developed its Computer Crime Policy, which can be written for any type of financial institution.

The Computer Crime Policy contains seven insuring agreements:

- Computer Systems Fraud—Covers loss caused by someone who has managed to enter or change electronic data or computer programs in the insured's computer system. However, this insuring agreement does not cover loss caused by employee dishonesty, which is covered by the financial institution bond.

- Data Processing Service Operations—Designed for insureds that perform data processing services for others under contract. It covers loss sustained by the insured's clients caused by fraudulent entries or changes in the insured's computer system if the insured is legally liable to its client.

- Voice Initiated Transfer Fraud—Covers the fraudulent transfer of funds based on telephone instructions given by someone pretending to be either a customer or an employee in another office. Security measures are required, and—when the transfer exceeds the amount specified in the policy—the transaction must be confirmed by a call-back to verify the instructions.

- Telefacsimile Transfer Fraud—Covers the fraudulent transfer of funds based on faxed instructions given by someone pretending to be either a customer or an employee in another office.

- Destruction of Data or Programs by Hacker—Covers destruction of, or damage to, electronic data or computer programs by a hacker.

- Destruction of Data or Programs by Virus—Covers destruction of, or damage to, electronic data or computer programs resulting from a computer virus.

- Voice Computer System Fraud—Covers loss resulting from unauthorized telephone long-distance toll charges. The charges can be caused by fraudulent use of codes or passwords to obtain access to parts of the insured's voice communications network.

Like financial institution bonds, the Computer Crime Policy covers on a discovery basis. The policy in effect when the loss is discovered provides coverage, regardless of when the loss occurred and whether the insured had insurance at that time.

Combination Safe Depository Policy

Many financial institutions provide safe-depository facilities for their customers and are therefore exposed to legal liability for loss of, or damage to, their customers' property. Additionally, the institutions may want to cover customers' property even when they are not legally liable for such losses in order to maintain customer goodwill. The **Combination Safe Depository Policy** can be used to provide coverage for these exposures.

The policy has two coverage agreements:

- Liability of Depository
- Loss of Customers' Property; Premises Damage

The Liability of the Depository agreement covers almost all causes of loss to the extent of the financial institution's legal liability. The Loss of Customers' Property—Premises Damage agreement includes coverage for two exposures:

- Loss of customers' property by actual or attempted burglary or robbery or destruction (regardless of the insured's legal liability)—Generally, safe deposit facilities are liable for such losses only if they result from their own negligence. However, many institutions want to provide this coverage to maintain customer goodwill in the event of a loss.

- Damage to the insured's premises and all furnishings, fixtures, fittings, equipment, safes, and vaults therein resulting from actual or attempted burglary or robbery, or vandalism or malicious mischief.

> **Combination Safe Depository Policy**
> A policy that enables a financial institution to cover loss of or damage to its customers' property in the insured's safe-depository facilities and damage to the insured's premises.

Other Coverages Designed for Financial Institutions

In addition to financial institution bonds, three additional coverages designed to meet specific needs of financial institutions that make or service mortgage loans are mortgage impairment insurance, mortgage guarantee insurance, and title insurance.

Mortgage Impairment Insurance

The Insurance Services Office (ISO) form for providing **mortgage impairment insurance** coverages is the Mortgageholders Errors and Omissions Coverage Form, which can be written as part of a commercial package policy.

Insurers specializing in this coverage have developed their own forms, usually referred to as mortgage impairment policies, which include similar coverages. Although some of the independently developed forms include enhancements not found in the ISO form, analyzing the ISO form is an effective approach to understanding what mortgage impairment policies typically cover. The ISO form contains four insuring agreements that can be purchased separately, depending on the insured's needs.

Coverage A—Mortgageholders Interest covers loss to the insured's interest as mortgageholder in covered property resulting from the insured's (or its

> **Mortgage impairment insurance**
> Insurance that protects a lending institution or mortgage servicing agency against losses arising out of the insured's failure to maintain insurance protecting mortgaged property, as well as other exposures connected with servicing mortgages.

representative's) error or accidental omission when following its customary procedure to require, procure, and maintain insurance on the mortgaged property. The covered causes of loss are those against which the mortgageholder customarily requires its mortgagors (borrowers) to provide insurance policies that protect the mortgageholder's interest in the property. The form excludes certain causes of loss, principally those excluded in the Causes of Loss—Special Form. Moreover, the form excludes (1) any event that occurs more than thirty days after the mortgageholder knows that an error or omission may have occurred and (2) errors or omissions involving title, mortgage guarantee, life, health, or accident insurance.

Coverage B—Property Owned or Held in Trust covers loss to property owned (such as a house on which a bank has foreclosed) or held in trust by the insured. If, through the insured's error or omission, such property is not covered by property insurance, the policy obligates the insurer to pay for loss resulting from a covered peril. The covered perils for Coverage B correspond to those of the Causes of Loss—Basic Form. Independently developed mortgage impairment policies often provide perils equal to those required of the mortgagee rather than just the basic form perils.

Coverage C—Mortgageholders Liability covers the insured's liability for damages arising from the insured's duties as a mortgage fiduciary or servicing agent. An insured who purchases this coverage might be either a mortgageholder that has agreed to obtain insurance on the mortgaged property or a servicing agent that has agreed to perform that duty on the mortgageholder's behalf. If, through error or omission, the insured fails to renew a required homeowners policy of a mortgagor and the dwelling is damaged by a covered peril, the mortgageholder's liability coverage will defend the insured against a claim or suit alleging covered loss and pay damages if the insured is legally liable.

Coverage D—Real Estate Tax Liability covers damages for which the insured becomes liable because it failed to pay a mortgagor's real estate taxes. This type of loss can occur when the mortgageholder, under an escrow agreement with the mortgagor, collects an amount of money from the mortgagor each month and agrees to use that money to pay the mortgagor's real estate taxes.

Mortgage Guarantee Insurance

Mortgage guarantee insurance can be written for banks, savings and loan associations, and other persons or organizations that provide mortgage loans. The policy covers the amount of the loan, interest on the loan, taxes, and insurance costs that the insured advanced to a borrower in connection with the loan transaction, and certain other expenses.

Title Insurance

Title insurance can be written for both mortgageholders and property owners. Title insurance is required by mortgagees and the typical title insurance policy

Mortgage guarantee insurance

Insurance that protects a mortgageholder from loss if the borrower fails to repay the mortgage loan.

Title insurance

Insurance that protects against loss resulting from defects in a title to real property.

covers only the mortgagee; however, it can be extended to cover the property owner for an additional premium.

Titles may be defective for various reasons, such as errors made by recorders of deeds, forged signatures on prior documents, or liens that contractors have placed on the property. Title insurance covers the cost of curing defects in the title or, in the worst case, the value of the property lost because of a defective title. Losses on title insurance policies are rare because title insurance firms search title records before issuing a policy and require that the problems they identify be either cured or excluded from coverage.

MARKET SEGMENTS PROGRAM

ISO's Market Segments Program includes a series of endorsements to expand commercial property and general liability coverages to meet the insurance needs of specific types of businesses. Although the Market Segments endorsements are designed for use with commercial package policies, the targeted businesses typically are small and midsize businesses, some of which may be eligible for businessowners policies.

ISO has developed one or more endorsements for each business type (including the market segments program types of businesses shown in the exhibit). Some insurers offer similar programs using their own coverage forms and endorsements. See the exhibit "Business Types Eligible for ISO Market Segments Program."

Business Types Eligible for ISO Market Segments Program

Apartment Building Owners	Landscapers
Auto Service Risks	Plumbing and HVAC Contractors
Dry Cleaning and Laundry Facilities	Personal Care Services
Funeral Homes	Pet Services
Florists	Restaurants
Hardware and Home Improvement Stores	Self-Storage Facilities
Hotels, Motels, and Inns	Supermarkets
Janitorial Services	Staffing Firms

[DA03701]

The provisions that ISO's Market Segment Program endorsements add to regular commercial property and general liability forms can be divided into three categories:

- Provisions that add higher limits for coverage extensions or additional coverages
- Provisions that add coverages available in other ISO forms
- Provisions that add coverages not found in any other ISO forms

Higher Limits for Extensions or Additional Coverages

Examples of provisions in the first category are an increase the Fire Department Service Charge limit to $5,000 (instead of $2,500) and an increase in the Pollutant Clean Up limit to $25,000 (instead of $10,000).

Coverages Available in Other ISO Forms

These are examples of provisions in the second category:

- Money and securities coverage of $25,000 per occurrence for loss at the described premises or within a bank or savings institution. The limit can be increased to any amount acceptable to the insurer.
- Money and securities coverage of $10,000 per occurrence for loss of covered property while in transit or at specified locations other than the insured premises.
- Employee dishonesty coverage of $10,000 per occurrence, which may be increased to $25,000 or $50,000.

Coverages Not Found in Any Other ISO Forms

These are examples of provisions in the third category (which provide coverages not found in current ISO forms):

- Ordinance or Law – Equipment covers the increased cost required by law to repair or replace covered equipment lost or damaged by a covered peril; the usual ISO ordinance or law endorsements apply only to building property. (Included in the Apartment Building Owners; Dry Cleaning and Laundry Facilities; Funeral Homes; Hotel, Motels, and Inns; Pet Services; Restaurants; Self-Storage Facilities; and Supermarkets endorsements.)
- Tenant Move Back Expenses indemnifies the insured for up to $15,000 for expenses it incurs to move tenants back to the insured premises when the tenants must temporarily vacate because of untenantability from loss or damage by a covered cause of loss. (Included in the Apartment Building Owners endorsement.)

- Sale and Disposal Liability covers the insured's liability for acts or omissions arising out of the lock-out, sale, removal or disposal of tenants' property when the tenant is evicted for failure to pay rent. The annual aggregate limit is $5,000. (Included in the Apartment Building Owners Program endorsement. A similar provision is included in the Dry Cleaning and Laundry Facilities endorsement and the Self-Storage Facilities endorsement.)

- Merchandise Withdrawal Expenses covers expenses associated with the recall or withdrawal of items sold or held for sale because of a known or suspected defect or a known or suspected tampering with the items, which has caused or is reasonably expected to cause bodily injury or damage to tangible property. The limit is $25,000 per occurrence, subject to a $250 per loss deductible. (Included in the Hardware and Home Improvement Stores; Restaurants; and Supermarkets endorsements.)

- Delivery Errors and Omissions coverage is provided for the failure to deliver, or the misdelivery of, customers' goods. The annual aggregate limit is $5,000, subject to a $250 deductible per loss. (Included in the Dry Cleaning and Laundry Facilities; Florists; Hardware and Home Improvement Stores; and Supermarkets endorsements.)

- Home Improvement Design Errors & Omissions covers the insured's legal liability for damages caused by a home improvement design error or omission by the insured. An annual aggregate limit of $10,000 applies, subject to a $250 deductible per loss. (Included in the Hardware and Home Improvement Stores endorsement. A similar provision is included in the Landscapers endorsement.)

- Guests' Evacuation Expense pays up to $25,000 limit to reimburse expenses the insured incurs to evacuate the premises because of imminent danger to the life or safety of the guests. (Included in the Hotels, Motels, and Inns endorsement.)

- Guests' Relocation Expense provides up to $500 per guest/$50,000 per occurrence for reimbursement of expenses incurred when guests are lodged at another facility when the insured location is rendered uninhabitable because of loss or damage by a covered cause of loss. Reimbursement is for the difference in lodging expenses and for the reasonable expense of traveling back and forth to the replacement lodging. (Included in the Hotels, Motels, and Inns endorsement.)

- Customers' Property Legal Liability covers the insured's liability for property damage to a customer's property while at the insured's self-storage facility. The annual aggregate limit is $100,000 subject to a $250 deductible per loss. This limit may be increased to any amount acceptable to the insurer. (Included in the Self-Storage Facilities endorsement.)

Many of these coverages are not commonly available in other forms. Even if the insured does not want to purchase the coverage, the endorsement can be a useful risk management tool for identifying loss exposures.

SUMMARY

The ISO farm program includes various forms and endorsements that can be combined into either a separate farm policy or a coverage part in a commercial package policy. There are three property coverage forms containing a total of seven insuring agreements. As in the commercial property coverage part, three levels of covered causes of loss can be purchased under the ISO farm program: basic, broad, and special.

Agricultural and related operations often need additional types of coverage that are not usually available in farm policies. These specialty coverages include crop hail insurance, Multiple Peril Crop Insurance, animal mortality insurance, feedlot insurance, and federal livestock insurance.

Financial institutions obtain crime insurance under specialized policies called financial institution bonds. Separate bond forms are available for different types of financial institutions. Financial Institution Bond Form No. 24, used to insure commercial banks, includes Insuring agreements A through G. Noteworthy provisions in Form 24 are its exclusions, discovery coverage trigger, notice of loss requirement, limits of liability, and deductible.

In addition to the basic financial institution bonds, these SFAA forms are available:

- The Computer Crime Policy is available to any type of financial institution to cover loss resulting from computer system fraud and related loss exposures.
- The Combination Safe Depository Policy is available for insuring a financial institution against liability for loss to customers' property kept in the insured's safe depository facilities.

Other noncrime coverages designed for financial institutions include mortgage impairment insurance, mortgage guarantee insurance, and title insurance.

ISO's Market Segment Program provides endorsements that broaden standard coverage forms for various types of businesses. It is designed for use with ISO commercial property and general liability forms and has a target market of smaller businesses.

ASSIGNMENT NOTES

1. For more information about the FCIC's livestock insurance programs, see the RMA Web site: http://www.rma.usda.gov/livestock/.
2. Includes copyrighted material of The Surety & Fidelity Association of America, used with its permission.
3. Teresa Dixon Murray and Karen Farkas, "Key Corp Bank Embezzlement Case Baffling," *Cleveland Plain Dealer*, November 21, 2006, www.securityinfowatch.com/press_release/10548096/keycorp-bank-embezzlement-case-baffling (accessed May 6, 2009).

13

Surety Bonds

Educational Objectives

After learning the content of this assignment, you should be able to:

▷ Describe the characteristics of surety bonds, including how surety bonds contrast with insurance.

▷ Describe the guarantees provided by the particular types of surety bonds within the following bond classifications:

- Contract bonds

- License and permit bonds

- Public official bonds

- Court bonds

- Miscellaneous bonds

▷ Recommend an appropriate surety bond for a described individual or organization.

Surety Bonds

13

SURETY BONDS CONTRASTED WITH INSURANCE

In its most fundamental form, suretyship represents the promise of one person (called the surety) to answer for the failure of another person (called the principal) to do something as promised.

Suretyship is usually conducted by insurers and is evidenced by a written contract called a **surety bond**. Surety bonds are used to provide a wide range of guarantees.

Although there are many different types of surety bonds, they share four qualities that distinguish them from most property and liability insurance policies:

- There are three parties to the contract.
- The principal is liable to the surety for losses paid by the surety.
- In theory, the surety should not sustain any losses on any surety contracts.
- The coverage period is indefinite.

Three Parties

A surety bond is a contract that involves three parties—the principal, the obligee, and the surety. The **principal** has primary responsibility to perform for the obligee's benefit. The **obligee** is the party to whom the surety bond is given and who is protected against loss. The **surety** (usually the insurer) answers to the obligee for the principal's failure to perform as required by the underlying contract, permit, or law. For example, a surety could guarantee that a construction contractor (principal) will complete a building for a property owner (obligee) in accordance with the construction contract.

Principal Liable to Surety

If the principal fails to fulfill the obligation, the surety must either fulfill the obligation or indemnify the obligee. However, the principal becomes liable to the surety to the extent of the surety's expenditures. The surety bond, in other words, pays the obligee's loss, not the principal's, even though the principal pays the premium.

Surety bond
A written contract that expresses one party's promise to answer for another party's failure to do something as promised.

Principal
The party to a surety bond whose obligation or performance the surety guarantees.

Obligee
The party to a surety bond that receives the surety's guarantee that the principal will fulfill an obligation or perform as promised.

Surety
The party (usually an insurer) to a surety bond that guarantees to the obligee that the principal will fulfill an obligation or perform as required by the underlying contract, permit, or law.

Surety Expects No Losses

Before issuing a surety bond, a surety examines the prospective principal's qualifications. A principal's qualifications are sometimes summed up as the "three Cs"—capital, capacity, and character:

- Capital—Does the principal have sufficient funds and credit to finance the project and all other ongoing work?
- Capacity—Does the principal have the skill, experience, staff, and equipment to execute the work successfully?
- Character—Does the principal have a reputation for honoring agreements even when there are adverse developments?

At least in theory, no surety bond is issued unless the surety is satisfied that the principal is capable of performing the obligation that is the subject of the surety bond. In issuing a surety bond, the surety is attesting to the principal's ability to perform. In practice, sureties do sustain losses when a principal fails to perform and the principal does not have the funds to repay the surety. In some cases, the surety will require that the principal post collateral to make sure that the principal will be able to repay the surety if the surety has to perform on behalf of the principal.

Indefinite Coverage Period

Surety bonds ordinarily do not terminate until the principal has fulfilled its obligations, which may take only a few days or as long as many years. Consequently, surety bonds are not issued as year-to-year contracts, and they normally do not allow either the surety or the principal to cancel them.

However, some types of surety bonds may be cancelable. Typically, bonds allowing cancellation require the surety to give notice of cancellation to the obligee. Cancellation becomes effective a certain number of days thereafter as stipulated in the bond itself or provided by law or regulation.

Other Characteristics of Surety Bonds

Other characteristics of surety bonds, which do not necessarily represent a contrast with property and liability insurance contracts, include the statutory nature of some surety bonds and the use of a limit.

Statutory Nature of Bonds

Many bonds are required by municipal ordinance or federal or state regulations or statutes. The provisions of these statutory bonds, and therefore the obligations of the three parties to the bond, are spelled out in the law. Other bonds are not required by statute. The need for a nonstatutory bond is usually established in the contract between the obligee and the principal. For example, a construction contract between a private owner and a contractor may require the contractor to obtain certain types of contract bonds.

Bond Limit

A bond is written for a set limit, sometimes called the "penalty." If the principal's obligation exceeds the limit, the surety will be liable only for the amount of the limit. However, like liability insurance policies, some bonds pay court costs and interest on judgments in addition to the stated limit. If the obligee's actual loss is less than the limit, most surety bonds provide only for the payment of the actual loss. Some surety bonds are issued on a forfeiture basis, meaning that the entire amount of the bond is paid if the principal defaults.

GENERAL TYPES OF SURETY BONDS

Many types of surety bonds are needed to address the variety of surety bonding needs.

Surety bonds are instruments that respond not only to the various contractual arrangements that arise between principal and obligee, but also to various legal and statutory requirements. **Suretyship** is usually conducted by insurers. Because surety bonds are used to provide a wide range of guarantees, many types exist. They fall into these categories:

Suretyship

The obligation of one entity to answer for the debt, default, or miscarriage of performance of duties by another entity.

- Contract bonds
- License and permit bonds
- Public official bonds
- Court bonds
- Miscellaneous bonds

Although the principal is responsible for furnishing the bonds required of the obligee, surety bond forms are frequently provided by the obligee. In some instances, the obligee may specify a bond form from an unrelated organization, such as the American Institute of Architects (AIA). If the obligee does not provide or specify a bond form, the surety may have a form that is acceptable to the obligee. In addition, the federal government has drafted and printed standard forms for contract bonds that are required by federal law.

Contract Bonds

Contract bond

A surety bond guaranteeing the fulfillment of obligations under construction contracts or other types of contracts.

Contract bonds are often required of individuals or organizations that are contractually obligated to perform work or service for others. They serve two broad purposes:

- The surety's willingness to furnish the bond is evidence that, in the surety's judgment, the principal is qualified to fulfill the terms of the contract.

- The surety guarantees that, even if the principal defaults, the obligations of the contract will be performed, or the surety will indemnify the obligee up to the penal amount of the bond.

The obligees of contract bonds may be private entities, but often are government entities because the bonds are frequently required by law. Primarily used for construction purposes, types of contract bonds include bid bonds, performance bonds, payment bonds, and maintenance bonds.

Performance bonds and payment bonds are key components of the Miller Act, a federal statute that governs contracts for the construction, alteration, or repair of any public buildings or public work for the federal government. This act requires that, when construction contracts exceed $100,000, a contractor must furnish a performance bond for the protection of the government and a payment bond for the protection of suppliers of labor and materials.

The government contracting officers may specify that the prime contractor provide alternative payment protection on construction projects between $25,000 and $100,000. Allowable alternatives to bonds could include escrow agreements, letters of credit, certificates of deposit, and deposits of other types of security.

The Miller Act does not provide for total payment to all creditors. The act's required payment bond protects two general categories of creditors, provided, of course, the bond limit is sufficient:

- Material suppliers, laborers, and subcontractors that deal directly with the prime contractor

- Those that have a direct relationship with a subcontractor but that do not have a contractual relationship, express or implied, with the prime contractor that furnishes the payment bond

Bid Bonds

Bid bond

A contract bond guaranteeing that a contractor bidding on a construction or supply contract will enter into the contract and will provide a performance bond if the bid is accepted.

The obligee to whom a **bid bond** is furnished is usually the owner of the proposed construction project. However, the obligee can also be a general contractor who requires subcontractors to give bonds for the general contractor's own benefit. The surety promises that the general contractor or subcontractor (principal) bidding for a contract will, if the bid is accepted, enter into a contract and furnish other necessary contract bonds. If the bid is accepted and the principal refuses to enter into the contract or fails to provide such bonds, the obligee, in most instances, is entitled to be paid (subject to the penal amount of the bond) the difference between the amount of the principal's bid and the next lowest bid the obligee finally accepts.

Generally, a claim against a bid bond arises only when, after being awarded the contract by the obligee, a contractor refuses to enter into the contract to perform the work or is unable to supply the required bonds. The contractor usually refuses for one of these reasons:

* The contractor determines that performance of the contract is virtually impossible at the quoted price.

* Economic conditions change, increasing the cost of performing the work and making the bid price inadequate. For example, a sharp increase in interest rates and unexpected inflation might bring about substantial increases in wages and material prices.

* The contractor discovers that a mistake was made in preparing the bid and does not make an effort to obtain relief from a procuring agency or a court, or such effort fails.

After a bid has been accepted, the chosen contractor must enter into a contract with the owner and furnish any other bonds required to secure the contractor's performance of the work. These other bonds usually include a performance bond and a payment bond. A maintenance bond might also be required.

Performance Bonds

After it is awarded a contract, the principal must usually provide a **performance bond**. The obligee can demand that the surety perform its obligation under a performance bond only after the principal has defaulted. Ordinarily, the performance bond form includes language that gives the surety a number of options if the principal has defaulted, including completing the contract using the existing contractor, completing the contract using a replacement contractor, or having the owner arrange for the completion of work, with the surety paying for the additional cost up to the bond's penal amount. Sureties often vigorously oppose bond forms or contract terms that limit their options in a claim situation, especially forms that compel the surety to complete the contract, which may expose the surety to a potential loss in excess of the bond's penal amount.

Whatever the outcome in the event of default, the surety always has the right to seek reimbursement from the principal. The surety can collect from the principal by an assignment of the obligee's rights to the surety, because of the written indemnity agreement (sometimes included in the bond application), or through subrogation.

Additionally, sureties may fulfill their obligations under performance bonds in other ways besides paying the penal amount of the bond. In some instances, they may attempt to provide an alternative remedy that satisfies the obligee and allows a project to be completed despite the default. For example, a

Performance bond
A contract bond guaranteeing that a contractor's work will be completed according to plans and specifications.

construction company contracted by a hotel to complete the expansion of its facilities in time for a major annual meeting defaults six months before the event. With the building's improvements incomplete, the surety intervenes and arranges for the hotel to work with a new contractor, who invests extra resources provided by the surety to finish the job on schedule.

Payment Bonds

Payment bond

A contract bond guaranteeing that the project will be free of liens.

A **payment bond** (or labor and materials payment bond) offers payment protection vital to private project owners because labor and material suppliers who go uncompensated can usually apply a mechanic's lien to the property. A mechanic's lien is a right granted by statute and is available to those who seek to secure the value of their work or services that have gone into the form of additions on real estate.[1] When a lien is placed on such property, the owner does not have clear title to the property until all debts are settled.

Maintenance Bonds

Maintenance bond

A contract bond guaranteeing that the work will be free from defects in materials and workmanship for a specified period after the project is completed.

Many statutes, ordinances, and contracts require the exercise of a certain degree of care in the construction of property. In addition, construction contracts often specify that contractors must remedy any faulty work or defective materials discovered within a specified period of time. To comply with these requirements, contractors must sometimes provide obligees with a **maintenance bond**.

Generally, a performance bond includes this maintenance guarantee, without additional premium, for one year after completion of performance. Even when a separate maintenance bond is required along with a performance bond, usually there is no additional charge by the surety for a maintenance bond, provided the duration is one year or less. The maintenance bond requires an additional charge when a contractor does not have to furnish a performance bond but still has to produce a maintenance bond, or when the contractor must guarantee certain work and materials for longer than one year.

Sureties are often reluctant to provide maintenance guarantees for longer than one year. After a lapse of time, determining the cause of defects becomes more difficult. Additionally, the sureties' reluctance to extend lengthy guarantees can be attributed to laws permitting property owners to recover from contractors for defects in completed work.

Miscellaneous Contract Bonds

Subdivision bond

A contract bond guaranteeing a local governmental authority that a subdivision developer will complete the subdivision in accordance with approved proposals and at the developer's expense.

Supply contract bond

A contract bond guaranteeing that a supplier will perform the designated supply contract according to specifications.

Contract bonds are also used to secure a variety of contracts other than construction contracts. The purposes for which such bonds may be required include mechanical equipment rental with or without operators, transportation of school children, snow and garbage removal, and street cleaning.

Two common types of miscellaneous contract bonds are **subdivision bonds** and **supply contract bonds**.

Land developers and real estate firms often subdivide tracts of property for housing developments. Before doing so, developers must agree to construct all improvements and provide proper sewage disposal systems, a water supply, and other utilities. Before construction can begin, developers are usually required to obtain permits and provide subdivision bonds to the local governmental authority. Developers are exposed to various risks that may cause them to run out of the funds needed to complete the promised subdivision improvements. For example, costs can escalate, original estimates can be too low, financing arrangements can fail to close, other ventures can consume cash, or properties may not sell as planned. Largely because of such hazards, a subdivision bond is difficult for developers to procure unless they can provide the type of qualifying credentials required by the surety.

A supply contract involves an agreement for furnishing and delivering materials or supplies at an agreed price. Most such contracts occur between private enterprises and federal, state, or local governmental entities, but some contracts involve private parties only. Those who wish to obtain supply contracts from purchasers invariably must submit bids. Typically, the lowest bidder is selected. When a successful bidder fails to furnish the required supplies according to the contract specifications, the purchaser stands to suffer a loss equal to the difference between the bid price and the higher cost of buying supplies in the open market. Although the bidder can ultimately be held liable for this amount, purchasers often require their suppliers to be bonded so that compensation by the defaulted bidder will be guaranteed. The appropriate bond for this situation is a supply contract bond. Because, for the most part, these bonds are required by the government, they are usually required by statute. See the exhibit "Surety Bond Guarantee Program for Small Contractors."

License and Permit Bonds

Many enterprises need licenses to operate. Licenses provide special privileges entitling their holders to do something that they would not otherwise be entitled to do.[2] Licenses are required by the federal government, states, counties, cities, and political subdivisions, for two primary reasons:

* They are a source of revenue.
* They help regulate license holders through statutes, regulations, or ordinances that exist for the safety and general welfare of the community.

Permits are somewhat like licenses. They are obtained from political subdivisions, and they serve as a means of regulation and as sources of revenue. Often they are needed as prerequisites for performing special functions that are incidental to business operations:

> ### Surety Bond Guarantee Program for Small Contractors
>
> Many small contractors lack some of the capital necessary to meet sureties' underwriting requirements for surety bonds. Assistance in obtaining surety bonds is available to such contractors through the Small Business Administration (SBA) under its Surety Bond Guarantee Program.
>
> The program is intended to give small, less-experienced contracting firms the opportunity to be bonded so that they can compete for bonded jobs and prove themselves by profitably performing work to specifications. A history of successful performance may, in turn, enable such firms to secure surety bonds for future jobs based on their own reputation and financial ability.
>
> The SBA program is limited to bonds listed in the contract bond section of the *Manual of Rules, Procedures and Classifications* published by the Surety Association of America. However, work requiring another type of bond is sometimes permissible if that bond is written in conjunction with a contract bond.
>
> For example, a license or permit bond required of a construction contractor working on a public highway may be included under this program because it is considered to be incidental to a contract bond.
>
> Under this program, the SBA does not issue surety bonds. It merely guarantees to reimburse a participating surety for a stipulated portion—such as 70, 80, or 90 percent—of any loss sustained. In addition to issuing the required bond or bonds, the participating surety must pay the SBA a fee for guaranteeing the bonds that are written.
>
> If a contract is breached by a contractor bonded under the SBA program and a claim or suit is brought against the surety, the SBA must be notified within a reasonable time. Even though the SBA requires notification of any breach, the surety is still responsible for handling all phases of the claim before being reimbursed by the SBA.
>
> More specific information about the SBA Surety Bond Guarantee Program is available at www.sba.gov/opc/pubs/fszi.html.

[DA05305]

Characteristics of License and Permit Bonds

License and permit bonds

Surety bonds that provide payment to the obligee (the state, city, or other public entity) for loss or damage resulting from violations of the duties and obligations imposed on the licensee or permit holder.

Whatever the type, licenses or permits frequently are not issued until those who need them furnish a surety bond to the appropriate public entity. **License and permit bonds** are usually written for a one-year term, although they can terminate sooner or run indefinitely until canceled, depending on the reasons for their use. Because the bonds are statutory, they contain language reflecting the requirements of the underlying statutes. Thus, whether these bonds are cancelable depends on the law for which they are issued or the cancellation provision in the bond form.

Classifications of License and Permit Bonds

The Surety & Fiduciary Association of America (SFAA) established classifications of license and permit bonds to create a basis for developing loss costs.

Guarantees provided by these bonds demonstrate the variety of guarantees provided by license and permit bonds:

- Compliance-only bonds—Principal will comply with the laws that apply to the activity for which the principal is licensed.

- Compliance bonds with third-party liability—Principal will comply with the laws that apply to the activity for which the principal is licensed and pay damages to any third party that suffers a loss because of the principal's failure to comply.

- Forfeiture bonds—Surety will pay (forfeit) the entire bond penalty if the principal fails to complete the bonded obligation.

- Payment of tax or fee bonds—Principal will properly account for and remit taxes or fees collected.

- Merchandising and dealer bonds—Principal will conduct merchandising activities according to the law and, on many bonds, properly account for any funds held in trust and transfer them to the appropriate party.

- Reclamation and environmental protection bonds—Principal will restore land to its original state after its operations are completed and clean up spills or runoff that pollute the land or water in the area of operation.

Public Official Bonds

Individuals who are appointed or elected to public office are obligated to discharge their duties faithfully, to the best of their abilities and to otherwise protect the public interest. When they hold public funds, they have the duty to account for them and turn them over to their successors in office. With few exceptions, laws generally hold public officials personally accountable for losses, shortages, and damage to public property. Some officials are also held responsible for the acts and omissions of their subordinates.

All such obligations are affirmed by public officials when they take an oath of office, which is one requirement they must fulfill before they can act in their official capacities. They must also furnish **public official bonds**, which guarantee honesty, faithful performance, or both.

Some bonds are for honesty only and are considered less hazardous than those that include faithful performance. For example, under the honesty guarantee, a treasurer accounts for the cash that he or she holds. Under the faithful performance guarantee, the treasurer could be held liable if he or she deposited tax collections in a noninterest bearing account rather than investing them to increase revenue. In some states, such as New York, the law requires sureties to provide both guarantees in public official bonds.

Public officials who are required to post bonds include officials whose duties are administrative, those whose duties involve handling public funds, and those whose duties require direct involvement with members of the public, such as constables, sheriffs, and public notaries. These duties determine the

Public official bond

A commercial surety bond guaranteeing that a public official will perform his or her duties faithfully and honestly.

guarantee provided under public officials bonds and affect the degree of hazard connected with the bonds.

Administrative Officials

Sureties willingly write bonds for officials who have administrative duties and who do not routinely handle money, because such principals (who include, for example, officers of public entities and charitable organizations, commissioners, assessors, judges, coroners, engineers, law enforcement officers, town clerks, city attorneys, and auditors) seldom default on their obligations. Sureties can incur losses on these bonds when officials make mistakes, are neglectful, exceed the authority granted, or handle money when the bond is classed as a nonmoney-handling officials bond.

Officials Who Handle Public Funds

Officials who handle public funds are legally charged with honesty and faithful performance of duty while handling money. In many jurisdictions, these officials are seen as insurers of public funds and are held liable for loss by burglary, robbery, or any other cause, except acts of God. Sureties guarantee payment for all such losses, making these bonds relatively hazardous.

Government entities that require bonds sometimes designate approved banks in which the official or employee should deposit public funds, called designated depositories, and establish limitations on the amounts deposited in any given bank. Most of these bonds guarantee payment for losses that occur when the principal fails to follow designated depository guidelines or when the bank where the principal deposits funds fails.

Sureties write these bonds for officers such as town, city, county, school, and state treasurers; tax collectors; court clerks; public institution superintendents; public administrators; and public guardians. Sureties pay losses on these bonds when principals handle their duties carelessly or negligently, make unlawful expenditures, fail to collect required taxes, or when subordinates in their offices cause losses through similar actions.

Officials With Direct Public Involvement

Officials who have direct involvement with members of the public include public notaries, sheriffs, deputies, marshals, constables, and peace officers who serve civil or criminal writs. These parties are legally responsible for the property and safety of others.

Sureties guarantee payment of third-party damages when principals breach authority or commit wrongful acts, such as making wrongful arrests, seizing the wrong goods, or failing to seize goods that should have been seized. Sureties write public notary bonds freely but consider the other bonds in this category to be hazardous. Sureties sometimes write them only as an accommodation to existing clients or producers or when conditions in a certain locality are particularly favorable.

Court Bonds

Court bonds guarantee that a person or an organization will faithfully perform certain duties prescribed by law or a court, or will demonstrate financial responsibility for the benefit of another until the final outcome of a court's decision. If the principal fails to meet such obligations, the surety must answer for damages. Court bonds are usually noncancelable and continuous. The two general classes of court bonds are judicial bonds and fiduciary bonds.

Judicial Bonds

Judicial bonds generally arise out of litigation. They are posted by a plaintiff or a defendant (the principal) in a court case to protect the opposing party in the event that the principal does not prevail in the court action.

Plaintiff bonds and defendant bonds are major types of judicial bonds. For example, a person bringing action against another to obtain an equitable remedy in court—such as the performance of a certain action, the repossession of property, or the fulfillment of a monetary obligation—may be required to post a plaintiff bond before the court will proceed with the complaint. This type of judicial bond guarantees that, if the court determines that the plaintiff's action was wrongfully taken, the plaintiff will pay any damages sustained by the defendant because of the action.

As another example, the court might require a defendant to post a bond (a defendant bond), such as when the plaintiff objects to some proposed action by the defendant or wishes to attach property held by the defendant. Such a bond guarantees to the court (obligee) that if the court decides in the plaintiff's favor, the defendant will refrain from the action, return the property, and/or pay damages sustained by the plaintiff.

These are examples of judicial bonds:

- Attachment bond—Before a court will attach property (that is, take it by legal authority) at the request of another, the plaintiff must give the court an **attachment bond**. If the court decides in the plaintiff's favor, the bond automatically terminates.
- Release of attachment bond—After a defendant's property is attached, it can be released to the defendant pending final outcome of the court's decision if the defendant gives the court a **release of attachment bond**. The defendant is required to furnish such a bond only if the defendant desires to maintain possession of the property until the dispute is settled. To secure the bond, the defendant must satisfy the surety that he or she is financially responsible. (Liability insurance policies commonly agree to pay the premiums for release of attachment bonds required in any suit for covered damages.)

Court bonds

A classification of surety bonds guaranteeing that a person or an organization will faithfully perform certain duties prescribed by law or by a court or will demonstrate financial responsibility for the benefit of another until the final outcome of a court's decision.

Attachment bond

A judicial bond guaranteeing that, if the court decides against a plaintiff who has requested attachment of the defendant's property, the defendant will be paid any damages that result from the property attachment.

Release of attachment bond

A bond that guarantees that the insured will pay any damages and court costs if the court should decide in the claimant's favor.

Appeal bond

A judicial bond guaranteeing that a plaintiff who appeals an adverse decision to a higher court will pay all court costs of the appeal.

Defendant's appeal bond (supersedeas bond)

A judicial bond guaranteeing that a defendant who appeals an adverse decision to a higher court will pay the entire judgment, plus court costs and interest, should the higher court sustain the initial judgment for the plaintiff.

- Appeal bond—An **appeal bond** is required of a plaintiff who decides to appeal an adverse decision to a higher court. The bond, when posted, guarantees payment of all court costs on the appeal.
- Defendant's appeal bond—When the defendant desires to appeal a case to a higher court, a **defendant's appeal bond** (or *supersedeas* bond) is required. Defendants' appeal bonds are another type of bond that liability insurers typically agree to pay the premium for when such bonds are required of their insureds in a covered lawsuit.

The exhibit describes these corresponding plaintiff and defendant bonds. See the exhibit "Summary of Selected Judicial Bonds."

Summary of Selected Judicial Bonds

Bond	Principal	Obligee	Guarantee
Attachment Bond	Plaintiff requesting attachment of property	The court, for the benefit of defendant	If court decides against plaintiff, plaintiff will pay any damages sustained by defendant as a result of having property attached.
Release of Attachment Bond	Defendant who wants to regain possession of property that has been attached by plaintiff	The court, for the benefit of plaintiff and court	If court decides in plaintiff's favor, defendant will return the property and will pay any damages and court costs.
Appeal Bond	Plaintiff who desires to appeal an adverse decision to a higher court	The court	Plaintiff will pay all required court costs on the appeal.
Defendant's Appeal Bond	Defendant who desires to appeal an adverse decision to a higher court	The court, for the benefit of plaintiff and court	If higher court sustains initial judgment, defendant will pay the entire judgment plus court costs and interest.

[DA05975]

Fiduciary Bonds

Fiduciary bonds hold the principals and the sureties jointly and severally liable to obligees for the faithful performance of specified duties. Fiduciary bonds remain in force until the proceedings are complete and the sureties and fiduciaries have been released by the court from further obligation. Both individuals and corporations can be selected to act as fiduciaries. Most problems involving fiduciary bonds deal with administrators of estates and guardians of minors and incompetents.

One type of fiduciary is a guardian, who is anyone with the legal responsibility to care for a person or a person's property (or both) because of that person's inability to manage his or her own affairs. A guardian is often appointed by a probate court to look after the affairs of a minor or an incompetent (a person who suffers from impaired judgment as determined by a probate court). The minor or an incompetent is called a "ward of the court." The guardian can be a parent, a relative, or some other competent person.

All jurisdictions have statutes that safeguard the rights and interests of minors and legally incompetent persons. Those statutes require a guardian to post a bond before assuming the role of fiduciary for a minor or an incompetent. The bond guarantees that the fiduciary will faithfully perform all duties, observe all directives of the court, and provide an accounting of all money and other property when required by the court to do so. Failing this, the fiduciary is liable to the court for all damages.

The surety is liable and pays the damages, up to the penalty of the bond. However, a surety might be required to pay, in excess of the penal amount, any court costs and any interest that has accrued from the time a judgment is rendered against the fiduciary. The fiduciary indemnifies the surety for any losses paid, as agreed in the indemnity agreement.

A surety can exercise control by supervising some or all of the assets of an estate. This supervision is called "joint control" because both the surety and the fiduciary control the assets. Sureties often require joint control primarily on long-term fiduciary bonds, such as guardian bonds.

Guardians of minors and conservators of incompetents can experience problems for a number of reasons, including these:

- Expenditures are improperly made.
- Funds are misappropriated.
- Funds or property are mismanaged.
- Records are inadequate.

A second type of fiduciary is an executor, who is a fiduciary named in a will to administer an estate. When a person dies intestate (without leaving a will), a court will appoint an administrator to settle the estate of the decedent.

Fiduciary bond

A court bond guaranteeing that a person appointed by a court to administer the property or interests of others will faithfully perform his or her duties.

The duties and obligations of administrators and executors are generally the same, but there are some distinctions. For example, administrators settle estates according to the directives of the courts, whereas executors settle estates as specified in wills, subject to approval of the courts. The duties and responsibilities of both types of fiduciaries include collecting all estate assets and preserving them from loss, paying all claims against the estate, and providing the court with an accounting of all transactions. Upon the court's approval of the accounting, the fiduciary distributes the remaining assets as specified by the will or statute. After satisfactorily completing these duties, the fiduciary is discharged by the court.

When a court requires an administrator or an executor to post a bond (the latter may be excused from doing so if the will so specifies), the bond guarantees the fiduciary's faithful performance as dictated by law or by the court. Although the fiduciary is liable for any default to the full extent of any damages, the surety must answer only to the extent of the bond penalty. In some cases, however, the surety may also be responsible for court costs and interest that accrues on any judgment rendered against the principal.

Claims involving administrators range from allegations of simple failure to perform to charges of mismanagement of estates' affairs because of ignorance, negligence, or dishonesty. Administrators and executors are obligated to exercise reasonable care in notifying all heirs of an impending probate proceeding. However, heirs are not always notified, and estates are sometimes settled without notification of all heirs. Courts have held administrators and their sureties accountable for not exercising reasonable care in notifying all heirs.

Administrators and executors are also obligated to give public notice of the estate proceedings for a certain period, usually six weeks, to give creditors an opportunity to file claims against the estate. Problems arise when fiduciaries begin to close the estate before this period expires. A related problem occurs when fiduciaries do not make payments to secured creditors and general (unsecured) creditors in legal order of priority.

Administrators who are direct heirs sometimes conceal funds or other estate property and exclude them from the distribution among other heirs, and fiduciaries sometimes fail to make a proper accounting for tax purposes—leading to subsequent government lawsuits.

A third type of fiduciary is a receiver or trustee in a bankruptcy proceeding. In U.S. bankruptcy proceedings, the U.S. Trustee appoints and supervises a panel of private trustees who are available to handle cases under the various chapters of the bankruptcy code. These trustees supervise the administration of cases. The law also allows the U.S. Trustee to establish a blanket bond in favor of the U.S., conditioned on the faithful performance of official duties by the panel of trustees. The U.S. Trustee establishes the penal amount. Such blanket bonds often include a "per case" limit and an aggregate limit per trustee.

In a Chapter 7 liquidation, the trustee reduces any assets to cash and distributes it among the debtor's creditors based on the priority of payments specified in the U.S. Bankruptcy Code. Under Chapter 11 reorganization, the court-appointed trustee develops a reorganization plan that satisfies the claims of creditors and interests of shareholders or others with business interests. The plan must comply with specifications in the Bankruptcy Act, be approved by the creditors, and be confirmed by the Bankruptcy Court. Following the proceedings, the debtor must continue the business according to the reorganization plan.

The Chapter 12 trustee sells only those assets that are unnecessary to a family farmer's business operation and distributes the proceeds to creditors according to the Bankruptcy Code. The debtor develops and files its own reorganization plan with the court and generally continues the daily operation of the farm. When the debtor fulfills the plan, it is excused from full performance of debts.

In most jurisdictions, the federal Bankruptcy Court appoints a standing trustee to handle all Chapter 13 bankruptcies. Chapter 13 allows individuals with a regular income to repay creditors, in full or in part, over a period of time. The debtor retains possession of assets and works out a payment program in which debts are paid to each creditor based on the proportion of debt owed them to the debtor's total debt.

Miscellaneous Bonds

The SFAA has classified some surety bonds as **miscellaneous bonds**. These bonds often support private relationships and unique business needs, and they represent a significant source of business for sureties that write them. Because of the specific nature of each bond obligation, underwriters must look beyond the bond form to the underlying agreement or law that required the bond. Many of these bonds contain a financial guarantee.

The number of bonds in this classification prohibits discussion of most of them, but three common examples of miscellaneous bonds are summarized in the exhibit. See the exhibit "Summary of Selected Miscellaneous Bonds."

Miscellaneous bond
Any bond that does not fit well under the other primary categories of surety bonds formulated by the Surety and Fidelity Association of America.

Summary of Selected Miscellaneous Bonds

Bond	Parties Protected	Principal	Guarantee Provided
Lost Securities Bonds	Entity that issues replacement securities*	Owner of the lost securities	Principal will indemnify obligee for any financial loss it suffers because of the duplicate securities it issues to the principal.
Hazardous Waste Removal Bonds	Federal or State government*	Owner or operator of hazardous waste facility	Principal will comply with Environmental Protection Agency (EPA) and state laws for closure and post-closure care of hazardous waste facilities.
Credit Enhancement Financial Guaranty Bonds	Investor	Governmental entities	Principal will pay interest to investors as promised and will return the principal at maturity of a debt instrument.

* Third parties that suffer damages because of the principal's failure to perform as required in the bond are also protected and have a right to sue the surety in their own names.

[DA03719]

SURETY BOND CASE STUDY

Surety bonds provide useful risk management techniques for loss exposures concerning fulfillment of contracts or obligations.

A surety bond can be a useful risk management technique to provide both risk control and risk transfer for certain types of loss exposures:

- Requiring the principal to furnish a surety bond is a form of risk control because the surety company provides prequalification of the principal to determine that the principal is able to fulfill the legal obligation to perform.

- By requiring the principal to furnish a surety bond, an organization (the obligee) may transfer the risk of loss to a professional risk bearer, the surety.

Case Facts

ABC, Inc. develops computer software programs that assist healthcare providers with medical records and billing. The business is growing, and the company needs to expand its office space. ABC purchased land and hired an architect to design a new office complex. The architectural plans are complete, the board has approved the concept, and the company is now ready to begin construction.

George, ABC's CFO, and Amy, ABC's risk manager, meet with their insurance broker, Gail. George and Amy explain to Gail that they are ready to solicit bids from construction companies to serve as the general contractor on the project.

George and Amy are not construction experts and are unfamiliar with the qualifications of different construction companies. Amy has no risk management experience in construction. It is important to ABC for construction to begin as soon as possible. The company has outgrown its current leased office, and George would like the construction to be complete on the new complex before the current lease expires. George and Amy discuss with Gail how they can be certain that the contractor they select through the bidding process will actually enter into a contract and begin construction.

What types of surety bonds should Gail recommend that George and Amy require from prospective contractors to address ABC's risk in the selection of a general contractor for the office construction project?

Case Analysis Tools and Information

Gail discusses with Amy and George the different types of surety bonds typically used for construction projects.

Contract bonds are often required for construction operations and serve two broad purposes:

- The bond is evidence that, in the judgment of the surety for the bond, the principal is qualified to fulfill the terms of the contract.

- The surety guarantees that if the principal defaults, either the contract obligations will be performed or the surety will indemnify the obligee up to the bond's penal amount.

There are four different types of contract bonds commonly used for construction projects:

- Bid bond
- Performance bond
- Payment bond
- Maintenance bond

Case Analysis Steps

Gail reviews the different types of contract bonds used for construction projects. A bid bond is a type of surety bond designed to assist individuals and organizations who are receiving bids on construction contracts. See the exhibit "Bid Bond."

Bid Bond

This surety promises that the general contractor bidding for a contract will, if the bid is accepted, enter into a contract and furnish other necessary contract bonds. If the bid is accepted and the principal refuses to enter into the contract or fails to provide such bonds, the obligee, in most instances, is entitled to be paid (subject to the penal amount of the bond) the difference between the amount of the principal's bid and the next lowest bid the obligee finally accepts.

[DA06049]

The bid bond will accomplish the two broad purposes of a contract bond:

- To provide evidence of the principal's qualifications
- To indemnify the obligee if the principal does not fulfill the contract

Gail discusses with George and Amy that the insurer issuing the bid bond will verify the qualifications of the bidder. This is the most important function of the bond for George and Amy, who want to be reasonably certain that they choose a qualified contractor. Gail explains that insurers generally do not expect to have to make payment on a surety bond. The underwriter will carefully consider whether the principal will be able to perform the requirements of the contract. This prequalification of the prospective contractors will serve as risk control for ABC in the selection process.

Although the prequalification will make it unlikely that the contractor awarded the bid will fail to either enter into the contract or start the work as agreed, the bond also provides risk transfer from ABC to the surety in the event of a default.

Gail also discusses with George and Amy that the bid bond will require the contractor, after being awarded the bid, to obtain a performance bond and a maintenance bond to guarantee the successful completion of the construction project. She mentions that the general contractor may want to use bid bonds with the subcontractors who bid to perform different aspects of the construction, such as the electrical; plumbing; and heating, ventilation, and air conditioning work. Gail also discusses with George and Amy that they may want to consider a wrap-up program in which either ABC or the general contractor provides the insurance for the project and deducts that cost from the bid price. Surety bonds could be included with the wrap-up insurance program or provided separately.

Surety bonds can assist organizations in managing various loss exposures throughout the different stages of a construction project. By requiring contractors to obtain bonds, owners as well as general contractors obtain prequalification and, as obligees, obtain indemnification if a contractor does not fulfill the obligations of a contract. See the exhibit "Surety Bond Recommendation for ABC, Inc.."

Surety Bond Recommendation for ABC, Inc.

A bid bond will be the most effective risk management technique for ABC, Inc.'s loss exposure as the company selects a general contractor for its office construction project through a competitive bidding process. The bid bonds will provide risk control by prequalification of the prospective contractors, who will be required to obtain the bonds in order to submit a bid. The prospective contractor will be the principal on the bid bond. The surety will indemnify ABC as the obligee if the contractor does not fulfill the obligation to enter into a contract with ABC to build the complex after being awarded the bid.

[DA06050]

This solution might not be the only viable solution. Other solutions could be exercised if justified by the analysis. In addition, specific circumstances and organizational needs or goals may enter into the evaluation, making an alternative action a better option.

SUMMARY

In a surety bond, the surety (usually an insurer) guarantees to the obligee that the principal will fulfill an obligation or perform as promised. If the principal does not perform as promised, the surety must fulfill the obligation or indemnify the obligee.

Most surety bonds fall into these categories:

- Contract bonds
- License and permit bonds
- Public official bonds
- Court bonds
- Miscellaneous bonds

Various types of surety bonds can provide risk management techniques in situations requiring fulfillment of a contract or an obligation. Contract bonds are types of surety bonds often used for construction projects. Bid bonds are contract bonds designed to guarantee the ability and willingness of a contractor to perform the work specified in a construction contract.

ASSIGNMENT NOTES

1. *American Jurisprudence*, 2d ed. (Rochester, N.Y.: Lawyers Cooperative, 1993), Section 1, p. 512.
2. American Jurisprudence, 2d, Section 1, p. 89.

Index

Page numbers in boldface refer to pages where the word or phrase is defined.